Significant changes to the sixth edition will provide you with greater coverage of major media developments in the past and help you comprehend the full impact and influence of media in maintaining social order and promoting change.

1. Reorganization of the text. The sixth edition has been reorganized to provide greater unity within and among the eight parts of the text.

2. Expanded coverage of major media developments in the past includes the role of printing in the rise of the modern state, and an expanded examination of communication in our own era of proliferating media forms—television, video, digital technology, and the internet.

3. Introductions to each section provide a rationale for that particular section, an explanation of key concepts and transitions, and background material to help you to better appreciate the individual essays.

4. New authors. New authors include Lisa Gitelman, Jonathan Sterne, John Durham Peters, Henry Jenkins, and Manuel Castells.

5. Updated essay selections. New selections address the development of sound recording, the emergence of the modalities of broadcasting, television in the new post-mass media environment and the expanding social significance of mobile communications and networks, providing you with a more all-encompassing view of the communication history.

PEARSON

SIXTH EDITION

COMMUNICATION IN HISTORY

TECHNOLOGY, CULTURE, SOCIETY

David Crowley

McGill University

Paul Heyer

Wilfrid Laurier University

Allyn & Bacon

Boston   Columbus   Indianapolis   New York   San Francisco   Upper Saddle River
Amsterdam   Cape Town   Dubai   London   Madrid   Milan   Munich   Paris   Montreal   Toronto
Delhi   Mexico City   Sao Paulo   Sydney   Hong Kong   Seoul   Singapore   Taipei   Tokyo

> ## TO THE MEMORY OF Don Theall
> ### *Teacher, Scholar, Friend*

Acquisitions Editor: Jeanne Zalesky
Assistant Editor: Megan Lentz
Marketing Manager: Blair Tuckman
Production Manager: Kathy Sleys
Creative Director: Jayne Conte
Cover Designer: Bruce Kenselaar
Manager, Rights and Permissions:
 Zina Arabia

Image Permission Coordinator: Kathy Gavilanes
Cover Art: Getty Images
Full-Service Project Management: Joseph Malcolm,
 GGS Higher Education Resources, PMG
Composition: GGS Higher Education Resources,
 PMG
Printer/Binder/Cover Printer: R.R. Donnelley &
 Sons

Credits appear on page 312, which constitutes an extension of the copyright page.

Library of Congress Cataloging-in-Publication Data
Communication in history : technology, culture, society / [edited by] David Crowley, Paul Heyer.—6th ed.
 p. cm.
Includes index.
ISBN-13: 978-0-205-69309-2
ISBN-10: 0-205-69309-1
1. Communication—History. 2. Mass media—History. I. Crowley, D. J. (David J.), 1945- II. Heyer, Paul, 1946-
P90.C62945 2010
302.209—dc22

 2010000105

10 9 8 7 6 5 4 3 2 1   DOH   13 12 11 10

**Allyn & Bacon
is an imprint of**

www.pearsonhighered.com

ISBN-10: 0-205-69309-1
ISBN-13: 978-0-205-69309-2

CONTENTS

PART VIII   New Media and Old in the Information Age 273

Foreword

Willard D. Rowland, Jr.

Willard D. Rowland, Jr., is dean and professor emeritus of the School of Journalism and Mass Communication, The University of Colorado, Boulder.

The historiography of communication is undergoing its second important shift. Students of contemporary media and culture are increasingly interested in the long-term environment of human experience that frames modern communication, and that interest is reshaping the study of history in the field. This anthology, by David Crowley and Paul Heyer, with its particular structure, is a crucial and long overdue contribution to that reformulation.

For much of its initial life, communication history was the story of the press, typically rendered as the biographies of great publishers or newspapers, or of other specific media institutions and major figures, as in the chronicles of particular networks, media moguls, or film genres. The best such work, though generally in the minority, tended to situate its narratives in a broader social context, examining, for instance, the relationship between the press and changing forms of democracy, between film and socio-cultural experience, or between the electronic media and political economic patterns. The first significant shift in communication historiography was to make such broader considerations of politics, law, economics, and culture much more regular, intimate elements, to weave their threads more tightly into the tapestries of particular journalism and media histories.

If that first major shift was to broaden the horizontal frame of reference, to situate media history in a wider range of social institutions, the second major shift is to extend the frame vertically, to consider the broader story of media institutions against a much deeper chronological backdrop of the whole of human history, to examine the role of communication in the development of the human species and its forms of civilization.

It is in light of that latter shift that this book should be considered. The editors take their clue from the pioneering work of such scholars as Walter Ong, Elizabeth Eisenstein, and Harold Innis. Those communication historians share a keen interest in the deep civilization context of all principal forms of communication technologies, thereby encouraging a much richer understanding of the present, rapidly changing experience.

There are several key principles of this school of communication historiography that are well reflected in this book. First, this approach perceives all contemporary media and communication technologies as extensions of basic, innate human communication capacities. It refuses to abstract contemporary forms of media hardware and uses television cameras, personal computers, and satellites, seeing them instead as part of a long, complex process by which human beings are continuing to work out their particularly strong skills and instincts for creating systems of meaning and symbolic interaction. In this light, modern media technologies are only the latest, albeit highly significant, forms of ancient human communication technologies that include speech, gesture, drama, and social ritual of all kinds.

Second, as those different "technologies" have variously held sway during different periods of human experience, they have had differential impact in the defining characteristics of the species' capacities. It appears that the very cognitive structure of the individual human being and the formal patterns of human social relations are intimately linked to the forms or systems of communication that are predominant in given eras. An oral culture, without writing, print, or electronic media, seems to be "biased" toward a particular pattern of sensory and expository capacity that encourages ways of seeing, hearing, and, indeed, knowing, that are remarkably different when other forms of communication are more prominent. Over time those tendencies seem in turn to favor and encourage major changes in social organization, influencing, if not defining, choices among options in political, legal, religious, and economic structures. The whole of human experience, therefore, seems to depend greatly upon the form or forms of communication that are most in ascendancy during any era.

Third, if these relationships between communication systems and broad patterns of human thought and experience are so strong, then the story of communication is much more central to human history than the formal academic discipline of history itself has recognized. Since the late nineteenth century, history in the academy has been conventionally apportioned among the other major fields of social and humanistic learning that were also invented at about the same time. That is, we have had several histories, as in political history, social history, economic history, and even cultural history. Each of these has contended for primacy of place as the essential history, the substructural history upon which all the others are built. But now with the advent of a deep-civilization perspective in communication history comes another contender. In its emerging form, contemporary communication history raises the prospect that communication patterns, systems, and technologies are not just important, but central and indispensable to human history, and that the other formal branches of history may have to be rewritten in its light.

Reduced to such principles, the current form of communication history has deep and far-reaching implications, not only for history itself, but also for communication research and media studies. At the very least it helps reiterate the importance in the academy of communication studies, underscoring the centrality of its questions to the overall understanding of human behavior and social experience. The readings in this book can therefore be seen as part of that broader project that is demonstrating the contribution of communication research to the increasingly important contemporary debates about culture and technology in society.

Those claims having been made, however, it should quickly become clear that the historical perspective advanced by this book raises a number of important new questions and cautions. For instance, if one is to take communication forms and media experience as central to the development of human experience, just how fundamental are they? To what extent does this argument flirt with a form of technological determinism that our more recent studies in both communication research and the philosophy of technology strongly caution us against?

Or, as another example, if we are to adopt a deeper chronological sense of communication history and push the matter back into the origins of human civilization, how much farther back must we go? We have customarily thought of the "evolution" of communication as a progression through a trilogy, from oral through print to electronic cultures. Yet much contemporary anthropological research suggests the possibility of a strong, pre-oral kinesic capacity. It may well be that systems of gesture, posture, movements, and signs antedate formal patterns of speech and language. Could it be that our classical Greek heritage and the long-standing influence of rhetoric in Western academic consciousness have over-privileged the oral tradition in the evolution of mind and culture? If so, the dimensions of a pre-oral culture will have to be mapped and added to the usual trilogy, making it at least a quartet.

However, the methodological problems therein are formidable. It has been difficult enough to describe the characteristics of oral cultures, because history is typically interpretation organized around documentary records. Periods of human experience before written documents or other tangible artifacts slide off into a vague, highly speculative prehistory. How do we develop a sophisticated capacity for inferring and knowing with any certainty the nature of the communication experience in such oral and pre-oral mists?

Meanwhile, what about the transitional periods? The trilogy or quartet models imagine a clear-cut distinction between one communication culture or tradition and another. Yet, the more we study the problem of change, the more we are struck by John Donne's problem of finding the line between day and night. Just how long was Western scribal culture? Just how oral was it; or to consider it the other way around, how much of what we consider print culture did it anticipate, if not determine? Such questions are not trivial in our own age when we are still in the quite early days of what we think is an electronic culture.

How, too, to compensate for the Western-centric character of our interpretation of communication experience? We know just enough about Eastern languages and media experiences to begin to feel uneasy about a chronology that is dominated by European and North American recitations. At the same time, we have barely scratched the surface of the many other great, Southern Hemisphere civilizations whose histories of speech and writing alone would probably add much rich and, perhaps even confounding, material to this task.

What, too, of the problem of progress? A print culture is typically seen as preferable to an oral or scribal tradition. But is it? Against what criteria? What is lost in the shift? Then, what are we to make of the contemporary changes? We swing wildly between messianic and demonic views about the nature and impact of modern communications technology. How are we to think carefully about what is better or worse in a given array of communication capacities? Indeed, how are we to account for the influence of the particular constellation of communication forms at the moment in even asking the question?

It is not as if the readings selected by Crowley and Heyer answer such questions, or that they should be expected to do so. But the perspective on communication history offered here is rich and compelling. It will make it considerably easier to teach ever more sophisticated histories of the media and communications technologies, giving them a much more sober and learned framework. It should also help energize a whole new generation of related scholarship within communication studies and even history itself.

Preface

Why does a new communication medium—the alphabet, printing, broadcasting, the internet—come into being? What impact does it have on the media that precede it? How does a new medium exert influence on the everyday life of society? And how, in turn, can society and culture influence media practices?

These are some of the questions Communication in History has been trying to address for over a decade. During that time numerous students and colleagues have told us that the subject area is becoming increasingly vital to their interests and professional development. Thanks to their encouragement and the support of Pearson Allyn & Bacon, we have created this new and expanded sixth edition. The new edition features more coverage of major media developments in the past, such as the role of printing in the rise of the modern state, and an expanded examination of communication in our own era of proliferating media forms—television, video, digital technology, and the internet. We have created this rich canvas using selections from writers considered to be at the vanguard of their respective fields. The goal of this new edition, however, has changed little from previous versions: to invite students to consider the development of human behavior and social experience as, in part, a response to the uses and consequences of communication media in the wider context of human history. The text lays out a journey that will help reveal how media have been influential both in maintaining social order and as powerful agents of change.

The issues raised by the role of media in history are broad-based, too broad we think to be easily encompassed in a single author textbook. From the beginning, we felt that the best way to go was with an anthology featuring an exemplary list of contributors, whose research relates directly to or complements one another. As with past editions, all the contributors try to tell us something about the characteristics and the human consequences of particular media and their development. It should not be surprising that the contributors come from a variety of disciplines. The history of communication, although most at home in the disciplines of communication and cultural studies, draws from and has relevance for a variety of fields, including architecture, archeology, anthropology, history, journalism, literary criticism, and sociology.

New to This Edition

New authors include Lisa Gitelman, Jonathan Sterne, John Durham Peters, Henry Jenkins, and Manuel Castells. New selections address the development of sound recording, the emergence of the modalities of broadcasting, television in the new post-mass media environment, and the expanding social significance of mobile communications and networks.

We have divided the sixth edition into eight parts, beginning with prehistory and ending with the contemporary information era. At times, contributors in a given section will cite each other's work as well as the work of a contributor in another part of the book. As a result, we think you will find considerable unity within and among the eight parts of the text.

To further help students appreciate these connections, and to afford an overview of the history of communication, we have provided an introduction to each of the eight sections. The purpose of the section introductions is to provide a rationale for that particular section, an explanation of key concepts and transitions, and to cite background material that might help the reader better appreciate the individual essays. At the end of the volume, we have included a short list of Suggestions for Further Reading.

Acknowledgments

Finally, we wish to mention a few of the many individuals who provided encouragement, and often assistance, for this ongoing project. Our thanks go to Alison Beale, Anouk Belanger, David Black, Rhianon Bury, Bill Buxton, Ella Chmielewska, Ian Chunn, Hart Cohen, Lon Dubinski, Derrick de Kerckhove, Jane Dickson, Elin Edwards, Bruce Ferguson, Jonathan Finn, Jib Fowles, Kathleen Galarneau, Robert Graham, Lynne Hissey, Sylvia Hoang, Richard Herbert Howe, Jesse Hunter, Iwona Irwin-Zarecka, Liss Jeffrey, James B. Johnston, Stephen Kern, Bill Leiss, Rolly Lorimer, Oya Majlesi, Shauna McCabe, David Mitchell, Ira Nayman, Jean Ogilvie, John Rowlandson, Lise Ouimet, Herbert Pimlot, Firoozeh Radjei, Gertrude Robinson, Wik Rowland, Leslie Shade, Brian Shoesmith, Ed Slopek, Steve Stack, Jonathan Sterne, Graham Thompson, Phil Vitone, James Wong, Darren Wershler, Gaius Gilbert, Lisa Sumner, Martin Dowding, Andrew Herman, Barbara Jenkins, Erin Macleod, and Peter Urquhart.

For their assistance, we would like to thank the National Archives of Canada, Art History and Communication Studies at McGill University, the Department of Communication Studies at Wilfrid Laurier University, the McLuhan Program in Culture and Technology at the University of Toronto, and The InterNet Group. Our thanks go as well to our editor, Jeanne Zalesky, and to Megan Lentz, Bayani DeLeon, Sarah Bylund, Sarah Sleys, Kathy Gavilanes at Pearson Allyn & Bacon and to Joseph Barnabas Malcolm at GGS Higher Education Resources and Lucy Palmieri at Pre-PressPMG and Jane Hilken and to all those who contributed to the new international edition.

PART ONE

The Media of Early Civilization

Painted limestone stela, from the twelfth Egyptian dynasty, about 1955 B.C. *The Metropolitan Museum of Art, gift of Edward S. Harkness, 1912 (12.184).* The Metropolitan Museum of Art, New York, NY, U.S.A. Image copyright © The Metropolitan Museum of Art/Art Resource, NY. The Metropolitan Museum of Art, New York, NY, U.S.A. Image copyright © The Metropolitan Museum of Art.

Whenever the terms "media" or "communications" are mentioned, many of us envision the pervasive technology of today's world. Students of communication may range further back historically and think of the newspaper over the past two hundred years, the invention of the printing press in the fifteenth century, or perhaps the origins of the alphabet in ancient Greece. Communications media, however, are older—much older. In this part we will look at some key aspects of their development, beginning with the emergence of the complex writing systems of ancient Mesopotamia and Egypt.

What was the first communications medium? This question may be impossible to answer scientifically. However, it is not impossible to imagine. Almost as soon as our prehistoric ancestors made tools of wood, bone, and stone to help them physically adapt to a changing environment, they probably made "tools for thought" as well. Perhaps the earliest device of this kind was a simple stick, notched to indicate the number of deer in a nearby herd or some rocks or logs arranged to mark the importance of a given territory. What was important was the process. Humankind enlarged its sphere of communication by creating communications.

Communication is an exchange of information and messages. It is an activity. About one hundred thousand years ago, our early ancestors communicated through nonverbal gestures and an evolving system of spoken language. As their world became increasingly complex, they needed more than just the shared memory of the group to recall important things. They needed what is sometimes called an extrasomatic memory, a memory outside of the body. Thus an increase in "communication" led to "communications," the development of media to store and retrieve the growing volume of information. The microchip of today is one such medium and a direct descendant of our hypothetical notched stick.

The later prehistoric period, from about fifty thousand to ten thousand B.C., has begun to yield impressive evidence of both communication and communications. For some time now, archeologists and other researchers have been engaged in reexamining some of the so-called art of the Old Stone Age, the bone tools, figurines, and the famous cave paintings that were found in Western Europe and date from the end of the last Ice Age. Whereas earlier researchers often saw these artifacts as ritual magic, or "art for art's sake," from a communications perspective we might ask whether they constitute an early systematic attempt at symbol-using to record information about the natural environment, in other words, communications media.

While contemporary research holds out the possibility that we will continue to add to our knowledge of the beginnings of the process that leads to the emergence of ancient writing systems, the more immediate historical origins of this phenomenon have been outlined in our first excerpt from Denise Schmandt-Besserat, "The Earliest Precursors of Writing." Schmandt-Besserat bases her argument not on the discovery of new archeological remains, but on reinterpreting previous finds in a new communications way. She begins about twelve thousand years ago and continues to the fourth millennium B.C. (Standard usage now is B.C.E—Before the Christian Era—although some essays in our book use the older designation) and the rise of the great Near Eastern civilizations in Mesopotamia and Egypt, which are often said to have been made possible through the invention of writing.

Schmandt-Besserat provides compelling evidence for her contention that before the emergence of writing, several Old World societies were recording economic transactions through the use of fired clay tokens one to three centimeters in size. Readers will be shown some fascinating archeological detective work as she comments on traditional interpretations of these artifacts as charms, toys, or tools, and then suggests an alternative communications view. In so doing she notes that many of the tokens resemble the characters known as ideograms, which are conventionalized signs that do not look like what they represent (a character that looks like what it represents is known as a pictogram). Ideograms were the basis of the world's first full-fledged writing system, the Sumerian, which arose in 3500 B.C. Thus if one accepts her hypothesis, the tokens were an abstract form of three-dimensional writing in response to social and economic changes necessitating a more complex way of life: civilization.

Our next excerpt, by Harold Innis, deals with what happened in the realm of communications and culture after the establishment of empires in Egypt and Mesopotamia. Innis (1894–1952) was a Canadian political economist turned communication theorist. The communication ideas he acquired in training at the University of Chicago surfaced periodically in his early economic writings. However, it was the work he produced shortly before his death, *Empire and Communications* (1950) and *The Bias of Communication* (1951), which marked his transformation to communications historian. More than any other twentieth-century figure, Innis argued that this field merits disciplinary or sub-disciplinary status. Although he explored almost every facet of the communications/history question, the bulk of his project deals with the role of media in the organization of ancient empires and early Western civilization.

Innis elaborated his history of communication around a series of core concepts, several of which are used in the excerpt we have included. Perhaps the most significant one pertains to time and space. Innis argued that each of the major Old World civilizations had a specific cultural orientation that was temporal or spatial. This orientation derived in part from the nature and use of the dominant medium it employed. For example, stone in ancient Egypt was a durable "time-biased" medium, favoring a centralized absolute government of divine kingship. This bias was further evident in the use of hieroglyphic writing to produce astonishingly accurate calendars, around which the agricultural cycle pivoted. With the coming of papyrus, a light portable "space-biased" medium suitable for administration over distance, the complexion of Egypt changed. The priestly class expanded its power as the acquisition of new territories gave rise to an extended empire needing an administrative bureaucracy versed in the new medium.

Our next selection, by Marcia and Robert Ascher, deals with an area of communications history ignored until recently by major scholars in the field—ancient New World civilizations. The Aschers focus on the Incas, who, unlike other New World states, the Maya and Aztec for example, did not have writing. But isn't writing essential to civilization and a complex state level organization? Ascher and Ascher debunk this still prevalent misconception. They convincingly show that it is not writing per se that allows for civilization, but some medium for the keeping of records which can function in an efficient and comprehensive manner. The quipu served this purpose among the Incas of ancient Peru. It was a series of cords of different length, thickness, and colors that was knotted and braided. Each of these elements constituted information, the kind used to record crop production, taxation, a census, and a variety of other kinds of information.

An intriguing point relevant to the excerpt by the Aschers, and the one preceding it by Innis, is that the quipu, being a light portable medium, was suitable for administration over distance and indeed was heavily used in this manner by the expansionist Inca empire. This is a classic example of Innis's notion of a space-biased medium, although Innis did not consider the Incas. Ascher and Ascher, however, were influenced by him, and their research sustains this interesting and useful concept.

The quipu notwithstanding, most of the world's early civilizations came into being using writing as their dominant medium of communication.

In our final selection, Andrew Robinson sketches out some of the issues, many still unresolved, in the relationship between earlier systems of three-dimensional accounting, such as the system of tokens, and the later development of two-dimensional systems of scripts and alphabets that characterize the evolution of writing worldwide. Robinson explores the controversy about the relationship of written and spoken language systems and the ways in which the linkage between written and spoken forms (logography and phonography) varies widely from language to language. He also raises the question of how the globalizing trends in society today might push the demand for new forms of communication (he points to the growing use of pictograms in public spaces) that are independent of both spoken and written languages. Robinson also shows us that some of the principles used in ancient scripts, such as hieroglyphs, are still with us in everything from road signs to computer keyboards. What further examples can you add to his list?

CHAPTER 1

The Earliest Precursor of Writing

Denise Schmandt-Besserat

Denise Schmandt-Besserat is an archaeologist working at the University of Texas at Austin. Her work on early symbol systems leading to the origin of writing is currently influencing students in a wide range of disciplines.

Individuals applied their minds to symbols rather than things and went beyond the world of concrete experience into the world of conceptual relations created within an enlarged time and space universe. The time world was extended beyond the range of remembered things and the space world beyond the range of known places.

—HAROLD A. INNIS[1]

It is the nature of archaeological research to deal with data and their interpretation. . . . I use the facts as well as the hypotheses I have presented on the token system to reflect more broadly on the significance of tokens with respect to communication, social structures, and cognitive skills.

[This reading] deals with the place of tokens among other prehistoric symbolic systems. After presenting relevant aspects of symbolism from the Paleolithic to the Neolithic period, I will analyze what the tokens owed to their antecedents, how they revolutionized the use of symbols, and how they presaged writing.

SYMBOLS AND SIGNS

Symbols are things whose special meaning allows us to conceive, express, and communicate ideas. In our society, for example, black is the symbol of death, the star-spangled banner stands for the United States of America, and the cross for Christianity.

Signs are a subcategory of symbols. Like symbols, signs are things that convey meaning, but they differ in carrying narrow, precise, and unambiguous information. Compare, for example, the color black, the symbol standing for death, with the sign "I." Black is a symbol loaded with a deep but diffuse significance, whereas "I" is a sign that stands unequivocally for the number "one." Symbols and signs are used differently: symbols help us to conceive and reflect on ideas, whereas signs are communication devices bound to action.[2]

Because the use of symbols is a characteristic of human behavior, it is by definition as old as humankind itself.[3] From the beginnings of humanity, symbols have encapsulated the knowledge, experience, and beliefs of all people. Humans, from the beginning, have also communicated by signs. Symbols and signs, therefore, are a major key to the understanding of cultures.

Symbols, however, are ephemeral and, as a rule, do not survive the societies that create them. For one thing, the meaning they carry is arbitrary. For instance, the color black, which evokes death in our culture, may just as well stand for life in another. It is a fundamental characteristic of symbols that their meaning cannot be perceived either by the senses or by logic but can only be learned from those who use them.[4] As a consequence, when a culture vanishes, the symbols left behind become enigmatic, for there is no longer anyone initiated into their significance. Thus, not only are symbolic relics from prehistoric societies extremely few, but those that are extant usually cannot be interpreted.

LOWER AND MIDDLE PALEOLITHIC SYMBOLS

Although humans were present in the Near East starting in the Lower Paleolithic period, as early as 600,000 years ago, no symbols have been preserved from these remote times. The first archaeological material attesting to the use of symbols in the Near East belongs to the epoch of Neanderthal humans, the Middle Paleolithic period, as late as 60,000 to 25,000 B.C. The data are threefold. First, pieces of ocher were recovered in the cave of Qafzeh, Israel.[5] There is, of course, no way of knowing what ocher was used for at the time, but the red pigment suggests a symbolic rather than a functional purpose, and some hypothesize it may have been used for body painting. The second set of evidence consists of funerary paraphernalia, such as flowers or antlers deposited in burial sites—for example, at Shanidar about 60,000 B.C.[6] and at Qafzeh.[7] Although we shall never know the significance that ocher, flowers, and antlers may have had for Neanderthal humans, it is generally assumed that the red pigment and the funerary deposits were symbols carrying a magico-religious connotation. Accordingly, some of the earliest evidence of the use of symbols in the Near East suggests a ritual function.

A third category of artifacts is bone fragments engraved with a series of notches usually arranged in a parallel fashion, such as were recovered in the cave of Kebara.[8] These incised bones are important for the present study because they constitute the earliest known examples of manmade

symbols in the Near East. Whereas at Shanidar Neanderthal humans conferred a meaning on pigments and flowers readily available in nature, the occupants of Kebara began modifying materials in order to translate ideas.

UPPER PALEOLITHIC AND MESOLITHIC SYMBOLS

The same symbolic tradition continues in the Upper Paleolithic and the Mesolithic. The use of ocher is frequently attested,[9] and notched bones are part of the assemblages at Hayonim in Israel, ca. 28,000 B.C.,[10] as well as at Jiita[11] and Ksar Akil in Lebanon, ca. 15,000–12,000 B.C. A bone awl from Ksar Akil measures about 10 cm in length and bears some 170 incisions grouped along the shaft into four separate columns. . . . Such artifacts are still present at Hayonim,[12] at other Natufian sites of the Levant,[13] and even as far away as the Negev around 10,000 B.C.[14] At the same time, sites from the Levant to Iraq produced pebbles and various limestone and bone implements engraved with parallel lines.[15]

A new category of iconic symbols is manifested in western Asia during the course of the Upper Paleolithic. At Hayonim, ca. 28,000 B.C., these symbols take the shape of stone slabs bearing fine lines that suggest a horse.[16] The cave of Beldibi, Turkey, dated about 15,000 to 12,000 B.C., produced images of a bull and a deer, traced with a flint on the cave wall[17] and on pebbles.[18]

The function of the Paleolithic and Mesolithic incised bones and animal representations can only be hypothesized. André Lcroi-Gourhan viewed the iconic representations as symbols of magico-religious significance. According to him, the animal images referred to the numinous, each species representing one manifestation of a complex cosmology.[19] Leroi-Gourhan argued that these animal figures were symbols loaded with a deep meaning, serving as instruments of thought and making it possible to grasp the abstract concepts of a cosmology. On the other hand, from the early days of archaeology, the notched bones have been interpreted as tallies, each notch representing one item of which to keep track.[20] According to a recent theory of Alexander Marshack, the artifacts were lunar calendars, each incised line recording one sighting of the moon.[21] The linear markings have been consistently viewed as referring to discrete and concrete entities. I suggest, therefore, that we consider the notches as signs promoting the accumulation of knowledge for specific ends. If these hypotheses are correct, the tallies constitute evidence that signs started being used in the Near East at least by the Middle Paleolithic period; and if the evidence reflects the facts, then the use of signs to communicate factual information followed the use of symbols in ritual.

If indeed the incised bones are tallies, the Paleolithic and Mesolithic linear markings of Kebara, Hayonim, Ksar Akil, and Jiita are of considerable interest because they represent the first attempt at storing and communicating concrete information in the Near East. This first step in "data processing" signified two remarkable contributions. First, the tallies departed from the use of ritual symbols by dealing with concrete data. They translated perceptible physical phenomena, such as the successive phases of the moon, rather than evoking intangible aspects of a cosmology. Second, the notched signs abstracted data in several ways:

1. They translated concrete information into abstract markings.
2. They removed the data from their context. For example, the sighting of the moon was abstracted from any simultaneous events, such as atmospheric or social conditions.
3. They separated the knowledge from the knower, presenting data, as we are told by Walter J. Ong[22] and Marshall McLuhan, in a "cold" and static visual form, rather than in the "hot" and flexible oral medium, that involves voice modulation and body gestures.[23]

As a result, the graphic signs of Ksar Akil and Jiita not only brought about a new way of recording, handling, and communicating data, but generated an unprecedented objectivity in dealing with information.

The tallies remained, however, a rudimentary device. For one thing, the notches were unspecific and could suggest an unlimited field of interpretations. Marshack postulates that the signs stood for phases of the moon; others have hypothesized that they served to keep a tally of animal kills. But there is no way to verify their meaning. In fact, the notched bones were limited to recording quantitative information concerning things known by the tallier but remaining enigmatic to anyone else. These quantities were entered according to the basic principle of one-to-one correspondence, which consisted of matching each unit of the group to be tallied with one notch. Moreover, because tallies used a single kind of marking—namely, notches—they could handle only one type of data at a time. One bone could keep track of one item, but a second bone was necessary in order to keep track of a second set of data. Therefore, this simple method of tallies would be adequate only in communities where just a few obvious items were being recorded, as seems to have been the case in the Upper Paleolithic period.

It is certainly possible, of course, that the bone tallies were not the only devices for storing information before 10,000 B.C. It is even likely that, as in many preliterate societies, people during the Paleolithic and Mesolithic periods used pebbles, twigs, or grains for counting. If this was so, then these counters shared the same inadequacies as tallies. First of all, pebbles, like the notches along the shaft of a bone, lacked the capacity to indicate what item was being counted. Only the individual who made the markings or piled up a number of pebbles knew what things were being recorded. Second, because they were nonspecific, pebbles and twigs did not allow one to keep track of more than a single category at a time. A pile of pebbles, or one bone, could keep track of a sequence of days, but another pile and another bone would be necessary to handle quantities of, say, animals. Third and finally, it may be presumed that the loose counters were used, like tallies, in the cumbersome method of one-to-one correspondence—each pebble or each twig standing for one unit, with no possibility of expressing abstract numbers. One day, for example, was represented by one pebble, two days by two pebbles, and so on. The loose counters facilitated data manipulation because they were easier to handle. On the other hand, the notched bones were more efficient for accumulating and preserving data, because the notches were permanent and could not be disassembled.

NEOLITHIC SYMBOLS

The first agricultural communities of the Near East carried on the age-old symbolic traditions. Early farmers placed antlers in house foundations and painted their floors with pigments.[24] They also performed burial rituals that sometimes involved red ocher.[25] At that time, too, human and animal forms were translated into clay figurines.[26] Finally, notched bones were still part of village assemblages.[27] However, the practice of agriculture generated new symbols—no doubt as a result of a new economy and a new way of life. The new symbols were different in form and content from anything used previously. These were the clay tokens modeled in distinctive shapes, each representing a precise quantity of a product.

A New Form

The primary singularity of the tokens was that they were entirely manmade. In contrast to pebbles, twigs, or grains put to a secondary use for counting, and in contrast to tallies, which communicated meaning by slightly altering a bone, tokens were artifacts created in specific shapes, such as cones, spheres, disks, cylinders, and tetrahedrons, from an amorphous clay mass for the unique purpose of communication and record keeping.

The tokens were an entirely new medium for conveying information. Here the conceptual leap was to endow each token shape, such as the cone, sphere, or disk, with a specific meaning. Consequently, unlike markings on tallies that had an infinite number of possible interpretations, each clay token was itself a distinct sign with a single, discrete, and unequivocal significance. While tallies were meaningless out of context, tokens could always be understood by anyone initiated into the system. The tokens, therefore, presaged pictography; each token stood for a single concept. Like the later Sumerian pictographs, the tokens were "concept signs."[28]

The greatest novelty of the new medium, however, was that it created a *system*. There was not just one type of token carrying a discrete meaning but an entire repertory of interrelated types of tokens, each with a corresponding discrete meaning. For example, besides the cone, which stood for a small measure of grain, the sphere represented a large measure of grain, the ovoid stood for a jar of oil, and so on. The system made it feasible to simultaneously manipulate information concerning different categories of items, resulting in a complexity of data processing never reached previously. It thus became possible to store with precision unlimited quantities of information concerning an infinite number of goods without the risk of depending on human memory. Furthermore, the system was open; that is to say, new signs were added when necessary by creating new token shapes, and the ever-increasing repertory constantly pushed the device to new frontiers of complexity.

The token system was, in fact, the first code—the earliest system of signs used for transmitting information. First of all, the repertory of shapes was systematized; that is to say, all the various tokens were systematically repeated in order to carry the same meaning. A sphere, for example, always signified a particular measure of grain. Second, it may be presumed that tokens were used according to a rudimentary syntax. It is likely, for example, that the counters were lined up on the accountant's table in a hierarchical order, starting on the right with tokens representing the largest units. That was how the Sumerians organized signs on a tablet, and it is logical to assume that the procedure was inherited from former usage in handling tokens. The fact that the tokens were systematized also had a great impact on their expansion. The token system was transmitted as a full-fledged code from community to community, ultimately spreading throughout the entire Near East, with each token form preserving the same meaning.

The token system owed little to the Paleolithic and Mesolithic periods. The choice of material for manufacturing the counters was a novelty; clay had been ignored by hunters and gatherers. Clay proved particularly advantageous since it is found abundantly in nature and is easy to work. Its remarkable plasticity when wet made it possible for villagers to create, with no tools and no great skill, an indefinite number of forms that became permanent when dried in the sun or baked in an open fire or oven.

The format of movable units was probably one of the very few features that tokens adopted from the past, perhaps having been inspired by a former usage of counting with pebbles, shells, twigs, or grains. Such a format enhanced data manipulation, since the small tokens could be arranged and rearranged at will into groups of any composition and size, while notches engraved on tallies were fixed and irreversible.

Otherwise, the various token shapes have no known Paleolithic or Mesolithic antecedents. But the counters have the merit of bringing together as a set, for the first time, each of the basic geometric shapes, such as the sphere, cone, cylinder, tetrahedron, triangle, quadrangle, and cube (the latter surprisingly rarely).[29] It is difficult to evaluate which of these forms were inspired by everyday life commodities and which were fully abstract. Among the latter, the cylinders and lenticular disks, which represented, alternatively, one unit and a group of animals, are visibly arbitrary. Others, such as the cone and ovoid, which stand respectively for a measure of grain and a unit of oil, were probably iconic, depicting a small cup and a pointed jar. Still other tokens, in the shape of animal heads, were naturalistic depictions.

A New Content

The token system was also unique in the kind of information it conveyed. Whereas Paleolithic iconic art probably evoked cosmological figures, and whereas Paleolithic or Mesolithic tallies may have counted time, the tokens dealt with economic data; each token stood for one precise amount of a commodity. As noted above, the cone and the sphere represented measures of grain probably equivalent to our liter and our bushel, respectively; the cylinder and lenticular disk showed numbers of animals; the tetrahedrons were units of work; and so on.

Moreover, unlike tallies, which recorded only quantitative information, the tokens also conveyed qualitative information. The type of item counted was indicated by the token shape, while the number of units involved was shown by the corresponding number of tokens. For example, one bushel of grain was represented by one sphere, two bushels of grain by two spheres, and [see photo] five bushels corresponded to five spheres. Therefore, like the previous tallies, the token system was based on the simple principle of one-to-one correspondence. This made it cumbersome to deal with large quantities of data, since humans can only identify small sets by pattern recognition. There are a few instances of tokens, though, which stood for a collection of items. Among them, the lenticular disk stood for a "flock" (presumably ten sheep). The large tetrahedron may have represented a week's work or the work of a gang—compared with the small tetrahedron, expressing one man-day's work.

The tokens lacked a capacity for dissociating the numbers from the items counted: one sphere stood for "one bushel of grain," and three spheres stood for "one bushel of grain, one bushel of grain, one bushel of grain." This inability to abstract numbers also contributed to the awkwardness of the system, since each collection counted required an equal number of tokens of a special shape. Furthermore, the number of types and subtypes of tokens multiplied over time in order to satisfy the growing need for more specificity in accounting. Thus, tokens for counting sheep were supplemented by special tokens for counting rams, ewes, and lambs. This proliferation of signs was bound to lead to the system's collapse.

The Neolithic symbolic system of clay tokens superseded the Paleolithic tallies throughout the Near East because it had the following advantages:

A. The system was simple.

1. Clay was a common material requiring no special skills or tools to be worked.
2. The forms of the tokens were plain and easy to duplicate.
3. The system was based on a one-to-one correspondence, which is the simplest method for dealing with quantities.
4. The tokens stood for units of goods. They were independent of phonetics and could be meaningful in any dialect.

B. The code allowed new performances in data processing and communication.

1. It was the first mnemonic device able to handle and store an unlimited quantity of data.
2. It brought more flexibility in the manipulation of information by making it possible to add, subtract, and rectify data at will.
3. It enhanced logic and rational decision-making by allowing the scrutiny of complex data.

. . . The code was also timely. It fulfilled new needs for counting and accounting created by agriculture. It was an intrinsic part of the "Neolithic Revolution" spreading throughout the entire region of the Near East, wherever agriculture became adopted.

A TURNING POINT IN COMMUNICATION AND DATA STORAGE

The Neolithic token system may be considered the second step in the evolution of communication and data processing. It followed the Paleolithic and Mesolithic mnemonic devices and preceded the invention of pictographic writing in the urban

Envelope from Susa, Iran, showing markings corresponding to the tokens enclosed. *Musee du Louvre/RMN Reunion des Musees Nationaux, France. SCALA/Art Resource, NY.*

period. The tokens are the link, therefore, between tallies and pictographs. They borrowed elements from such Paleolithic antecedents as the tallies or pebbles used for counting. On the other hand, the counters already presaged writing in many important ways.

The main debt of the token system to Paleolithic and Mesolithic tallies was the principle of abstracting data. Like tallies, tokens translated concrete information into abstract markings, removed the data from their context, separated the knowledge from the knower, and increased objectivity. The format of small movable counters was probably inherited from a former usage of counting with pebbles, shells, or seeds. Most important, the tokens acquired from tallies and pebbles their cumbersome way of translating quantity in one-to-one correspondence.

On the other hand, the tokens were new symbols that laid the groundwork for the invention of pictographic writing. In particular, they presaged the Sumerian writing system by the following features:[30]

1. *Semanticity:* Each token was meaningful and communicated information.
2. *Discreteness:* The information conveyed was specific. Each token shape, like each pictograph, was bestowed a unique meaning. The incised ovoid, for example, like the sign ATU 733, stood for a unit of oil.
3. *Systematization:* Each of the token shapes was systematically repeated in order to carry the same meaning. An incised ovoid, for example, always signified the same measure of oil.
4. *Codification:* The token system consisted of a multiplicity of interrelated elements. Besides the cone, which stood for a small measure of grain, the sphere represented a larger measure of grain, the ovoid meant a jar of oil, the cylinder an animal, and so on. Consequently, the token system made it feasible, for the first time, to deal simultaneously with information concerning different items.
5. *Openness:* The repertory of tokens could be expanded at will by creating further shapes representing new concepts. The tokens could also be combined to form any possible set. This made it feasible to store an unlimited quantity of information concerning an unlimited number of items.
6. *Arbitrariness:* Many of the token forms were abstract; for example, the cylinder and lenticular disk stood respectively for one and ten(?) animals. Others were arbitrary representations; for instance, the head of an animal bearing a collar symbolized the dog.
7. *Discontinuity:* Tokens of closely related shapes could refer to unrelated concepts. For example, the lenticular disk stood for ten(?) animals, whereas the flat disk referred to a large measure of grain.
8. *Independence of phonetics:* The tokens were concept signs standing for units of goods. They were independent of spoken language and phonetics and thus could be understood by people speaking different tongues.
9. *Syntax:* The tokens were organized according to set rules. There is evidence, for example, that tokens were arranged in lines of counters of the same kind, with the largest units placed at the right.
10. *Economic content:* The tokens, like the earliest written texts, were limited to handling information concerning real goods. It is only centuries later, about 2900 B.C., that writing began to record historical events and religious texts.

The chief drawback of the token system was its format. On the one hand, three-dimensionality gave the device the advantage of being tangible and easy to manipulate. On the other hand, the volume of the tokens constituted a major shortcoming. Although they were small, the counters were also cumbersome when used in large quantities. Consequently, as is illustrated by the small number of tokens held in each envelope, the system was restricted to keeping track of small amounts of goods. The tokens were also difficult to use for permanent records, since a group of small objects can easily be separated and can hardly be kept in a particular order for any length of time. Finally, the system was inefficient because each commodity was expressed by a special token and thus required an ever-growing repertory of counters. In short, because the token system consisted of loose, three-dimensional counters, it was sufficient to record transactions dealing with small quantities of various goods but ill-suited for communicating more complex messages. Other means, such as seals, were relied upon to identify the patron/recipient in a transaction.

In turn, the pictographic tablets inherited from tokens the system of a code based on concept signs, a basic syntax, and an economic content. Writing did away with the greatest inadequacies of the token system by bringing four major innovations to data storage and communication. First, unlike a group of loose, three-dimensional tokens, pictographs held information permanently. Second, the tablets accommodated more diversified information by assigning specific parts of the field for the recording of particular data. For example, signs representing the sponsor/recipient of the transaction were systematically placed below the symbols indicating goods. In this fashion, the scribe was able to transcribe information, such as "ten sheep (received from) Kurli" even though no particular signs were available to indicate verbs and prepositions. Third, writing put an end to the repetition in one-to-one correspondence of symbols representing commodities such as "sheep" (ATU 761/ZATU 571) or "oil" (ATU 733/ZATU 393). Numerals were created. From then on, these new symbols, placed in conjunction with the signs for particular goods, indicated the quantities involved. Fourth, and finally, writing overcame the system of concept signs by becoming phonetic and, by doing so, not only reduced the repertory of symbols but opened writing to all subjects of human endeavor.

The first traces of visual symbols in the prehistoric Near East date to the Mousterian period, ca. 60,000–25,000 B.C. These symbols, which consisted of funerary offerings and perhaps body paintings, show that Neanderthal humans had developed rituals in order to express abstract concepts.[31] The earliest evidence of signs(?), in the form of notched tallies, also date from the Middle Paleolithic. Assuming that the archaeological data reflect the facts, those data suggest that symbolism was used both in rituals and, at the same time, for the compilation of concrete information.

From its beginnings in about 30,000 B.C., the evolution of information processing in the prehistoric Near East proceeded in three major phases, each dealing with data of increasing specificity. First, during the Middle and late Upper Paleolithic, ca. 30,000–12,000 B.C., tallies referred to one unit of an unspecified item. Second, in the early Neolithic, ca. 8000 B.C., the tokens indicated a precise unit of a particular good. With the invention of writing, which took place in the urban period, ca. 3100 B.C., it was possible to record and communicate the name of the sponsor/recipient of the merchandise, formerly indicated by seals.

The Neolithic tokens constitute a second step, and a major turning point, in information processing. They inherited from Paleolithic devices the method of abstracting data. The system of tokens can be credited as the first use of signs to manipulate concrete commodities of daily life, whereas Paleolithic symbols dealt with ritual and tallies (perhaps) recorded time. The simple but brilliant invention of clay symbols that represented basic concepts provided the first means of supplementing language. It opened new avenues of tremendous importance for communication, providing the immediate background for the invention of writing.

NOTES

1. Harold A. Innis, *Empire and Communication* (Oxford: Clarendon Press, 1950), p. 11.
2. Suzanne K. Langer, *Philosophy in a New Key* (Cambridge: Harvard University Press, 1960), pp. 41–43.
3. Jerome S. Bruner, "On Cognitive Growth II," in Jerome S. Bruner et al., *Studies in Cognitive*

Growth (New York: John Wiley and Sons, 1966), p. 47.

4. Ibid., p. 31.

5. B. Vandermeersch, "Ce que révèlent les sépultures moustériennes de Qafzeh en Israël," *Archeologia* 45 (1972): 12.

6. Ralph S. Solecki, *Shanidar* (London: Allen Lane, Penguin Press, 1972), pp. 174–178.

7. Vandermeersch, "Ce que révèlent les sépultures," p. 5.

8. Simon Davis, "Incised Bones from the Mousterian of Kebara Cave (Mount Carmel) and the Aurignacian of Ha-Yonim Cave (Western Galilee), Israel," *Paléorient* 2, no. 1 (1974): 181–182.

9. Among the sites involved are Ksar Akil, Yabrud II, Hayonim, and Abu-Halka. Ofer Bar-Yosef and Anna Belfer-Cohen, "The Early Upper Paleolithic in Levantine Caves," in J. F. Hoffecker and C. A. Wolf, eds., *The Early Upper Paleolithic: Evidence from Europe and the Near East*, BAR International Series 437 (Oxford, 1988), p. 29.

10. Davis, "Incised Bones," pp. 181–182.

11. Loraine Copeland and Francis Hours, "Engraved and Plain Bone Tools from Jiita (Lebanon) and Their Early Kebaran Context," *Proceedings of the Prehistoric Society*, vol. 43 (1977), pp. 295–301.

12. Ofer Bar-Yosef and N. Goren, "Natufians Remains in Hayonim Cave," *Paléorient* 1 (1973): fig. 8: 16–17.

13. Jean Perrot, "Le Gisement natufien de Mallaha (Eynan), Israel," *L'Anthropologie* 70, nos. 5–6 (1966): fig. 22: 26. An incised bone radius from Kharaneh IV, phase D, may also date from the same period. Mujahed Muheisen, "The Epipalaeolithic Phases of Kharaneh IV," *Colloque International CNRS, Préhistoire du Levant* 2 (Lyons, 1988), p. 11, fig. 7.

14. Donald O. Henry, "Preagricultural Sedentism: The Natufian Example," in T. Douglas Price and James A. Brown, eds., *Prehistoric Hunter-Gatherers* (New York: Academic Press, 1985), p. 376.

15. Phillip C. Edwards, "Late Pleistocene Occupation in Wadi al-Hammeh, Jordan Valley," Ph.D. dissertation, University of Sydney, 1987, fig. 4.29: 3–8; Rose L. Solecki, *An Early Village Site at Zawi Chemi Shanidar*, Bibliotheca Mesopotamica, vol. 13 (Malibu, Calif.: Undena Publications, 1981), pp. 43, 48, 50, pl. 8r, fig. 15p.

16. Anna Belfer-Cohen and Ofer Bar-Yosef, "The Aurignacian at Hayonim Cave," *Paléorient* 7, no. 2 (1981): fig. 8.

17. Enver Y. Bostanci, "Researches on the Mediterranean Coast of Anatolia, a New Paleolithic Site at Beldibi near Antalya," *Anatolia* 4 (1959): 140, pl. 11.

18. Enver Y. Bostanci, "Important Artistic Objects from the Beldibi Excavations," *Antropoloji* 1, no. 2 (1964): 25–31.

19. André Leroi-Gourhan, *Préhistoire de l'art occidental* (Paris: Editions Lucien Mazenod, 1971), pp. 119–121.

20. Denis Peyrony, *Eléments de préhistoire* (Ussel: G. Eyoulet et Fils, 1927), p. 54.

21. Alexander Marshack, *The Roots of Civilization* (New York: McGraw-Hill, 1972).

22. Walter J. Ong, *Orality and Literacy* (New York: Methuen, 1982), p. 46.

23. Marshall McLuhan, *Understanding Media* (New York: New American Library, 1964), pp. 81–90.

24. Jacques Cauvin, *Les Premiers Villages de Syrie-Palestine du IXème au VIIème Millénaire avant J. C.*, Collection de la Maison de l'Orient Méditerranéen Ancien no. 4, Série Archéologique 3 (Lyons: Maison de l'Orient, 1978), p. 111; Jacques Cauvin, "Nouvelles fouilles à Mureybet (Syrie) 1971–72, Rapport préliminaire," *Annales Archéologiques Arabes Syriennes* (1972): 110.

25. Robert J. Braidwood, Bruce Howe, and Charles A. Reed, "The Iranian Prehistoric Project," *Science* 133, no. 3469 (1961): 2008.

26. Denise Schmandt-Besserat: "The Use of Clay before Pottery in the Zagros," *Expedition* 16, no. 2 (1974): 11–12; "The Earliest Uses of Clay in Syria," *Expedition* 19, no. 3 (1977): 30–31.

27. Charles L. Redman, *The Rise of Civilization* (San Francisco: W. H. Freeman and Company, 1978), p. 163, fig. 5–18: A.

28. Ignace J. Gelb, *A Study of Writing* (Chicago: University of Chicago Press, 1974), p. 65.

29. Cyril S. Smith, "A Matter of Form," *Isis* 76, no. 4 (1985): 586.

30. C. F. Hockett, "The Origin of Speech," *Scientific American* 203 (1960): 90–91.

31. M. Shackley, *Neanderthal Man* (Hamden, Conn.: Archon Books, 1980), p. 113.

CHAPTER 2

Media in Ancient Empires

Harold Innis

Harold Innis (1894–1952) was a Canadian scholar of world renown. He was trained in economics at the University of Chicago and, toward the close of his life, extensively explored the field of communication history. Two of his books on the subject have become classics, Empire and Communications *and* The Bias of Communication.

FROM STONE TO PAPYRUS

The profound disturbances in Egyptian civilization involved in the shift from absolute monarchy to a more democratic organization coincided with a shift in emphasis on stone as a medium of communication or as a basis of prestige, as shown in the pyramids, to an emphasis on papyrus.[1] Papyrus sheets dated from the first dynasty and inscribed sheets dated from the fifth dynasty (2680–2540 B.C. or 2750–2625 B.C.).

Papyrus Technology

In contrast with stone, papyrus as a writing medium was extremely light. It was made from a plant (*Cyperus papyrus*) that was restricted in its habitat to the Nile delta, and was manufactured into writing material near the marshes where it was found. Fresh green stems of the plant were cut into suitable lengths and the green rind stripped off. They were then cut into thick strips and laid parallel to each other and slightly overlapping on absorbent cloth. A similar layer was laid above and across them, and the whole was covered by another cloth. This was hammered with a mallet for about two hours and then the sheets were welded into a single mass that was finally pressed and dried. Sheets were fastened to each other to make rolls, in some cases of great length. As a light

commodity it could be transported over wide areas.[2]

Brushes made from a kind of rush (*Funcus maritimus*) were used for writing. Lengths ranged from 6 to 16 inches and diameters from 1/16 to 1/10 of an inch. The rushes were cut slantingly at one end and bruised to separate the fibres.[3] The scribe's palette had two cups for black and red ink and a water pot. He wrote in hieratic characters from right to left, arranging the text in vertical columns or horizontal lines of equal size that formed pages. The rest of the papyrus was kept rolled up in his left hand.[4]

Thought Gained Lightness

Writing on stone was characterized by straightness or circularity of line, rectangularity of form, and an upright position, whereas writing on papyrus permitted cursive forms suited to rapid writing. "When hieroglyphs were chiselled on stone monuments they were very carefully formed and decorative in character. When written on wood or papyrus they became simpler and more rounded in form . . . The cursive or hieratic style was still more hastily written, slurring over or abbreviating and running together . . . they ceased to resemble pictures and became script."[5]

"By escaping from the heavy medium of stone" thought gained lightness. "All the circumstances arouse interest, observation, reflection."[6] A marked increase in writing by hand was accompanied by the secularization of writing, thought, and activity. The social revolution between the Old and the New Kingdom was marked by a flow of eloquence and a displacement of religious by secular literature.

The Organization of Scribes

Writing had been restricted to governmental, fiscal, magical, and religious purposes. With the increased use of papyrus and the simplification of hieroglyphic script into hieratic characters—in response to the demands of a quicker, cursive hand and the growth of writing and reading—administration became more efficient. Scribes and officials charged with the collection and administration of revenues, rents, and tributes from the peasants became members of an organized civil service and prepared accounts intelligible to their colleagues and to an earthly god, their supreme master.

After 2000 B.C. the central administration employed an army of scribes, and literacy was valued as a stepping-stone to prosperity and social rank. Scribes became a restricted class and writing a privileged profession. "The scribe comes to sit among the members of the assemblies . . . no scribe fails to eat the victuals of the king's house."[7] "Put writing in your heart that you may protect yourself from hard labour of any kind and be a magistrate of high repute. The scribe is released from manual tasks."[8] "But the scribe, he directeth the work of all men. For him there are no taxes, for he payeth tribute in writing, and there are no dues for him."[9]

EFFECTS OF WRITING AND EQUALITY

New Religions

The spread of writing after the democratic revolution was accompanied by the emergence of new religions in the immortality cult of Horus and Osiris. Ra worship had become too purely political, and individuals found a final meaning and a fulfillment of life beyond the vicissitudes of the political arbitrator.[10] Osiris, the god of the Nile, became the Good Being slain for the salvation of men, the ancestral king and model for his son Horus. As an agricultural god, he had faced death and conquered it. His wife Isis, the magician, made codes of law and ruled when Osiris was conquering the world. She persuaded the Sun-god Ra to disclose his name, and since knowledge of a person's name[11] gave to him who possessed it magical power over the person himself, she acquired power over Ra and other gods. In the twelfth dynasty, Osiris became the soul of Ra, the great hidden name that resided in him. With Ra, he shared supremacy in religion and reflected the twofold influence of the Nile and the Sun. Night and day were joined as complementary—Osiris, yesterday and death; Ra, tomorrow and life. Funerary rites invented by Isis were first applied to Osiris. Conferring immortality, they have been described by Moret as "the most precious revelation which any Egyptian god had ever made to the world."[12]

Magic and Writing

Osiris was served by Thoth as vizier, sacred scribe, and administrator. As the inventory of speech and writing, "Lord of the creative voice, master of words and books,"[13] he became the inventor of magic writings. Osiris became the center of a popular and priestly literature to instruct people in the divine rights and duties. Words were imbued with power. The names of gods were part of the essence of being, and the influence of the scribe was reflected in the deities. Since religion and magic alike were sacred, they became independent. The priest used prayers and offerings to the gods, whereas the magician circumvented them by force or trickery. Family worship survived in the Osirian cult, and because of a practical interest, magic was used by the people. To know the name of a being was to have the means of mastering him; to pronounce the name was to fashion the spiritual image by the voice; and to write it, especially with hieroglyphics, was to draw a material image. In the manifold activity of the creative word, magic permeated metaphysics. Polytheism persisted, and names were among the spiritual manifestations of the gods. Magical literature and popular tales preserved the traditions of the great gods of the universe.

Redistribution of Power

The king gained from the revolution as the incarnation of the king gods: Falcon; Horus-Seth; Ra; Ra-Harakhti; Osiris; Horus, son of Isis; and Amon-Ra, who ruled Egypt. The king's devotion created a great wave of faith among the people. Ritual enabled him to appoint a proxy to act as prophet. Power was delegated to professional priests, who first incarnated themselves in the king and performed the ceremonies in every temple every day. The worship of Ra and the celestial gods was confined to priests and temples. The priests of Atum condensed revelation in the rituals of divine worship, and a cult supplied the needs of living images in statues in the temple.

EFFECTS OF CHANGE

Invasion

The shift from dependence on stone to dependence on papyrus and the changes in political and religious institutions imposed an enormous strain on Egyptian civilization. Egypt quickly succumbed to invasion from peoples equipped with new instruments of attack. Invaders with the sword and the bow and long-range weapons broke through Egyptian defense that was dependent on the battle-axe and dagger. With the use of bronze and, possibly, iron weapons, horses, and chariots, Syrian Semitic peoples under the Hyksos or Shepherd kings captured and held Egypt from 1660 to 1580 B.C.

Cultural Resistance

Egyptian cultural elements resisted alien encroachments and facilitated reorganization and

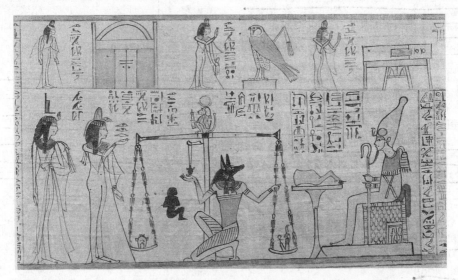

A detail from an Egyptian painted papyrus, known as the Papyrus of Nany. The complete illustration is 17 feet in length and 2.5 inches wide, ca. 1039–991 B.C. *Museum Excavations, 1928–1929 and Rogers Fund, 1039–991 B.C. (30.3.31) Image. The Metropolitan Museum of Art, New York, NY, U.S.A. Image copyright © The Metropolitan Museum of Art / Art Resource, NY.*

the launching of a counterattack. The conquerors adopted hieroglyphic writing and Egyptian customs, but the complexity of these enabled the Egyptians to resist and expel the invaders. They probably acquired horses[14] and light four-spoked chariots from the Libyans to the west, and after 1580 B.C. the Nile valley was liberated. In a great victory at Megiddo in 1478 B.C.,[15] Thutmose III gave a final blow to Hyksos's power. Under rulers of the eighteenth dynasty (1580–1345 B.C.), the New Theban Kingdom was established.

Priests, Property, and Power

In the New Kingdom, the Pharaohs at Thebes (the capital and metropolis of the civilized East) had resumed their sovereign rights, taken possession of the goods of the temples, and brought clerical vassalage to an end. Monarchical centralization was accompanied by religious centralization. The gods were "solarized," and Amon, the God of the Theban family, reigned over all the gods of Egypt as Amon-Ra after 1600 B.C. As a result of the success of war in imperial expansion, the priests became securely established in territorial property and assumed increasing influence. Problems of dynastic right in the royal family gave them additional power.

Magic and Medicine

The use of papyrus rapidly increased after the expulsion of the Hyksos. The cult of Thoth had played an important role in the New Kingdom and in the expulsion of the Hyksos. Thoth became the god of magic. His epithets had great power and strength, and certain formulae were regarded as potent in the resistance to, or in the expulsion of, malicious spirits. To about 2200 B.C., medicine and surgery had advanced, since mummification had familiarized the popular mind with dissection of the human body and had overcome an almost universal prejudice. But after the Hyksos invasion, medicine became a matter of rites and formulae[16] and opened the way to Greek physicians and anatomists in Alexandria. . . .

THE CITY-STATES OF SUMER

In Egypt, the ability to measure time and to predict the dates of floods of the Nile became the basis of power. In the Tigris and Euphrates valleys in southern Mesopotamia, the rivers[17] were adapted to irrigation and organized control, and less exacting demands were made on the capacity to predict time. Sumer was a land of small city-states in which the chief priest of the temple was the direct representative of the god. The god of the city was king, and the human ruler was a tenant farmer with the position and powers of a civil governor.

It has been suggested that writing was invented in Sumer to keep tallies and to make lists and, hence, was an outgrowth of mathematics. The earliest clay tablets include large numbers of legal contracts, deeds of sale, and land transfers, and they reflect a secular and utilitarian interest. Lists, inventories, records, and accounts of temples and small city-states suggest the concerns of the god as capitalist, landlord, and bank. Increased revenues necessitated complex systems of accounting and writing intelligible to colleagues and successors. Temple offices became continuing and permanent corporations. The growth of temple organizations and the increase in land ownership were accompanied by the accumulation of resources and the differentiation of functions. Specialization and increased wealth brought rivalry and conflict.

CLAY AND CUNEIFORM

Alluvial clay found in Babylonia and Assyria was used for making brick and as a medium in writing. Modern discoveries of large numbers of records facilitate a description of important characteristics of Sumerian and later civilizations, but they may reflect a bias incidental to the character of the material used for communication. On the other hand, such a bias points to salient features in the civilization.

Old Babylonian period cylinder seal and its impression. Amurru the son of (The God) *With permission of the Royal Ontario Museum © ROM).*

In preparation for writing, fine clay was well kneaded and made into biscuits or tablets. Since moist clay was necessary and since the tablet dried quickly, it was important to write with speed and accuracy.[18] Pictographs of fine lines made by an almost knife-sharp reed were probably followed by linear writing such as might be easily cut on stone records. But the making of straight lines tended to pull up the clay, and a cylindrical reed stylus was stamped perpendicularly or obliquely on the tablet. A triangular stylus of about the size of a small pencil with four flat sides and one bevelled end was introduced, probably in the second half of the third millennium. It was laid on a sharp edge, and if the tip was pressed deeply, a true wedge or cuneiform appeared on the tablet. If the stylus was pressed lightly, a large number of short strokes was necessary to make a single sign.

Economy of effort demanded a reduction in the number of strokes, and the remnants of pictorial writing disappeared. As a medium, clay demanded a shift from the pictograph to formal patterns. "The gap between picture and word is bridged."[19] Cuneiform writing was characterized by triangles and the massing of parallel lines. The complexity of a group of wedges of different sizes and thicknesses and an increase in the size of the tablets, which changed the angle at which they were held in the writer's hand, hastened the tendency toward conventionalization. A change in the direction of the angle[20] meant a change in the direction of the strokes or wedges and hastened the transition from pictographs to signs.[21] Conventionalization of pictographs began with signs most frequently used and advanced rapidly with the replacement of strokes by wedges. Pictographic expression became inadequate for the writing of connected religious or historical texts, and many signs were taken to represent syllables.

By 2900 B.C. the form of the script and the use of signs had been fully developed, and by 2825 B.C. the direction of writing and the arrangement of words according to their logical position in the sentence had been established. Signs were arranged in compartments on large tablets. The writing ran from left to right, and the lines followed horizontally. Cylinders could be rolled on wet clay to give a continuous impression, and cylinder seals of hard stone were introduced. Engraved with various designs, they served as personal symbols and were used as marks of identification of ownership in a community in which large numbers were unable to read and write. Seals were carried around the neck and served to stamp signatures on contracts concerning property and ownership.

Concrete pictographs involved an elaborate vocabulary with large numbers of items. To show modifications of the original meaning, signs were added to the pictures. As many as 2,000 signs were used. By 2900 B.C. the introduction of syllabic signs in a vocabulary that was largely monosyllabic had reduced the number of signs to about 600. Of these signs, about 100 represented vowels, but no system was devised for representing single consonantal sounds or creating an alphabet. Cuneiform writing was partly syllabic and partly ideographic, or representative of single words. Many of the signs were polyphonic or had more than one meaning. Sumerian had no distinctions of gender and often omitted those of number, persons, and tenses. An idea had not fully developed to the symbol of a word or syllable. Pictographs and ideograms took on abstract phonetic values, and the study of script became linked to the study of language.

Sun-dried tablets could be altered easily; this danger was overcome by baking in fire. Indestructibility assured inviolability for commercial and personal correspondence. Though admirably adapted by its durability to use over a long period of time, clay as a heavy material was less suited as a medium of communication over large areas. Its general character favored the collection of permanent records in widely scattered communities.

CLAY AND SOCIAL ORGANIZATION

Religious Power

Adaptability to communication over long distances emphasized uniformity in writing and the development of an established and authorized canon of signs. Extensive commercial activity required a large number of professional scribes or those who could read and write. In turn, the difficulties of writing a complex language implied a long period of training and the development of schools. Temple accounts and sign lists with the names of priests inventing the signs were made into school texts. In order to train scribes and administrators, schools and centers of learning were built up in connection with temples, and special emphasis was given to grammar and mathematics.

Since the art of writing as the basis of education was controlled by priests, scribes, teachers,

Clay tablet and envelope, later Persian period about 400 B.C. *With permission of the Royal Ontario Museum © ROM.*

and judges, the religious point of view in general knowledge and in legal decisions was assumed. Scribes kept the voluminous accounts of the temples and recorded the details of regulations in priestly courts. Practically every act of civil life was a matter of law that was recorded and confirmed by the seals of contracting parties and witnesses. In each city, decisions of the courts became the basis of civil law. The growth of temples and an extension in the power of the cult enhanced the power and authority of priests. The characteristics of clay favored the conventionalization of writing, decentralization of cities, the growth of continuing organization in the temples, and religious control. Abstraction was furthered by the necessity of keeping accounts and the use of mathematics, particularly in trade between communities.

The accumulation of wealth and power in the hands of the priests and the temple organization, which accompanied the development of mathematics and writing, was probably followed by ruthless warfare between city-states and the emergence of military specialization and mercenary service. It has been suggested that the control of religion over writing and education entailed a neglect of technological change and military strength. Temple government or committees of priests were unable to direct organized warfare, and temporal potentates appeared beside the priest. The latter enjoyed a prerogative and led the prince into the presence of the deity.

NOTES

1. In particular, heavy emphasis on papyrus as a basis of feudalism in contrast with the alphabet and bureaucracy of the Roman Empire.
2. Napthali Lewis, *L'industrie du papyrus dans L'Egypte Gréco-Romain* (Paris, 1834), p. 117. See F. G. Kenyon, *Ancient Books and Modern Discoveries* (Chicago, 1927).
3. Alfred Lucas, *Ancient Egyptian Materials and Industries* (London, 1934), p. 133 *ff*.
4. Alexander Moret, *The Nile and Egyptian Civilization* (London, 1927), p. 457 n.

5. Lynn Thorndike, *A Short History of Civilization* (New York, 1927), pp. 37–38.
6. Moret, *The Nile and Egyptian Civilization*, p. 457.

   Till to astonish'd realms PAPYRA taught
   To paint in mystic colours Sound and Thought.
   With Wisdom's voice to print the page sublime.
   And mark in adamant the steps of Time.
   (Erasmus Darwin, The Loves of the Plants, 1789).

7. Cited in Moret, *The Nile and Egyptian Civilization*, p. 270.
8. Cited in V. Gordon Childe, *Man Makes Himself* (London, 1936), p. 211.
9. Cited in V. Eric Peet, *A Comparative Study of the Literature of Egypt, Palestine, and Mesopotamia* (London, 1931), pp. 105–06.
10. Reinhold Niebuhr, *The Children of Light and the Children of Darkness* (New York, 1945), p. 80.
11. Cassirer had described language and myth as in original and indissoluble correlation with one another and emerging as independent elements. Mythology reflected the power exercised by language on thought. The word became a primary force in which all being and doing originate. Verbal structures appeared as mythical entities endowed with mythical powers. The word in language revealed to man that world that was closer to him than any world of material objects. Mind passed from a belief in the physio-magical power comprised in the word to a realization of its spiritual power. Through language the concept of the deity received its first concrete development. The cult of mysticism grappled with the task of comprehending the Divine in its totality and highest inward reality and yet avoided any name or sign. It was directed to the world of silence beyond language. But the spiritual depth and power of language was shown in the fact that speech itself prepared the way for the last step by which it was transcended. The demand for unity of the Deity took its stand on the linguistic expression of Being and found its surest support in the word. The Divine excluded from itself all particular attributes and could be predicated only of itself.
12. Moret, *The Nile and Egyptian Civilization*, p. 383.
13. Ibid., p. 403.
14. Sir William Ridgeway, *The Origin and Influence of the Thoroughbred Horse* (Cambridge, 1903). On the significance of the Hyksos invasion in introducing

the horse and chariot, see H. E. Wenlock, *The Rise and Fall of the Middle Kingdom in Thebes* (New York, 1947), ch. 8.

15. h 1479 (?) Breasted.

16. See Herman Ranke, "Medicine and Surgery in Ancient Egypt," *Studies in the History of Science* (Philadelphia, 1941), pp. 31–42.

17. Flooding irregular and incalculable.

18. Administrators wrote on ledgers all at one time.

19. *Studies in the History of Science.*

20. Angle changed 90 degrees and perpendicular columns turned so that characters were scribes read from on their sides and left to right—shift from space to time arrangement.

21. S. H. Hooke, "The Early History of Writing" (*Antiquity,* XI, 1937, p. 275).

CHAPTER **3**

Civilization without Writing— The Incas and the Quipu

Marcia Ascher and Robert Ascher

Marcia Ascher is a mathematician and Robert Ascher is an anthropologist with an interest in how a major New World culture, the Incas, developed "civilization" without writing—using the quipu described in the excerpt to follow. Their book, Code of the Quipu, *should be of interest to all students of communication media.*

A quipu is a collection of cords with knots tied in them. The cords were usually made of cotton, and they were often dyed one or more colors. When held in the hands, a quipu is unimpressive; surely, in our culture, it might be mistaken for a tangled old mop [see photo]. For the Spanish, the Inca quipu was the equivalent of the Western airplane for native Australians.

In earlier times, when the Incas moved in upon an area, a census was taken and the results were put on quipus. The output of gold mines, the composition of workforces, the amount and kinds of tribute, the contents of storehouses—down to the last sandal—were all recorded on quipus. At the time of the transfer of power from one Sapa Inca to the next, information stored on quipus was called upon to recount the accomplishments of the new leader's predecessors. Quipus probably predate the coming to power of the Incas. But under the Incas, they became a part of state-craft. Cieza, who attributed much to the action of kings, concluded his chapter on quipus this way: "Their orderly system in Peru is the work of the Lord-Incas who rule it and in every way brought it so high, as those of us here see from this and other greater things. With this, let us proceed."

There are several extremely important properties of quipus . . . . First of all, *quipus can be assigned horizontal direction.* When seeing a film, there usually are credits at one end and the word END at the other. Even if the meaning of these

An example of the quipu, the early communication medium used by the ancient Incan empire throughout the Andean region of South America. *The Peabody Museum of Archaeology and Ethnology, Harvard University. Reprinted by permission.*

third level, and so on. Quipus are made up of cords and spaces between cords. Cords can easily be moved until the last step in their attachment when they are fixed into position. Therefore, larger or smaller spaces between cords are an intentional part of the overall construction.

The importance of these properties is that cords can be associated with different meanings depending on their vertical direction, on their level, on their relative positions along the main cord, and, if they are subsidiaries, on their relative positions within the same level. And, just as one suspects having missed the beginning of a film when walking in on action rather than credits, quipu readers can doubt a specimen complete if the main cord doesn't have both a looped and a knotted end and can surmise that suspended cords are incomplete if they lack knotted tapered ends.

As well as having a particular placement, each cord has a color. Color is fundamental to the symbolic system of the quipu. Color coding, that is, using colors, to represent something other than themselves, is a familiar idea. But color systems are used in different ways.

The colors red and green used in traffic signals have a universal meaning in Western culture. It is generally understood that red is stop and green is go. Moreover, this common understanding is incorporated into the traffic regulations of Western governments. The color system is simple and specific, and certainly no driver is free to assign his or her own meanings to these colors.

Several more elaborate color systems are used elsewhere in Western culture, for example, in the electronics field. The color system for resistors, espoused by the International Electrotechnical Commission, has been adopted as standard practice in many countries. Resistors are ubiquitous in electrical equipment because the amount of electrical current in different parts of the circuitry can be regulated by their placement. In this international system, four bands of color appear on each resistor. Each of twelve colors is associated with a

were not understood, they could still be used when faced with a jumble of filmstrips. With them, all the filmstrips could be oriented in the same direction. All viewing and analysis would be based on the same running direction. Therefore, terms like *before* and *after* could be applied. Similarly, a main cord has direction. Quipumakers knew which end was which; we will assume that they start at the looped ends and proceed to the knotted ends. *Quipus also can be assigned vertical direction.* Pendant cords and top cords are vertically opposite to each other with pendant cords considered to go downward and top cords upward. Terms like *above* and *below,* therefore, also become applicable. Quipus *have levels.* Cords attached to the main cord are on one level; their subsidiaries form a second level. Subsidiaries to these subsidiaries form a

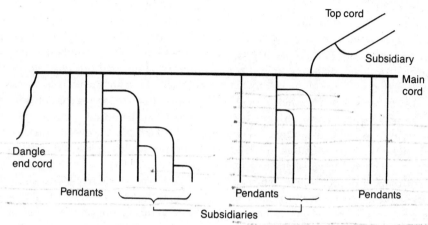

Quipu use. *Reprinted by permission of the authors.*

specific numerical value, and each of the bands is associated with a particular meaning. The first two bands are read as digits (for example, violet = 7 and white = 9 so /violet/white/ = 79); the next band tells how many times to multiply by 10 (for example, red = 2 so /violet/white/red = 79 × 10 × 10); and the last describes the accuracy (for example, silver = 10 percent, so /violet/white/red/silver = 7,900 ohms plus or minus 10 percent). By combining meanings for colors with meanings for the positions, the information that can be represented has been greatly increased.

Clearly, lettered signs for traffic messages and printed words on resistors would be less effective than colors. In the case of traffic messages, visibility from a distance and eliciting a rapid response are the important criteria. Locating and reading letters small enough to fit on a resistor when these components are intermingled with others in compact spaces would be difficult. Directing one's fingers to the right component is what is important, and with color coding this can be more readily done. As useful as they are, these systems are inflexible. Some group, not the individual users, defines the system and, therefore, sets its limits.

Consider another form of representation, the use of letters in physics formulas:

$$V = \frac{RT}{P}; \quad V = IR; \quad V = \frac{ds}{dt}.$$

In these formulas, the letter V is shorthand for volume, or voltage, or velocity, because the formulas come from three different contexts within physics. Their contexts are a discussion of gases, electricity, and motion respectively. What V stands for or what each formula means, of course, depends on a knowledge of context. We are, however, free to change the shorthand. In the first formula, which represents Boyle's Law, instead of V, T, P, R, we could use, say a = volume, b = temperature, c = pressure, and d = universal gas constant. But, because of the behavior of gases, we are not free to change the relationship between a, b, c, d to, say,

$$a = \frac{dc}{b}.$$

So, too, a color system increases in complexity as the number of contexts it describes increases and as statements of relationship become involved.

In the context of the traffic and resistor color systems, there is *an* answer to the question, What does red mean? But *V* has no fixed meaning in physics and red is associated with no specific lobsterman in Maine. However, in their local context, be it a discussion of gases or a particular port and in association with other letters or colors, the meaning is sufficiently clear. The quipu color system, like the latter systems, is rich and flexible and of the type for which there is no one answer to such questions. Basically, the quipumaker designed each quipu using color coding to relate some cords together and to distinguish them from other cords. The number of colors on a particular quipu depends on the number of distinctions that are being made. The overall patterning of the colors exhibits the relationships that are being represented. The color coding of cords that are compactly connected together and likely to become intertwined, shares with the resistor color system the function of uniting the visual with the tactile. Also, recall that quipu cords can be on different levels, have different directions, and have relative positions. Another feature shared with the resistor color system is that meanings for color and meanings for positions are used in combination with each other.

Yarns dyed different colors were available to the quipumaker. Additional cord colors were created by spinning the colored yarns together. Two solid colors twisted together gives a candy cane effect, two of these twisted together using the opposite twist direction gives a mottled effect, and the two solid colors can be joined so that part of the cord is one color and the rest of it is another color. The cord colors thus created can then be spun together creating new cord colors. With just three yarn colors, say red, yellow, and blue, and the three operations of candy striping, mottling, and joining, consider the distinctly different cord colors that are possible. There is red alone, yellow alone, blue alone; red and yellow striped, red and blue striped, yellow and blue striped; red and yellow mottled, red and blue mottled, yellow and blue mottled; red above yellow, yellow above red, red above blue, blue above red, yellow above blue, and blue above yellow. Selecting from these fifteen

and using the same operations on them, there are many more.

In some cases, the quipumaker extended the subtlety of the color coding by having a two-color combination on one cord retain the significance of both colors rather than taking on a significance of its own. In these cases, a cord made of one color yarn had a small portion striped or mottled with a second color. Thus the overall cord color had one significance while the inserted color had another significance.

For the most part, cords had knots tied along them, and the knots represented numbers. But we are certain that before knots were tied in the cords, the entire blank quipu was prepared. The overall planning and construction of the quipu was done first, including the types of cord connections, the relative placement of cords, the selection of cord colors, and even individual decorative finishings. In a few cases, quipus were found in groups mingled with other cords. Some of these quipu groups contain quipus in different stages of preparation from bundles of prepared blank quipu cords, to completely constructed blank quipus, to completely constructed quipus with some or all cords knotted. Cords with knots tied in them are only found detached when they are evidently broken.

What particular abilities did a person need to be a quipumaker? What was his position in the Inca bureaucracy? In what ways did one quipumaker differ from another? And what did the quipumaker have to know? These are interesting questions, and they are going to be answered. The route to the answers will often appear to be a thin line of scant information, or a dotted line—information with many gaps—or a broken line as when, for example, information from another culture is introduced. At the end, all questions having been answered, there will emerge a still too darkly shaded picture of the quipumaker.

His material—colored strings of cotton and sometimes wool—will give us some notion of the abilities the quipumaker needed. They become apparent when we contrast his material with those of his counterparts in other civilizations.

Many different substances have been used for recording. Stone, animal skin, clay, silk, and various parts of plants including slips of wood, bark, leaves, and pulp are some of them. The material used for a medium in a civilization is often derived from a substance that is common and abundant in its environment. (The simultaneous use of several mediums in one area is a recent development. Even if two were used, one tended to dominate the other and gradually replaced it.) Each kind of material calls forth a somewhat different set of abilities. For contrast with the quipumaker's cotton and wool, we choose to detail the clay of the Sumerian scribe and the papyrus of the Egyptian record keeper.

The Sumerian scribe lived in the southern part of what today is called Iraq, between, say 2700 and 1700 B.C.E. The clay he used came from the banks of rivers. He kneaded it into a tablet that varied in size from a postage stamp to a pillow. (For special purposes, the clay was shaped into a tag, a prism, or a barrel.) Pulling a piece of thread across the clay, he made rulings on the tablet. He was then prepared to record. This he did with a stylus, a piece of reed about the size of a small pencil shaped at one end so that it made wedgelike impressions in the soft, damp clay. If he lived toward the early part of the thousand-year time interval, he made impressions vertically, from top to bottom. Later on, they were made from left to right across the tablet. Having finished one side, he turned the tablet over by bringing the lower edge to the top, continuing the record on the obverse side. He had to work fast; the clay dried out and hardened quickly; when that happened, erasures, additions, and other changes were no longer possible. If he ran short of space on the tablet or if the tablet dried out before he was done, he started a second one. When he was finished recording, the tablet or tablets were dried in the sun or baked in a kiln, permanently fixing the impressions . . . .

In Egypt, at about the same time, the scribe used papyrus. Its source was the interior of the stem of a tall sedge that flourished in swampy depressions. Fresh stems were cut, the rinds were removed, and the soft interiors were laid out and beaten until they were formed into sheets. The natural gum of the pith was the adhesive. A papyrus sheet was about six inches wide and nine inches high. It was white or faintly colored, the surface was shiny and smooth, and it was flexible. Dry sheets could be joined with a prepared adhesive; twenty of them, for example, made a surface six feet long. The Egyptian scribe used brush and ink. To make a brush, he cut a rush about one foot in length; then, he cut one end at an angle and bruised it to separate the fibers. His inks were actually small cakes resembling modern watercolors, and they were used in much the same way. Black cakes were made with soot scraped from cooking vessels; red cakes, from ocher. Moving from right to left, the Egyptian scribe brushed his record onto the papyrus.

An obvious contrast between the quipumaker and his Sumerian and Egyptian counterparts is that the former used no instruments to record. The quipumaker composed his recording by tracing fingers in space as when, for example, he turned a string in an ever-changing direction in the process of tying a knot. All of this was not preparatory to making a record; it was part of the very process of recording. The stylus and the brush were held in the hand, their use had to be learned, and the learning involved a sense of touch. But the quipumaker's way of recording— direct construction—required tactile sensitivity to a much greater degree. In fact, the overall aesthetic of the quipu is related to the tactile: the manner of recording and the recording itself are decidedly rhythmic; the first in the activity, the second in the effect. We seldom realize the potential of our sense of touch, and we are usually unaware of its association with rhythm. Yet anyone familiar with the activity of caressing will immediately see the connection between touch and rhythm. In fact, tactile sensitivity begins in the rhythmic pulsating environment of the unborn child far in advance of the development of other senses.

Color is another point of contrast: the Sumerian used none, the Egyptians two (black and red), and the quipumakers used hundreds. All three needed keen vision; the quipumaker alone had to recognize and recall color differences and use them to his advantage. His color vocabulary was large; it was not simply red, green, white, and so on, but various reds, greens, and whites. Drawing upon this color vocabulary, his task was to choose, combine, and arrange colors in varied patterns to express the relationships in whatever it was that he was recording. Confronted with a quipu, it is not easy to grasp immediately, if at all, the complex use of colors. The quipumaker, and the people of the Andean world who were a part of his everyday experience, understood complex color usage because they were accustomed to it in the textiles they saw, just as we comprehend polyphonic music because we hear it often enough. This appeal to musical imagery comes from an art historian; others in our culture have also turned to musical composition to translate their understanding of Andean color composition. At the base of their musical imagery is the formal patterning and structure that can also be translated into mathematical language.

The third contrast is perhaps the most important. Both the Sumerian and the Egyptian recorded on planar surfaces. In this regard, papyrus had certain advantages over clay. For example, sheets could be added or deleted, thus changing the dimensions of the surface; the dimensions of the clay surface were fixed once the tablet was formed. By contrast to both papyrus and clay, the quipumaker's strings present no surface at all. Recording in papyrus or clay involved filling the space in a more or less continuous process either up or down, or from right to left, or from left to right. This is linear composition. By contrast, the quipumaker's recording was nonlinear. The nonlinearity is a consequence of the soft material he used. A group of strings occupies a space that has no definite orientation; as the quipumaker connected strings to each other, the space became defined by the points where the strings were attached. The establishment of these points did not have to follow any set left-to-right or right-to-left sequence. The relative positions of the strings are set by their points of attachment, and it is the relative position, along with the colors and the knots, that renders the recording meaningful. Essentially then, the quipumaker had to have the ability to conceive and execute a recording in three dimensions with color.

The quipumaker fits somewhere in the bureaucracy that developed in the Inca state: the question is, Where? In theory, his position was one of privilege. As for the facts in the case, the one good piece of evidence that exists supports what one would expect from theory.

Hand in hand with massive construction, standing armies, and all the other attributes of the state, there is always a bureaucracy to administer its affairs. And bureaucratic administration, in the words of Max Weber ". . . means fundamentally the exercise of control on the basis of knowledge." The knowledge is stored in records. These, together with people who have "official functions," form the "office" that carries on the state's affairs. The bureaucracy keeps records of everything that can be recorded, but especially things that are quantifiable: the number of people living at a certain place, the tribute that was collected in a village, the day the river flooded. The bureaucracy believes in its rationality; its records give assurance to those who wield power. The more records there are, and the more the bureaucracy has experience with them, the more power to the state. A bureaucracy's records are peculiar to itself, and bureaucrats try very hard to keep it that way.

In the Inca state, the quipumaker composed the records for the bureaucracy. He might know, for example, how many men in a group of villages were suitable for army service, how many could work in the mines, and much else of interest. He worked with privileged information, so he was privileged. We expect that he was more important than an ordinary man, yet he was not as important as the really important men who held authority in the community where he lived or the Incas who watched over them.

CHAPTER 4

The Origins of Writing

Andrew Robinson

Andrew Robinson is a King's Scholar at Eton College and Literary Editor of The Times Higher Education Supplement. *His books include* The Shape of the World: The Mapping and Discovery of the Earth *and* The Story of Writing, *from which the present excerpt is taken.*

Writing is among the greatest inventions in human history, perhaps *the* greatest invention, since it made history possible. Yet it is a skill most writers take for granted. We learn it at school, building on the alphabet or (if we live in China or Japan) the Chinese characters. As adults we seldom stop to think about the mental-cum-physical process that turns our thoughts into symbols on a piece of paper or on a video screen, or bytes of information in a computer disc. Few of us have any clear recollection of how we learned to write.

A page of text in a foreign script, totally incomprehensible to us, reminds us forcibly of the nature of our achievement. An extinct script, such as Egyptian hieroglyphs or cuneiform from the ancient Near East, strikes us as little short of miraculous. By what means did these pioneering writers of 4000–5000 years ago learn to write? How did their symbols encode their speech and thought? How do we decipher (or attempt to decipher) the symbols after centuries of silence? Do today's writing systems work in a completely different way from the ancient scripts? What about the Chinese and Japanese scripts? Are they like ancient hieroglyphs? Do hieroglyphs have any advantages over alphabets? Finally, what kind of people were the early writers, and what kind of information, idea, and feelings did they make permanent?

THE FUNCTION OF WRITING

Writing and literacy are generally seen as forces for good. It hardly needs saying that a person who can read and write has greater opportunities for fulfilment than one who is illiterate. But there is also a dark side to the spread of writing that is present throughout its history, if somewhat less obvious. Writing has been used to tell

Hieroglyphic inscription on a fragment of limestone, Egypt, Third Dynasty, 2686–2613 B.C. *With permission of the Royal Ontario Museum © ROM.*

lies as well as truth, to bamboozle and exploit as well as to educate, to make minds lazy as well as to stretch them.

Socrates pinpointed our ambivalence toward writing in his story of the Egyptian god Thoth, the inventor of writing, who came to see the king seeking royal blessing on his enlightening invention. The king told Thoth: "You, who are the father of letters, have been led by your affection to ascribe to them a power the opposite of that which they really possess . . . You have invented an elixir not of memory, but of reminding; and you offer your pupils the appearance of wisdom, not true wisdom, for they will read many things without instruction and will therefore seem to know many things, when they are for the most part ignorant." In a late twentieth-century world drenched with written information and surrounded by information technologies of astonishing speed, convenience, and power, these words spoken in antiquity have a distinctly contemporary ring.

Political leaders have always used writing for propaganda purposes. Nearly 4000 years and a totally different script separate the famous black basalt law code of Hammurabi of Babylon from the slogans and billboards of 1990s Iraq, but the message is similar. Hammurabi called himself "mighty King, King of Babylon, King of the whole country of Amurru, King of Sumer and Akkad, King of the Four Quarters of the World"; and he promised that if his laws were obeyed, then all his people would benefit. "Writing," wrote H. G. Wells in his *Short History of the World,* "put agreements, laws, commandments on record. It made the growth of states larger than the old city-states possible. The command of the priest or king and his seal could go far beyond his sight and voice and could survive his death."

Yes, regrettably, Babylonian and Assyrian cuneiform, Egyptian hieroglyphs, and the Mayan glyphs of Central America, carved on palace and temple walls, were used much as Stalin used posters about Lenin in the Soviet Union: to remind the people who was the boss, how great were his triumphs, how firmly based in the most

high was his authority. At Karnak, in Egypt, on the outer wall of a temple, there are carved representations of the battle at Kadesh fought by Ramesses II against the Hittites, around 1285 B.C. Hieroglyphs recount a peace treaty between the pharaoh and the Hittite king and celebrate a great Egyptian victory. But another version of the same treaty found at the Hittite capital Boghazköy turns the battle into a win for the Hittites!

The urge for immortality has always been of the first importance to writers. Most of the thousands of known fragments written by the Etruscans, for instance, are funerary inscriptions. We can read the name, date, and place of death because they are written in an adaptation of the Greek alphabet; but that is about all we know of the enigmatic language of this important people, who borrowed the alphabet from Greece, handed it on to the Romans, who in turn gave it to the rest of Europe. Decipherment of the Etruscan language is like trying to learn English by reading nothing but gravestones.

Another purpose for writing was to predict the future. All ancient societies were obsessed with what was to come. Writing allowed them to codify their worries. Among the Maya it took the form of bark-paper books elaborately painted in color and bound in jaguar skin; the prognostications were based on a written calendrical system so sophisticated it extended as far back as 5 billion years ago, more than our present scientifically estimated age for the earth. In China, on the other hand, during the Bronze Age Shang dynasty, questions about the future were written on turtle shells and ox bones, so-called "oracle bones." The bone was heated with a brand until it cracked, the meaning of the shape of the crack was divined, and the answer to the question was inscribed. Later, what actually transpired might be added to the bone.

But of course most writing was comparatively mundane. It provided, for instance, the equivalent of an ancient identity card or a property marker. The cartouche enclosing the name of Tutankhamun was found on objects throughout his tomb, from the grandest of thrones to the smallest of boxes. Anyone who was anyone among ancient rulers required a personal seal for signing clay tablets and other inscriptions. So did any merchant or other person of substance. (Today in Japan, a seal, rather than a western-style signature, is standard practice for signing business and legal documents.) Such name-tagging has been found as far apart as Mesopotamia, China, and Central America. The stone seals from the Indus Valley civilization, which flourished around 2000 B.C., are especially interesting: not only are they exquisitely carved—depicting, among other motifs, a mysterious unicorn—the symbols written on them are undeciphered. Unlike the script of Babylonia, the Indus Valley writing does not appear on walls as public inscriptions. Instead the seals have been found scattered around the houses and streets of the "capital" city. They were probably worn on a cord or thong and used as a personal "signature" or to indicate a person's office or the social or professional group to which he or she belonged.

Writing used for accountancy was much commoner than that on seals and tags. The earliest writing of all, on Sumerian clay tablets from Mesopotamia, concerns lists of raw materials and products, such as barley and beer, lists of laborers and their tasks, lists of field areas and their owners, the income and outgoings of temples, and so forth—all with calculations concerning production levels, delivery dates, locations, and debts. And the same is true, generally speaking, of the earliest deciphered European writing, tablets from pre-Homeric Greece and Crete written in Linear B script. The tablet that clinched the decipherment of Linear B in 1953 was simply an inventory of tripod cauldrons (one of them with its legs burnt off) and of goblets of varying sizes and numbers of handles.

THE ORIGIN(S) OF WRITING

Most scholars now accept that writing began with accountancy, even though accountancy is little in evidence in the surviving writing of ancient Egypt, China, and Central America. To quote an expert on early Sumerian tablets, writing developed "as a direct consequence of the compelling demands of an expanding economy." In other words, some time in the late fourth millennium B.C., the complexity of trade and administration in the early cities of Mesopotamia reached a point at which it outstripped the power of memory of the governing élite. To record transactions in a dependable, permanent form became essential. Administrators and merchants could then say the Sumerian equivalents of "I shall put it in writing" and "Can I have this in writing?"

But this does not explain how writing actually emerged out of no-writing. Divine origin, in favor until the Enlightenment in the eighteenth century, has given way to the theory of a pictographic origin. The first written symbols are generally thought to have been pictograms, pictorial representations of concrete objects. Some scholars believe that writing was the result of a conscious search by an unknown Sumerian individual in the city of Uruk (biblical Erech) in about 3300 B.C. Others believe it was the work of a group, presumably of clever administrators and merchants. Still others think it was not an invention at all, but an accidental discovery. Many regard it as the result of evolution over a long period, rather than a flash of inspiration. One particularly well-aired theory holds that writing grew out of a long-standing counting system of clay "tokens" (such "tokens," exact purpose unknown, have been found in many Middle Eastern archaeological sites); the substitution of two-dimensional signs for these tokens, with the signs resembling the shapes of the tokens, was a first step toward writing, according to this theory.

In any case, essential to the development of full writing, as opposed to the limited, purely pictographic writing of North American Indians and others, was the discovery of the rebus principle. This was the radical idea that a pictographic symbol could be used for its phonetic value. Thus a drawing of an owl in Egyptian hieroglyphs could represent a consonantal sound with an inherent *m;* and in English a picture of a bee with a picture of a leaf might (if one were so minded) represent the word belief.

THE DEVELOPMENT OF WRITING

Once invented, accidentally discovered, or evolved—take your pick—did writing then diffuse throughout the globe from Mesopotamia? The earliest Egyptian writing dates from 3100 B.C., that of the Indus Valley from 2500 B.C., that of Crete from 1900 B.C., that of China from 1200 B.C., that of Central America from 600 B.C. (all dates are approximate). On this basis, it seems reasonable that the idea of writing, but not the particular symbols of a script, did spread gradually from culture to distant culture. It took 600 or 700 years for the idea of printing to reach Europe from China and even longer for the idea of paper: why should writing not have reached China from Mesopotamia over an even longer period?

Nevertheless, in the absence of solid evidence for transmission of the idea (even in the case of the much nearer civilizations of Mesopotamia and Egypt), a majority of scholars prefer to think that writing developed independently in the major civilizations of the ancient world. The optimist, or at any rate the anti-imperialist, will prefer to emphasize the intelligence and inventiveness of human societies; the pessimist, who takes a more conservative view of history, will tend to assume that humans prefer to copy what already exists, as faithfully as they can, restricting their innovations to cases of absolute necessity. The latter is the preferred explanation for how the Greeks borrowed the alphabet from the Phoenicians, adding in the process the vowels not expressed in the Phoenician script.

There can be no doubt about certain script borrowings, such as the Romans taking the Etruscan script, the Japanese taking the Chinese characters and, in our own time, the Turks (under Kemal Atatürk) abandoning the Arabic script in favor of the Latin script. Changes are made to a borrowed script because the new language has sounds in it that are not found in the language for which the script was being used (hence the umlaut on the "u" of Atatürk). This idea is easy enough to grasp when the two languages are similar, but it can be extremely awkward to follow when the two languages differ vastly, as Japanese does from Chinese. In order to cope with the differences, the Japanese script has *two* entirely distinct sets of symbols: Chinese characters (thousands) and Japanese syllabic signs (about 50) that symbolize the basic sounds of Japanese speech. A Japanese sentence therefore mixes Chinese characters and Japanese syllabic signs in what is generally regarded as the most complicated system of writing in the world.

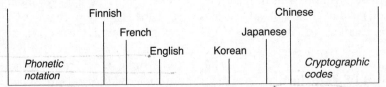

PURE PHONOGRAPHY   PURE LOGOGRAPHY

Finnish   French   English   Korean   Japanese   Chinese

Phonetic notation   Cryptographic codes

Phonography to logography. Written versus spoken language (after DeFrancis and Unger). Writing systems are shown on a theoretical continuum of writing between pure phonography and pure logography, with Finnish script as the most phonetically efficient and Chinese script the least efficient. *Reprinted by permission of Thames & Hudson.*

SCRIPT, SPEECH, AND LANGUAGE

Europeans and Americans of ordinary literacy must recognize and write around fifty-two alphabetic signs and sundry other symbols, such as numerals, punctuation marks, and "whole-word" semantic symbols, for example, +, &, £, $, 2, which are sometimes called logograms. Their Japanese counterparts, by contrast, are supposed to know and be able to write some 2,000 symbols, and, if they are highly educated, must recognize 5,000 symbols or more. The two situations, in Europe/America and in Japan, appear to be poles apart. But in fact, the positions resemble each other more than it appears.

All scripts that are full writing—that is, a "system of graphic symbols that can be used to convey any and all thought" (to quote John DeFrancis, a distinguished American student of Chinese)—operate on one basic principle, contrary to what most people think, some scholars included. Both alphabets and the Chinese and Japanese scripts use symbols to represent sounds (i.e., phonetic signs), and all writing systems use a mixture of phonetic and semantic signs. What differs—apart from the outward forms of the symbols, of course—is the *proportion* of phonetic to semantic signs. The higher the proportion, the easier it is to guess the pronunciation of a word. In English the proportion is high, in Chinese it is low. Thus English spelling represents English speech sound by sound more accurately than Chinese characters represent Mandarin speech, but Finnish spelling represents the Finnish language better than either of them. The Finnish script is highly efficient phonetically, while the Chinese (and Japanese) script is phonetically seriously deficient.

The difficulty of learning the Chinese and Japanese scripts cannot be denied. In Japan, in the mid-1950s, a peak in teenage suicides seems to have been connected with the expansion of mass education post war, using the full-blown Japanese script with its several thousand characters. It takes a Chinese or Japanese person several years longer than a western counterpart to achieve fluency in reading.

That said, there are many millions of westerners who have failed to learn to read and write. The level of literacy in Japan is higher than in the West (though probably not as high as is claimed). The intricacy of the Japanese script has not stopped the Japanese from becoming a great economic power nor has it caused them to abandon their use of Chinese characters in favor of a much smaller set of signs based on their already-existing syllabic signs—a theoretically feasible move.

MODERN "HIEROGLYPHS"

Are the huge claims made for the efficiency of the alphabet then perhaps misguided? Maybe writing and reading would work best if alphabetic scripts contained more logograms standing for whole words, as in Chinese and Japanese writing and (less so) in Egyptian hieroglyphs. Why is it necessarily desirable to have a *sound*-based script? What, after all, has sound got to do with the actual process of writing and reading?

Modern hieroglyphs.

We have only to look around us to see that "hieroglyphs" are striking back—beside highways, at airports, on maps, in weather forecasts, on clothes labels, on computer screens and on electronic goods including the keyboard of one's word processor. Instead of "move cursor to right," there is a simple ⇒. The hieroglyphs tell us where we must not overtake, where the nearest telephone is, which road is a motorway, whether it is likely to rain tomorrow, how we should (and should not) clean a garment, and how we should rewind a tape. Some people, beginning with the philosopher and mathematician Leibniz in the seventeenth century, even like to imagine that we can invent an entire written language for universal communication. It would aim to be independent of any of the spoken languages of the world, dependent only upon the concepts essential to high-level philosophical, political, and scientific communication. If music and mathematics can achieve it, so the thought goes—why not more generally?

Writing: A Chronicle

Ice Ages (after 25,000 BC)	Proto-writing, i.e., pictographic communication, in use
8000 BC onward	Clay "tokens" in use as counters, Middle East
3300 BC	Sumerian clay tablets with writing, Uruk, Iraq
3100 BC	Cuneiform inscriptions begin, Mesopotamia
3100–3000 BC	Hieroglyphic inscriptions begin, Egypt
2500 BC	Indus script begins, Pakistan/N.W. India
18th cent. BC	Cretan Linear A inscriptions begin
1792–1750 BC	Hammurabi, king of Babylon, reigns; inscribes law code on stela
17th–16th cent. BC	First known alphabet, Palestine
1450 BC	Cretan Linear B inscriptions begin
14th cent. BC	Alphabetic cuneiform inscriptions, Ugarit, Syria
1361–1352 BC	Tutankhamun reigns, Egypt
c. 1285 BC	Battle of Kadesh celebrated by both Ramesses II and Hittites
1200 BC	Oracle bone inscriptions in Chinese characters begin
1000 BC	Phoenician alphabeticinscriptions begin, Mediterranean area
730 BC	Greek alphabetic inscriptions begin
c. 8th cent. BC	Etruscan alphabet appears, northern Italy
650 BC	Demotic inscriptions, derived fromhieroglyphs, begin, Egypt
600 BC	Glyphic inscriptions begin, Mesoamerica
521–486 BC	Darius, king of the Persians, reigns; creates Behistun inscription (key to decipherment of cuneiform)
400 BC	Ionian alphabet becomes standard Greek alphabet
c. 270–c. 232 BC	Ashoka creates rock edicts in Brahmi and Kharosthi script, northern India
221 BC	Qin dynasty reforms Chinese character spelling
c. 2nd cent. BC	Paper invented, China
1st cent. AD	Dead Sea Scrolls written in Aramaic/Hebrew script
75 AD	Last inscription written in cuneiform
2nd cent.	Runic inscriptions begin, northern Europe
394	Last inscription written in Egyptian hieroglyphs
615–683	Pacal, Classic Maya ruler of Palenque, Mexico
712	*Kojiki*, earliest work of Japanese literature (in Chinese characters)
Before 800	Printing invented, China

9th cent.	Cyrillic alphabet invented, Russia
1418–1450	Sejong, king of Korea, reigns; invents Hangul alphabet
15th cent.	Movable type invented, Europe
1560s	Diego de Landa records Mayan "alphabet," Yucatán
1799	Rosetta stone discovered, Egypt
1821	Cherokee "alphabet" invented by Sequoya, USA
1823	Egyptian hieroglyphs deciphered by Champollion
1840s onward	Mesopotamian cuneiform deciphered by Rawlinson, Hincks, and others
1867	Typewriter invented
1899	Oracle bone inscriptions discovered, China
1900	Knossos discovered by Evans, who identifies Cretan Linear A and B
1905	Proto-Sinaitic inscriptions discovered by Petrie, Serabit el-Khadim, Sinai
1908	Phaistos Disc discovered, Crete
1920s	Indus civilization discovered
1940s	Electronic computers invented
1948	Hebrew becomes a national language in Israel
1953	Linear B deciphered by Ventris
1950s onward	Mayan glyphs deciphered
1958	Pinyin spelling introduced in China
1980s	Word processors invented; writing becomes electronic
23 Dec. 2012	Current Maya Great Cycle of time due to end

PART TWO

The Tradition
of Western Literacy

Saint Mark illumination, from a Gospel lectionery. MS. M.639,f218. *Art Resource/The Pierpont Morgan Library.*

As we have just seen, the first writing systems initiated a major communications revolution. Writing made possible the storage and retrieval of vast amounts of information. It enabled the civilizations employing it to achieve a size and complexity unparalleled previously. These early scripts were primarily used for economic and political purposes. Their individual signs represented ideas, objects, and actions, not speech. Eventually however, in places like Egypt and Babylonia, writing developed an auditory dimension. For example, a picture in hieroglyphics, or a cuneiform character, came to indicate not the object represented, but the sound (usually the main syllable) uttered when the object was spoken.

The use of these sound signs, known as phonograms, added to the possibilities of writing. Myths and histories began to be transcribed. Nevertheless the scripts remained complex and difficult; an elite group of full-time scribes was still necessary. This situation was challenged by the emergence of the twenty-two-character Phoenician alphabet around 1500 B.C. Unlike the Egyptians and Babylonians, the Phoenicians did not build an empire. They were a seafaring trading people based in the western Mediterranean. Each character in their alphabet represented a consonant linked to several possible syllables. The proper one to "read" was deduced through the context of the adjacent "letters". This is a slow process compared to the way we read today, and one that makes it difficult for us to read a Phoenician text in a manner that is faithful to the spoken language on which it was based.

The Phoenician alphabet was economical and provided a rough approximation of speech. When introduced to the Greek-speaking peoples of Asia Minor it underwent significant modifications. Vowels were added. This converted the former consonant syllables into pure consonants—abstract bits of sound—which when combined with vowel letters produced an immediately recognizable range of syllables and words. This new way of writing, although not a perfect representation of speech, was a rich approximation, and the ancestor of all the subsequent scripts of the West.

The extraordinary vistas opened up by the Greek alphabet are dealt with by Eric Havelock in our first selection. He argues that the new literacy, born of the Greek experience, challenged the "craft-literacy" of the ancient empires. It created the common reader: large numbers of literate people not part of an elite scribal tradition. Havelock also comments on the psychological implications of the alphabet, how it affected memory and cognition. Finally, he assesses specific media, such as wax tablets and papyrus, which the Greeks used to produce written texts. An important point to keep in mind, as he reminds us, is that Greek literacy is still not modern literacy as we know it. Texts such as those by Plato were in part transcribed from an earlier oral tradition. At the same time such texts provide a glimpse of the conceptual directions that would become dominant after the advent of moveable type printing.

Building on the work of Havelock, Robert Logan's selection shows how systems for writing and abstract numerals evolved from token logograms and suggests how a variety of alphabets and numbering systems cross-influenced each other. The essays of Havelock and Logan allude to a preliterate oral tradition. Elsewhere they write—as do Innis, McLuhan Ong and a host of other communication scholars whose work is represented in this anthology—with considerable respect regarding the intelligence of people who live in such societies. Therefore, readers should not assume that literate is superior to oral in terms of some absolute measure of intelligence. The differences are cultural, not hierarchical. We gain new insight with the acquisition of literacy, but we also lose. The world of primary oral cultures is rich in metaphor, nonlineal creative thought, and memory stepped in a multi-sensory apprehension of the world. Genius is a legacy of both the oral and literate worlds. After all, Homer could not write. His epics were transcribed by others. Yet for generations, as Havelock shows, it was assumed that such artistry was only possible in a literate mind.

In our next selection, Walter Ong highlights some of these differences. He assesses the psychodynamics of orality: the way the world is perceived by cultures that have not had the benefits, or limitations, of knowledge based on literacy's visual and linear bias. Understanding this oral tradition, Ong contends, is a necessary starting point for grasping the subsequent impact of writing and print, a view shared by many of our contributors. He concludes by showing how "secondary orality" has become a key element in the way electronic media operate.

James Burke and Robert Ornstein conclude this section with a look at culture and communication during the Middle Ages. Literacy based knowledge at this time was largely controlled by the Catholic Church. Monasteries scattered throughout Europe served as educational and administrative centers. Books were written by hand in Latin on parchment (treated animal skins). For the most part they were sacred teachings. However, by the twelfth century, secular texts from Greco-Roman antiquity, preserved in Islamic libraries that were much larger than those in Christendom, gradually began making their way into Europe. Writings that were consonant with or could be adapted to Christian teaching were reproduced by the scribes; those texts that were deemed heretical were either hidden away or destroyed—many would resurface later with the advent of print in the fifteenth century. Burke and Ornstein also show us the practical side of monastic culture that would eventually spread to the secular world: a factory-like regimentation of labor organized around the mechanical clock.

CHAPTER 5

The Greek Legacy

Eric Havelock

Eric Havelock (1903–1989) was professor of classics at Yale University. A one-time colleague of Harold Innis, Havelock wrote extensively on the impact of literacy on the history of the West, especially with reference to the legacy of Greek alphabetization.

The introduction of the Greek letters into inscription somewhere about 700 B.C. was to alter the character of human culture, placing a gulf between all alphabetic societies and their precursors. The Greeks did not just invent an alphabet, they invented literacy and the literate basis of modern thought. Under modern conditions there seems to be only a short time lag between the invention of a device and its full social or industrial application, and we have got used to this idea as a fact of technology. This was not true of the alphabet. The letter shapes and values had to pass through a period of localization before being standardized throughout Greece. Even after the technology was standardized or relatively so— there were always two competing versions, the Eastern and the Western—its effects were registered slowly in Greece, were then partly cancelled during the European Middle Ages, and have been fully realized only since the further invention of the printing press. But it is useful here and now to set forth the full theoretic possibilities that would accrue from the use of the Greek alphabet, supposing that all human impediments to their realization could be removed, in order to place the invention in its proper historical perspective.

It democratized literacy, or rather made democratization possible. This point is often made, but in simplistic terms, as though it were merely a matter of learning a limited number of letters, that is, learning to write them. Hence even

the Semitic system has often been erroneously credited with this advantage. If Semitic societies in antiquity showed democratic tendencies, this was not because they were literate. On the contrary, to the extent that their democracy was modified by theocracy, with considerable prestige and power vested in priesthoods, they exhibited all the symptoms of craft literacy. The Greek system by its superior analysis of sound placed the skill of reading theoretically within the reach of children at the stage where they are still learning the sounds of their oral vocabulary. If acquired in childhood, the skill was convertible into an automatic reflex and thus distributable over a majority of a given population provided it was applied to the spoken vernacular. But this meant that democratization would depend not only upon the invention but also upon the organization and maintenance of school instruction in reading at the elementary level. This second requirement is social rather than technological. It was not met in Greece for perhaps three hundred years after the technological problem was solved, and was abandoned again in Europe for a long period after the fall of Rome. When operative, it rendered the role of the scribe or the clerk obsolete, and removed the elitist status of literacy characteristic of craft-literate epochs.

Have the outward social and political effects of full literacy really been as important and profound as is sometimes claimed? Our later examination of oral cultures and the way they function may throw some doubt on this. What the new script may have done in the long run was to change somewhat the content of the human mind. This is a conclusion which will not be argued fully here. But this much should be said at once. The acoustic efficiency of the script had a result which was psychological: once it was learned you did not have to think about it. Though a visible thing, a series of marks, it created to interpose itself as an object of thought between the reader and his recollection of the spoken tongue. The script therefore came to resemble an electric current communicating a recollection of the sounds of the spoken word directly to the brain so that the meaning resounded as it were in the consciousness without reference to the properties of the letters used. The script was reduced to a gimmick; it had no intrinsic value in itself as a script and this marked it off from all previous systems. It was characteristic of the alphabet that the names of the Greek letters, borrowed from the Phoenician, for the first time became meaningless: *alpha, beta, gamma,* etc. constitutes simply a nursery chant designed to imprint the mechanical sounds of the letters, by using what is called the acrophonic principle, in a fixed series on the child's brain, while simultaneously tightly correlating them with his vision of a fixed series of shapes which he looks at as he pronounces the acoustic values. These names in the original Semitic were names of common objects like "house" and "camel" and so on. Uncritical students of the history of writing will even make it a reproach against the Greek system that the names became "meaningless" in Greek. The reproach is very foolish. A true alphabet, the sole basis of future literacy, could only become operative when its components were robbed of any independent meaning whatever, in order to become convertible in to a mechanical mnemonic device.

The fluency of reading that could result depended upon fluency of recognition and this in turn as we have seen upon the removal so far as possible of all choices upon the part of the reader, all ambiguities. Such an automatic system brought within reach the capacity to transcribe the complete vernacular of any given language, anything whatever that could be said in the language, with a guarantee that the reader would recognize the unique acoustic values of the signs, and so the unique statements conveyed thereby, whatever they happened to be. The need for authorized versions restricted to statements of a familiar and accepted nature was removed. Moreover the new system could identify the phonemes of any language with accuracy. Thus the possibility arose of placing two or several languages within the same type of script and so greatly accelerating the process of cross-translation between them. This is the technological secret which made possible the construction of a Roman literature upon Greek models—the first such enterprise in the history of mankind. For the most part, however, this advantage of interchange between written communications has accrued to the later alphabetic cultures of Europe. By way of contrast, the historian Thucydides in the Greek period records an episode where the documents of a captured Persian emissary had to be "translated" into Greek. That is how the word is interpreted by the commentators who explain this passage. But Thucydides does not say "translated." What the would-be translators had first to do was to "change the letters" of the original syllabic script into the Greek alphabet. How could they have done this? I suggest that it was done only with the previous assistance of the spoken tongue, not the written. That is, an orally bilingual Persian who was also craft-literate in the Persian sense, that is, knew his cuneiform, would read aloud what the document said, translating as he went into spoken Greek. His opposite number would then transcribe from his dictation into the Greek alphabet, unless there was a Persian available who could use both cuneiform and alphabet. Then the Persian dispatch, now in Greek alphabetic form, could be carried to Athens and read there. In the United Nations today some such procedure is still required for cross-communication between the alphabetic cultures and the non-alphabetic ones like the Arabic, Chinese, and Japanese, leading as it often does to ambiguities and even misunderstandings of a special sort that do not arise between the alphabetic cultures, misunderstandings which can even have political consequences.

These effects, to repeat, were theoretically attainable. For reasons to be explained later, the full vernacular was not in fact the first thing to be transcribed. The alphabet was not originally put at the service of ordinary human conversation. Rather it was first used to record a progressively complete version of the "oral literature" of Greece, if the paradox may be permitted, which had been nourished in the non-literate period and which indeed had sustained the identity of the previous oral culture of Greece. Although today we "read" our Homer, our Pindar, or our Euripides, a great deal of what we are "listening to" is a fairly accurate acoustic transcription of all the contrived forms in which oral speech had hitherto been preserved. This phenomenon as it occurs in the formation of what we call Greek literature has been imperfectly understood and will be explored in depth when the Greeks are at last allowed, as they will be, to take over the course and direction of this history.

And yet, though fluent transcription of the oral record became the primary use to which the alphabet was put, the secondary purpose which it came to serve was historically more important. I could say that it made possible the invention of fluent prose, but this would be misleading, since obviously the larger component of oral discourse even in an oral culture is prosaic. What is effectively brought into being was prose recorded and preserved in quantity. To interpret this innovation as merely stylistic would be to miss the point of a profound change occurring in the character of the content of what could be preserved. A revolution was underway both psychological and epistemological. The important and influential statement in any culture is the one that is preserved. Under conditions of non-literacy in Greece, and of craft literacy in pre-Greek cultures, the conditions for preservation were mnemonic, and this involved the use of verbal and musical rhythm, for any

statement that was to be remembered and repeated. The alphabet, making available a visualized record which was complete, in place of an acoustic one, abolished the need for memorization and hence for rhythm. Rhythm had hitherto placed severe limitations upon the verbal arrangement of what might be said, or thought. More than that, the need to remember had used up a degree of brain power—of psychic energy—which now was no longer needed. The statement need not be memorized. It could lie around as an artifact, to be read when needed; no penalty for forgetting—that is, so far as preservation was concerned. The mental energies thus released, by this economy of memory, have probably been extensive, contributing to an immense expansion of knowledge available to the human mind.

These theoretic possibilities were exploited only cautiously in Graeco-Roman antiquity, and are being fully realized only today. If I stress them here in their twofold significance, namely, that all possible discourse became translatable into script and that simultaneously the burden of memorization was lifted from the mind, it is to bring out the further fact that the alphabet therewith made possible the production of novel or unexpected statement, previously unfamiliar and even "unthought." The advance of knowledge, both humane and scientific, depends upon the human ability to think about something unexpected—a "new idea," as we loosely but conveniently say. Such novel thought only achieves completed existence when it becomes novel statement, and a novel statement cannot realize its potential until it can be preserved for further use. Previous transcription, because of the ambiguities of the script, discouraged attempts to record novel statements. This indirectly discouraged the attempt to frame them even orally, for what use were they likely to be, or what influence were they likely to have, if confined within the ephemeral range of casual vernacular conversation? The alphabet, by encouraging the production of unfamiliar statement, stimulated the thinking of novel thought, which could lie around in inscribed form, be recognized, be read and readers, and so spread its influence among readers. It is no accident that the pre-alphabetic cultures of the world were also in a large sense the pre-scientific cultures, pre-philosophical, and pre-literary. The power of novel statement is not restricted to the arrangement of scientific observation. It covers the gamut of the human experience. There were new inventible ways of speaking about human life, and therefore of thinking about it, which became slowly possible for man only when they became inscribed and preservable and extendable in the alphabetic literatures of Europe. . . .

READERSHIP BEFORE THE PRINTING PRESS

There were limits set to classical literacy by the character of the materials and the methods employed to manufacture the written word. The alphabet did not fully come into its own until Western Europe had learned to copy the letter shapes in movable type and until progress in industrial technique made possible the manufacture of cheap paper. So-called book production in antiquity and the various styles of writing employed have received substantial scholarly attention, the results of which need not be recapitulated here except as they throw light on the material difficulties which any extension of popular literacy was bound to encounter. For literacy is not built upon a fund of inscriptions. In Greece, where stone and baked clay initially provide our earliest testimony to the use of the alphabet, what we would like to know more about is the availability of those perishable surfaces which could perform the casual and copious services now supplied by the paper which we moderns so thoughtlessly consume and throw away. Herodotus reports that the earliest material of this nature in use was parchment, that is, animal skins, obviously a very limited resource, quantitatively speaking, though qualitatively superior as later

antiquity was to realize. The other basic surface was that of the papyrus sheet available in Egypt. How soon did Greece import papyrus in quantity? The texts of Homer, so we were told by late tradition, received a recension of some sort in the period when Pisistratus ruled Athens about the middle of the sixth century. In what form were these texts available? Were they inscribed on papyrus? Certainly the first half of the fifth century saw the increasing use of papyrus in Athens, and also of the waxed tablet for making notes on. References in the plays of Aeschylus make this certain. But it is possible to deduce that the references are there because the use of such items was novel rather than familiar. The words "biblos" or "byblos" are translatable as either "papyrus" the material, or as the object consisting of papyrus on which writing is placed. The common translation "book" is misleading. Individual sheets of papyrus, as is well known, could be gummed together at the edges in series, thus forming a continuously extended surface which could be rolled up. To find the place you had to unroll until you came to it. "Biblion," the diminutive, meant neither book nor roll but a simple folded sheet or conceivably two or three such, folded once over together. Such details as these, coupled with the certain scarcity of material when judged by modern standards, serve to remind us that the would-be reader in ancient Athens encountered certain obstacles to his reading which we would regard as constricting. In estimating the degree of literacy and the rate of its spread, how far should such material limitations be taken into account? Should they not make us more cautious in this matter than Hellenists usually are? To give just one example: Plato in his *Apology* makes Socrates refer to the *biblia* of Anaxagoras the philosopher, "purchasable for a drachma at most," which he says "are chockfull" (*gemei*) of such statements (*logoi*) as the prosecution has referred to. Are these books? Of course not. The reference is to those summary pronouncements of the philosopher's doctrine which still survive in quotation from later antiquity and which we now call the "fragments" of the philosopher. They are compressed in style and even oracular and, we suggest, were published as a guide to the philosopher's system to be used as a supplement to oral teaching. Such summaries could be inscribed in installments upon separate sheets of papyrus purchasable for a drachma per sheet. But a good deal has been made of his reference in describing the supposed Athenian book trade of the period and also in affirming a sophisticated literacy which is presupposed by the misleading translation "book."

This is not to discount the degree of literacy achieved in Athens in the last third of the fifth century before Christ but to emphasize that however general the management of the alphabet became, the habit of rapid which we are accustomed to identify as the hallmark of a verbally competent person would be very difficult to implement. There was no large volume of documentation to practice on. If Plato's Academy in the fourth century B.C. had a library, how many shelves were filled? The very term "library" is almost a mistranslation, considering the modern connotation, as when we are told that Euripides possessed the first library. This tradition appears to base itself upon an inference drawn from a piece of burlesque concocted by Aristophanes in his play *The Frogs* at the poet's expense. Euripides and his poetry, in a contest with Aeschylus in Hades, have to be "weighed," so he is told to get into the scale pan, after "picking up his papyri," indicating that the poet could be expected to carry a parcel with him. He is satirized as a composer who had turned himself into a reader and who made poetry out of what he had read, in supposed contrast to his antagonist who is orally oriented.

On what materials did Athenian children in elementary school learn their letters? Probably sand and slate, rather than papyrus, both being media quantitatively copious, since they admit of continual reuse through erasure. A "school scene" which predates the age of social literacy in Athens portrays an older man using a waxed tablet. Such

waxed tablets but not paper are actually featured in the plots of a few plays of Euripides produced in the last third of the century when the delivery of a message or letter is called for. Aeschylus is aware only of their use for memoranda. In either case the material used would favor brevity of composition. It also could of course be reused, which again implies continual erasure of the written word. Documents can be flourished in a comedy of Aristophanes to back up an oral statement with the implication that only shysters would use this resource; the written word is still under some suspicion or is a little ridiculous. All in all, one concludes that the reading of the literate Athenian was confined within limits that we would think narrow, but what he did read he read deliberately and carefully. Speed of recognition, the secret of the alphabetic invention, was still likely to be slow relative to modern practice and thus likelihood bears on the acknowledged attention which writers and readers of the high classical period gave to words and their weighing. Inscribed language was not being manufactured at a rate great enough to dull the attention or impair verbal taste. The written word carried the value of a commodity in limited supply. The literature of the period bears the hallmark of a verbal nicety never excelled and rarely equalled in European practice.

As a corollary to this verbal sophistication (which was reinforced by residual habits of oral composition), the writers of the classical period consulted each other's works and wrote what they had to say out of what others had written before them to a degree difficult for a modern author to appreciate. The world of literature, because quantitatively so restricted, could constitute itself a sort of large club, the members of which were familiar with each other's words even though separated by spans of historic time. A good deal of what was written therefore called upon the reader to recognize echoes from other works in circulation. If the modern scholar thinks he is able to trace influences and interconnections which seem excessive by modern standards of free composition, he is not necessarily deluding himself. The world of the alphabet in antiquity was like that.

Books and documentation multiplied in the Hellenistic and Roman periods. Papyrological discoveries indicate that papyrus was in ready supply in Hellenistic Egypt, where indeed one would expect to find it. But up to the end of antiquity and beyond that through the medieval centuries, extending through the invention of the codex or book proper, so much easier to handle and consult, the distinction between our modern paper literacy, if I may call it, and the literacy of our ancestors still holds. It is a distinction determined in part by the sheer quantitative limitations placed in antiquity upon the materials available for inscription. The use of the palimpsest—the document hoarded and then erased and reused, sometimes twice over—is eloquent testimony to the scarcity and the preciousness of the material surfaces upon which alphabetic script could be written.

But scarcity of materials aside, the production of script and hence the resources available for readership were bound to remain restricted beyond the imagination of any modern reader as long as such production remained a handicraft. This set a second quantitative limitation upon the creation of all documentation, whether for literary or business purposes, as is obvious. A decree or law could not be promulgated in a newspaper; copies of accounts could not be distributed to shareholders; an author could not commit his manuscript to a publisher for mass manufacture and sale.

But the qualitative restrictions thus imposed were if anything more drastic. Strict uniformity of letter shapes was rendered impossible by the vagaries of personal handwriting. A degree of standardization was theoretically possible and certainly aimed at in the Graeco-Roman period.

It quickly broke up thereafter. A handicraft may and does produce a custom-made product of fine quality, and in the case of those artifacts that we use and consume in daily living such competitive excellence becomes esteemed and valuable. But the production of custom-built products on the same lines when the goal is the manufacture of communication becomes self-defeating. To the extent that the scribes formed schools or guilds, formal or otherwise, to foster the elaboration of local hands and embellish competing styles of writing, readership of that sort which alone furnishes the basis of a literate culture was bound to be impaired. Calligraphy, as already noted above, becomes the enemy of literacy and hence also of literature and of science.

Alphabetic literacy, in order to overcome these limitations of method and so achieve its full potential, had to await the invention of the printing press. The original achievement, the Greek one, had solved an empirical problem by applying abstract analysis. But the material means for maximizing the result required the assistance of further inventions and had to await a long time for it. Such necessary combination of technologies is characteristic of scientific advance. To realize that there is energy available when water is converted into steam was one thing. To harness the energy successfully was another, requiring the parallel construction of machine tools capable of producing fine tolerances to fit piston to cylinder, the manufacture of lubricants capable of sealing the fit, the parallel invention of slide-rod mechanisms to control the periods of steam pressure, and of crank and connecting rod to convert the thrust into rotation. The energy of the alphabet likewise had to await the assistance provided by the dawning age of scientific advance in Europe in order to be fully released.

CHAPTER 6

Writing and the Alphabet Effect

Robert K. Logan

Robert K. Logan is a professor of physics at the University of Toronto and a professor of education at the Ontario Institute for Studies in Education. He is the author of several works on communication history, including The Alphabet Effect *and* The Sixth Language, *from which the present excerpt is taken.*

WRITING AND THE ALPHABET EFFECT: A NEW MODE OF INFORMATION PROCESSING

Writing goes beyond the mere transcription of spoken language. Although writing is a medium whose content is spoken language, its uses differ from those of speech. It organizes and stores information quite differently than speech; in effect, it is a different form of language. Written language has evolved in ways quite different from speech. The rules for the construction of speech and prose are quite different. Prose is not recorded speech but a much more formal organization of information. The closest form of writing to speech is poetry, which is meant to be heard. Prose is not meant to be heard and, in fact, the most efficient form of accessing the information contained in prose writing is to read it silently.

The epic poems of Homer provide a unique opportunity to compare the oral and the written forms of language. The poems were composed and presented orally long before they were transcribed in their present form "sometime between 700 and 550 BCE" (Havelock 1978, 3). Before their transcription, there was no particular order in which the various episodes were presented by the bard who performed them. Once the verses were committed to writing, however, they became objectified, an artifact that could be studied and scanned visually, their components compared, and then edited into some temporal order, as is the case with Homer's verses. "The story pieces are sorted out and numbered so as to achieve the effect of a single overall time sequence which moves forward but with interruptions, flashbacks, and digression to an appointed end. Thus arose the arrangement of our present text . . . this arrangement being the work of the eye, not the ear, a work achievable only when the various portions of the soundtrack had been alphabetized" (Havelock 1978, 19).

The very act of transcribing an oral composition requires an ordering. The text becomes a physical artifact that can be "looked at, reflected upon, modified, looked at repeatedly, shown to others, etc." (Havelock 1978). The medium helps determine the mode of organization: "Due to the transitory character of the acoustic medium, spoken language is organized by continuity, connectivity, and integration . . . in addition to intonation. By contrast, because of the visual medium, written language is organized by discreteness, and segmentation" (Ludwig 1983, 39).

The objectification of information, or the separation of the knower from the knowledge that writing permitted, encouraged abstraction, systematization, and the objectivity of scientific thought. Phonetic writing, particularly alphabetic writing, encouraged classification and codification of information. Alphabetizing provided a natural way of ordering verbal information. It is interesting to note that the order of the letters of the alphabet never changed despite the fact that it was passed from one culture to another and adopted by so many different languages. The names and shapes of the letters changed but not the order of their presentation when the alphabet is recited as "abcdef."

The use of the alphabet as a writing code promoted and encouraged the skills of analysis, coding, decoding, and classification. Each spoken word to be transcribed had to be broken down into its phonemic components, each of which was then represented by a unique letter of the alphabet. The impact of information processing due to alphabetic writing was enormous because it introduced a new level of abstraction, analysis, and classification into Western thinking: At the same time that the Hebrews adopted alphabetic writing, they codified their law in the form of the Ten Commandments and introduced, for the first time in the history of humankind, monotheism and the notion of a prime mover or first cause.

The Greeks also made enormous intellectual strides shortly after their adoption of the Phoenician alphabet and its modification to include vowels. They were the first culture to develop deductive logic, abstract science, and rational philosophy. The Hebrews and the Greeks were also the first societies to write fairly objective histories of their own nations.

While none of these intellectual developments can be causally linked, Marshall McLuhan and I postulated (1977) that the use of phonetic writing systems created an environment conducive to the development of codified law, monotheism, abstract science, deductive logic, objective history, and individualism. All of these cultural innovations occurred primarily between 2000 and 500 BCE in the closely linked cultures found between the Tigris-Euphrates river system and the Aegean Sea. The introduction of the phonetic alphabet represents a break boundary

because of the tremendous intellectual and cultural fallout that followed from its use (Logan 1986).

ZERO AND THE PLACE NUMBER SYSTEM

One of the themes of this [reading] has been the way in which one notational system influences the development of another through a process of evolution. We have also seen that although the notation systems for writing and abstract numerals are independent, they arose together from impressed token logograms. Without abstract numerals, there might not have been writing, and without writing, there might not have been abstract numerals. The two systems of notation share a number of features. Writing employs a basic set of visual signs (for example, a set of logograms, a syllabary, or an alphabet) to transcribe or record the sounds of a spoken language into an array of visual signs. The language of mathematics also notates numbers and mathematical operations with a set of visual signs. For example, the operation of addition is represented with the + sign. At first, writing and mathematical notation were used to store the verbal or mathematical utterances of spoken language. As their use expanded, however, literature and mathematics emerged as languages in themselves, with their own peculiar techniques for processing, retrieving, and organizing information quite distinct from that of speech.

The cross-pollination between the two systems of notation continued, as writing evolved its more sophisticated phonetic elements. The alphabet influenced quantitative analysis because it stimulated an analytic and rational approach to the organization of qualitative information. This led to the development of abstract science and deductive logic by the ancient Greeks. In turn, logic and science stimulated the need for exact and precise quantitative analysis and measurement. This led to axiomatic geometry, the elements of Euclid, the quantitative astronomy of

Ptolemy and Aristarchus, the Pythagorean obsession with numbers, the mechanics of Archimedes, and the botanical and biological classification schemes of Aristotle.

The Semitic alphabet stimulated quantitative analysis directly by becoming the basis of a number system in which each letter was assigned a numerical value. The first nine letters represented 1 through 9, and the next nine letters represented 10, 20, . . . through 90. There were also letters for 100 and 1000. Any number between 1 and 100 could be represented by a maximum of two letters. For example, 18 would be written as חי where (ח) is 8 and (י) is 10. The Semitic number system was not a place number system in that 81 was not written (יח) but rather as (עא) where (א) is 1 and (ע) is 80. The system was a forerunner of the place number system in that it contained one of the essential features for such a system; namely, that all numbers between 1 and 9 had their own unique ideographic signs. The element lacking from the alphabetic number system (which the Greeks and Hindus also employed with their alphabets) that prevented it from serving as a place number system was the concept of zero and the zero symbol.

The place number system and the concept of zero were inventions of Hindu mathematicians as early as 200 BCE. The Hindu writing system at the time was alphabetic, as was their number system. Once the Hindu mathematicians developed the notion of zero, or *sunya*, as they called it, they quickly devised a place number system.

Sunya means "leave a place" in Sanskrit and indicates that the zero or sunya concept arose from recording abacus calculations. If the result of a calculation was 503, this could not be written as "5" "3" because it would be read as either 53 or 530, but if instead the result was written as "5" "leave a place" "3", the number being designated would be interpreted properly as 5 hundreds, no tens, and 3 units. "Leave a place," or sunya, soon evolved into the abstract number of zero, 0.

The Arabs used the Hindu system and transmitted it to Europe, where it arrived in the fifteenth century. The Arabs had translated sunya, or "leave a place," into the Arabic *sifr,* or cipher, the name we still use for zero as well as the name for the whole place number system itself. Our present-day term "zero" derives from the shortened version of the Latin term for cipher, *zepharino.* The place number system brought with it many advances in mathematics, including simple algorithms for arithmetic, negative numbers, algebra, and the concept of the infinite and the infinitesimal, and hence, calculus.

One of the mysteries associated with the invention of the place number system is why the Greeks, the inventors of vowels, who made such great advances in geometry and logic, did not discover zero. The explanation lies in the Greeks' overly strict adherence to logic, which led Parmenides to the conclusion that non-being (and hence, nothing) could not "be" because it was a logical contradiction. The Hindus, on the other hand, had no such inhibition about non-zero. In fact, they were positively inclined to the concept of non-being since it constituted their notion of nirvana (Logan 1986; Logan 1979, 16).

THE LANGUAGE OF MATHEMATICS

Numeric notation, like writing, grew out of the system for recording the payment of tributes with clay tokens. The language of mathematics grew out of spoken language and the need for a mathematical notation for enumeration. The mathematical statements expressed in the numerals and the signs for mathematical operations can always be translated into spoken language or writing. For example, the equation $1 + 2 = 3$ may be spoken or written as, "One plus two is three." The language of mathematics may be regarded as a medium whose content is the mathematical concepts of spoken language, namely, abstract numbers and mathematical operations, such as addition, subtraction, multiplication, and division. Once a mathematical language or notation emerged, however, it took on an existence of its own and evolved in ways quite different from either speech or writing due to the unique methods of processing information that its use stimulated.

A mathematics notation allowed abstract mathematical operations that could never have been carried out in a person's head to emerge. The notation became a tool of investigation and invention. It suggested ways of generalizing results, and thus led to new concepts. The concept of and notation for zero provides a good example. In addition to the place number system, the concept of zero, originally notated as a dot and then later as a small circle, resulted in a number of new mathematical ideas. Not long after introducing zero, the Hindu mathematicians invented negative numbers which they notated by placing a dot above a number (Logan 1986; Logan 1979). For example, $3°$ represented minus three or three below zero, which the notation literally suggests, as the 3 sits under the zero sign.

The zero sign, sunya—"leave a place"—was also used to represent the unknown. This allowed the development of algebra because the mathematician was able to "leave a place" for the unknown and deal with it as though it were also a number. Here, we see clearly how the existence of a notation (for zero, in this case) allowed the ideas of negative numbers and algebra to develop. The notation for zero caused mathematicians to think of zero as a number like 1 or 2 and hence to consider mathematical operations with this number such as addition, subtraction, multiplication, and division. The addition or subtraction of zero leads to no change and multiplication by zero yields zero, but the division of a number by zero leads to an interesting result: infinity, another new concept or invention of the Hindu mathematicians. The idea of infinity led them also to the notion of the infinitesimal, a concept that was an essential element in the development of calculus (Logan 1986; Logan 1979).

THE IMPACT OF QUANTITATIVE AND QUALITATIVE NOTATION AND ANALYSIS

There is no way short of speculation to determine how the idea for numerals and writing arose from the impressed token logograms. Because of the difficulty of establishing causal relations among cognitive processes, even when historical data are readily available, it is difficult to determine how qualitative and quantitative notational systems influenced each other's development. It is evident, however, that the new level of abstraction that pictographic writing established created an environment conducive to the development of abstract numbers and vice versa. It is clear from Schmandt-Besserat's work that the processes of literacy and numeracy are more closely linked than is commonly acknowledged. Numbers and phonetic writing emerged from a single progenitor, the clay token, in which both quantitative and qualitative information had been merged. The separation of this information into two distinct streams of written words on the one hand, and numerals on the other, opened new avenues of abstract thought and information processing. Ideographic and phonetic writing represented the first means of supplementing and extending verbal language. Numerals representing abstract numbers made possible new techniques of quantitative analysis. Both these developments mark the beginning of objective learning or the separation of the knower from the knowledge (Schmandt-Besserat 1985, 149–54).

The quantitative (from the Latin *quantus*—how great) and the qualitative (from the Latin *qualis*—of what kind) are two key categories of Western thinking that have, from the philosophical thoughts of the ancient Greeks to contemporary social science, been regarded as distinct and independent modes of analysis. The common origin of quantitative and qualitative notation from clay tokens argues against the notion that these two categories form a dichotomy. The fact that the two forms of notation emerged at the same point in history indicates the cognitive power that the interplay between the quantitative and qualitative can release.

Other breakthroughs in information processing can be associated with this interplay. The letters of the alphabet were used to notate abstract numerals until the Hindus, under the influence of alphabetic literacy, invented zero and developed the cipher system (Logan 1986; Logan 1979). It is not an accident that zero and the place number system were the invention of mathematicians who used the alphabet. The place number system and the alphabet share a number of features that contribute to their abstract nature:

1. Each system contains a small number of elements: twenty-six letters (for the English alphabet) and ten numerals.
2. They form a complete set so that the total set of possible spoken words can be represented alphabetically, and any number, no matter how large or small, can be expressed in terms of some combination of the ten numerals.
3. The individual elements of the two systems, the letters and the numerals, are atomic—that is, they are identical and repeatable.
4. The values (sound or numerical) of the aggregate elements (words or numbers) of the system depend not only on their atomistic components (the letters or numerals of which they are composed) but also on their order or syntax. In other words, both the letters and their order determine a word, and the numerals and their order determine a number. For example, ON is not the same as NO, nor is 18 the same as 81.

These similarities in the two systems illustrate two points: the alphabet was probably a stimulus to the development of the place number system; and quantitative and qualitative notational schemes are not all that different and require many of the same fundamental cognitive skills.

The common origin and emergence of quantitative and qualitative notation is only one of the indicators of the overlap of these two categories. An abstract number denotes the quantity of objects in a set, but it can also describe a quality of the set. In addition to their numerical values, the abstract numbers 1, 2, or 3 also denote the qualities of oneness, twoness, or threeness. For example, in the saying "Two's company and three's a crowd," the numbers 2 and 3 are abstract numbers and yet also describe qualities. The relationships described are quite independent of the actual 2 or 3 individuals who constitute "company" or the "crowd."

Abstract numbers themselves possess both quantitative and qualitative features. The difference between the abstract numbers 3 and 4 is quantitative in the sense that 4 is one more than 3, but the difference is not purely quantitative; it is also qualitative in that 3 is a prime number and 4 is not, but rather a perfect square. Another overlap of the two categories of letters and numerals is the way in which their use is combined for the purposes of creating classification schemes; for example, the call numbers for library books and license plates where letters and numbers are used together.

The link or overlap we have established both empirically and theoretically between the qualitative and the quantitative is confirmed etymologically when the terms used for the profession of writing or numerical accounting are examined. In ancient Babylonian or Hebrew, the term for one who writes and one who counts is identical, namely *spr* (Demsky 1972). There is a similar overlap of meaning of these words in English. A "teller" is one who counts or tells, and the expression "to give an account" can mean either to provide a narrative or an enumeration depending on the context in which the word is used. One finds a similar overlap in other languages. In German, the word *zahlen* has a double meaning denoting either counting or telling.

Numeracy, the ability to conduct mathematical calculations, is a cognitive skill that emerged as a result of the development of quantitative notation. Although there are individuals who can do calculations in their head without using notated figures, the origin of these calculational techniques required the existence of numerals. While literacy and numeracy are quite distinct cognitive skills, it is obvious that there is a strong overlap between them. The claim that some individuals are gifted with words but not numbers or vice versa has little basis in our understanding of the origins of these skills. Marked differences in an individual's literate and numerate skills could be due to a disparity in interest rather than intrinsic abilities. Historical research has indicated that literate and numerate skills are related and associated with each other. Split-brain research supports this hypothesis, as both the literate and the numerate activities seem to be concentrated in the left hemisphere of the brain.

The importance of these observations for contemporary education is not obvious. The observations do indicate, however, that current instruction in primary school of reading and writing, on the one hand, and mathematics on the other, requires greater integration. Drawing parallels between the two notational systems could certainly help students to understand the abstract nature of the alphabet and the place number system. It might help those who are strong in math but weak in reading, or vice versa, to use their strengths with one notational system to better understand the other. These suggestions are purely speculative but certainly worthy of further examination and research. The use of the computer in education might provide exactly the correct environment for such an integration as the computer treats all abstract notation in more or less the same manner. In fact, the computer may be regarded as a device for the manipulation of abstract symbols, whether they are alphabetic or numerical.

BIBLIOGRAPHY

Demsky, Aaron. 1972. "Scroll." *Encyclopedia Judaica.* Jerusalem.

Havelock, Eric. 1978. "The Alphabetization of Homer." In *Communications Arts in the Ancient World,* ed. E. Havelock and J. Hershbell. New York: Hasting House.

Logan, Robert K. 1979. "The Mystery of the Discovery of Zero." *Etcetera* 36.

Logan, Robert K. 1986. *The Alphabet Effect.* New York: William Morrow.

Ludwig, O. 1983. "Writing Systems and Written Language." In *Focus,* ed. F. Coulmas and K. Erlich. New York: Mouton.

McLuhan, Marshall, and R. K. Logan. 1977. "Alphabet, Mother of Invention." *Etcetera* 34.

Schmandt-Besserat, D. 1985. "Clay Symbols for Data Storage in the VIII Millennium BC." In *Studiti Palentologia in onore di Salvatore M. Puglisi.* La Spaienza: Universita di Roma.

CHAPTER 7

Orality, Literacy, and Modern Media

Walter Ong

The late Walter Ong was Professor of humanities at Saint Louis University. He wrote extensively on the orality/literacy question, as well as on the communications dimension of the shift from the medieval to the modern era.

Fully literate persons can only with great difficulty imagine what a primary oral culture is like, that is, a culture with no knowledge whatsoever of writing or even of the possibility of writing. Try to imagine a culture where no one has even "looked up" anything. In a primary oral culture, the expression "to look up something" is an empty phrase: it would have no conceivable meaning. Without writing, words as such have no visual presence, even when the objects they represent are visual. They are sounds. You might "call" them back—"recall" them. But there is nowhere to "look" for them. They have no focus and no trace (a visual metaphor, showing dependency on writing), not even a trajectory. They are occurrences, events.

To learn what a primary oral culture is and what the nature of our problem is regarding such a culture, it helps first to reflect on the nature of sound itself as sound (Ong 1967b, pp. 111–38). All sensation takes place in time, but sound has a special relationship to time unlike that of the other fields that register in human sensation. Sound exists only when it is going out of existence. It is not simply perishable but essentially evanescent, and it is sensed as evanescent. When I pronounce the word "permanence," by the time I get to the "-nence," the "perma-" is gone, and has to be gone.

There is no way to stop sound and have sound. I can stop a moving picture camera and hold one frame fixed on the screen. If I stop the movement of sound, I have nothing—only silence, no sound at all. All sensation takes place in time, but no other sensory field totally resists a holding action, stabilization, in quite this way. Vision can register motion, but it can also register immobility. Indeed, it favors immobility, for to examine something closely by vision, we prefer to have it quiet. We often reduce motion to a series of still shots the better to see what motion is. There is no equivalent of a still shot for sound. An oscillogram is silent. It lies outside the sound world.

For anyone who has a sense of what words are in a primary oral culture, or a culture not far removed from primary orality, it is not surprising that the Hebrew term *dabar* means "word" and "event." Malinowski (1923, pp. 451, 470–81) has made the point that among "primitive" (oral) peoples generally language is a mode of action and not simply a countersign of thought, though he had trouble explaining what he was getting at . . ., since understanding of the psychodynamics of orality was virtually nonexistent in 1923. Neither is it surprising that oral peoples commonly, and probably universally, consider words to have great power. Sound cannot be sounding without the use of power. A hunter can see a buffalo, smell, taste, and touch a buffalo when the buffalo is completely inert, even dead, but if he hears a buffalo, he had better watch out: something is going on. In this sense, all sound, and especially oral utterance, which comes from inside living organisms, is "dynamic."

The fact that oral peoples commonly and in all likelihood universally consider words to have magical potency is clearly tied in, at least unconsciously, with their sense of the word as necessarily spoken, sounded, and hence power-driven. Deeply typographic folk forget to think of words as primarily oral, as events, and hence as necessarily powered: for them, words tend rather to be assimilated to things, "out there" on a flat surface. Such "things" are not so readily associated with magic, for they are not actions, but are in a radical sense dead, though subject to dynamic resurrection (Ong 1977, pp. 230–71).

Oral peoples commonly think of names (one kind of words) as conveying power over things. Explanations of Adam's naming of the animals in Genesis 2:20 usually call condescending attention to this presumably quaint archaic belief. Such a belief is in fact far less quaint than it seems to unreflective chirographic and typographic folk. First of all, names do give human beings power over what they name: without learning a vast store of names, one is simply powerless to understand, for example, chemistry and to practice chemical engineering. And so with all other intellectual knowledge. Secondly, chirographic and typographic folk tend to think of names as labels, written or printed tags imaginatively affixed to an object named. Oral folk have no sense of a name as a tag, for they have no idea of a name as something that can be seen. Written or printed representations of words can be labels; real, spoken words cannot be.

You Know What You Can Recall: Mnemonics and Formulas

In an oral culture, restriction of words to sound determines not only modes of expression but also thought processes.

You know what you can recall. When we say we know Euclidean geometry, we mean not that we have in mind at the moment every one of its propositions and proofs but rather that we can bring them to mind readily. We can recall them. The theorem "You know what you can recall" applies also to an oral culture. But how do persons in an oral culture recall? The organized knowledge that literates today study so that they "know" it, that is, can recall it, has, with very few if any exceptions, been assembled and made available to them in writing. This is the case not only with Euclidean geometry but also with American Revolutionary history or even baseball batting averages or traffic regulations.

An oral culture has no texts. How does it get together organized material for recall? This is the same as asking, "What does it or can it know in an organized fashion?"

Suppose a person in an oral culture would undertake to think through a particular complex problem and would finally manage to articulate a solution which itself is relatively complex, consisting, let us say, of a few hundred words. How does he or she retain for later recall the verbalization so painstakingly elaborated? In the total absence of any writing, there is nothing outside the thinker, no text, to enable him or her to produce the same line of thought again or even to verify whether he or she has done so or not. *Aides-mémoire* such as

notched sticks or a series of carefully arranged objects will not of themselves retrieve a complicated series of assertions. How, in fact, could a lengthy, analytic solution ever be assembled in the first place? An interlocutor is virtually essential: it is hard to talk to yourself for hours on end. Sustained thought in an oral culture is tied to communication.

But even with a listener to stimulate and ground your thought, the bits and pieces of your thought cannot be preserved in jotted notes. How could you ever call back to mind what you had so laboriously worked out? The only answer is: Think memorable thoughts. In a primary oral culture, to solve effectively the problem of retaining and retrieving carefully articulated thought, you have to do your thinking in mnemonic patterns, shaped for ready oral recurrence. Your thought must come into being in heavily rhythmic, balanced patterns, in repetitions or antitheses, in alliterations and assonances, in epithetic and other formulary expressions, in standard thematic settings (the assembly, the meal, the duel, the hero's "helper," and so on), in proverbs which are constantly heard by everyone so that they come to mind readily and which themselves are patterned for retention and ready recall or in other mnemonic form. Serious thought is intertwined with memory systems. Mnemonic needs determine even syntax (Havelock 1963, pp. 87–96, 131–2, 294–6).

Protracted orally based thought, even when not in formal verse, tends to be highly rhythmic, for rhythm aids recall, even physiologically. Jousse (1978) has shown the intimate linkage between rhythmic oral patterns, the breathing process, gesture, and the bilateral symmetry of the human body in ancient Aramaic and Hellenic targums, and thus also in ancient Hebrew. Among the ancient Greeks, Hesiod, who was intermediate between oral Homeric Greece and fully developed Greek literacy, delivered quasi-philosophic material in the formulaic verse forms that structured it into the oral culture from which he had emerged (Havelock 1963, pp. 97–8, 294–301).

Formulas help implement rhythmic discourse and also act as mnemonic aids in their own right, as set expressions circulating through the mouths and ears of all. "Red in the morning, the sailor's warning; red in the night, the sailor's delight." "Divide and conquer." "To err is human, to forgive is divine." "Sorrow is better than laughter, because when the face is sad the heart grows wiser" (Ecclesiastes 7:3). "The clinging vine." "The sturdy oak." "Chase off nature and she returns at a gallop." Fixed, often rhythmically balanced, expressions of this sort and of other sorts can be found occasionally in print, indeed can be "looked up" in books of sayings, but in oral cultures they are not occasional. They are incessant. They form the substance of thought itself. Thought in any extended form is impossible without them, for it consists in them.

The more sophisticated orally patterned thought is, the more it is likely to be marked by set expressions skillfully used. This is true of oral cultures generally from those of Homeric Greece to those of the present day across the globe. Havelock's *Preface to Plato* (1963) and fictional works such as Chinua Achebe's novel *No Longer at Ease* (1961), which draws directly on Ibo oral tradition in West Africa, alike provide abundant instances of thought patterns of orally educated characters who move in these oral, mnemonically tooled grooves, as the speakers reflect, with high intelligence and sophistication, on the situations in which they find themselves involved. The law itself in oral cultures is enshrined in formulaic sayings, proverbs, which are not mere jurisprudential decorations, but themselves constitute the law. A judge in an oral culture is often called on to articulate sets of relevant proverbs out of which he can produce equitable decisions in the cases under formal litigation before him. . . .

In an oral culture, to think through something in non-formulaic, non-patterned, non-mnemonic terms, even if it were possible, would be a waste of time, for such thought, once worked through, could never be recovered with any effectiveness, as it could be with the aid of writing. It would not be abiding knowledge but simply a passing thought, however complex. Heavy patterning and communal fixed formulas in oral cultures serve some of the purposes of writing in chirographic cultures, but in doing so they of course determine the kind of thinking that can be done, the way experience is intellectually organized. In an oral culture, experience is intellectualized mnemonically. This is one reason why, for a St Augustine of Hippo (A.D. 354–430), as for other savants living in a culture that knew some literacy but still carried an overwhelmingly massive oral residue, memory bulks so large when he treats of the powers of the mind.

Of course, all expression and all thought is to a degree formulaic in the sense that every word and every concept conveyed in a word is a kind of formula, a fixed way of processing the data of experience, determining the way experience and reflection are intellectually organized, and acting as a mnemonic device of sorts. Putting experience into any words (which means transforming it at least a little bit—not the same as falsifying it) can implement its recall. The formulas characterizing orality are more elaborate, however, than are individual words, though some may be relatively simple: the *Beowulf*-poet's "whale-road" is a formula (metaphorical) for the sea in a sense in which the term "sea" is not.

THE INTERIORITY OF SOUND

In treating some psychodynamics of orality, we have thus far attended chiefly to one characteristic of sound itself, its evanescence, its relationship to time. Sound exists only when it is going out of existence. Other characteristics of sound also determine or influence oral psychodynamics. The principal one of these other characteristics is the unique relationship of sound to interiority when sound is compared to the rest of the senses. This relationship is important because of the interiority of human consciousness and of human communication itself. It can be discussed only summarily here. I have treated the matter in greater fullness and depth in *The Presence of the Word*, to which the interested reader is referred (1967, Bibliography).

To test the physical interior of an object as interior, no sense works so directly as sound. The human sense of sight is adapted best to light diffusely reflected from surfaces. (Diffuse reflection, as from a printed page or a landscape, contrasts with specular reflection, as from a mirror.) A source of light, such as a fire, may be intriguing but it is optically baffling: the eye cannot get a "fix" on anything within the fire. Similarly, a translucent object, such as alabaster, is intriguing because, although it is not a source of light, the eye cannot get a "fix" on it either. Depth can be perceived by the eye, but most satisfactorily as a series of surfaces: the trunks of trees in a grove, for example, or chairs in an auditorium. The eye does not perceive an interior strictly as an interior: inside a room, the walls it perceives are still surfaces, outsides.

Taste and smell are not much help in registering interiority or exteriority. Touch is. But touch partially destroys interiority in the process of perceiving it. If I wish to discover by touch whether a box is empty or full, I have to make a hole in the box to insert a hand or finger: this means that the box is to that extent open, to that extent less an interior.

Hearing can register interiority without violating it. I can rap a box to find whether it is empty or full or a wall to find whether it is hollow or solid inside. Or I can ring a coin to learn whether it is silver or lead.

Sounds all register the interior structures of whatever it is that produces them. A violin filled with concrete will not sound like a normal violin. A saxophone sounds differently from a flute: it is structured differently inside. And above all, the human voice comes from inside the human organism which provides the voice's resonances.

Sight isolates, sound incorporates. Whereas sight situates the observer outside what he views, at a distance, sound pours into the hearer. Vision dissects, as Merleau-Ponty has observed (1961).

Vision comes to a human being from one direction at a time: to look at a room or a landscape, I must move my eyes around from one part to another. When I hear, however, I gather sound simultaneously from every direction at once: I am at the center of my auditory world, which envelops me, establishing me at a kind of core of sensation and existence. This centering effect of sound is what high-fidelity sound reproduction exploits with intense sophistication. You can immerse yourself in hearing, in sound. There is no way to immerse yourself similarly in sight.

By contrast with vision, the dissecting sense, sound is thus a unifying sense. A typical visual ideal is clarity and distinctness, a taking apart (Descartes' campaigning for clarity and distinctness registered an intensification of vision in the human sensorium—Ong 1967, pp. 63, 221). The auditory ideal, by contrast, is harmony, a putting together.

Interiority and harmony are characteristics of human consciousness. The consciousness of each human person is totally interiorized, known to the person from the inside and inaccessible to any other person directly from the inside. Everyone who says "I" means something different by it from what every other person means. What is "I" to me is only "you" to you. And this "I" incorporates experience into itself by "getting it all together." Knowledge is ultimately not a fractioning but a unifying phenomenon, a striving for harmony. Without harmony, an interior condition, the psyche is in bad health.

It should be noted that the concepts interior and exterior are not mathematical concepts and cannot be differentiated mathematically. They are existentially grounded concepts, based on experience of one's own body, which is both inside me (I do not ask you to stop kicking my body but to stop kicking *me*) and outside me (I feel myself as in some sense inside my body). The body is a frontier between myself and everything else. What we mean by "interior" and "exterior" can be conveyed only by reference to experience of bodiliness. Attempted definitions of "interior" and "exterior" are inevitably tautological: "interior" is defined by "in," which is defined by "between," which is defined by "inside," and so on round and round the tautological circle. The same is true with "exterior." When we speak of interior and exterior, even in the case of physical objects, we are referring to our own sense of ourselves: I am *inside* here and everything else is *outside*. By interior and exterior we point to our own experience of bodiliness (Ong 1967, pp. 117–22, 176–9, 228, 231) and analyze other objects by reference to this experience.

In a primary oral culture, where the word has its existence only in sound, with no reference whatsoever to any visually perceptible text, and no awareness of even the possibility of such a text, the phenomenology of sound enters deeply into human beings' feel for existence, as processed by the spoken word. For the way in which the word is experienced is always momentous in psychic life. The centering action of sound (the field of sound is not spread out before me but is all around me) affects man's sense of the cosmos. For oral cultures, the cosmos is an ongoing event with man at its center. Man is the *umbilicus mundi,* the navel of the world (Eliade 1958, pp. 231–5, etc.). Only after print and the extensive experience with maps that print implemented would human beings, when they thought about the cosmos or universe or "world," think primarily of something laid out before their eyes, as in a modern printed atlas, a vast surface or assemblage of surfaces (vision presents surfaces) ready to be "explored." The ancient oral world knew few "explorers," though it did know many itinerants, travelers, voyagers, adventurers, and pilgrims.

It will be seen that most of the characteristics of orally based thought and expression discussed earlier in this chapter relate intimately to the unifying, centralizing, interiorizing economy of sound as perceived by human beings. A sound-dominated verbal economy is consonant with aggregative (harmonizing) tendencies rather than with analytic, dissecting tendencies (which would come with the inscribed, visualized word: vision is a dissecting sense). It is consonant also with the conservative holism (the homeostatic present that

must be kept intact, the formulary expressions that must be kept intact), with situational thinking (again holistic, with human action at the center) rather than abstract thinking, with a certain humanistic organization of knowledge around the actions of human and anthromorphic beings interiorized persons, rather than around impersonal things.

The denominators used here to describe the primary oral world will be useful again later to describe what happened to human consciousness when writing and print reduced the oral–aural world to a world of visualized pages.

SECONDARY ORALITY

. . . With telephone, radio, television and various kinds of sound tape, electronic technology has brought us into the age of "secondary orality." This new orality has striking resemblances to the old in its participatory mystique, its fostering of a communal sense, its concentration on the present moment, and even its use of formulas (Ong 1971, pp. 284–303; 1977, pp. 16–49, 305–41). But it is essentially a more deliberate and self-conscious orality, based permanently on the use of writing and print, which are essential for the manufacture and operation of the equipment and for its use as well.

Secondary orality is both remarkably like and remarkably unlike primary orality. Like primary orality, secondary orality has generated a strong group sense, for listening to spoken words forms hearers into a group, a true audience, just as reading written or printed texts turns individuals in on themselves. But secondary orality generates a sense for groups immeasurably larger than those of primary oral culture—McLuhan's "global village." Moreover, before writing, oral folk were group-minded because no feasible alternative had presented itself. In our age of secondary orality, we are group-minded self-consciously and programmatically. The individual feels that he or she, as an individual, must be socially sensitive. Unlike members of a primary oral culture, who are turned outward because they have had little occasion to turn inward, we are turned outward because we have turned inward. In a like vein, where primary orality promotes spontaneity because the analytic reflectiveness implemented by writing is unavailable, secondary orality promotes spontaneity because through analytic reflection we have decided that spontaneity is a good thing. We plan our happenings carefully to be sure that they are thoroughly spontaneous.

The contrast between oratory in the past and in today's world well highlights the contrast between primary and secondary orality. Radio and television have brought major political figures as public speakers to a larger public than was ever possible before modern electronic developments. Thus in a sense orality has come into its own more than ever before. But it is not the old orality. The old-style oratory coming from primary orality is gone forever. In the Lincoln–Douglas debates of 1858, the combatants—for that is what they clearly and truly were—faced one another often in the scorching Illinois summer sun outdoors, before wildly responsive audiences of as many as 12,000 or 15,000 persons (at Ottawa and Freeport, Illinois, respectively—Sparks 1908, pp. 137–8, 189–90), speaking for an hour and a half each. The first speaker had one hour, the second an hour and a half, and the first another half hour of rebuttal—all this with no amplifying equipment. Primary orality made itself felt in the additive, redundant, carefully balanced, highly agonistic style, and the intense interplay between speaker and audience. The debaters were hoarse and physically exhausted at the end of each bout. Presidential debates on television today are completely out of this older oral world. The audience is absent, invisible, inaudible. The candidates are ensconced in tight little booths, make short presentations, and engage in crisp little conversations with each other in which any agonistic edge is deliberately kept dull. Electronic media do not tolerate a show of open antagonism. Despite their cultivated air of spontaneity, these media are totally dominated by a sense of closure which is the heritage of print: a show of hostility might break open the closure, the tight control. Candidates

accommodate themselves to the psychology of the media. Genteel, literate domesticity is rampant. Only quite elderly persons today can remember what oratory was like when it was still in living contact with its primary oral roots. Others perhaps hear more oratory, or at least more talk, from major public figures than people commonly heard a century ago. But what they hear will give them very little idea of the old oratory reaching back from preelectronic times through two millennia and far beyond, or of the oral lifestyle and oral thought structures out of which such oratory grew.

BIBLIOGRAPHY

Achebe, Chinua (1961) *No Longer at Ease* (New York: Ivan Obolensky).

Eliade, Mircea (1958) *Patterns in Comparative Religion*, trans. by Willard R. Trask (New York: Sheed & Ward).

Havelock, Eric A. (1963) *Preface to Plato* (Cambridge, MA: Belknap Press of Harvard University Press).

Jousse, Marcel (1925) *Le Style oval rhythmique et mnemotechnique chez les Verbomoteurs* (Paris: G. Beauchesne).

Jousse, Marcel (1978) *Le Parlant, la parole, et le souffle*, preface by Maurice Houis, Ecole Pratique des Hautes Etudes, *L'Anthropologie du gest* (Paris: Gallimard).

Malinowski, Bronislaw (1923) "The Problem of Meaning in Primitive Languages," in C. K. Ogden and I. A. Richards (eds.), *The Meaning of Meaning* (New York: Harcourt Brace; London: Kegan Paul, Trench, Trubner).

Merleau-Ponty, Maurice (1961) "L'Oeil et l'esprit," *Les Temps modernes*, 18, 184–5. Numéro spécial: "Maurice Merleau-Ponty," 193–227.

Ong, Walter (1967) *The Presence of the Word* (New Haven and London: Yale University Press).

——— (1971) *Rhetoric, Romance, and Technology* (Ithaca and London: Cornell University Press).

——— (1977) *Interface of the Word* (Ithaca and London: Cornell University Press).

Sparks, Edwin Erle (ed.) (1908) *The Lincoln-Douglas Debates of 1858*, Collections of the Illinois State Historical Library, Vol. III, Lincoln Series, vol. 1 (Springfield, IL: Illinois State Historical Library).

CHAPTER 8

Communication and Faith in the Middle Ages

James Burke and Robert Ornstein

James Burke is a well-known author and educator and the host of several television series, including Connections *and* The Day the Universe Changed. *Robert Ornstein is the author of many books, including* New World, New Mind, *and* The Psychology of Consciousness.

In the dying years of Rome, the Christian hierarchy modeled their organization on the Imperial administration, where groups of city governments formed provinces and groups of provinces formed vicariates. In the church, the basic unit became the diocese ruled by a bishop. Dioceses were grouped together to form church provinces presided over by archbishops, and provinces were grouped under the direction of metropolitan archbishops, or primates. Ruling the metropolitans were the patriarchs of Rome, Constantinople, Antioch, Alexandria, and Jerusalem.

This tightly knit structure lasted through the centuries of darkness that followed the fall of Rome because its members had the means to keep in contact and share what little knowledge survived the cataclysm. Taking as their text Daniel 12.4: "Many shall run to and fro, and knowledge shall be increased" (or perhaps taking a look around at the crumbling Empire), the early medieval church organized special congregations of priests and lay people to repair local roads, build bridges, set up messenger relays, and even establish hostels for travelers.

The church's magic power was also able to persuade people that if they visited holy shrines they would be granted numinous contact with the relics of Saints. These faithful travelers also acted as messengers for the church, whose lines of communication were kept open at most times throughout this entire period. A widespread and well-organized message network, operating from bishop to bishop, was set up by Pope Gregory the Great in the seventh century.

A hundred years later, St. Boniface used priests to carry his regular and numerous letters from Germany to England and Rome. In them, Boniface referred to items he either wanted delivered or had already received. While he was in Germany, books were sent to him by Abbess Eadburga in England; Boniface asked for details of any books in the library of Abbot Duddo that might be useful; he ordered a copy of the epistles of St. Peter written in gold letters to impress his congregation with honor and reverence; late in life he sought a copy of the Prophets, written out in large letters and without abbreviations, because of his failing eyesight.

The ability to read and write and to communicate over distance raised the Christian hierarchs to an extremely powerful position over illiterate kings and princes, who relied totally on the clergy to help them administer their territories. This was when new phrases came into the language, such as "auditing" accounts and holding "hearings," where oral evidence was presented because most of those involved, including the highest in lay society, were illiterate and could only understand the spoken word. But when a cardinal corrected the Latin of the Emperor Sigismund he replied, *Ego sum rex Romanus et super grammatica* ("I am the Roman Emperor and I am above grammar").

It was easy for the church, primarily through its monastic communities and bishops, to control an illiterate world. By the early Middle Ages, Roman state schooling had vanished and nothing replaced it that might compete with the educational system controlled by the church. Knowledge was now in the hands of a tiny fraction of the population, it was exclusively religious in purpose, and gave the church a monopoly of control over those aspects of social life that required literary and learning.

Pope Gregory made art a propaganda tool. He said:

> Pictorial representation is made use of in churches for this reason: that such as are ignorant of letters may at least read by looking at the walls what they cannot read in books. To the end that both those who are ignorant of letters might have wherewith to gather a knowledge of the history and that the people might by no means sin by adoration of a pictorial representation. . . . For what writing presents to readers, this a picture presents to the unlearned to behold, since in it even the ignorant see what they ought to follow. In it the illiterate read. Hence, and chiefly to the nations . . . a picture is instead of reading.

In the later Middle Ages, art would be used variously to publicize papal authority over secular rulers. Emperors and anti-popes are repeatedly shown trodden underfoot by a triumphant supreme pontiff sitting on an ever-larger throne. Much later it became common for the popes to be portrayed somewhere in every work of art they commissioned. . . .

Ecclesiastical control, based on their literate abilities, inserted the clergy into every aspect of secular life. Bishops and abbots received grants of land from kings and noblemen, although royal appointment often placed them in an inferior position to the monarch. But it did enhance their political and economic power in all the kingdoms of the West, giving them power-of-landlord over thousands of peasants. Throughout this period, bishops and abbots sat in royal councils, were influential in drafting secular law codes, and took a major part in affairs of state. During the ninth and tenth centuries, churchmen also frequently became involved in military organization, since from the ninth century onwards a number of conditions began to be attached to grants of land, often including an obligation that the church recipients should muster a specified number of troops when requested for their benefactor's service.

By the eleventh century the church's grip on Western society was, firm, although not uncontested. Churches had been established in all major areas of settlement throughout northern Europe, and this made possible the growth of a parish system. Everybody living in a town or village in western Europe had a local church.

The church then took social control to new levels, achieving unprecedented mastery over the thoughts and feelings of every individual through one of the most effective systems for social discipline ever devised: the confession. By the twelfth century, any sins or offenses committed against church doctrine had to be privately divulged to a priest, and failure to do so could lead to punishment, even to the ultimate sanction of excommunication from the Christian community, which would deprive the guilty party of all forms of protection under civil or canon law. The practice probably began in Celtic monastic penitential practices, where a monk or hermit confessed his sins to his "soul-friend," as the texts called this moral guide.

Slowly the system became commonplace to the point where the Lateran Council of 1215 decreed that everybody had to confess once a year to the parish priest. This was one of the most important steps taken in over a thousand years to enforce the Christianization of hearts and minds. Mental control, first exercised over monks by other monks, came to be exercised over everybody by the secular clergy responsible for spiritual care. From this point on, nothing would remain hidden from the church. However, as things turned out, the church would need every control system it could marshal to deal with the threat (to Christendom and above all to papal mind-control) that had been building up in the Middle East since the seventh century.

By this time, Alexandrine Greek knowledge had begun to transfer to Islam, where it would be processed before returning once again to Western culture. The transfer was triggered by a heretic Christian sect, the Nestorians, who had been expelled from Byzantium centuries earlier and had wandered Asia Minor until settling at a place in Jundishapur in the mountains of southern Iran, a few miles from what would become the site of the first Arab capital, Baghdad.

In seventh century Baghdad, Caliph Al Mansur was looking for a cure to his gastric problems and sent servants to the Nestorian monastery to ask for medicines. His retainers reported the presence in the monastery of an immense library. Al Mansur subsequently discovered that the Nestorians had preserved virtually intact the work of all the major thinkers at the Alexandrine Museion as well as that of their Classical Greek predecessors. The caliph and his successors ordered almost all the texts translated and found themselves in possession of a treasure trove of Greek axemaker knowledge.

The transfer of the Greek data reached its height during the eighth and ninth centuries in Baghdad under the Abbasid Caliphs, with the translation of Aristotle and Plato, Hippocrates and Galen, Ptolemy, Euclid and Archimedes, Apollonius, Aristarchus, and others. Nothing was absorbed into Islamic culture until it had been checked for theological acceptability. This work was done in libraries, hospitals, and observatories, and it stimulated Arab axemakers to their own investigations of the world. Astronomy told them the hours of prayer and the direction of Mecca; medicine was a valuable applied science, linked to astronomy through the astrological nature of treatment; philology aided the analysis of sacred writings.

Gradually, however, Islam drew a distinction between religious subjects (law and religious custom), the subjects to be used in the service of religion, such as astronomy and grammar, and the secular sciences of math, astronomy, and medicine. Islamic societies turned Greek theory into applied technology that would help them and their clerical masters to survive and prosper. They achieved important advances in hydraulics and applied them to irrigation systems so that their deserts bloomed with the magnificent gardens of their rulers' palaces.

The highly centralized nature of Islamic society, which placed tight constraints on the individual's freedom of intellectual movement, made innovative thinking possible but its application strictly controlled. The same was true of medieval Chinese society, where at this time other axemaker knowledge was being generated, which would, like Islamic advances, eventually find its way West. In China, the state controlled all activity, and the comprehensive social organization originally required for irrigation and other large-scale public works gave Chinese life a collective character.

All individual activity in China was subordinate to the common good and thus defined by the bureaucrats. From earliest times, power had rested exclusively in the hands of a shaman ruler, who was the divine son of heaven. He was supported by an extensive, all-powerful Mandarin bureaucracy, entry to which was by merit and most of whom followed the teachings of the fifth-century B.C.E. thinker Confucius. To the Mandarins, Confucian thought was the "Great Way of Life," whose tenets controlled all social and political activity, as well as keeping tight constraints on the activities of the free-thinking analytical mind.

The Confucian view was another good example of the self-fulfilling nature of axemaker processes. According to the Confucian tenet, the only purpose of education was to prepare for service to the state, so the aim of the educated man was to involve himself primarily in the maintenance of stable government. No knowledge was derived from supernatural revelation; rather it was reached through the use of reason, which also made explicit the guidelines for ethical conduct, which in turn was defined by the state.

In this closed loop, there was no way for scientific theory to become technological practice because the state decreed that no contact was permitted between one discipline and another, so theory was not expected to relate to practice. The Mandarins believed the most powerful tool for social management was classification and record keeping of everything and everybody, so everything was categorized, and the application of knowledge was only permitted within its own category. While all the requisite information was available, a revolution did not happen in China because it was all separated.

When the immense repository of Islamic (and through Islam, Chinese) and Alexandrine Greek knowledge finally reached the West at the time when Europe first made contact with the Arabs in Spain, Sicily, and Jerusalem, it would first of all put unprecedented power of cut-and-control into the hands of the Catholic leadership, thanks to the Christian belief that they had a God-given right to subjugate the world.

According to both the Old and New Testaments, man had been, given dominion over nature. Genesis said: "Every living thing shall; be meat for you . . . the fear of you and dread of you shall be upon every beast of the Earth . . . Into your hand they are delivered . . . Have dominion over the Earth and subdue it." When these early statements were originally made, they were probably intended to regulate and maybe celebrate what had been happening since the axemakers had made possible settlement in the prehistoric Levant and principally to memorialize the domestication of animals and the first agriculture.

In many other religions, nature was divine, or it shared divinity, but Christian doctrine gave humankind a position separate in nature from the rest of created things. Greek cosmologists had also shared this view that nature was not sacred, so when Arab translations of Aristotle's work arrived in the Christian West in the early Middle Ages, his statement that animal life only existed for man's sake added extra authority to Christian practice.

The dominant Christian view was that since animals and plants did not have souls, this precluded their eligibility for humane treatment. Manipulation of nature (which could include the enhancement of its value and beauty) was mankind's right and duty because "improvement" of the world involved the exercise of power derived from God for that very purpose.

The medieval Christian believed in Aristotle's "Great Chain of Being," the hierarchical structure created at Creation by God or, as Aristotle would have put it, the "Prime Mover." The Great Chain linked all species, one to the next, from the simplest organism all the way up to humans and angels and was based on the concept that lower forms existed only for the sake of higher forms.

Eleventh-century Benedictine monks were among the first systematically to apply these views of nature to their daily life and to begin a process of "improvement" of nature, which would be reflected in axemaker activity for centuries to come. The Rule of St. Benedict had ordered members of the Order to seek out monastic sites "far from the haunts of men," in wild and isolated places, and then to apply their knowledge to cultivation of the land so that it would provide enough food to support them.

One particular family of Benedictines, the Cistercians, whose motto was "Work is prayer," succeeded best of all in this task. Most of what little technology survived the centuries after the fall of Rome emerged in the Middle Ages from Cistercian monasteries that were more like small factories, filled with water-driven looms, mills, saws, grinding stones, and trip-hammers.

In the twelfth century, St. Bernard of Clairvaux in France described the landscape at his Cistercian monastery as having been "given meaning," since human ingenuity had brought order to the wilderness and had dammed the river, diverting its flow to drive the monastery's waterwheels. . . .

Twelfth-century Cistercian monasteries were the most advanced technical complexes on the European continent, with the most developed agricultural techniques and the most productive factories and mines. It was their dynamic "go forth and improve" doctrine that was eventually to give secular authorities of the late medieval West the technology to achieve efficient means of social control.

One of the new control systems arose out of the liturgical needs of the monasteries in Northern Europe, where monks needed to know what time it was because there were specific rules scheduling daily collective prayer for the souls of the multitude that it was a monk's duty to perform. There were seven set times at which prayers were to be said, some of them in the middle of the night. At first, water clocks and candles had served to indicate when the monastery bells should be tolled to mark prayer time, but water clocks froze in winter and candles blew out.

For the monastery overseers in the monastic proto-factories, timekeeping was also an indispensable method of organization. So it may have been the expansion of this technology-oriented religious order of axemakers that intensified the search for a better form of timekeeping and spurred the development of the mechanical, weight-driven clock in the thirteenth century.

The gift of the clock immediately made possible new forms of wider, more effective marshaling of social forces. Demand for clocks from royal courts and from the growing number of towns throughout Europe was overwhelming. Town clocks gave guilds and governments the means to regulate all behavior. In Brussels, textile workers rose at a dawn bell, weavers and twisters ended their day with an evening bell, and there was a special clock for cobblers. In 1355, in Amiens, France, the city government would issue an ordinance "concerning the time when the workers . . . should go each morning to work, when they should eat and when to return to work after eating; and also in the evening when they should quit work for the day," and they used a special bell for this purpose. . . .

Then in 1277 the discussion of anything remotely related to rationalism was forbidden, while Rome looked for a means out of the apparent impasse. The way was found in the person of a Dominican intellectual who had studied under Albertus Magnus in Paris and whose name was Thomas Aquinas.

Aquinas papered over the cracks between faith and reason in his *Summa Theologica*. In it he argued that philosophy examined the supernatural order in the light of reason and theology examined it in the light of revelation. Although reason was used in theology, revelation did not fall within the province of philosophy, and philosophy could not contradict theology because truth could not contradict truth. Human reason could demonstrate some truths of revelation and it could show that other truths were supra- rather than antirational, but faith was a realm in which reason could not hold sway.

For Aquinas, faith and knowledge were, therefore, not mutually exclusive. He said that belief took over at the point where knowledge ended. The goal of both reason and theology was "Being," and although reason could not finally grasp "Being," it could make faith plausible. In this way, he showed that faith and knowledge were not antithetical. Aquinas summed up his view: "To believe is to think with assent."

Aquinas showed the lack of tolerance to opponents that might be expected from a defender of the establishment, justifying excommunication and execution and arguing that since their sin affected the soul, they should be more quickly and severely punished than forgers and robbers. However, the church should admonish them twice, hoping for their return, before excommunicating them and turning them over to secular powers for execution.

With this *Summa,* Aquinas released the full power of the gift of rationalism into secular hands. He bowed to the power of geometry, admitting that God could not make the sum of the internal angles of a triangle add up to more than two right angles. In the future there would be two kinds of knowledge: that which related to revelation (which would be the province of theology) and that which dealt with the natural world (which reason and philosophy could handle).

With this decision the church created another opportunity for axemakers to go forth and multiply. The result would one day become known as "science." But the unshackling of rationalism in this way was only a matter of appearances. No "science" would be free of ecclesiastical control for centuries. Indeed, for most of the time up to the modern world, most scientists would be churchmen, and as late as Darwin science would continue to work in support of established religion.

One of the earliest expressions of the new, more secular view came at the end of the thirteenth century from an English cleric called Roger Bacon, in his *Opus Maius*. Writing about Peter of Maricourt, another traveler to Arab lands who was already famous for his work on magnetism, Bacon said: "What others strive to see dimly and blindly, like bats in twilight, he gazes at in the full light of day because he is a master of experiments. Through experiment he gains knowledge of natural things medical, chemical and indeed of everything in the heavens or Earth."

Bacon's major "scientific" writings were not pieces of natural philosophy but passionate attempts to warn the church hierarchy (in works addressed to the pope) against suppressing the new learning expressed in Aristotelian philosophy and in all the new literature relating to natural philosophy, mathematical science, and medicine. Bacon argued that the new philosophy was a divine gift, capable of proving articles of faith and persuading the unconverted; that scientific knowledge contributed vitally to the interpretation of Scripture; that astronomy was essential for establishing the religious calendar; that astrology enabled man to predict the future; that "experimental science" taught how to prolong life; and that optics enabled the creation of devices that would terrorize unbelievers and lead to their conversion.

There was "one perfect wisdom," Bacon argued in his *Opus Maius,* "and this is contained in holy Scripture, in which all truth is rooted.

I say, therefore, that one discipline is mistress of the others, namely, theology, for which the others are integral necessities and that cannot achieve its ends without them. And it lays claim to their virtues and subordinates them to its nod and command." So theology did not oppress these sciences but put them to work, directing them to their proper end.

Bacon's experimental technique, which would give axemakers a new technique for manufacturing knowledge, became known as "resolution and composition." It was a direct descendant of the mode of thought made possible by the alphabet because it applied the cut-and-control analytical method to the solution of problems. "Resolution" defined a complex phenomenon and its causal conditions by breaking it down into the elements or principles involved in its appearance. "Composition" then used this data to show how these causes brought the phenomenon about, thus revealing the conditions that were necessary and sufficient to produce the phenomenon.

The first experiments along these lines were carried out by Bacon and his English contemporary Robert Grosseteste (the first Chancellor of Oxford), as well as Theodoric of Freiburg and others. The aim was to find "mechanisms to make the phenomenon," by experimentally creating the conditions for a phenomenon to exist. Theodoric sprayed water droplets in order to simulate the conditions for a rainbow, then investigated the optical properties of the droplets by creating models of them with spherical flasks full of water and arrived at an explanation of the geometry of light refraction.

Starting in the thirteenth century, the new experimenters began for the first time to refer to nature as if it were a machine that functioned according to discoverable, measurable "mechanisms." In Paris, Nicholas Oresme compared the universe to a clock. The investigators began to describe phenomena as "primary" (physical activity that produced light, heat, or sound) and "secondary" (sensations produced when these phenomena affected the senses).

They were laying the groundwork for an entirely new body of knowledge that would enormously expand the power and influence of institutions and individuals with access to it. In the fourteenth century these new techniques for manufacturing knowledge were still limited to tiny, isolated groups of clerics. But their isolation would end with explosive results a hundred years later, when in 1439 a German goldsmith would get the date wrong. The consequences of his mistake would shake the authority of Rome to its foundations and create an entirely new kind of axemaker.

PART THREE

The Print Revolution

Dutch Printing office.

A Dutch printing office from the sixteenth century. The Development of Printing, plate 5 from "Nova Reperta". *The Bridgeman Art Library International.*

In closing the previous section, Burke and Ornstein took us to the fifteenth century and the beginnings of the print revolution. Their belief that print was the major cultural/technological transformation in the history of the West is shared by several of our contributors. Traditionally, the view has been that printing, along with numerous other developments, marked the transition between the end of the Middle Ages and the dawn of the modern era. However, the more we study this remarkable invention, the more we realize that it was not just one factor among many. Although we hesitate to argue for historical "prime-movers," certainly the printing press comes close to what is meant by this term. It was a technology that influenced other technologies—a prototype for mass production—and one that impacted directly on the world of ideas by making knowledge widely available and creating a space in which new forms of expression could flourish.

The repercussions of the printing press in early modern Europe did not come about in an inherently deterministic manner. Rather, they resulted from the existence of conditions whereby print could enhance a context receptive to its potential. We must not forget that there *was* change in the Middle Ages, although slower than in subsequent centuries, and that several earlier shifts in communications prepared the way for and accelerated the influence of print: vernacular literacy, the use of paper, and the adoption of Arabic numbers.

Vernacular literacy, as noted in the previous section, emerged during the twelfth and thirteenth centuries. It challenged the church's monopoly on written communication. The acquisition of literacy now became a one-step process, whereas with Latin it entailed the learning of a second language. Vernacular writings instilled in their audiences, both those that were literate and nonliterates who were read to aloud, a sense of cultural tradition and regional place. This was facilitated through the use of a new medium, paper, less costly than parchment.

Paper was invented in China perhaps as early as the first century A.D. It entered Western Europe in the twelfth century and began to be manufactured there in the thirteenth. By 1500 every major European city had a paper mill, without which the growing demand for printed books in the vernacular could not have been met. Paper also helped spread a new language, mathematics, using Arabic numbers. This system was superior for doing calculations. It had entered Europe in the twelfth century. Yet for the next four hundred years its potential was infrequently realized. The scribal/manuscript tradition failed to standardize the form of the numbers or produce adequate instructional texts explaining their use. The printing press did both. Science and commercialism directly benefited.

Europe not only owed China a debt as regards the gift of paper. Printing from carved wooden blocks, an essential precursor to the moveable-type press, was likewise Chinese in origin. As Thomas Carter underscores in the first selection, China was not only a literate civilization (using ideograms), but one capable of research and development as well. Paper was created to offset the inadequacies of other media, notably silk and bamboo, and subsequently improved upon. Block printing began in the eighth century. Thus, when Europe was in the so-called "Dark Ages," China was producing large numbers of printed paper books. Europe started to use block printing in the fourteenth century, acquiring the idea via the trade routes set up in the wake of the Mongol conquests.

One final point regarding printing in China. Chinese printing sometimes employed moveable type and thus anticipated Gutenberg by over five centuries. However, baked clay rather than metal characters were used, in order to replicated a nonalphabetic script composed of thousands of characters. In such circumstances a Chinese print shop could be a complex facility! For most purposes, however, carving a page of text on a wooden block remained both more expedient and aesthetically pleasing.

With the coming of the printing press to Europe, as Lewis Mumford argues in our second selection, the reproduction of written texts became mechanized. At first, printers tried to reproduce writing as it appeared in earlier manuscripts. However, in time it was realized that a less ornate and more standardized style was desirable. As the art and craft of calligraphy declined, a new world of mass produced knowledge based on typography replaced it. This loss of the scribe was, for Mumford, "a reasonable price to pay" for the increased access to books made possible by print.

As Elizabeth Eisenstein points out in our next selection, the reproduction of written materials moved from the copyist's desk to the printer's workshop. She begins by setting the stage for a concerted examination of this problem. Prior to print, what was the world of the scribe like? How can we access such an understanding, when to do so we must use standardized texts, charts and maps that were alien to the period we are trying to fathom? To use the same historical strategy for different epochs may obscure more than it reveals. Take nothing for granted, she suggests, and in so doing the enormity of the transformation will become apparent.

Eisenstein goes on to show us how printing brought forth a new class of intellectuals, "men of letters." Previously those who produced knowledge worked under the auspices of the church, or acquired a patron from the nobility or wealthy merchant class. The printer became a new kind of patron, one linked to a growing market economy. As a result the nature of texts changed.

An important point to keep in mind when considering the print revolution is that it did not occur in one generation. Two hundred years were necessary for most of the definitive changes to knowledge and society produced by print to fall into place. This illustrates a tendency we examined in the previous part: how new media, before they exert their distinctive influence, often do what was done by older forms. In the case of printed books, the first wave, known as *incunabula*, included many of the older manuscript titles. However, texts on the new science and philosophy would soon become a major aspect of the printing industry.

The print revolution helped bring about changes in the characteristics of texts and also in the way readers appropriated them. Rapid silent reading, a rarity in the Middle Ages, became widespread. This was accompanied and facilitated by marked changes in books, which we frequently take for granted. The index is a case in point. Indices were rare in manuscripts, where auditory recall helped orient readers to texts. In the print era, indices helped support the book as a work of reference, which could be periodically consulted without having to be mastered in its entirety. The quintessential expression of this trend was the rise of dictionaries, encyclopedias and grammatical texts. All contributed to standardizing the language in ways alien to the Middle Ages.

One of the most significant consequences of printing was its influence on the Protestant Reformation. Harvey Graff explores this relationship in our next piece. Print allowed for the rapid dissemination of the ideas of Martin Luther as well as their easy entry into the vernacular. Graff is quick to point out that the new medium did not cause, in a deterministic sense, the Reformation's many changes. However, it did facilitate them in profound ways. He concludes with a look at how the legacy of the Reformation and the new culture of the printed book, affected literacy, education and religion in colonial North America.

Print also made possible the widespread dissemination of news. In our final selection John Thompson traces the early history of printed newspapers, from the first weeklies, to the dailies that are still with us. News, of course, circulated before print, mainly through word of mouth, troubadour performances, and hand-written news sheets that could be read aloud to the illiterate. However, with the advent of printed news, individual citizens had rapid and widespread access to information, especially economic and political information, upon which they could act.

By the end of the eighteen century in both Europe and North America, what could be called an information society had emerged around the circulation of books, journals, and especially forms of news. In addition to officially approved sources of published news, which were subject to censorship in many countries, numerous unofficial and inventive modes also flourished. It is worth stressing that news and information were distinctly public activities at this time, so that meeting to talk about the news was an essential part of its circulation. Letters, poems and songs were also important modes for disseminating information and these were often recited or performed in public gathering places such as cafes, taverns, and public gardens. Reading rooms, bookstores, and salons afforded other more formal settings in which people gathered to discuss the world in print.

The long development of literacy and print culture into a worldwide phenomenon helps underscore a point made throughout this text—that media do indeed take on distinctive characteristics as regions, peoples and cultures work out what to do with them, and so define their own ways of information production, circulation, and control. Over time such systems become a formidable force in how the events of the day take on the shape and public understanding they do.

CHAPTER 9

Paper and Block Printing— From China to Europe

Thomas F. Carter

Thomas Francis Carter (1882–1925) was a professor of Chinese at Columbia University. His book, The Invention of Printing in China and Its Spread Westward, *has done much to reveal to Westerners the importance of the Chinese legacy, in terms of both the invention of printing and the invention of paper.*

Back of the invention of printing lies the use of paper, which is the most certain and the most complete of China's inventions. While other nations may dispute with China the honor of those discoveries where China found only the germ, to be developed and made useful to mankind in the West, the manufacture of paper was sent forth from the Chinese dominions as a fully developed art. Paper of rags, paper of hemp, paper of various plant fibers, paper of cellulose, paper sized and loaded to improve its quality for writing, paper of various colors, writing paper, wrapping paper, even paper napkins and toilet paper—all were in general use in China during the early centuries of our era. The paper, the secret of whose manufacture was taught by Chinese prisoners to their Arab captors at Samarkand in the eighth century, and which in turn was passed on by Moorish subjects to their Spanish conquerors in the twelfth and thirteenth centuries, is in all essential particulars the paper that we use today. And even in our own times China has continued to furnish new developments in paper manufacture, both the so-called "India paper" and papier-mâché having been introduced from China into the West during the nineteenth century.

Though the invention of paper is carefully dated in the dynastic records as belonging to the year A.D. 105, the date is evidently chosen rather arbitrarily, and this invention, like most inventions, was a gradual process. Up to the end of the Chou dynasty (256 B.C.), through China's classical period, writing was done with a bamboo pen, with ink of soot, or lampblack, upon slips of bamboo or wood. Wood was used largely for short messages, bamboo for longer writings and for books. The bamboo was cut into strips about nine inches long and wide enough for a single column of characters. The wood was sometimes in the same form, sometimes wider. The bamboo strips, being stronger, could be perforated at one end and strung together, either with silken cords or with leather thongs, to form books. Both the wooden strips and those of bamboo are carefully described in books on antiquities, written in the early centuries of the Christian era. The abundance of wooden and bamboo slips excavated in Turkestan conforms exactly to the early descriptions.

The invention of the writing brush of hair, attributed to general Mêng T'ien in the third century B.C., worked a transformation in writing materials. This transformation is indicated by two changes in the language. The word for chapter used after this time means "roll"; the word for writing materials becomes "bamboo and silk" instead of "bamboo and wood." There is evidence that the silk used for writing during the early part of the Han dynasty consisted of actual silk fabric. Letters on silk, dating possibly from Han times, have been found together with paper in a watch-tower of a spur of the Great Wall.

But as the dynastic records of the time state, "silk was too expensive and bamboo too heavy." The philosopher Mo Ti, when he traveled from state to state, carried with him many books in the cart tail. The emperor Ch'in Shih Huang set himself the task of going over daily a hundred and twenty pounds of state documents. Clearly a new writing material was needed.

The first step was probably a sort of paper or near-paper made of raw silk. This is indicated by the character for paper, which has the silk radical showing material, and by the definition of that character in the *Shuo wên*, a dictionary that was finished about the year A.D. 100.

The year A.D. 105 is usually set as the date of the invention of paper, for in that year the invention was officially reported to the emperor by the eunuch Ts'ai Lun. Whether Ts'ai Lun was the real inventor or only the person in official position who became the patron of the invention (as Fêng Tao did later with printing) is uncertain. In any case his name is indelibly connected with the invention in the mind of the Chinese people. He has even been deified as the god of papermakers and in the T'ang dynasty the mortar which Ts'ai Lun was supposed to have used for macerating his old rags and fish nets was brought with great ceremony from Hunan to the capital and placed in the imperial museum. The following is the account of the invention, as written by Fan Yeh in the fifth century in the official history of the Han dynasty, among the biographies of famous eunuchs:

During the period Chien-ch'u (A.D. 76–84), Ts'ai Lun was a eunuch. The emperor Ho, on coming to the throne (A.D. 89), knowing that Ts'ai Lun was a man full of talent and zeal, appointed him a *chung ch'ang shih*. In this position he did not

hesitate to bestow either praise or blame upon His Majesty.

In the ninth year of the period Yung-yüan (A.D. 97) Ts'ai Lun became *shang fang ling*. Under his instruction workmen made, always with the best of materials, swords and arrows of various sorts, which were models to later generations.

In ancient times writing was generally on bamboo or on pieces of silk, which were then called *chih*. But silk being expensive and bamboo heavy, these two materials were not convenient. Then Ts'ai Lun thought of using tree bark, hemp, rags, and fish nets. In the first year of the Yüan-hsing period (A.D. 105) he made a report to the emperor on the process of papermaking, and received high praise for his ability. From this time paper has been in use everywhere and is called the "paper of Marquis Ts'ai."

The biographical note goes on to tell how Ts'ai Lun became involved in intrigues between the empress and the grandmother of the emperor, as a consequence of which, in order to avoid appearing before judges to answer for statements that he had made, "he went home, took a bath, combed his hair, put on his best robes, and drank poison."

Two statements in this quotation have received ample confirmation from discoveries along the Great Wall and in Turkestan. In March, 1931, while exploring a Han ruin on the Edsin-gol, not far from Kharakhoto, the Swedish archeologist Folke Bergman discovered what is probably the oldest paper in the world. It was found along with a Chinese iron knife stuck in a leather sheath, a badly shriveled water sack of leather, a crossbow arrow with bronze head and reed shaft, many manuscripts on wood, silk rags (including a piece of polychrome silk), and an almost complete raincoat made of twisted grass strings. Lao Kan, who later made a report on this precious piece of paper, informs us that of the seventy-eight manuscripts on wood the great majority were dated between the fifth and seventh years of Yung-yüan (a reign period covering the years A.D. 89–105). On the latest was written: "5th day of the 1st moon of the 10th year of Yung-yüan," or February 24, A.D. 98. Mr. Lao agrees that, just because the last of the dated wooden slips bears a dated inscription, one cannot conclude that everything in the hoard was cached away in that year. Nevertheless, he surmises that about this time, possibly a few years later (whether before or after Ts'ai Lun's historic announcement will never be known), the paper was manufactured and dispatched to this lonely spot in modern Ninghsia province. Other pieces of paper of early times discovered in Turkestan date from about a century and a half after the announcement by Ts'ai Lun.

The statement concerning the materials used has also been thoroughly confirmed. Examination of paper from Turkestan, dating from the third to the eighth centuries of our era, shows that the materials used are the bark of the mulberry tree; hemp, both raw fibers and those which have been fabricated (fish nets, etc.); and various plant fibers, especially China grass (*Boehmeria nivea*), not in their raw form but taken from rags.

The discovery of rag paper in Turkestan, while confirming the statement in the Chinese records, came as a surprise to many Western scholars. From the time of Marco Polo until some seventy years ago, all oriental paper had been known as "cotton paper," and it had been supposed that rag paper was a German or Italian invention of the fifteenth century. Wiesner and Karabacek in 1885–87 showed, as a result of microscopic analysis, that the large quantity of Egyptian paper which had at that time recently been brought to Vienna, and which dated from about A.D. 800 to 1388, was almost all rag paper. A subsequent examination of the earliest European papers showed that they, too, were made in the main from rags. The theory was then advanced and generally believed that the Arabs of Samarkand were the inventors of rag paper, having been driven to it by their inability to find in Central Asia the materials that had been used by the Chinese. In 1904, this theory suffered a rude shock. Dr. Stein had submitted to Dr. Wiesner of Vienna some of the paper he had found during his first expedition to Turkestan, and Dr. Wiesner, while finding in it no pure rag paper, did find paper in which rags

were used as a surrogate, the main material being the bark of the paper mulberry. The theory was changed to suit the facts. The Arabs of Samarkand were no longer the first to have used rags in the production of paper, but the first to have produced paper *solely* of rags. Finally, in 1911, after Dr. Stein's second expedition, paper of the first years of the fourth century was laid before Dr. Wiesner and was found to be a pure rag paper! Rag paper, supposed until 1885 to have been invented in Europe in the fifteenth century, supposed until 1911 to have been invented by the Arabs of Samarkand in the eighth century, was carried back to the Chinese of the early fourth century, and the Chinese record, stating that rag paper was invented in China at the beginning of the second century, was substantially confirmed.

The use of paper, so far superior to bamboo and silk as a writing material, made rapid headway. It was still, however, regarded as a cheap substitute. Extensive improvements in its manufacture were made by Tso Po, a younger contemporary of Ts'ai Lun. The records of the next centuries contain abundant references to the use of paper and to certain special fancy and beautiful papers that appeared from time to time. In Turkestan, at each point where excavations have been undertaken, the time when wooden stationery gave way to paper can be fairly accurately dated. By the time of the invention of block printing all of Chinese Turkestan, so far as excavations show, was using paper. The use of paper in China proper had apparently become general much earlier.

The papers found in Turkestan show a certain amount of progress, especially in the art of loading and sizing to make writing more easy. The earliest papers are simply a net of rag fibers with no sizing. The first attempt to improve the paper so that it would absorb ink more readily consisted of giving the paper a coat of gypsum. Then followed the use of a glue or gelatine made from lichen. Next came the impregnation of the paper with raw dry starch flour. Finally this starch flour was mixed with a thin starch paste, or else the paste was used alone. Better methods of maceration also came into use that proved less destructive of the fibers and produced a stronger paper. All these improvements were perfected before the invention was passed on to the Arabs in the eighth century and before the first block printing in China began. So far as an invention can ever be said to be completed, it was a completed invention that was handed over to the Arabs at Samarkand. The papermaking taught by the Arabs to the Spaniards and Italians in the thirteenth century was almost exactly as they had learned it in the eighth. The paper used by the first printers of Europe differed very slightly from that used by the first Chinese block printers five centuries or more before. . . .

THE BEGINNINGS OF BLOCK PRINTING

The period of the T'ang dynasty (618–906)—the period during which Chinese printing had its birth—was one of the most glorious in the history of China. The four centuries of disunion and weakness—China's Dark Ages—had been brought to an end some thirty years before the T'ang era commenced. Under the first emperors of the new dynasty, during the seventh century and the early part of the eighth, the ancient glory of the empire was revived and enhanced. Not only China itself, but East Turkestan, Korea, and a large part of Indochina were at one time or another brought under the control of the court of Ch'ang-an, while armies were sent over the passes of the Himalayas into Kashmir against certain Indian states and over the T'ien Shan range into the region of Samarkand against the rising power of the Arabs. The early T'ang emperors of the century or more before Charlemagne did in China much the same work that Charlemagne did in Europe in restoring the old Empire on a new basis and bringing to an end the long era of chaos and disorder. But the chaos of China's Dark Ages had never been so complete as that of Europe, and classical civilization was first restored, then

surpassed, far more quickly than in the Western world.

The early emperors of the T'ang dynasty were great patrons of literature, of art, and of religion, and ruled over a people whose mental vision was rapidly expanding. Under T'ai Tsung (627–49), a library was erected at the capital which contained some fifty-four thousand rolls. At the same time, China's attainment in the domain of painting was rapidly approaching its high-water mark.

For impartiality in religious toleration, T'ai Tsung and his immediate followers have seldom been surpassed in history. While they themselves leaned toward Taoism and considered their family to be of the lineage of Lao-tzŭ, they were liberal patrons of Confucian scholarship and welcomed with open hand every foreign faith. Within the space of thirty years, in the early part of the seventh century, the court at Ch'ang-an had the opportunity to welcome the first Christian missionaries, to give refuge to the deposed king of Persia and his Mazdean priests, and to do honor to Hsüan-tsang, the greatest of all the apostles of Chinese Buddhism, who returned from India to give new impetus to the Buddhist faith. All received the heartiest welcome. All propagated their respective faiths with the emperor's favor and help. Contact with men of many lands and of varied opinions produced an alertness, a renewing of youth in the land, such as China had never before known.

This Augustan age lasted for more than a century. It culminated in the reign of Ming Huang (712–56) in whose time the Hanlin Academy was founded, and about whose court gathered such men as Li Po and Tu Fu, Wu Tao-tzŭ, and Wang Wei, the greatest poets and the greatest artists whom China in all her long history has known.

During this golden age of Chinese genius, a great variety of devices was being evolved in the Buddhist monasteries and elsewhere for the reduplication of sacred books and texts—an activity that reached its climax in block printing some time before the end of the "golden age."

One of the earliest indications of the multiplication of illustrations in the East comes from the great Chinese Buddhist pilgrim I-ching (635–713). After a sojourn in India (673–85), he spent several years translating Sanskrit texts on the island of Sumatra, whence in 692 he sent to China his report. One sentence of the report runs as follows: "The Priests and the laymen in India make Kaityas or images with earth, or impress the Buddha's image on silk or paper, and worship it with offerings wherever they go." It is puzzling to find I-ching applying this practice to India, where there was silk but where paper was rare. For China and its nearest neighbors, however, it seems entirely reasonable.

This activity in devising methods of multiplication can best be studied from the findings of Tun-huang and those of Turfan, the two places where the manuscript records of early Buddhism on the borders of China have been preserved. Here are found not only rubbings from stone inscriptions, but also stencils and pounces, printed textiles, seals and seal impressions, and a great profusion of little stamped figures of Buddha, all of which led the way directly to the art of the block printer.

The rubbing from stone was in the main the Confucian preparation for printing. But discoveries at Tun-huang show that the Buddhists used the device, too, and by means of it printed one of their favorite scriptures, the *Diamond Sutra*.

The stencil or pounce was a means of reduplication of which the Buddhist monasteries were especially fond. Several of these paper stencils have been found, with large heads of Buddha first drawn with a brush, then outlined with needle pricks like a modern embroidery transfer pattern. Among the finds are also stenciled pictures—on paper, on silk, and on plastered walls.

Printed textiles appear in considerable number at Tun-huang. These are sometimes in two colors, sometimes in several. The designs are all conventional and nonreligious, an entire contrast to all other early printing and pre-printing in the Far East. Conventionalized animal designs—horses, deer, and ducks—are popular. There is also one example of design-printing on paper. It looks like heavy modern wallpaper, with a dark blue geometric design.

Small stamped figures of Buddha mark the transition from the seal impression to the woodcut. Thousands upon thousands of these stamped impressions have been found at Tun-huang, at Turfan, and at other places in Turkestan. Sometimes they appear at the head of each column of a manuscript. Sometimes great rolls are filled with them—one such roll in the British Museum is seventeen feet long and contains four hundred and sixty-eight impressions of the same stamp. The only difference between these Buddha figures and true woodcuts, other than the primitive workmanship shown, is that the impressions are very small, and hence were evidently made by hand pressure like the impressions from seals. The stamps found have handles for this purpose. When the idea occurred to some inventive genius to turn his stamp upside down, lay the paper on it, and rub it with a brush, the way was open for making impressions of any size desired, and the way was open also for such improvement of technique as made the new invention a force in the advancement of civilization. But first it seems to have brought about only the making of better Buddha figures. One roll at London, though similar in many respects to the others, was evidently made not by stamping but by rubbing, for it shows much larger and better Buddha impressions. A perfected woodcut in the Louvre shows a still further advance—a number of Buddha figures in concentric circles of varying form, and all made from one block.

Such are some of the steps—rubbing from stone, printed silk, stencil, seal, and stamp—that were leading at the same time toward the block print. All these objects have been found in Buddhist monasteries, and back of all, or most of them, lies that duplicating impulse that has always been a characteristic of Buddhism. That these actual objects found at Tun-huang and Turfan are earlier than the first block books is by no means certain. None bears clear indication of date except one stone rubbing and one stamp. But there is every indication that those which are not themselves earlier than the first block printing at least represent survivals of earlier and more primitive processes.

The exact date at which true block printing began is shrouded in mystery. A supposed reference to printing as having taken place under the emperor Wên in 594, before the beginning of the T'ang dynasty—a statement that has found its way into almost everything that has been written in European languages on the subject of Chinese printing—is apparently based on an error by a Chinese writer of the sixteenth century.

At this point it is necessary to mention that one fragment of paper, found near the then Chinese frontier, which bears a date equivalent to A.D. 594, has recently been reported as a printed item. Discovered by Sir Aurel Stein during his third expedition to Central Asia in the years 1913–16 amongst the ruins of a Buddhist temple at the village of Toyuk (or Toyukh) in the neighborhood of Kara Khoja, it was turned over for study—after World War I—to Professor Henri Maspero, along with all other documents on wood and paper. Unfortunately for the world of scholarship, Maspero's manuscript of some 600 pages, completed in 1936 and sent to London that same year, has only just been published. But a few years ago Dr. Bruno Schindler was entrusted with the preparation of a résumé of Maspero's findings and announced that this was a poster, printed in Chinese, "complete at top and bottom, but cut on right and left side. . . . The text reads (in translation): '. . . 34th year yen-ch'ang (=A.D. 594), year chia-yin. There is a vicious dog in the house. Passers-by to take care.'" This astounding information now appears to be in error. On the authority of Dr. Harold James Plenderleith, Keeper, Department of Research Laboratory, the British Museum, who has examined it, the document shows no indication of printing. Dr. Schindler too has withdrawn his earlier assertion, and considers that Maspero made a mistake.

The difficulty of dating the beginning of block printing is enhanced by the fact that the evolution of the art was so gradual as to be almost imperceptible. The earliest well-defined block print extant dates from 770 and comes from Japan. The earliest printed book comes from China and is dated 868. But that printed book is a highly developed product. It is evident that the feverish activity in devising new ways of reduplication, which was going on in the Buddhist monasteries and elsewhere before this time, must have culminated in some sort of block printing before 770, and long enough before that date to have been by that time carried across to Japan. Perhaps the nearest approach to an approximate date that can be given would be the reign of Ming Huang (712–56), the time when China's national greatness and China's cultural achievement reached their height.

The reign of Ming Huang ended in a disastrous revolution. The glories of the T'ang dynasty from that time began to fade. The policy of perfect toleration for all religious faiths that marked the reigns of T'ai Tsung and Ming Huang was abandoned, and in its stead there grew up a policy of persecution of foreign faiths, including Buddhism. This persecution culminated in the famous edict of 845, by which 4,600 Buddhist temples were destroyed and 260,500 Buddhist monks and nuns forced to return to lay life. It is owing to this destruction of temples, as well as to the civil wars of the last century of the T'ang dynasty, that most of the great works of art of the T'ang period have perished. It is doubtless due to the same cause that no Chinese printing earlier than the *Diamond Sutra* of 868 has survived, and that for the earliest extant block prints it is necessary to turn to Japan.

SELECTED BIBLIOGRAPHY

The following are the abbreviations for the various journals that are cited.

HJAS   *Harvard Journal of Asiatic Studies, Cambridge*
JA   *Journal asiatique, Paris*

JAOS   *Journal of the American Oriental Society, New Haven*
MS   *Monumenta Serica, Peiping*
TP   *T'oung Pao, Leiden*

Bergman, Folke. "Travels and Archeological Field-Work in Mongolia and Sinkiang—A Diary of the Years 1927–1934," *History of the Expedition in Asia, 1927–1935*, Vol. 4 (Publication No. 26 of the Sino-Swedish Expedition). Stockholm, 1945.

Blanchet, Augustin. *Essai sur l'histoire du papier.* Paris, 1900.

Blue, Rhea C. "The Argumentation of the *Shih-huo chih*," *HJAS II* (1948), 1–118.

Chavannes, Edouard (trans.). "Les livres chinois avant l'invention du papier," *JA*, Series 10, 5 (1905), 1–75.

Day, Florence E. "Silks of the Near East," *Bulletin of the Metropolitan Museum of Art* 9, No. 4 (Dec. 1950), 108–17.

Duyvendak, J. J. L. "Bibliographie," *TP* 38 (1947), 314.

Erkes, Edward. "The Use of Writing in Ancient China," *JAOS* 61 (1941), 127–30.

Fan Yeh (398–445) *et al. Hou Han shu* (History of the Later Han Dynasty). 1739 ed.

Feifel, Eugene. "Specimen of Early Brush Writing," *MS* 6 (1941), 390–91.

Giles, H. A. (trans.). *The Travels of Fa-hsien (399–414 A.D.).* Cambridge, 1923.

Goodrich, L. C. "Paper: A Note on Its Origin," *Isis* 42, Part 2, No. 128 (June, 1951), 145.

Grohmann, Adolf. *Corpus Papyrorum Raineri III. Series Arabica, I. I Allgemeine Einführung in die Arabischen Papyri.* Vienna, 1924.

Hou Han shu. See Fan Yeh.

Hummel, Arthur W. "The Development of the Book in China," *JAOS* 61 (1941), 71–76.

Hunter, Dard. *Papermaking: The History and Technique of an Ancient Craft.* 2d ed. rev. and enl. New York, 1947.

Julien, Stanislas. "Documents sur l'art d'imprimer à l'aide de planches au bois, de planches au pierre et de types mobiles," *JA*, Series 4, 9 (1847), 508–518.

Lao Kan. "Lun Chung-kuo tsao chih shu chih yüan shih" (On the Origin of the Art of Making Paper in China). *Bulletin of the Institute of History and Philosophy, Academia Sinica* 19 (1948), 489–498.

Laufer, Berthold. "Review of Carter, *The Invention of Printing in China*," *JAOS* 47 (1927), 71–76.

Liebenthal, Walter. "Sanskrit Inscriptions from Yünnan I," *MS* 12 (1947), 1–40. Cited as Liebenthal, 1947a.

———. "A Sanskrit Inscription from Yünnan," *Sino-Indian Studies* 3 (1947), 10–12. Cited as Liebenthal, 1947b.

Maspero, Henri. *Les documents chinois découverts par Aurel Stein.* London, 1953.

Pelliot, Paul. *Les débuts de l'imprimerie en Chine.* ("Oeuvres Posthumes de Paul Pelliot," IV.) Edited by Robert des Rotours, with additional notes and appendix by Paul Demiéville. Paris, 1953.

Reichwein, Adolf. *China and Europe: Intellectual and Artistic Contacts in the Eighteenth Century.* Translated by J. C. Powell. New York, 1925.

Reinaud, M. *Relation des voyages faits par les Arabes et les Persans dans l'Inde et dans la Chine.* Paris, 1845.

Renaudot, Eusebius. *Anciennes relations des Indes et de la Chine de deux voyageurs Mohametans.* Paris, 1718.

Sanborn, Kate. *Old Time Wall Papers: An Account of the Pictorial Papers on Our Forefathers' Walls.* Greenwich, Conn., 1905.

Sauvaget, Jean. *Relation de la Chine et de l'Inde.* Paris, 1948.

Schindler, Bruno. "Preliminary Account of the Work of Henri Maspero Concerning the Chinese Documents on Wood and Paper Discovered by Sir Aurel Stein on His Third Expedition in Central Asia," *Asia Major*, n.s. 1, Part 2 (1949), 216–264.

———. "Concerning Fragment Stein Br. Mus. Toy. 046 (Maspero, No. 365)," *Asia Major*, n.s. 3, Part 2 (1952–53), 222–223.

Stein, Marc Aurel. *Serindia.* 4 vols. Oxford, 1921.

———. *Innermost Asia.* 3 vols. Oxford, 1928.

Takakusu, Junjiro (trans.). *A Record of the Buddhist Religion as Practised in India and the Malay Archipelago (A.D. 671–95) by I-tsing.* Oxford, 1896.

Wang Chi-Chên. "Notes on Chinese Ink," *Metropolitan Museum Studies* 3, Part 1 (December, 1930), 114–133.

White, Bishop William C. "Knowledge of Early Chinese Culture Revolutionized," *Illustrated London News*, Oct. 28, 1933, 698–701.

———. *Tombs of Old Loyang.* Shanghai, 1934.

Wylie, Alexander. *Chinese Researches.* Shanghai, 1897.

———. *Notes on Chinese Literature.* Shanghai, 1867; reprint of 1922.

Yetts, W. Perceval. *The George Eumorfopoulos Collection: Catalogue of the Chinese and Corean Bronzes.* I. London, 1929.

CHAPTER 10

The Invention of Printing

Lewis Mumford

The late Lewis Mumford is among the most respected of twentieth-century humanist scholars who have addressed the issues of communication history. Many of his works deal in some manner with the link between culture and technology.

The invention of printing from movable types is second only to the clock in its critical effect upon our civilization; and in its own right exemplifies the much broader passage, constantly going on in our own day, from the tool to the hand-worked machine, and from the machine to the completely automatic self-regulating device from which, at the end, almost every intervention of the human person is eliminated, except at the very beginning, in the arrangement of the works, and at the very end, in the consumption of the product. Finally, and not least, I have chosen printing because it shows, in the course of its own development, how art and technics may be brought together, and how necessary it is, even for technical development, to have the person that presides over the process refresh himself constantly at those sources in life from which the symbol, in its purest forms, comes forth.

Probably many people in this audience know, at least in outline, the story of printing, so admirably put together by Thomas Carter, the veritable unraveling of a mystery from which only the very last link in the chain seems still to be absent. For one thing, though it is in the nature of mechanical inventions to spread widely from their original center, the spread of printing and the accessory arts upon which it depends, like that of papermaking, is one that wove into a single web the cultures of the East and West, with each part contributing its share to the final product.

In a special sense, therefore, printing is a universal art, prophetic of that One World which our technical instruments make it possible for man now to achieve—though we do not yet know whether it will be one world blasted and ruined by atomic bombs or one world pushed to a higher plane of development through the abundant practice of mutual aid. At all events, printing swept across the world, from China and Korea, where movable types were first invented, into Europe, in the course of a century. We can trace its progress in a series of steps, by way of Persia and Turkey and Russia, till we find the first printed book in Holland and the first European book printed from movable types in Germany. This art had many beginnings in earlier civilizations, from signet rings to coins. It *might* have been applied to the printing of books at almost any moment for the last 2500 years. But before the method was applied to books a new social medium was necessary: a community that had abandoned slavery and was ready, indeed eager, to equalize cultural advantages once reserved for a ruling caste, so that the rise of free cities of urban democracy, of an increasingly literate group of citizens gave an incentive to a method for manifolding and cheapening the process of producing books.

And here again—you must forgive me if I drive this point home a little insistently, to compensate for the more dominant opposite view— here again the esthetic symbol preceded the practical use. For the first application of printing was in the domain of art, the printing of woodcuts: it was only at a later stage that the interest in the word led to that consummate invention, so advanced, so modern at every point—the invention of movable type. For note what was involved in the concept of setting up a line of type by using separate letters cast on a uniform pattern in a mold: the movable type is the original model of the standardized, replaceable part, which some forgetful historians are inclined to attribute to a much later inventor, Eli Whitney, in his perfection of the standardized gun. Finally, the printing press itself, first hand-operated, then, in the nineteenth century power-driven, became one of the earliest pieces of standardized, increasingly automatic, machinery. Within a century of the invention of printing, the calligrapher, the hand-copyist, had been driven out the field of book production over which he had long presided; and yet, so far from this being a serious loss, it was in its initial stages a mighty gain, since all that was good in the handwork was preserved, while some part of what was bad, the inevitable monotony and tedium, was eliminated. Within a generation of Gutenberg's invention, the book in fact reached a perfection in type, impression, and general form that has not in fact been surpassed by any later efforts.

To understand what was involved in this change-over from writing to printing, we must compare the difference visible at an earlier stage between cursive handwriting, longhand, and the more highly formed hand-printed letter. Though there is a typical element in all handwriting—so that one can identify the clerical hand or the humanist hand, the civil service hand or the Palmer method hand or the boarding school hand—there is no form of art that tells one so much, at every stroke, about the individuality of the writer, about his tone and his temper and his general habits of life. So truly is handwriting a key to the human personality that when one wants to refer to the highest type of individuation in art, we refer to the artist's signature. As you know, Chinese calligraphy usually accompanies a picture, done in the same style—visually a part of it. But this very individuality of handwriting is itself a handicap to the widest kind of communication. Reading would be a most laborious art if, on every page, one had to struggle with a new personality and master his vagaries of written expression as well as his thought. For the sake of general legibility and universality it was important that the human being who copied a book should achieve a certain kind of neutrality and impersonality, that he should sacrifice expressiveness to order, subduing his idiosyncrasies, making each letter conform to a common type, rigorously standardizing the product. The typical and the repeatable—what is that but the province of the machine? After a copyist repeated the same letter a thousand times, his letters would achieve that impersonal quality. And by habit and repetition, by restraint and humility, he brought the manuscript to a point of mechanical perfection at which the letters themselves could readily be transferred into movable types.

But note how perverse art itself can be when divorced from other equally central human purposes. From the standpoint of effective communication, the handwrought manuscript tended by its very elaboration to lose sight of its essential reason for existence. In this respect, its development was very similar to that we often find in other arts, a tendency on the part of human fantasy, once it is emancipated from the restraint of practical needs, to run riot, to seek to prolong the esthetic moment beyond any reasonable duration. In medieval cathedrals this sometimes went so far that Ruskin even discovered carving in places where no human eye but his own—if we except the original worker—had probably ever beheld it. Quite evidently this desire to prolong a pleasurable occupation, while it makes for a good life, has its own kind of shortcoming; and in the case of the book, the very esthetic excellence of the illuminators and illustrators served also to retard the process of copying and so limit the circulation of books. Even if the hand labor had been rough and quick, it would have produced too few; but since it was actually measured and meticulous, it served as a further brake on the spread of learning. How unique and precious books were, how well respected they were as works of art, we know from the state they come down to us in: no scrawls in the margins! no dirty fingerprints! no dog ears! But as long as art held production in check, there were never enough books, even in an illiterate age, to go round. So eventually, in the development of the manuscript, there came a point where the two impulses, the technical and the esthetic, came to a parting of the ways. The esthetic and personal part of copying was getting in the way of the practical offices of the book; and for the sake of increasing the circulation of ideas, it was time for the two sides of the art to separate. At that point, the machine entered, to take over the repetitive part of the process. As a result, printing itself reached maturity almost overnight.

Unfortunately, it took a long time to discover that, to be an art in its own right, the machine need not, in fact *must not,* attempt to imitate the special graces of handicraft art. If viewed from the ideal standpoint of the illuminator, aiming at purely esthetic effects, printing was indeed a poor makeshift; and the early printers themselves must have felt the force of this traditional judgment, for very often, right down to the nineteenth century, they gave the printed page many of the illuminator's embellishments: a certain floridness, a certain ornateness of figure and arabesque on the title page and the initial letters, surrounded the serene austerity of the text itself. But printing, even before the steam press and the linotype machine completely mechanized it, was essentially a new art, with its own special canons of taste, its own standards of esthetic expression. The early printers hesitated to let the type speak for itself. They thought machine ornaments were better than no ornaments, whereas they should have realized that a certain chastity of statement, a certain reserve and underemphasis, is characteristic of good machine art; it is the function itself that addresses us, and the esthetic appeal must always be within the compass of a rational judgment. If the essence of machine art is the expression of

function—if beauty here, in Horatio Greenough's memorable words, is the "promise of function"—then the main effort of the printer must be to convey the meaning of the writer to the reader, with the least intrusion of his own personality.

Behind the appearance of printing from movable types, apparently so sudden, and on superficial analysis just a great mechanical feat, we find a thousand years of self-discipline and esthetic training, which went along with the effort to respect the gifts of the spirit and to deepen the inner life. Some of that training still is important for those who would design typography. You might think that, once printing was achieved, it would be possible to cut loose entirely from these earlier sources; but in fact the continued interdependence of art and technics could not be better illustrated than in this wholly mechanical art. The great fonts of type, the platonic forms from which all later types down to our own day have been derived, were almost all cast within a century of the invention of printing. Sometimes the early books printed in these fonts seem a little too compact and crowded for our modern taste in reading, as if the designer still felt that the paper was as precious as parchment, and if he was to have wide margins, the lines themselves must be crowded together. But in general, nothing more perfect, as print, has been achieved than the work of the early type designers and printers like the great Nicholas Jenson: people who were still under the spell of the old manuscripts. As soon as the art of the calligrapher fell into decay, the art of type design became more difficult, for in aiming at mechanical accuracy and finish, the designer often lost the precious touch of the hand itself. Once utilitarian and rational interests predominated over esthetic ones, as they did in the nineteenth century, there followed a series of lapses both in type itself and in the layout of the printed page: the Bounderbys and the Gradgrinds of Victorian capitalism, confusing ugliness with efficiency, seem to have preferred ill proportioned, illegible, or downright ugly types.

The two great results of the invention of mechanical printing have been characteristic, in some degree, of similar advances in all the industrial arts: they have been to standardize in a more rigorous fashion a product that was already standardized, and to progressively eliminate the craftsman himself in the act of freeing him from the drudgery of hand labor patterned on a mechanical model. If there was a certain loss in that changeover, it nevertheless was, I submit, a reasonable price to pay for the benefit that printing conferred on the word—and the world; for, if it suppressed the copyist, it released the writer and conferred on him the privilege of talking directly to a greater number of fellow men than he had ever addressed before. Printing broke the class monopoly of the written word, and it provided the common man with a means of gaining access to the culture of the world, at least, all of that culture as had been translated into words or other printable symbols; doing so, it increased every man's range in time and space, bringing together times past and times to come, near and distant, peoples long dead and peoples still unborn. Recent generations have perhaps overestimated the benefits of literacy, for these benefits do not come about automatically, and they may be accompanied, if unwisely used, by a loss of firsthand experiences and contacts, a loss of both sense and sensibility, with an increase of pride and prejudice. But it is hardly possible to overestimate the handicaps of illiteracy; for that chains one to the world of the here and now, a form of cultural solitary confinement, fatal to human development. Again, though print undoubtedly accentuated man's natural eye-mindedness, to the point of actually impairing his vision by overstraining the eye, it also freed the mind from the retarding effects of irrelevant concreteness. Only now that we are falling back into a state of vacuous illiteracy, through the overdevelopment of radio and television, can we realize on what a low level of abstraction we should live without the benefit of the printed word. The swiftness and economy of print, compared with the interminable prolixity of the spoken word, more than made up for the other human qualities that were forfeited through the invention of the printing press.

What further innovations remain to be made in printing, other than the possibilities I have mentioned, are mainly on the technical side. They are similar to what has been happening in other departments of technics. One improvement that is surely coming, now that practically all manuscripts are in their final stages typewritten, is a completion of the automatic process with the aid of a scanner which will automatically set up type without the intervention of the typographer. When that final invention takes place in printing, this art will have achieved its theoretical limit of perfection, the limit long ago envisaged by Aristotle, when he observed, in words I am fond of quoting, that slavery would disappear when musical instruments would play by themselves and looms would weave by themselves: for then, he added, "chief workmen would not need helpers, nor masters slaves." The other possibility, also a technical one, would lead in the other direction, not toward automatism and large-scale mass production, but in the direction of making printing or its equivalent possible by a more simple and direct method, lending itself to small-scale production and therefore to a larger measure of personal expression. Many such processes, from mimeographic to photographic offset printing, are already available. William Blake was perhaps only a little ahead of his time in his personal method of reproducing his poems in small quantities. Thanks to my friendly Japanese translator, Professor Tsutomu Ikuta, I have in my possession a charming version of Edmund Blunden's poems, done in Japan, hand-lettered and then photographed and reproduced by the offset process, a sort of modern version of the earliest method of wood-block printing; and the directness and simplicity and beauty of the product, its exquisite fitness to the work in hand, with its modest demands for material support, perhaps indicates a way in which we can overcome the banal effects of mass production, with its abject dependence upon a large market. This means of printing will perhaps be one of the answers to the modern publisher's barbarous reluctance to consider the publication of poetry, for example, as anything but a painful personal favor on his part.

CHAPTER 11

Aspects of the Printing Revolution

Elizabeth Eisenstein

Elizabeth Eisenstein is a historian whose book The Printing Press as an Agent of Change *has been hailed by people in many disciplines as a landmark study of how a particular technology has influenced history.*

In the late fifteenth century, the reproduction of written materials began to move from the copyist's desk to the printer's workshop. This shift, which revolutionized all forms of learning, was particularly important for historical scholarship. Ever since then historians have been indebted to Gutenberg's invention; print enters their work from start to finish, from consulting card files to reading page proofs. Because historians are usually eager to investigate major changes and this change transformed the conditions of their own craft, one would expect the shift to attract some attention from the profession as a whole. Yet any historiographical survey will show the contrary to be true. It is symbolic that Clio has retained her handwritten scroll. So little has been made of the move into the new workshops that after five hundred years, the muse of history still remains outside. "History bears witness," writes a sociologist, "to the cataclysmic effect on society of inventions of new media for the transmission of information among persons. The development of writing, and later the development of printing, are examples." Insofar as flesh-and-blood historians who turn out articles and books actually bear witness to what happened in the past, the effect on society of the development of printing, far from appearing cataclysmic, is remarkably inconspicuous. Many studies of developments during the last five centuries say nothing about it at all.

There is, to be sure, a large, ever-growing literature on the history of printing and related topics. Several works that synthesize and summarize parts of this large literature have appeared. Thus Rudolf Hirsch surveys problems associated with "printing, selling, reading," during the first century after Gutenberg. A more extensive, well-organized volume by Febvre and Martin, which skillfully covers the first three centuries of printing and was first published in a French series devoted to "the evolution of humanity," has recently been translated into English. An even broader coverage, embracing "five hundred years," is provided by Steinberg's remarkably succinct semi-popular survey. All three of these books summarize data drawn from many scattered studies. But although the broader historical implications of these data are occasionally hinted at, they are never really spelled out. Like the section on printing in the *New Cambridge Modern History,* the contents of these surveys rarely enter into treatments of other aspects of the evolution of humanity.

According to Steinberg: "The history of printing is an integral part of the general history of civilization." Unfortunately, the statement is not applicable to written history as it stands, although it is probably true enough of the actual course of human affairs. Far from being integrated into other works, studies dealing with the history of printing are isolated and artificially sealed off from the rest of historical literature. In theory, these studies center on a topic that impinges on many other fields. In fact, they are seldom consulted by scholars who work in any other field, perhaps because their relevance to other fields is still not clear. "The exact nature of the impact which the invention and spread of printing had on Western civilization remains subject to interpretation even today." This seems to understate the case. There are few interpretations even of an inexact or approximate nature upon which scholars may draw when pursuing other inquiries. The effects produced by printing have aroused little controversy, not because views on the topic coincide, but because almost none has been set forth in an explicit and systematic form. Indeed, those who seem to agree that momentous changes were entailed always seem to stop short of telling us just what they were.

"Neither political, constitutional, ecclesiastical, and economic events, nor sociological, philosophical, and literary movements can be fully understood," writes Steinberg, "without taking into account the influence the printing press has exerted upon them." All these events and movements have been subjected to close scrutiny by generations of scholars with the aim of understanding them more fully. If the printing press exerted some influence upon them, why is this influence so often unnoted, so rarely even hinted at, let alone discussed? The question is worth posing if only to suggest that the effects produced by printing are by no means self-evident. Insofar as they may be encountered by scholars exploring different fields, they are apt to pass unrecognized at present. To track them down and set them forth—in an outline or some other form—is much easier said than done.

When authors such as Steinberg refer to the impact of printing on every field of human enterprise—political, economic, philosophical, and so forth—it is by no means clear just what they have in mind. In part at least they seem to be pointing to indirect consequences which have to be inferred and which are associated with the consumption of printed products or with changed mental habits. Such consequences are, of course, of major historical significance and impinge on most forms of human enterprise. Nevertheless, it is difficult to describe them precisely or even to determine exactly what they are. It is one thing to describe how methods of book production changed after the mid-fifteenth century or to estimate rates of increased output. It is another thing to describe how access to a greater abundance or variety of written records affected ways of learning, thinking, and perceiving among literate elites. Similarly, it is one thing to show that standardization was a consequence of printing. It is another to decide how laws, languages, or mental constructs were affected by more uniform texts. Even at present, despite all the data being obtained from living responsive subjects; despite all the efforts being made by public opinion analysts, pollsters, or behavioral scientists; we still know very little about how access to printed materials affected human behavior. (A glance at recent controversies on the desirability of censoring pornography shows how ignorant we are.) Historians who have to reach out beyond the grave to reconstruct past forms of consciousness are especially disadvantaged in dealing with such issues. Theories about unevenly phased changes affecting learning processes, attitudes, and expectations do not lend themselves, in any event, to simple, clear-cut formulations that can be easily tested or integrated into conventional historical narratives.

Problems posed by some of the more indirect effects produced by the shift from script to print probably can never be overcome entirely. But such problems could be confronted more squarely if other impediments did not stand in the way. Among the far-reaching effects that need to be noted are many that still affect present observations and that operate with particularly great force upon every professional scholar. Thus constant access to printed materials is a prerequisite for the practice of the historian's own craft. It is difficult to observe processes that enter so intimately into our own observations. In order to access changes ushered in by printing, for example, we need to survey the conditions that prevailed before its advent. Yet the conditions of scribal culture can only be observed through a veil of print.

Even a cursory acquaintance with the findings of anthropologists or casual observations of preschool-age children may help to remind us of the gulf that exists between oral and literate cultures. Several studies, accordingly, have illuminated the difference between mentalities shaped by reliance on the spoken as opposed to the written word. The gulf that separates our experience from that of literate elites who relied exclusively on hand-copied texts is much more difficult to fathom. There is nothing analogous in our experience or in that of any living creature within the Western world at present. The conditions of scribal culture thus have to be artificially reconstructed by recourse to history books and reference guides. Yet for the most part, these works are more likely to conceal than to reveal the object of such a search. Scribal themes are carried forward, postprint trends are traced backward, in a manner that makes it difficult to envisage the existence of a distinctive literary culture based on hand copying. There is not even an agreed-upon term in common use which designates the system of written communications which prevailed before print.

Schoolchildren who are asked to trace early overseas voyages on identical outline maps are likely to become absent-minded about the fact that there were no uniform world maps in the era when the voyages were made. A similar absent-mindedness on a more sophisticated level is encouraged by increasingly refined techniques for collating manuscripts and producing authoritative editions of them. Each successive edition tells us more than was previously known about how a given manuscript was composed and copied. By the same token, each makes it more difficult to envisage how a given manuscript appeared to a scribal scholar who had only one hand-copied version to consult and no certain guidance as to its place or date of composition, its title or author. Historians are trained to discriminate between manuscript sources and printed texts; but they are not trained to think with equal care about how manuscripts appeared when this sort of discrimination was inconceivable. Similarly, the more thoroughly we are trained to master the events and dates contained in modern history books, the less likely we are to appreciate the difficulties confronting scribal scholars who had access to assorted written records, but lacked uniform chronologies, maps, and all the other reference guides which are now in common use.

Efforts to reconstruct the circumstances that preceded printing thus lead to a scholarly predicament. Reconstruction requires recourse to printed materials, thereby blurring clear perception of the conditions that prevailed before these materials were available. Even when the predicament is partly resolved by sensitive scholars who manage to develop a genuine "feel" for the times after handling countless documents, efforts at reconstruction are still bound to be frustratingly incomplete.

For the very texture of scribal culture was so fluctuating, uneven, and multiform that few long-range trends can be traced. Conditions that prevailed near the bookshops of ancient Rome, in the Alexandrian Library, or in certain medieval monasteries and university towns, made it possible for literate elites to develop a relatively sophisticated "bookish" culture. Yet all library collections were subject to contraction, and all texts in manuscript were liable to get corrupted after being copied over the course of time. Outside certain transitory special centers, moreover, the texture of scribal culture was so thin that heavy reliance was placed on oral transmission even by literate elites. Insofar as dictation governed copying in scriptoria and literary compositions were "published" by being read aloud, even "book" learning was governed by reliance on the spoken word—producing a hybrid half-oral, half-literate culture that has no precise counterpart today. Just what publication meant before printing or just how messages got transmitted in the age of scribes are questions that cannot be answered in general. Findings are bound to vary enormously depending on date and place. Contradictory verdicts are especially likely to proliferate with regard to the last century before printing—an interval when paper had become available and the literate man was more likely to become his own scribe.

Specialists in the field of incunabula, who are confronted by ragged evidence, are likely to insist that a similar lack of uniformity characterizes procedures used by early printers. To generalize about early printing is undoubtedly hazardous, and one should be on guard against projecting the output of modern standard editions too far back into the past. Yet one must also be on guard against blurring a major difference between the last century of scribal culture and the first century after Gutenberg. Early print culture is sufficiently uniform to permit us to measure its diversity. We can estimate output, arrive at averages, trace trends. For example, we have rough estimates of the total output of all printed materials during the so-called age of incunabula (that is, the interval between the 1450s and 1500). Similarly, we can say that the "average" early edition ranged between two hundred and one thousand copies. There are no comparable figures for the last fifty years of scribal culture. Indeed, we have no figures at all. What is the "average edition" turned out between 1400 and 1450? The question verges on nonsense. The term "edition" comes close to being an anachronism when applied to copies of a manuscript book.

As the difficulties of trying to estimate scribal output suggest, quantification is not suited to the conditions of scribal culture. The production figures which are most often cited, on the basis of the memoirs of a Florentine manuscript bookdealer, turn out to be entirely untrustworthy. Quattrocento Florence, in any case, is scarcely typical of other Italian centers (such as Bologna), let alone of regions beyond the Alps. But then *no* region is typical. There is no "typical" bookdealer, scribe, or even manuscript. Even if we set aside problems presented by secular book producers and markets as hopelessly complex and consider only the needs of churchmen on the eve of printing, we are still faced by a remarkable diversity of procedures. Book provisions for diverse monastic orders varied; mendicant friars had different arrangements from monks. Popes and cardinals often turned to the "multifarious activities" of the Italian *cartolai;* preachers made their own anthologies of sermons; semi-lay orders attempted to provide primers and catechisms for everyman.

The absence of an average output or a typical procedure poses a stumbling block when we try to set the stage for the advent of print. Let us take, for example, a deceptively simple summary statement which I made when first trying to describe the printing revolution. Fifteenth-century book production, I asserted, moved from scriptoria to printing shops. The assertion was criticized for leaving out of account a previous move from scriptoria to stationers' shops. In the course of the twelfth century, lay stationers began to replace monastic scribes. Books needed by university faculties and the mendicant orders were supplied by a "putting-out" system. Copyists were no longer assembled in a single room, but worked on different portions of a given text, receiving payment from the stationer for each piece (the so-called pecia system). Book production, according to my critic, had thus moved out of scriptoria three centuries *before* the advent of print.

The objection seems worth further thought. Certainly one ought to pay attention to the rise of the lay stationer in university towns and other urban centers during the twelfth and thirteenth centuries. The contrast between the free labor of monks working for remission of sins and the wage labor of lay copyists is an important one. Recent research has stressed the use of a putting-out system and has also called into question long-lived assumptions about the existence of lay scriptoria attached to stationers' shops. Thus one must be especially cautious about using the term scriptoria to apply to conditions in the later Middle Ages—more cautious than I was in my preliminary version.

Yet, on the other hand, one must also be wary about placing too much emphasis on trends launched in twelfth-century Paris, Oxford, Bologna, and other university towns where copies were multiplied rapidly to serve special institutional needs. Caution is needed when extending university regulations designed to control copyists to the actual practices of university stationers—let alone to bookdealers serving nonuniversity clientele. That relatively clear thirteenth-century patterns get smudged by the late fourteenth century must also be kept in mind. During the interval between 1350 and 1450—the crucial century when setting our stage—conditions were unusually anarchic, and some presumably obsolete habits were revived. Monastic scriptoria, for example, were beginning to experience their "last golden age."

The existence of monastic scriptoria right down to and even beyond the days of early printing is most intriguingly demonstrated by a treatise which is often cited as a curiosity in books on early printing: Johannes Trithemius's *De laude scriptorum*. In this treatise, the Abbot of Sponheim not only exhorted his monks to copy books, but also explained why "monks should not stop copying because of the invention of printing." Among other arguments (the usefulness of keeping idle hands busy, encouraging diligence, devotion, knowledge of Scripture, and so on), Trithemius somewhat illogically compared the written word on parchment which would last one thousand years with the printed word on paper which would have a shorter life span. The possible use of paper (and scraped parchment) by copyists, or of skin for a special printed version, went unmentioned. As a Christian scholar, the abbot was clearly familiar with earlier writings which had set durable parchment against perishable papyrus. His arguments show his concern about preserving a form of manual labor which seemed especially suitable for monks. Whether he was genuinely worried about an increased use of paper—as an ardent bibliophile and in the light of ancient warnings—is an open question. But his activities show clearly that as an author he did not favor handwork over presswork. He had his *Praise of Scribes* promptly printed, as he did his weightier works. Indeed, he used one Mainz print shop so frequently that "it could almost be called the Sponheim Abbey Press."

Even before 1494, when the Abbot of Sponheim made his trip from scriptorium to printing shop, the Carthusians of Saint Barbara's Charterhouse in Cologne were turning to local printers to extend their efforts, as a cloistered order bound by vows of silence, to preach "with their hands." As many accounts note, the same thing happened outside Cologne and not just among the Carthusians. A variety of reformed Benedictine orders also kept local printers busy, and in some cases monks and nuns ran monastic presses themselves. The possible significance of this intrusion of a capitalist enterprise into consecrated space is surely worth further consideration. Thus, to rule out the formula "scriptorium to printing shop" completely seems almost as unwise as to attempt to apply it in a blanket form. Even while acknowledging the significance of changes affecting twelfth-century book production, we should not equate them with the sort of "book revolution" that occurred in the fifteenth century. The latter, unlike the former, assumed a cumulative and irreversible form. The revival of monastic scriptoria during the century before Gutenberg was the last revival of its kind. . . .

The Rise of the Reading Public

Given the religious, linguistic, and socioeconomic diversity of European readers, it is difficult to imagine just what figure Marshall McLuhan had in mind when he wrote about the "making of typographical man." By making us more alert to the possibility that the advent of printing had social and psychological consequences, McLuhan performed, in my view at least, a valuable service. But he also glossed over multiple interactions that occurred under widely varying circumstances. Granted that the replacement of discourse by silent scanning, of face-to-face contacts by more impersonal interactions, probably did have important consequences, it follows that we need to think less metaphorically and abstractly, more historically and concretely, about the sorts of effects that were entailed and how different groups were affected. Even at first glance both issues appear to be very complex.

We will not pause for long over one complication that has recently attracted attention: namely, Paul Saenger's demonstration that habits of silent reading developed during the Middle Ages. It is now clear that McLuhan and the scholars upon whom he relied overstated the oral character of medieval interchanges and mistakenly assigned to printing responsibility for introducing habits of silent scanning which had already developed among some literate groups in the age of scribes. But although printing did not introduce silent reading, it did encourage an increasing recourse to "silent instructors, which nowadays carry farther than do public lectures" (in the words of a sixteenth-century professor of medicine). To show that the habit predated Gutenberg does not diminish the significance of its becoming increasingly more pervasive and ever more elaborately institutionalized after the shift from script to print.

Even while insisting on this point, we shall need to be cautious about assuming, as did McLuhan and other authorities, that the spread of habits of silent scanning invariably diminished recourse to the spoken word. Although the textbook industry flourished, classroom lectures never died. Printed sermons and orations did not remove preachers from their pulpits or speakers from their podiums. To the contrary, priests and orators both benefited from the way their personal charisma could be augmented and amplified by the printed word.

The increased recourse to silent publication undoubtedly altered the character of some spoken words. Exchanges between members of parliament, for example, were probably affected by the printing of parliamentary debates. The printing of poems, plays, and songs altered the way "lines" were recited, composed, and sung. On the one hand, some "dying speeches" were fabricated for printing and never did get delivered; on the other, printed publicity enabled evangelists and demagogues to practice traditional arts outdoors before an expanded hearing public. A literary culture created by typography was conveyed to the ear, not the eye, by repertory companies and poetry readings. No simple formula will cover the changes these new activities reflect.

The same is true of how different groups were affected. Most rural villagers, for example, probably belonged to an exclusively hearing public down to the nineteenth century. Yet what they heard had, in many instances, been transformed by printing two centuries earlier. For the storyteller was replaced by the exceptional literate villager who read out loud from a stack of cheap books and ballad sheets turned out anonymously for distribution by peddlers. A fairly sleazy "popular" culture, based on the mass production of antiquated vernacular medieval romances, was thus produced well before the steam press and mass literacy movements of the nineteenth century. Yet the bulk of this output was consumed by a hearing public, separated by a psychological gulf from their contemporaries who belonged to a reading one.

The disjunction between the new mode of production and older modes of consumption is only one of many complications that need further study. Members of the same reading public, who confronted the same innovation in the same region at the same time, were nonetheless affected by it in markedly different ways. Trends pointing both to modernism and to fundamentalism, for example, were launched by Bible printing—as later discussion suggests. Pornography as well as piety assumed new forms. Book reading did not stop short with guides to godly living or practical manuals and texts, any more than printers stopped short at producing them. The same silence, solitude, and contemplative attitudes associated formerly with spiritual devotion also accompanied the perusal of scandal sheets, "lewd Ballads," "merry books of Italie," and other "corrupted tales in Inke and Paper." Not a desire to withdraw from a worldly society or the city of man, but a gregarious curiosity about them, could be satisfied by silent perusal of journals, gazettes, or newsletters. Complaints about the "sullen silence" of newspaper readers in seventeenth-century coffeehouses point to the intrusive effects of printed materials on some forms of sociability.

As communion with the Sunday paper has replaced church-going, there is a tendency to forget that sermons had at one time been coupled with news about local and foreign affairs, real estate transactions, and other mundane matters. After printing, however, news gathering and circulation were handled more efficiently under lay auspices. As contemporaries observed, there were resemblances between coffeehouse and conventicle. But the pipe-smoking habitues of the former gave otherworldly concerns low priority. Such considerations might be noted when thinking about the "secularization" or "desacralization" of Western Christendom. For in all regions (to go beyond the eighteenth century for a moment) the pulpit was ultimately displaced by the periodical press, and the dictum "nothing sacred" came to characterize the journalist's career. Pitted against "the furious itch of novelty" and the "general thirst after news," efforts by Catholic moralists and Protestant evangelicals, even Sunday schools and other Sabbatarian measures proved of little avail. The monthly gazette was succeeded by the weekly and finally by the daily paper. More and more provincial newspapers were founded. By the last century, gossiping churchgoers could often learn about local affairs by scanning columns of newsprint in silence at home.

The displacement of pulpit by press is significant not only in connection with secularization but also because it points to an explanation for the weakening of local community ties. To hear an address delivered, people have to come together; to read a printed report encourages individuals to draw apart. "What the orators of Rome and Athens were in the midst of a people *assembled*," said Malesherbes in an address of 1775, "men of letters are in the midst of a *dispersed* people." His observation suggests how the shift in communications may have changed the sense of what it meant to participate in public affairs. The wide distribution of identical bits of information provided an impersonal link between people who were unknown to each other.

By its very nature, a reading public was not only more dispersed; it was also more atomistic and individualistic than a hearing one. To catch the contrast, Walter Ong suggests that we imagine a speaker addressing an audience equipped with texts and stopping at one point with the request that a textual passage be read silently. When the readers look up again, the fragmented audience has to be reassembled into a collectivity. Insofar as a traditional sense of community entailed frequent gathering together to receive a given message, this sense was probably weakened by the duplication of identical messages which brought the solitary reader to the fore. To be sure, bookshops, coffeehouses, reading rooms provided new kinds of communal gathering places. Yet subscription lists and corresponding societies represented relatively impersonal group formations, while the reception of printed messages in any place still required temporary isolation—just as it does in a library now. The notion that society may be regarded as a bundle of discrete units or that the individual is prior to the social group seems to be more compatible with a reading public than with a hearing one. The nature of man as a political animal was less likely to conform to classical models after tribunes of the people were transmuted from orators in public squares to editors of news sheets and gazettes.

Even while communal solidarity was diminished, vicarious participation in more distant events was also enhanced; and even while local ties were loosened, links to larger collective units were being forged. Printed materials encouraged silent adherence to causes whose advocates could not be found in any one parish and who addressed an invisible public from afar. New forms of group identity began to compete with an older, more localized nexus of loyalties. Urban populations were not only pulled apart, they were also linked in new ways by the more impersonal channels of communication. The exchange of goods and services, real estate transactions, the provision of charity were all eventually affected. Personal attendance was increasingly supplemented by vicarious participation in civic functions and municipal affairs. Cheap versions of the magnificent prints which commemorated civic ceremonies, such as royal entries, enabled some stay-at-homes to experience "public" festivals.

The features of individual rulers and of members of their entourage came into sharper focus for scattered subjects in a given realm. The circulation of prints and engravings made it possible for a reigning dynasty to impress a personal presence on mass consciousness in a new way. The effect of duplicating images and portraits of rulers—which were eventually framed and hung in peasant hovels throughout Catholic Europe, along with saints and icons—has yet to be assessed by political scientists. The mass following of a single leader and the nationwide extension of his or her charismatic appeal, at all events, are possible by-products of the new communications systems which ought to be further explored. Joseph Klaits's study of Louis XIV's propaganda efforts describes how early modern rulers deliberately set out to exploit the new presses:

> Princes who had employed the cumbersome methods of manuscript to communicate with their subjects switched quickly to print to announce declarations of war, publish battle accounts, promulgate treaties or argue disputed points in pamphlet form. Theirs was an effort . . . "to win the psychological war which prepared and accompanied the military operations" of rulers . . . The English crown under Henry VIII and Thomas Cromwell made systematic use of both Parliament and press to win public support for the Reformation . . .
>
> In France the regency of Louis XIII saw the last meeting of the Estates General before 1789; it also

saw the founding of the first royally sponsored newspaper in Europe. The replacement of the volatile assembly by the controlled weekly *Gazette* is a concurrence symptomatic of the importance Cardinal Richelieu attached to print in his state-building objectives.

As these references to Richelieu and Thomas Cromwell suggest, even while making room for the heightened visibility of individual rulers, we also need to note how the powers of officials and bureaucrats were extended once government regulations became subject to the duplicative powers of print. The expansion of leviathan states, as might be expected, provoked countermeasures from parliaments and assemblies. Traditional tensions between court and country, crown and estates, were exacerbated by propaganda wars. A greater uniformity began to characterize provincial demands, with the circulation of model petitions and lists of grievances.

Recently some historians have begun to abandon, as fruitless, older debates about the "rise" of a new class to political power in early modern times. They seek to focus attention instead on the reeducation and regroupment of older governing elites—and have, thereby, precipitated new debates. Both lines of inquiry might be reconciled and fruitfully pursued if the consequences of printing received more attention.

SELECTED READINGS

Febvre, Lucien, and Martin, H-J. *The Coming of the Book,* trans. David Gerard (London, 1976). First ed.: *L'Apparition du livre* (Paris, 1958). Readers competent in French should get the original 1958 French version, which is superior in every way (including its bibliography and index) to this recent English translation. The book (which was written almost entirely by Martin) is a masterful survey and has more comprehensive coverage than any other title on this list.

Hirsch, Rudolf. *Printing, Selling, and Reading 1450–1550* (Wiesbaden, 1967; rev. ed. 1974). Crammed with facts; emphasis on German developments. By a rare-book librarian who is especially knowledgeable about European book-selling and printing.

McLuhan, Marshall. *The Gutenberg Galaxy: The Making of Typographical Man* (Toronto, 1962). Deliberately departs from conventional book format. Bizarre "mosaic" of citations drawn from diverse texts designed to stimulate thought about effects of printing. By a recently deceased Canadian literary scholar turned media analyst. Careless handling of historical data may mislead uninformed readers. Surprisingly useful bibliography.

Saenger, Paul. "Silent Reading: Its Impact on Late Medieval Script and Society." *Viator* 13 (1982), 367–414. Presents evidence showing that silent reading occurred before advent of printing. Overstates novelty of practice in late Middle Ages and ignores the extent to which silent reading was reinforced and institutionalized after printing.

Steinberg, S. H. *Five Hundred Years of Printing*, rev. ed. (Bristol, 1961). Remarkably succinct survey. Better coverage of first century of printing than of later ones.

CHAPTER **12**

Early Modern Literacies

Harvey J. Graff

Harvey J. Graff is professor of history and humanities at the University of Texas at Dallas and author of several acclaimed books on literacy, including The Literacy Myth *and* Literacy in History.

PRINT, REFORM, AND REFORMATION

In the history of the West, the Protestant Reformation is said to be one of the greatest positive forces toward the spread of literacy and schooling. It can easily be viewed as an educational reform movement. "The basic assumptions of the reformers were that one must start with the young, that indoctrination is necessary for religious and moral improvement . . . , that this indoctrination must be done in public schools. . . ."[1] The Reformation involved factors far beyond the religious and theological. Its roots lay in the Middle Ages; economic, political, cultural, and social issues inextricably intertwined to give rise to a deep and bitterly divisive mass movement. Its conflicts lasted through much of the sixteenth and seventeenth centuries; the reformation of social life was

a long-term endeavor in Western society and culture, to which literacy was often central.

Ecclesiastical reform movements were the central cause of the Reformation, which was triggered by the "publication" of Martin Luther's ninety-five theses in 1518. Increasing dissatisfaction with the church and papacy resulted in a slow, but steady, development of active dissent in the first half of the sixteenth century.

The major reform movements that helped to shape the context for the Reformation shared a common concern with moral criteria and a common approach: except for the "Devotio Moderna," the movements all looked to secular authorities for aid, took arguments and inspiration from the Bible, and appealed to the early church. They sought the reaffirmation of community, the reorganization of lay piety and religion, and the reintegration of the outer and inner self. The Northern Renaissance, with its central current of humanism, was probably the most important. Humanism benefited from such new factors as the role of printing, the urban and articulate commercial classes, and the increasingly literate laity; it offered an optimistic, progressive reform program.[2]

Early-sixteenth-century humanism appealed to the educated laity in their search for more religion and a more active piety. But the impact of the doctrines of the religious reformers went beyond theology alone; in addition, political changes in the territorial states necessitated major social and economic adjustments. Some turned to the new Protestantism, others toward Catholicism and the church. Townspeople, nobility, and even the peasants responded to the calls for reform or counter reform.

Martin Luther's own reform began as a university-based effort to transform the curriculum, replacing Aristotle and scholasticism with the Bible and St. Augustine. He was aware of the sensitive nature of his theses and made his challenge patiently through official channels. When no response arrived, he sent handwritten copies of the theses to some friends for clarification. Those copies were reproduced and circulated, and were even translated into German. They spread widely, and soon all of Germany, and then all of Christendom, had been aroused by Luther's theses.[3]

Two of the most significant developments of the Reformation were the contribution of the printing press and the use of the vernacular. These seminal currents were especially relevant to the history of literacy, yet their contributions were not always direct or immediately recognized. Neither Luther and his theses, the church's hierarchy, the social context, the printing press, nor any single factor or development *caused* the events that permanently split the world of Western Christendom and firmly ended the Middle Ages.

The contribution of movable typography to the religious revolution of the sixteenth century is easily exaggerated. At the beginning of the century, traditional moral and religious books were popular, but newly developing literary forms were also being published before the Reformation, including collections of sermons and the works of the church fathers. A large number of religious works were being published, but they constituted a smaller percentage of the total production. They may not have reached a larger public after the turn of the century than before.

The situation changed rapidly in Germany by 1517. Religious issues quickly took on the utmost importance. The first propaganda campaign with the help of the printing press was conducted, as the power of the press to influence public thought and opinion was realized. An attempt was made "to place within the reach of everyone and in the vernacular the Holy Writ which provided the basis of the reformed and restored religion."

The printing press did not determine the Reformation, for it had been technologically prepared for some time. Pious materials had been printed for many years—Bibles, books of simple piety, posters, handbills, and broadsheets. The press, rather, prepared the coming of the Reformation, providing a tried and tested vehicle for both reformers and their opposition to spread their ideas.

Leaflets and, especially, posters helped to keep the public informed. Illiterates could receive the message by having a poster read to them. The availability of printed matter did not cause an increase in literacy; it increased the flow of communications and raised the probability of more and more persons, receiving information. The use of printing insured that Luther's theses and later writings were rapidly and widely circulated.[4]

The contribution of print was dramatic. Notices posted on walls, church doors, and gateways were read with interest. Luther's own writings were in demand, and he and his colleagues produced more and more literature in the vernacular, hoping to reach the widest audience possible. In support and response came pamphlets caricaturing the church fathers and monks. More important, the number of books printed in

Germany rose quickly. The presses of Germany were kept busy with the business of the Reformation until well past mid-century.

Colporteurs and book peddlers carried Reformation propaganda into the countryside. In this way, printing was a direct influence in the Peasants' Revolt of 1524–1525. That revolt marked a watershed in the Lutheran Reformation, as reform leaders recognized dangers to social order and drew back in their calls for mass participation. A greater effort at formal, more cautious institutional and religious change was made—more directed and controlled. The number of pamphlets and polemical works declined as printing became a more controlled measure of propaganda. Reform-related printing became more narrowly religious and theological, but publishing in the vernacular remained a major preoccupation.[5]

Luther continued his translation of the Bible into German, and it was a great success. Some buyers were probably unable to read or comprehend it for themselves; to many it was more a symbol of faith, piety, and, perhaps, status. Despite a relatively high rate of literacy in urban areas, the ensuing educational campaign of the Reformation indicates that popular reading habits and skills were far from satisfactory.

Recognizing that rising lay literacy was one of the preconditions for the reform and that the struggles for reform depended upon print, and hence reading, requires no determinism about their roles. They were vehicles among many others; their larger importance was realized through the interactive potentials of print and literacy. Some readers could "enlighten" many others; high levels of literacy were hardly a requirement for embracing the Scriptures and making faith real. The roles of literacy and print, in a popular rather than an intellectual or theological sense, must be placed in sixteenth-century sociocultural settings.

The ideas of the Reformation were spread through various channels. One way was through personal contact. Luther and his supporters were responsible for some of the diffusion, but more significant were itinerant middlemen—preachers, salesmen, and journeymen. Print and literacy surely contributed here.

The message was also disseminated through print and writing—the distribution of books, manuscripts, pictures, personal letters, and songs. More was involved than literacy alone; sales of Reformation literature could yield high profits, and as this literature was bought in one place and reprinted and sold to other towns and cities, Lutheran ideas were spread without direct personal contact. Illiterates were attracted to Luther's ideas through visual devices (woodcuts and copperplates) and oral communications.

Institutions, including universities and political administrations, also helped to circulate evangelical ideas, supplementing and reinforcing personal contacts. Professors and students frequently returned to their home areas after their university studies and spread the new gospel through preaching, official service, or active citizenship. Other institutional contributions came from servants in imperial and territorial city administrations and similar agencies. Literacy and print acted in concert with personal and institutional contacts and exchanges to spread the Reformation. The sermon movement and preachers played an important role. From this basis, we begin to grasp the fuller nature of communications linkages and the mixture of media in sixteenth-century society. Print and literacy, while important, were parts of a larger whole. Personal relations, printing and writing, oral communications, institutions: each played a part, separately and interactively. The meaning of literacy to the reform effort, and its opposition, lies precisely in the nature of these relationships.[6]

The roles played by print and other media and channels were not exceptional to Germany. Similar processes within the international reform movement occurred in France, Switzerland, England, the Low Countries, and Scandinavia. The Reformation was brought to the New World by colonists.[7]

On a different level, among intellectuals and churchmen, the advent of printing had an important, contradictory impact. The use of printing assisted the movement for reform within the church, advanced the standardization of texts and observances within liturgical practices, influenced habits of sermonizing, and duplicated all sorts of literature, new and old. While changed by print, none of that was new. On the other hand, these uses of the press were not determined in advance; virtually all of them worked toward the efforts of the church or its critics. Printed texts could standardize church practices and improve them; or they could reveal, to literates at least, the gap between official doctrine and clerical practice. "With typographical fixity, moreover, positions once taken were more difficult to reverse. Battles of books prolonged polarization, and pamphlet wars quickened the press."

Despite the many claims advanced for the powers of "typographical fixity," the force has stopped few writers from changing their minds or positions in print, revising their work, or even, knowingly or unknowingly, contradicting themselves. Many of the reformers, from Luther on, did so. The battles of words, on printed pages, had a force that earlier, manuscript debates did not. Reducing face-to-face debates and disputations, they carried the issues, the divisions, the vehemence far beyond that possible in the age of script. Printing made propaganda, in a modern sense, possible; the Reformation was an early example, although perhaps not the first. Humanists and the church had engaged in such pursuits before the first international age of reform erupted.

One of the principal eruptions centered on the vernacular Bible, which the church was unwilling to countenance. One of the most important innovations furthered by the Reformers, it was a principal use of print. A tremendous incentive for literacy and a great boost to the vernacular followed. Yet, it is necessary to distinguish Bible study as scholarly exegesis from Bible study as lay Bible reading. Protestantism supported both; Catholicism promoted only the former.

Thus, Protestant doctrines stressing Bible reading for salvation generated special incentives toward literacy. That is a stereotypical view now, almost a myth, and *almost* true. Protestantism *was* a vital force toward the propagation of literacy among the populace in the West. But Catholicism has suffered a too negative, too unilaterally condemnatory press on this issue.[8] The written texts of the Bible had been a sacred and extraordinarily highly valued part of Christianity from its earliest days. It was Christianity more generally, long before Protestantism, that stressed the need to circulate *written* versions of the Bible despite the fact that severely restricted educational opportunities and literacy prevented the overwhelming number of adherents from confronting the great book for themselves. For this reason—and the fact that the Bible was not withheld from adherents who mastered Latin—comparisons with the Koran, on one hand, and strict Protestant-Catholic dichotomies, on the other, misrepresent realities that are more complex and interesting. The Bible was never restricted to a set of holy priests who recited it in the ways of the Koran and Islam; the Catholic church did not forbid the learned lay person from access to the Scriptures. Other issues were more central.

Post-Tridentine (Council of Trent, 1546) policies differed from those of the medieval church. A dramatic hardening of policy occurred, with vernacular Bibles prohibited, removing the Holy Scriptures from the direct access of virtually all adherents—an access marked by ability to read and perhaps even understand it. The Scriptures long assumed the qualities of sacred untouchable symbols to the Catholic laity. Trent curiously endorsed some forms of educational advancement and lay learning, but proscribed direct access to the Bible through the vernacular languages. The consequences were many. Not only were lay congregations further removed from clergy and texts, but an end was put to serious translations by Catholics for almost two centuries. Venetian printers were severely hit by the loss of some of their most salable products. Only in countries in which the Roman Catholic church was threatened by Protestant traditions was publication of vernacular Bibles permitted.[9]

In contrast, vernacular Bibles, prayer books, and catechisms were adopted by all the reformed and reforming churches. These materials, more traditional than innovative, served as a basis for schooling and literacy instruction, now in the native tongue. Educational and religious promotion were combined and reciprocally reinforced. Linguistic uniformity, as a part of nation building, was also advanced.[10]

The difference in support for public or popular schooling and promotion of literacy between lands Catholic and Protestant is often exaggerated, and the peculiar mix of local factors unexplored. Protestant promotion of literacy had social morality and secularized religious concerns at its core, rather than individualized, liberating, independent, self-advancement goals. The individual applications of literacy, of course, could not always be controlled, although the promoted ones were often dominant. Contrary to many generalizations, neither printing *alone* nor Protestantism *alone* shaped outcomes during the sixteenth century or the early modern period. Just as one should not be divorced from the other, neither should either be removed from its context or special mix of factors, local and national, that gave it meaning and shaped its use.

In this respect, it is important to note that by the second half of the sixteenth century, the post-Tridentine Catholic church had successfully and consciously mobilized printers for its counter-reform offensive. They, too, used print for proselytizing, produced devotional materials for clerics and laity, and contributed to printers' profits. In England, "Catholic printers proved as skillful as their Puritan counterparts in handling problems posed by the surreptitious printing and the clandestine marketing of books." Although their limits differed and their enthusiasm was restrained by a greater ambivalence, Catholic reformers had to promote lay literacy to combat the Protestants and struggle for their place in the new religious pluralism.[11] Printing comprised issues religious, economic, *and* political; so did literacy and its provision. . . .

LITERACY IN COLONIAL NORTH AMERICA

Contrary to historical stereotype, North American colonial settlers were born neither modern nor universally literate. Their origins were European, primarily English.[12] American students of American history, in stressing the exceptionality and uniqueness of these "plantations" of the Old World, have distorted the transatlantic connection that the colonists themselves held so dearly. A new, more contextually accurate and sophisticated understanding has recently developed, seeing the colonists as linked to the world in which the first generation was born and socialized and to a culture that shaped not only their lives but the lives of their children. Attitudes toward education, values of literacy, and notions about institutions, as well as the larger cultural universe, were brought from one side of the Atlantic to the other with the immigrants, but changes also occurred in the process of founding and developing a society in the wilderness of the North Atlantic coastal regions.[13]

The literacy levels of seventeenth-century colonists were relatively high. The rate of male literacy in New England was around 60 percent, as compared to a rate in contemporary England of no higher than 40 percent.[14] Puritanism was one reason. A religion of the Word and of the Book, it had a dynamic propelling its adherents toward literacy. This impetus was complex; in some ways it played a direct, almost linear, role in increasing rates and uses of literacy.[15] But more than Puritanism was responsible for the level of literacy among the first generation. Migratory selectivity was most important; persons more likely to be literate for religious, familial, occupational, demographic, geographic, or economic reasons, and/or from places with higher-than-average rates of literacy, were more likely to migrate over the long transatlantic distance. Both kinds of selectivity joined to constitute a population of movers whose ability to sign was perhaps (among males) one and one-half times the level at home—and possibly even higher.[16]

The situation of early French settlers in Quebec was similar. During the second half of the seventeenth century, migrants from the old country had relatively high levels of literacy. Marriage registers show that of those born in France and marrying between 1657 and 1715, 38 percent of men and 32 percent of women were able to sign. In contrast to British North American colonies, formal parish schooling was satisfactorily initiated. Of marriage partners born in the colony, 46 percent of grooms and 43 percent of brides signed, higher rates but also less differentiated by gender. The second generation progressed in this urban place in a way that was far more difficult in more rural, agrarian areas, whether in Quebec or in the English colonies. Here, too, schooling was traditional, and it was distinguished by class, gender, and geographic locale.[17]

For many English persons, especially Puritans, education, schooling, and literacy were acquiring a new importance by the early seventeenth century. That this value was transported with the colonists should be expected. English Protestant concern with schooling intersected with the Puritan stress on the importance of individual access to the Book and the Word among the New England settlers. Within a relatively few years of settlement in the Massachusetts colonies, the famous school laws were enacted requiring schooling for all children. An expression of piety, not a fearful reaction to the colonial wilderness, the laws derived from traditional Puritan motives, which were instrumental in raising literacy rates in England and which, when compulsory, seemed a powerful force for education. Literacy was a universal prerequisite to spiritual preparation, the central duty of the covenant about which Puritans were deeply concerned.[18]

Colonial New England witnessed a rise in literacy from little more than one-half of males to almost all men between the mid-seventeenth century and the end of the eighteenth. In the seventeenth century, literacy's progress was slow and uneven. Overall, levels of literacy barely moved during the lifetime of the second generation,

those dying around the year 1710 and educated during the 1660s. The rise of high levels of literacy, part of a trend in much of the West, came only after a slow start. The success of New England's literacy campaign, largely through local, town, or parish schools (the English model), came mainly in the eighteenth century.[19]

Women's literacy was also relatively high in colonial New England. About one-third of the women who died prior to 1670, and who left wills, could sign their names. This rate, about one-half that of males, may have been about one and one-half times that of women in England, the same proportional advantage as among the men. However, the seventeenth century was not a time of opportunities for schooling; not until the eighteenth century does it seem that the teaching of literacy to girls as well as boys was frequently attempted. The literacy of a woman's parents had no effect on her own literacy. Church membership was the only variable significantly related to women's literacy. A traditional Puritan concern with religion was felt on the individual as well as the societal level. The only families in which daughters were literate in most cases had two parents who were full members of the church. Familiar wealth was not related to daughters' literacy, as it was for sons. For women, not even elite status was a guarantee of literacy.[20]

The desired rise in literacy, a skill not practically useful to most settlers, took place primarily after the turn of the eighteenth century. The increasing level of signatures most likely resulted from a rising inclination *and* ability of families to send their children, especially sons, to schools, and from the increasing availability of schools, due in large part to population density and the processes of social development. With rising levels of commercialization and urbanization came for more men a need for and advantages from reading and writing. In this way, social development intersected with original intentions to drive the rates of literacy from about two-thirds of men to almost all men. This progress was more conservative than revolutionary or "liberating," and was essentially a movement among previously less literate peoples and regions that began to negate the traditional association of literacy with social status but not with economic standing.

In the seventeenth century, the social and geographic distribution of literacy was much more "traditional" than it would become. The more urban residents and higher-ranking persons, as in the Old World, were much more likely to be literate than lower-ranking and rural persons. As in England, literacy was linked directly to social standing. Social status, in wealth, occupation, deference, and the like, was brought with the settlers; it shaped literacy levels.

A number of historians have implied that literacy was instrumental to the formation of modern personality characteristics in the new colonies: activism, participation, optimism, awareness, cosmopolitanism, and larger loyalties. The presumed result was a more rational, planning, and calculating sort of person.[21] With regard to charitable behavior, however, studies have shown no modernization of attitudes occurring in colonial New England. Rather than literate men showing an increasing tendency to give to the needs of society, especially outside their families; to give to abstract causes and institutions rather than to persons; to give beyond their home villages and towns; or to give to rehabilitate rather than to alleviate, the analysis of charitable gifts revealed no such pattern, either for all givers or as a distinction between literate and illiterate givers. Literates, with their greater wealth, tended to give more often than illiterates, but when wealth is controlled, virtually no distinction existed.

The reason for charitable giving was usually traditional, to aid the poor or to further religion. Very few gifts were meant to rehabilitate the poor or turn religion to constructive secular needs; hardly any went to educate men or improve society. Literacy, it seems, did not press mightily upon men's beliefs or attitudes.[22]

Literacy did equip men with a skill that could be useful. But the quality of literacy and the environment limited and restrained its uses. In the seventeenth century many persons were not literate, but a high level of universal literacy was not required. Most transactions were localized and personal contacts; Puritans had a strong oral culture that shaped and received their value of the importance of individual access to the Book and the Word. Reading and writing were not often required in daily affairs outside the needs of devotion and piety. Land was obtained from towns by grant, and deeds were usually registered locally by clerks. "The gap between the literacy of the population and the functional demands of the society was not great."[23] High levels of literacy did not assist colonial New Englanders in dealing with the confusion that regularly plagued their social and cultural maturation and road to revolution.

As in England, the oral and the literate culture intertwined. The oral medium was employed to disseminate much of print culture. Illustrations in books helped to carry ideas to illiterates, as did books designed to be read aloud. The substance of the world of print was transmitted and broadcast well beyond the relatively narrow boundaries of the individual, silent reader.[24]

Printing existed in New England from 1630, a year after the first press arrived. The establishment of this press, in Cambridge, Massachusetts, probably was influenced by events at home, especially the extension of control over the press from censorship within England to pressure over publishing of Puritan works in the Netherlands. The presses started out slowly; most production was religious or administrative. Booksellers peddled their wares gradually. Their books were primarily religious; they also sold popular almanacs, medical manuals, and some literature—classics, histories, and other practical books. Other books were brought directly by the wealthiest or most educated settlers, who had the most important private libraries in seventeenth-century New England.[25] Primarily, only college graduates had collections that justified the label of library. The print culture of the early settlers, the limited evidence suggests, was not a vibrant, lively, and enlivening secular culture. Most print material related to religion.

The history of schooling in New England belongs more to the end of the seventeenth and the eighteenth centuries than to this period. The evidence of literacy and the limited reconstruction of educational activities join in suggesting that schooling, in a fairly systematic, regularized, and institutional way, came *after* initial plantation founding and society building. The social structure of literacy, for the seventeenth century, tended to vary mainly with the literacy levels of the founders themselves; levels of population concentration, wealth, commercialization, and "institutional maturity" related more closely to the presence of schools than did the facts of settlement per se. That English men and women brought English and Puritan motives, values, and plans for schooling with them is clear; it is also likely that they were not able to erect many schools at first. The compulsory schools required by the laws do not seem to have been established.[26] More developed areas and towns were able to sustain schools, but many simply were not.

The schooling that took place was traditional and religiously oriented. Children learned much as they had in England, from hornbooks and/or primers, either in schoolhouses under a schoolmaster or from their pastors. Catechisms were central to the curriculum. Primers, such as the famous *New England Primer,* were filled with religious material. Moral and religious training and knowledge were the most prized accomplishments of schooling.

Education was to begin as soon as the child was able to absorb it. The very young were to be prepared by oral instruction and moral comments on their actions. The household's piety and morality were to condition the child from the earliest moments of awareness. As the child grew, more formal instruction was to replace informal socialization. Other teaching took place in the church, and when possible in a school. At school, training was more intellectual, to provide the pupil with the tools, such as literacy, for acquiring religious knowledge. By the age of five, boys might be attending reading or dame schools. These elementary schools of colonial New England supplemented the lessons of the church.[27] As soon as they were old enough, children were taken regularly to church, to learn their religious knowledge from the pulpit. In theory, all aspects of education and literacy aimed at one central lesson.

In the Southern colonies of Virginia and Maryland, the male literacy rate in the seventeenth century was around 50 percent, again indicating the literacy selectivity of the generation migrating to the North American colonies. The rich were almost all literate, but only about half of the farmers and a third of the poor could sign. The level of literacy rose to about two-thirds by the middle of the eighteenth century, then stopped, at the same time that New England was achieving near-universal rates of male literacy.

A lack of intense Protestantism and the resulting school laws contributed to this stagnation, but other factors were equally important. The Puritan connection between individual literacy and reading the Scriptures was absent here. Piety and devotion were of interest, but education was viewed as academic and practical, as a means of teaching trades to boys and of giving domestic training to girls. An academic education was based on an ability "to read distinctly in the Bible"; pupils learned how to make a living and gained firsthand knowledge of the Bible at the same time. Schooling was also clearly class-biased. The paucity of formal education in the Colonial South was also due partly to the low population density, but more to the short life expectancy of the settlers. Parents often did not live long enough to see to their children's education.

Education of children in this area had little bearing on their success as adults. Literacy was not necessary for economic prosperity; occupation and age were more important. "The wealth differences between literates and illiterates among those engaged in agriculture and common laboring pursuits indicate that society did not provide much economic incentive for literacy for those people."

Although there were persistent desires for schools, and the early laws of each colony called for schooling of all children, few institutions followed. Literacy rose slightly through the period, but mainly through selective migration streams; the progress of educational development was slow.

One problem in places such as Virginia and Maryland was that the dispersed nature of geographic settlement required for the land- and labor-intensive plantation system greatly reduced the possibilities of formal schools, being founded and maintained. In huge parishes, some as large as a hundred square miles, churches reached only a portion of the population. "And, with residences scattered across the countryside, schools became uneconomical, for lack of both funds and scholars. Indeed, even the formal education of communal life was missing. . . ." Some Virginians hoped that towns, concentrating settlement and resources, would solve some of the problems, but for all their administrative, economic, and cultural importance, towns never played this role on a level sufficient for mass schooling.

Despite conviction, interest, and intention, schools remained restricted in the Southern colonies. That is as true for free and charity schooling for the poor as for other formal educational foundation. Little institutional progress took place until the second century of development. Education for the elite and wealthy was more successful before 1700 than were plans and desires for more inclusive schooling, with the exception of a handful of bequests for free and charity schools. Apprenticeship apparently developed on the English model, but fulfillment of its educational requirements proved a constant source of complaints and litigation.[28] The systematic program that came with time in the Puritan areas never developed in the Southern colonies.

Books and other elements of print culture were imported with the Southern colonists. Tastes were largely traditional, with major interests in religious literature, followed by a diversity of other materials. Indigenous printing developed more slowly than in New England; English products were even more pervasive. Book ownership and libraries were limited overwhelmingly to elites. . . .

NOTES

1. Gerald Strauss, *Luther's House of Learning* (Baltimore: Johns Hopkins Press, 1978).
2. John Headley, "The Continental Reformation," in Richard L. DeMolen, ed., *The Meaning of the Renaissance and Reformation* (Boston: Houghton Mifflin, 1974). . . .
3. Headley, "Continental," pp. 150–51; . . . Richard Crofts, "Books, Reform, and the Reformation," *Archives for Reformation History* 7 (1980): 21–36.
4. Louise Holborn, "Printing and the Growth of a Protestant Movement in Germany," *Church History* 11 (1942): 123. . . .
5. Lucien Febvre and H-J Martin, *The Coming of the Book* (London: NLB, 1976), pp. 287–88, 288, 289, 289–95, 290, 291, 291–92, 292–93, 292–95; A. G. Dickens, *Reformation and Society in Sixteenth-Century Europe* (London: Thames and Hudson, 1966), p. 51. . . .
6. Manfred Hanneman, *The Diffusion of the Reformation in Southwestern Germany,* Department of Geography, Research Paper no. 167 (Chicago: University of Chicago, 1975), pp. 9, 7–9, chaps. 5–7, pp. 12, 9–13, 12–13, 13 212. Conclusion. . . .
7. Febvre and Martin, *Coming,* pp. 295ff. . . .
8. Elizabeth Eisenstein, *The Printing Press as an Agent of Change* (Cambridge: Cambridge University Press, 1979), chap. 4, pp. 310, 326, chap. 4, sec. 2, p. 333. . . .
9. Eisenstein, *Printing Press,* pp. 344, 348; see also Febvre and Martin, *Coming.* . . .
10. Eisenstein, *Printing Press,* p. 349, passim. . . .
11. Eisenstein, *Printing Press,* p. 354. . . .
12. On the equation of modernity with literacy for this period, see Bernard Bailyn, *Education in the Forming of American Society* (Chapel Hill: University of North Carolina Press, 1960); Lawrence Cremin, *American Education: The Colonial Experience* (New York: Harper and Row, 1970); Richard D. Brown, "Modernization and the Formation of the Modern Personality in Early America, 1600–1865: A Sketch of a Synthesis," *Journal of Interdisciplinary History* 2 (1972): 201–228. . . .
13. For useful introductions and evidence, see Bailyn, *Education;* Cremin, *American Education;* Kenneth A. Lockridge, *Literacy in Colonial New England* (New York: Norton, 1974). . . . On schooling, see R. R. Reeder, *The Historical Development of School Readers and of Method in Teaching Reading,* Columbia

University Contributions to Philosophy, Psychology, and Education, vol. 8 (New York: Macmillan, 1900); Sanford Fleming; *Children and Puritanism* (New Haven: Yale University Press, 1933); Herbert Baxter Adams, *The Church and Popular Education,* Johns Hopkins University Studies in Historical and Political Science, vol. 28 (Baltimore, 1900).

14. See, in particular, the work of Lockridge.

15. Lockridge, *Literacy,* pp. 43, 99.

16. Kenneth A. Lockridge, "L'alphabétisation en Amérique," *Annales: e, s, c* 32 (1977); p. 509. . . . For example, see Alex Inkeles and David H. Smith, *Becoming Modern* (Cambridge, Mass.: Harvard University Press, 1974); Goody and Watt, "Consequences." . . .

17. Louise Dechêne, *Habitants et Marchants de Montreal au XVIIIe siècle* (Paris and Montreal: Plon, 1974), pp. 465–67.

18. Lockridge, *Literacy,* pp. 49–50 (his quotation is from Bailyn, *Education,* p. 27). . . .

19. Lockridge, *Literacy,* p. 15. . . .

20. Lockridge, *Literacy,* p. 38, passim. . . .

21. Lockridge, *Literacy,* pp. 15, 17, 22, 29; Bailyn, *Education,* pp. 48–49; Cremin, *American Education,* pp. 546–50. . . .

22. Lockridge, *Literacy,* pp. 33, 35–36. More recently, John Frye ("Class, Generation, and Social Change: A Case in Salem, Massachusetts, 1636–1656," *Journal of Popular Culture* 11 [1977]: 743–51) argues that a deviant subculture existed in New England communities, which included literates as well as illiterates.

23. Jon Butler, "Magic, Astrology, and the Early American Religious Heritage, 1600–1760," *American Historical Review* 84 (1979): 317–46; Lockridge, *Literacy,* p. 37; John Frye, "Class, Generation, and Social Change: A Case in Salem, Massachusetts, 1636–1656," *Journal of Popular Culture* II (1977): 743–51.

24. David D. Hall, "The World of Print and Collective Mentality in Seventeenth Century New England," in *New Directions in American Intellectual History,* eds. John Higham and Paul Contein (Baltimore: Johns Hopkins University Press, 1979), pp. 167, 169. . . .

25. Samuel Blist Morison, *The Intellectual Life of Colonial New England* (Ithaca: Cornell University Press, 1956), pp. 113, 115, 115–27, 127–32, chap. 6.

26. Morison, *Intellectual,* p. 71.

27. Edmund Morgan, *The Puritan Family* (New York: Harper and Row, 1965), pp. 88, 98, . . . 101. . . .

28. Cremin, *American Education,* pp. 240–41, bk. 1, pt. 2, passim. . . .

CHAPTER **13**

The Trade in News

John B. Thompson

John B. Thompson is a reader in sociology at the University of Cambridge and a fellow of Jesus College, Cambridge. He is the author of several works on social theory, including The Media and Modernity, *from which the present excerpt is taken. He is also an editor and a founding member of Polity Press.*

There is another way in which the development of printing transformed the patterns of communication in early modern Europe: it gave rise to a variety of periodical publications which reported events and conveyed information of a political and commercial character. Prior to the advent of printing, a number of regularized networks of communication had been established throughout

Europe. We can distinguish at least four distinct types of pre-print communication network. First, there was an extensive network of communication, established and controlled by the Catholic Church. This network enabled the papacy in Rome to maintain contact with the clergy and political elites dispersed throughout the loosely knit realm of Christendom. Second, there were networks of communication established by the political authorities of states and principalities; these networks operated both within the territories of particular states, facilitating administration and pacification, and between states which maintained some form of diplomatic communication with one another. A third type of network was linked to the expansion of commercial activity. As trade and manufacturing increased, new networks of communication were established within the business community and between the major trading centres. Commercial and banking houses—like the Fugger family of Augsburg and the great merchant houses of Florence—built up extensive systems of communication and began to supply information to clients on a commercial basis. Finally, information was also transmitted to towns and villages via networks of merchants, pedlars, and travelling entertainers, such as storytellers and ballad singers. As individuals gathered in market-places or taverns and interacted with merchants and travellers, they picked up news about events which took place in distant locales.

In the course of the fifteenth, sixteenth and seventeenth centuries, these networks of communication were affected by two key developments. In the first place, some states began to establish regular postal services which became increasingly available for general use. In France Louis XI established a royal post in 1464; private individuals could use the post by special permission and payment of a fee.[1] In central Europe Maximilian I developed an extensive postal network which linked the heartland of the Habsburg empire with cities throughout Europe. In 1490 he appointed Franz and Johann von Taxis as chief postmasters, thus establishing an imperial postal system that remained under the control of the von Taxis family

for several centuries.[2] In England a royal post was established early in the reign of Henry VIII, and a postmaster was appointed around 1516, although the development of regular postal services for general public use did not occur until the early seventeenth century.[3] Gradually in the course of the seventeenth and eighteenth centuries, an integrated network of public postal communication emerged, providing common carrier services for both domestic and foreign post. Of course, by twentieth-century standards, postal communication in early modern Europe was very slow. Messages were transported by horse and carriage at a time when the roads in many parts of Europe were of poor quality. Mail rarely travelled at more than 10 miles per hour over extended distances. In the late eighteenth century, Edinburgh was still a journey of 60 hours from London, and it 24 hours to travel from London to Manchester. It was not until the early nineteenth century, with the development of the railways, that the time required to transmit messages through the post was sharply reduced.

The second development which profoundly affected the established networks of communication in early modern Europe was the application of printing to the production and dissemination of news. Soon after the advent of printing in the mid-fifteenth century, a variety of printed information leaflets, posters and broadsheets began to appear. These were a mixture of official or semi-official statements of government decrees; polemical tracts; descriptions of particular events, such as military encounters or natural disasters; and sensationalized accounts of extraordinary or supernatural phenomena, like giants, comets and apparitions. These leaflets and news sheets were generally one-off or irregular publications. They were printed by the thousands and sold in the streets by hawkers and pedlars. They provided individuals with a valuable source of information about current and distant events.

Periodical publications of news and information began to appear in the second half of the sixteenth century, but the origins of the modern

Etching of a Parris Café scene. *Frederick Barnard (1846–1896)/Public Domain.*

newspaper are usually traced to the first two decades of the seventeenth century, when regular journals of news began to appear on a weekly basis with some degree of reliability.[4] In 1609 weekly journals were published in several German cities, including Augsburg, Strasbourg and Wolfenbüttel, and there is some evidence to suggest that a weekly paper may have appeared somewhat earlier (1607) in Amsterdam. Printed weeklies—or "corantos," as these early compilations of news were called at the time—soon appeared in other cities and languages. The cities located along the major European trading routes, such as Cologne, Frankfurt, Antwerp and Berlin, became early centres of newspaper production. The news which made up the corantos was often supplied by postmasters, who collected the news in their regions and then forwarded it to the major cities. A single individual could then assemble and edit the postmasters' reports, printing them in the form of a series of short paragraphs with details of the date and place of origin of the information. The weeklies could also be translated into other languages and sold in different cities and countries.

By 1620 Amsterdam had become the centre of a rapidly expanding trade in news. There was a growing public interest in the Thirty Years' War and this provided a major stimulus to the development of the fledgling newspaper industry. The first newspaper to appear in English was probably produced in Amsterdam in 1620 by the Dutch printer and map engraver Pieter van den Keere and exported to London.[5] Between 2 December 1620 and 18 September 1621, 15 issues of van den Keere's coranto appeared. Although it was not published weekly, it did appear fairly frequently and it provided regular coverage of the Thirty Years' War. The first coranto printed in England was probably produced by the London stationer Thomas Archer in 1621. Archer was subsequently imprisoned for publishing an unlicensed news sheet on the war in the Palatinate, but other English corantos and news pamphlets soon appeared.

Most of these early forms of newspaper were concerned primarily with foreign news, that is, with events which were taking place (or had taken place) in distant locales. The individuals who read these papers, or listened to them being read aloud by others, would learn of events taking place in distant parts of Europe—events they could not witness directly, in places they would never, in all likelihood, visit. Hence the circulation of the early forms of newspaper helped to create a sense of a world of events which lay beyond the individual's immediate milieu, but which had some relevance to, and potentially some bearing on, his or her life. Of course, the geographical scope of this world remained quite limited in the early seventeenth century: it rarely extended beyond the major cities and countries of Europe. Moreover, the circulation of the early newspapers was very low by present-day standards (one estimate puts the minimum print run of the early newspapers at 400 copies,[6] and in many cases it was probably not much more than that), although papers were no doubt read by more than one individual, and were commonly read aloud. But the importance of this new mode of information diffusion, through which printed reports of distant events were made available on a

regular basis to an unlimited number of recipients, should not be underestimated.

While the early corantos were concerned mainly with foreign news, it was not long before newspapers began to devote more attention to domestic events. In England this development had to wait until 1640, when the government's strict control of the press began to weaken. Since 1586 a Star Chamber decree had established a comprehensive system of licensing and censorship (supplemented by a further decree of 1637), which limited the number of printers in England and subjected them to specific censors for each type of publication. But as the crisis between Charles I and Parliament deepened, it became increasingly difficult for the Crown to enforce its control of the press, and in July 1641 the Star Chamber was abolished. The crisis also stimulated a public demand for up-to-date news of domestic political affairs. Between mid-November 1641 and the end of December 1641 three domestic weekly newspapers appeared, each providing summaries of the proceedings of Parliament; and in the first three months of 1642 another eight newspapers appeared, though some did not last for long.[7] This was the beginning of a period of relatively uncontrolled and intensive publication of newspapers, newsbooks and pamphlets dealing with the events of the Civil War and the issues surrounding it. During most weeks of 1645, 14 newspapers were on sale in the streets of London, as well as a multitude of other pamphlets and political tracts. While strict controls were reimposed by Charles II after the restoration of the monarchy in 1660, the period between 1641 and the restoration was an important one in the history of the press. For it was during this time that periodical publications emerged as key players in the affairs of state, providing a continuous flow of information on current events and expressing a range of differing views—sometimes sharply conflicting views—on matters of public concern.

The development of a commercially based periodical press which was independent of state power, and yet was capable of providing information and critical commentary on issues of general concern, entered a new phase in eighteenth-century England. The system of licensing, which had been re-established by Charles II in 1662, fell into abeyance at the end of the seventeenth century and was followed by a spate of new periodical publications. The first daily newspaper in England, Samuel Buckley's *Daily Courant,* appeared in 1702 and was soon joined by others. A variety of more specialized periodicals appeared, some concentrating on entertainment and cultural events, some on financial and commercial news, and others on social and political commentary. The latter included a number of journals which popularized the genre of the political essay, like the *Tatler,* the *Spectator,* Nicholas Amhurst's *Craftsman,* Daniel Defoe's *Review* and Jonathan Swift's *Examiner.* By 1750 London had five well-established daily papers, six thrice-weeklies, five weeklies and several other cut-price periodicals, with a total circulation between them of around 100,000 copies per week.[8] The papers were distributed in the city by networks of hawkers and agents, as well as by a loose federation of coffee houses which acquired the major papers and made them available for their customers to read. Since many papers were read in public places like taverns and coffee houses, their readership was almost certainly much higher than their circulation—perhaps as much as ten times higher. London papers were also distributed to the provinces by rapidly improving stage coach and postal services.

The political authorities sought to exercise some control over the proliferation of newspapers and periodicals by imposing special taxes, which would, it was thought, serve to restrict production and force the more marginal periodicals out of business, while at the same time raising additional revenue for the Crown. The Stamp Act of 1712 required newspaper proprietors to pay one penny for every printed sheet and one shilling for every advertisement. Subsequent Acts increased the amounts and broadened the basis for the application of the law. The Stamp Acts were bitterly opposed and became a rallying point in the struggle for the freedom of the press. It was not until the 1830s that the taxes were progressively reduced, and in the 1860s they were eventually abolished. Elsewhere in Europe the periodical press of the eighteenth century was controlled and censored with varying degrees of severity.[9] In the United Provinces the press remained relatively free, although it was discouraged from discussing local politics and was occasionally subjected to bouts of intensive censorship. In France a centralized and highly restrictive system of licensing, supervision and censorship existed until the Revolution; a brief post-revolutionary period of press freedom was finally brought to an end by Napoleon, who instituted a strict system of censorship and control. In the states and principalities of Germany and Italy the degree of official control varied from one state to another, but newspapers were generally allowed more leeway in reporting foreign news than in discussing domestic politics.

There is considerable force in the argument that the struggle for an independent press, capable of reporting and commenting on events with a minimum of state interference and control, played a key role in the development of the modern constitutional state. Some of the early liberal and liberal democratic thinkers, such as Jeremy Bentham, James Mill and John Stuart Mill, were fervent advocates of the liberty of the press. They saw the free expression of opinion through the organs of an independent press as a vital safeguard against the despotic use of state power.[10] It is significant that, following their successful war of independence against the British Crown, the American colonists incorporated the right of press freedom in the First Amendment to the Constitution. Similarly, the post-revolutionary French constitutions of 1791 and 1793, building on the Declaration des Droits de l'Homme of 1789, explicitly protected the freedom of expression (even if this freedom was subsequently abolished by Napoleon). Statutory guarantees of freedom of expression were eventually adopted by various European governments so that by the end of the nineteenth century the freedom of the press had become a constitutional feature of many Western states.

NOTES

1. See Howard Robinson, *The British Post Office: A History* (Princeton: Princeton University Press, 1948), p. 4.
2. For an account of the "Thurn und Taxis" postal service, as it became known, see Martin Dallmeier, *Quellen zur Geschichte des Europäischen Postwesens, 1501–1806*, Part 1: *Quellen-Literatur Einleitung* (Kallmünz: Michael Lassleben, 1977), pp. 49–220.
3. Robinson, *The British Post Office*, chs 1–3; J. Crofts, *Packhorse, Waggon and Post: Land Carriage and Communications under the Tudors and Stuarts* (London: Routledge and Kegan Paul, 1967), chs. 8–17.
4. The identification of what could be called "the first newspaper" is a matter of dispute, though most historians would agree that something resembling the modern newspaper first appeared around 1610. See Eric W. Allen, "International Origins of the Newspapers: The Establishment of Periodicity in Print," *Journalism Quarterly*, 7 (1930), pp. 307–19; Joseph Frank, *The Beginnings of the English Newspaper, 1620–1660* (Cambridge, Mass.: Harvard University Press, 1961), ch. 1.
5. Frank, *The Beginnings of the English Newspaper*, p. 3.
6. Folke Dahl, *A Bibliography of English Corantos and Periodical Newsbooks, 1620–1642* (London: Bibliographical Society, 1952), p. 22.
7. Frank, *The Beginnings of the English Newspaper*, pp. 21–2.
8. Anthony Smith, *The Newspaper: An International History* (London: Thames and Hudson, 1979), pp. 56–7.
9. For more detailed discussions of the history of political control and censorship of the press, see F. S. Siebert, *Freedom of the Press in England, 1476–1776* (Urbana: University of Illinois Press, 1952); A. Aspinall, *Politics and the Press, c.1780–1850* (Brighton: Harvester, 1973); Smith, *The Newspaper*, chs. 3–5.
10. See especially James Mill, "Liberty of the Press," in his *Essays on Government, Jurisprudence, Liberty of the Press and Law of Nations* (New York: Kelly, 1967); John Stuart Mill, "On Liberty," in his *Utilitarianism, On Liberty and Considerations on Representative Government*, ed. H. B. Acton (London: Dent, 1972).

PART FOUR

Electricity Creates the Wired World

A glimpse inside an early twentieth century telephone exchange in Paris where operators connect callers to one another through a switchboard. *AKG-Images.*

Up to this point we have looked at the history of communications in terms of a variety of media that physically carried certain kinds of information. To move the information one moved the medium. The book and manuscript passed from place to place in much the same fashion as did clay tablets, tokens and the quipu. With the advent of harnessable electricity, a major shift occurred: the telegraph and telephone became the first wave of a new communications revolution. To paraphrase Marshall McLuhan, beginning with the telegraph, messages could travel faster than messengers. Communication over distance was no longer tied to the available means of transportation. The effects of this breakthrough are still occurring. Through the use of faxes and emails, for example, a letter can now be freed from a dependency on the mails for speedy delivery.

This leap, from what is called a "transportation" model of communication to a "transmission" one, was not without precursors. Talking drums, smoke signals and the use of polished metal to direct sunlight (heliograph) were early ways of sending messages without messengers. The ancient Greeks developed a system of torch signals between towers several miles apart that could relay the letters of the alphabet. Well before the invention of the telegraph, ship-to-ship and ship-to-shore semaphore had inspired the construction of land-based systems of towers that used mechanical arms to signal alphabet letters. In one such system in France, called the Chappe telegraph after its builder, messages of several sentences could be sent from the south of France to Paris in under four hours. There were even plans in the United States during the 1830s (when Samuel Morse was working on his telegraph) to establish a similar "optical telegraph" from Washington to New Orleans. Investments in such unusual delivery systems should alert us to the way in which the significance of more rapid communication was gaining wider recognition. Electricity and the telegraph quickly displaced the optical telegraph.

With the coming of the telegraph in the 1840s, words were transformed into electrical impulses—the dots and dashes of Morse code—that passed through a network that eventually wired the continent. With this development, communication was, in theory, separable from modes of transportation. In reality, the two worked hand-in-hand. Almost everywhere that the railroad went, the telegraph followed. Initially it was mutual benefit that made partners of the railroad and the telegraph. Telegraph companies found it convenient to use an already established right-of-way. The railroads benefited as well through the telegraph's ability to monitor rail traffic and warn of breakdowns. Paralleling these specific services, the telegraph also functioned as a background director of commerce. It forwarded orders, coordinated shipments, and reported transactions.

Tom Standage explores the telegraph's early development in our first selection. Beginning in the 1840s, the telegraph emerged as a powerful instrument of continental communication in the United States and Europe, and thanks in part to the development of trans-oceanic cable technology it became a global system before the end of the century. An important point to note in the development of telegraphy is how the American government, over the objections of the postal service, chose not to own and operate the telegraph—the opposite of what would occur in Europe. This gave rise to one of the first corporate monopolies in the United States, Western Union, and set the stage for a future of private media ownership.

Among the changes that flowed from telegraphy, was the influence it had on the newspaper and the development of journalistic practices. Michael Schudson's essay concentrates on the new forms of news that emerged in the second half of the nineteenth century. Schudson sketches out two kinds of journalism that prevailed: the information press and entertainment press. The former was oriented to political and economic news and the business community, the latter to the dramatic, scandalous and everyday life world of a growing urban working class. Both were tied to a new system of reportage: feeding stories into major centres where they could be pooled and forwarded elsewhere through the growing influence of the telegraph-based wire services, such as the Associated Press. Schudson shows us how newspapers created new forms of meaning in response to social and technological changes that yielded a new reading public, one that would eventually lead to the rise of mass society in the twentieth century.

After the telegraph, the next major electric communications medium to develop was the telephone. It emerged in the third quarter of the nineteenth century. Based on voice transmission, it overcame several limitations of the telegraph. The most notable one was that, unlike the telegraph, the telephone was not restricted to transmitting mostly written documents. Also, since the telegraph required skilled mastery of Morse code, as well as literacy, its potential spread into the home did not seem viable.

Like telegraphy, telephony's early use was in the urban context of business and government, the same areas where telegraphy got its start. This illustrates a recurring theme in the history of communications. A new medium often tries to do what was already the preserve of earlier one, but in ways that *bypass* some of the problems and complexities of its predecessor. The telephone in this case could be described as bypassing the telegraph because voice transmission eliminated the need for literate telegraphers skilled in Morse code.

It should also be noted that in its early operation the telephone was as much complementary to the telegraph as competitive. The telephone allowed for a rapid two-way exchange, which could speed up business decisions. The telegraph facilitated the sending of detailed and often quantitative information that could be collected at specific points for later action. The telegraph favored a linear logic of one thing at a time. The telephone was an immediately interactive medium. By the late 1880s the ease and efficiency of the telephone led to its use in wealthy private homes. As the cost of units dropped around the turn of the century, it began to spread throughout society, creating new dimensions of interpersonal interaction.

In our next excerpt, Claude Fischer gives us the story of Alexander Graham Bell and the Bell companies as they tried to build a viable business around early telephone technology. Fischer notes how in the 1840s the telephone had been more a novelty than a practical tool—it was easier to draw a Sunday audience for an exhibition of the "singing telephone" than to attract business users. There was, of course, the telegraph, with its local offices, messenger boys, and the beginnings of reliable service nationally and internationally. Fischer also makes the interesting point that the earliest users of the telephone were concerned with simple two-point communications, between two buildings of the same firm, or between the home and office of an executive.

The installation of switchboards on a large scale made the telephone competitive with the telegraph. From the 1880s onward the telephone grew as rapidly as exchanges could be installed. The base of customers expanded among business and professional users. By the 1890s, significant growth in residential services had occurred. The Bell companies in these decades succeeded in both promoting the adoption of the telephone and in policing the system they built against rivals. Fischer's essay is especially useful in alerting us to the emerging role of the customer, who influenced the development of telephony by demanding new and innovative applications of the medium.

The telephone was important in other ways. Electricity-based communication gave rise to its own forms of expertise that had to be both invented and promulgated. Trade and technical journals arose to support the standardizing and dissemination of expert knowledge. Trade associations and trade schools and eventually higher education helped establish "electrical literacy," in the process building a culture of electrical insiders. At the same time, the popular press and a variety of smaller publications contributed to constructing a climate of public opinion and popular culture around the application and experience of the medium itself.

In final selection, James Carey uses a discussion of the telegraph to reflect on a theme that resonates through many of the essays in this text, the impact of a new media on culture and society. Carey's perspective is influenced by the concepts of Harold Innis, whom we encountered in Part One. Carey applies Innis' emphasis on space and time to suggest how the telegraph—and by extension the telephone—helped reshaped a range of business practices. He shows, for instance, how the telegraph brought diverse regional centers of buying and selling under a unified price and market system, and he considers the implications of the creation of standard time zones. Carey's work is especially valuable in helping us see the way in which technology and cultural practices are entwined. His perspective encourages us to looks for the ways in which the "wired world" of the telegraph initiated, or foreshadowed, cultural technological changes that we often take for granted.

CHAPTER 14

Telegraphy—The Victorian Internet

Tom Standage

Tom Standage is a science and technology journalist, currently with The Economist *in London.*

"We are one!" said the nations, and hand met hand,
in a thrill electric from land to land.
— FROM "THE VICTORY," A POEM WRITTEN
IN TRIBUTE TO SAMUEL MORSE, 1872

No invention of modern times has extended its influence so rapidly as that of the electric telegraph," declared *Scientific American* in 1852. "The spread of the telegraph is about as wonderful a thing as the noble invention itself."

The growth of the telegraph network was, in fact, nothing short of explosive; it grew so fast that it was almost impossible to keep track of its size. "No schedule of telegraphic lines can now be relied upon for a month in succession," complained one writer in 1848, "as hundreds of miles may be added in that space of time. It is anticipated that the whole of the populous parts of the United States will, within two or three years, be covered with net-work like a spider's web."

Enthusiasm had swiftly displaced skepticism. The technology that in 1845 "had been a scarecrow and chimera, began to be treated as a confidential servant," noted a report compiled by the Atlantic and Ohio Telegraph Company in 1849. "Lines of telegraph are no longer experiments," declared the *Weekly Missouri Statesman* in 1850.

Expansion was fastest in the United States, where the only working line at the beginning of 1846 was Morse's experimental line, which ran 40 miles between Washington and Baltimore. Two years later there were approximately 2,000 miles of wire, and by 1850 there were over 12,000 miles operated by twenty different companies. The telegraph industry even merited twelve pages to itself in the 1852 U.S. Census.

"The telegraph system [in the United States] is carried to a greater extent than in any other part of the world," wrote the superintendent of the Census, "and numerous lines are now in full operation for a net-work over the length and breadth of the land." Eleven separate lines radiated out from New York, where it was not uncommon for some bankers to send and receive six or ten messages each day. Some companies were spending as much as $1,000 a year on telegraphy. By this stage there were over 23,000 miles of line in the United States, with another 10,000 under construction; in the six years between 1846 and 1852 the network had grown 600-fold.

"Telegraphing, in this country, has reached that point, by its great stretch of wires and great facilities for transmission of communications, as to almost rival the mail in the quantity of matter sent over it," wrote Laurence Turnbull in the preface to his 1852 book, *The Electro-Magnetic Telegraph*. Hundreds of messages per day were being sent along the main lines, and this, wrote Turnbull, showed "how important an agent the telegraph has become in the transmission of business communications. It is every day coming more into use, and every day adding to its power to be useful."

Arguably the single most graphic example of the telegraph's superiority over conventional means of delivering messages was to come a few years later, in October 1861, with the completion of the transcontinental telegraph line across the United States to California. Before the line was completed, the only link between East and West was provided by the Pony Express, a mail delivery system involving horse and rider relays. Colorful

characters like William "Buffalo Bill" Cody and "Pony Bob" Haslam took about 10 days to carry messages over the 1,800 miles between St. Joseph, Missouri and Sacramento. But as soon as the telegraph line along the route was in place, messages could be sent instantly, and the Pony Express was closed down.

In Britain, where the telegraph was doing well but had not been quite so rapidly embraced, there was some bemusement at the enthusiasm with which it had been adopted on the other side of the Atlantic. "The American telegraph, invented by Professor Morse, appears to be far more cosmopolitan in the purposes to which it is applied than our telegraph," remarked one British writer, not without disapproval. "It is employed in transmitting messages to and from bankers, merchants, members of Congress, officers of government, brokers, and police officers: parties who by agreement have to meet each other at the two stations, or have been sent for by one of the parties: items of news, election returns, announcements of deaths, inquiries respecting the health of families and individuals, daily proceedings of the Senate and the House of Representatives, orders for goods, inquiries respecting the sailing of vessels, proceedings of cases in various courts, summoning of witnesses, messages for express trains, invitations, the receipt of money at one station and its payment at another; for persons requesting the transmission of funds from debtors, consultation of physicians, and messages of every character usually sent by the mail. The confidence in the efficiency of telegraphic communication has now become so complete, that the most important commercial transactions daily transpire by its means between correspondents several hundred miles apart."

Instalation of telephone post in North America. *National Archives of Canada.*

Just as the old optical telegraphs were understood to be the preserve of the Royal Navy, the new electric telegraph was associated in British minds with the railways. By 1848, about half of the country's railway tracks had telegraph wires running alongside them. By 1850, there were 2,215 miles of wire in Britain, but it was the following year that things really took off. The domination enjoyed by Ricardo and Cooke's Electric Telegraph Company came to an end as rival companies arrived on the scene, and thirteen telegraph instruments based on a variety of designs were displayed at the Great Exhibition of 1851 in London, fueling further interest in the new technology. These developments gave the nascent industry the jolt it needed to emerge from the shadow of the railways.

The telegraph was doing well in other countries, too. By 1852, there was a network of 1,493 miles of wire in Prussia, radiating out from Berlin. Turnbull, who compiled a survey of telegraph systems around the world, noted that instead of stringing telegraph wires from poles, "the Prussian method of burying wires beneath the surface protects them from destruction by malice, and makes them less liable to injury by lightning." Austria had 1,053 miles of wire, and Canada 983 miles; there were also electric telegraphs in operation in Tuscany, Saxony and Bavaria, Spain, Russia, and Holland, and networks were being established in Australia, Cuba, and the Valparaiso region of Chile. Competition thrived between the inventors of rival telegraph instruments and signaling codes as networks sprung up in different countries and the technology matured.

Turnbull was pleased to note that the wonders of the telegraph had managed to rouse the "lethargic" inhabitants of India into building a network. He was even ruder about the French, whom he described as "inferior in telegraphic enterprise to most of the other European companies." This view was unfounded, for the French had not only invented the telegraph but named it too. But their lead in the field of optical telegraphy had actually worked against them, and the French were reluctant to abandon the old technology in favor of the new. François Moigno, a French writer, compiled a treatise on the state of the French electric telegraph network, whose size he put at a total of 750 miles in 1852—and which he condemned for leading to the demise of the old optical telegraphs.

Sending and receiving messages—which by the early 1850s had been dubbed "telegrams"— soon became part of everyday life for many people around the world. But because this service was expensive, only the rich could afford to use the network to send trivial messages; most people used the telegraph strictly to convey really urgent news.

Sending a message was a matter of going into the office of one of the telegraph companies and filling in a form giving the postal address of the recipient and a message expressed as briefly as possible, since messages were charged by the word, as well as by the distance from sender to receiver. Once the message was ready to go, it would be handed to the clerk, who would transmit it up the line.

Telegraph lines radiated out from central telegraph offices in major towns, with each line passing through several local offices, and long-distance wires linking central offices in different towns. Each telegraph office could only communicate with offices on the same spoke of the network, and the central telegraph office at the end of the line. This meant that messages from one office to another on the same spoke could be transmitted directly, but that all other messages had to be telegraphed to the central office and were then retransmitted down another spoke of the network toward their final destination.

Once received at the nearest telegraph office, the message was transcribed on a paper slip and taken on foot by a messenger boy directly to the recipient. A reply, if one was given, would then be taken back to the office; some telegraph companies offered special rates for a message plus a prepaid reply.

Young men were eager to enter the business as messengers, since it was often a stepping-stone to better things. One of the duties of messenger boys was to sweep out the operating room in the mornings, and this provided an opportunity to tinker on the apparatus and learn the telegrapher's craft. Thomas Edison and steel magnate and philanthropist Andrew Carnegie both started out as telegraph messenger boys. "A messenger boy in those days had many pleasures," wrote Carnegie in his autobiography, which includes rather rose-tinted reminiscences of the life of a messenger boy in the 1850s. "There were wholesale fruit stores, where a pocketful of apples was sometimes to be had for the prompt delivery of a message; bakers and confectioners' shops where sweet cakes were sometimes given to him. He met very kind men to whom he looked up with respect; they spoke a pleasant word and complimented him on his promptness, perhaps asking him to deliver a message on the way back to the office. I do not know a situation in which a boy is more apt to attract attention, which is all a really clever boy requires in order to rise."

Though its business was the sending and receiving of messages, much like e-mail today, the actual operation of the telegraph had more in common with an on-line chat room. Operators did more than just send messages back and forth; they had to call up certain stations, ask for messages to be repeated, and verify the reception of messages. In countries where Morse's apparatus was used, skilled operators quickly learned to read incoming messages by listening to the clicking of the apparatus, rather than reading the dots and dashes marked on the paper tape, and this practice soon became the standard means of receiving. It also encouraged more social interaction over the wires, and a new telegraphic jargon quickly emerged.

Rather than spell out every word ("PHILADELPHIA CALLING NEW YORK") letter by letter in laborious detail, conventions arose by which telegraphers talked to each other over the wires using short abbreviations. There was no single standard: different dialects or customs arose on different telegraph lines. However, one listing of common abbreviations compiled in 1859 includes "I I" (dot dot, dot dot) for "I AM READY"; "G A" (dash dash dot, dot dash) for "GO AHEAD"; "S F D" for "STOP FOR DINNER"; "G M" for "GOOD MORNING." This system enabled telegraphers to greet one another and handle most common situations as easily as if they were in the same room.

Numbers were also used as abbreviations: 1 meant "WAIT A MOMENT"; 2, "GET ANSWER IMMEDIATELY"; 33, "ANSWER PAID HERE." All telegraph offices on a branch line shared one wire, so at any time there could be several telegraphers listening in to wait for the line to become available. They could also chat, play chess, or tell jokes during quiet periods.

Although the telegraph, unlike later forms of electrical communication, did not require the consumer who was sending or receiving a message to own any special equipment—or understand how to use it—it was still a source of confusion to those unfamiliar with it. And just like the apocryphal story of the woman who tried to send her husband tomato soup by pouring it into the telephone handset, there are numerous stories of telegraph-inspired confusion and misunderstanding.

One magazine article, "Strange Notions of the Telegraph," gives several examples of incomprehension: "One wiseacre imagined that the wires were hollow, and that papers on which the communications were written were blown through them, like peas through a pea shooter. Another decided that the wires were speaking tubes." And one man in Nebraska thought the telegraph wires were a kind of tightrope; he watched the line carefully "to see the man run along the wires with the letter bags."

In one case a man came into a telegraph office in Maine, filled in a telegraph form, and asked for his message to be sent immediately. The telegraph operator tapped it out in Morse to send it up the line and then spiked the form on the "sent" hook. Seeing the paper on the hook, the man assumed that it had yet to be transmitted. After waiting a few minutes, he asked the telegrapher, "Aren't you going to send that dispatch?" The operator explained that he already had. "No, you haven't," said the man, "there it is now on the hook."

Another story concerned a woman in Karlsruhe, Prussia, who went to a telegraph office in 1870 with a dish full of sauerkraut, which she asked to have telegraphed to her son, who was a soldier fighting in the war between Prussia and France. The operator had great difficulty convincing her that the telegraph was not capable of transmitting objects. But the woman insisted that she had heard of soldiers being ordered to the front by telegraph. "How could so many soldiers have been sent to France by telegraph?" she asked.

As one magazine article of the time pointed out, much confusion resulted from the new electric jargon, which imposed new meanings on existing words. "Thus, when it is said that a current of electricity flows along a wire, that the wire or the current carries a message, the speaker takes language universally understood, relating to a fluid moving from one place to another, and a parcel or a letter transported from place to place." One young girl asked her mother how the messages "get past the poles without being torn." The mother is said to have replied, "They are sent in a fluid state, my dear."

And there was a widespread belief that it was possible to hear the messages as they passed along the wires. According to a book, *Anecdotes of the Telegraph,* published in 1848, "a very general but erroneous idea, even among the better order of folks, is that the humming aeolian harp-like effect of the wind on the suspended wire is caused by the messages passing." A typical story concerned a telegraph operator who worked in a station in the Catskill Mountains, where the wind often whistled through the wires. One day a local man asked how business was doing. "Lively," said the operator. "Well, I didn't think so," said the man, "I ain't heard a dispatch go up in three or four days."

The retranscription of the message at the receiving station also confused some people. One woman preparing to send a telegram is said to have remarked as she filled out the telegraph form, "I must write this out afresh, as I don't want Mrs. M. to receive this untidy telegram." Another woman, on receiving a telegram from her son asking for money, said she was not so easily taken in; she knew her son's handwriting very well, she said, and the message, transcribed at the receiving office, obviously hadn't come from him.

As telegraph networks sprung up in different countries, the benefits of joining them soon became apparent. The first interconnection treaty was signed on October 3, 1849, between Prussia and Austria, so that messages could be sent from Vienna to Berlin. It was an inefficient system; rather than running a wire across the border, a special joint telegraph office was constructed, staffed by representatives of each country's telegraph company, who were connected to their respective national networks. When a message needed to be passed from one country to another, it was transcribed by the clerks at one end of the office, who then physically handed it over to their opposite numbers at the other end of the office for retransmission.

Similar agreements were soon in place between Prussia and Saxony, and Austria and Bavaria. In 1850, the four states established the Austro-German Telegraph Union to regulate tariffs and set common rules for interconnection. The following year, the Morse telegraph system was adopted as a standard to allow direct connections to be established between the four networks. Soon interconnection agreements had also been signed between France, Belgium, Switzerland, Spain, and Sardinia. But if Britain was to be connected to the growing European network, a significant barrier would have to be overcome: the English Channel.

Actually, experiments with sending messages along underwater telegraph cables had been going on almost since the earliest days of electric telegraphy. Wheatstone had tried it out in Wales, sending messages from a boat to a lighthouse, and in 1840 he proposed the establishment of a cross-Channel telegraph. But at that time the telegraph had yet to prove itself over short distances on land, let alone across water.

Morse, too, had a go at underwater telegraphy. In 1843, after coating a wire in rubber and encasing it in a lead pipe, he sent messages along a submerged cable between Castle Garden and Governors Island in New York Harbor. He also succeeded in using water itself as the conductor, with metal plates dipped in the water on each bank of a river and connected to the telegraph wires. (Wheatstone did some similar experiments across the river Thames in the presence of Prince Albert the same year.) At any rate, Morse was sufficiently pleased with the results across a few feet of water that, in typical indefatigable Morse fashion, he predicted that it wouldn't be long before there would be telegraph wires across the Atlantic.

For advocates of cross-Channel telegraphy, however, there were practical problems to be overcome. Laying a rubber-coated wire inside a lead pipe was possible in New York Harbor; laying a pipe along the seabed across the English Channel was another matter entirely. And if the cable was to last any length of time, an alternative to coating it in rubber would have to be found, since rubber quickly deteriorated in water.

The solution was to use gutta-percha, a kind of rubbery gum obtained from the gutta-percha tree, which grows in the jungles of Southeast Asia. One useful property of gutta-percha is that it is hard at room temperature but softens when immersed in hot water and can be molded into any shape. The Victorians used it much as we use plastic today. Dolls, chess pieces, and ear trumpets were all made of gutta-percha. And although it was expensive, it turned out to be ideal for insulating cables.

Once the question of what to use for insulation had been resolved, John Brett, a retired antique dealer, and his younger brother Jacob, an engineer, decided to embark upon building a telegraph link between England and France. They got the appropriate permission from the British and French governments and ordered a wire coated with a quarter of an inch of gutta-percha from the Gutta Percha Company in London. Their plan was breathtakingly low-tech: They intended to spool the wire (which was about the thickness of the power cable of a modern domestic appliance) out of the stern of a boat as it steamed across the Channel. They would then connect telegraph instruments at each end, and their company, the grandly named General Oceanic and Subterranean

Electric Printing Telegraph Company, would be in business. On August 28, 1850, with their cable wound onto a vast drum and mounted on the back of a small steam tug, the *Goliath*, they set out for France.

Things did not go according to plan. For starters, the wire was so thin that it wouldn't sink; it simply floated pathetically in the water behind the boat. The Bretts' response was to clamp weights around the wire at regular intervals to get it to sink. By the evening, they had arrived at Cap Gris-Nez near Calais in France, where they wired up their newfangled telegraph instrument—the very latest automatic printing model—and waited for the first test message to be sent from England. It came out as gibberish.

The cable was working, but the messages were being garbled because the surrounding water changed the cable's electrical properties in a way that was poorly understood at the time. Effectively, it meant that the staccato pulses of electricity were smoothed out, and the Bretts' high-speed automatic machines transmitted so fast that succeeding pulses overlapped and became indistinct. But, using an old-fashioned single-needle telegraph, they were eventually able to send a few messages manually, in much the same way that a preacher in a resonant cathedral must speak slowly and distinctly in order to be understood. However, the next day the cable met a watery end; a French fisherman snagged it in his net, and when he brought it to the surface he hacked off a piece to see what it was. Deciding that it was a hitherto unknown form of seaweed with a gold center, he took it to show his friends in Boulogne.

It took the Bretts over a year to raise the money for another cable, and they would probably have had to give up altogether but for the intervention of Thomas Crampton, a railway engineer. He put up half the £15,000 needed, and also designed the new cable. He wanted to protect his investment, so the new cable consisted of four gutta-percha-covered wires twisted together and wrapped in tar-covered hemp, and then encased in a cladding of tar-covered iron cords. It was far tougher than the first cable, and it weighed thirty times as much. This meant it was harder to lay—not because it wouldn't sink, like the first cable, but because it was so heavy it ran off the drum on the back of the boat faster than the Bretts wanted it to. It was so hard to control, in fact, that all the cable had been paid out before the boat carrying it reached France. Fortunately, the Bretts had brought along a spare piece of cable, which they spliced on, and in November 1851, after a few weeks of testing, the cable was opened to the public. The first direct message from London to Paris was sent in 1852.

The success of the Channel cable led to a boom in submarine telegraphy—to the delight of the directors of the Gutta Percha Company. With a virtual monopoly on the supply of gutta-percha, they suddenly found they were sitting on a gold mine. The problem of laying a telegraph link across a stretch of water seemed to have been

cracked: It was simply a matter of making sure that the cable was properly insulated, strong enough not to break, and heavy enough to sink, and that messages weren't sent too quickly along it. Before long Dover had been linked to Ostend, and after two failed attempts England was linked to Ireland in 1853. Further underwater links across the North Sea directly connected Britain with the coasts of Germany, Russia, and Holland. John Brett soon turned his attention to linking Europe with Africa and succeeded in connecting Corsica and Sardinia to Genoa on the European mainland in 1854. But the following year, he failed in his attempt to reach the North African coast, which involved laying a cable across the deepest and most mountainous part of the Mediterranean seabed. Brett lost a lot of money, and his failure proved that there were limits to submarine telegraphy after all. The prospect of linking Europe and North America seemed as far away as ever.

CHAPTER **15**

The New Journalism

Michael Schudson

Michael Schudson is a professor of communications and a historian of the development of the institutions of mass communication in the United States. In this excerpt from his book Discovering the News, *he demonstrates how the familiar models of news as information and news as entertainment grew significantly out of the organizational struggles of the New York press for readership in the late nineteenth century.*

Reporting was an invention of the end of the nineteenth century, but it was a two-part invention: the emergence of the new occupation played off against the industrialization of the newspaper. And while there was much that united the

ideology of reporters, there was much that divided the identities of the newspapers for which they worked. In New York, most of the major papers were direct descendants of the penny press: the *Sun*, the *Herald*, the *Tribune*, and the *Times*. Of papers that antedated the penny press, only the *Evening Post* still had an important following. The two largest papers were the *World*, begun in 1859 and revived by Joseph Pulitzer in 1883, and the *Journal*, begun in 1882 by Pulitzer's brother but escorted to the stage of history when William Randolph Hearst bought it in 1895. Both of these papers were sharply distinguished from the others; they represented what contemporaries generally referred to as "the new journalism." The established papers found their competition and their manners deeply disturbing and wrote of them with the same moral horror that had greeted their own arrival in New York journalism fifty years before.

While reporters subscribed concurrently to the ideals of factuality and of entertainment in writing the news, some of the papers they worked for chose identities that strongly emphasized one ideal or the other. The *World* and the *Journal* chose to be entertaining; the old penny press, especially the *Times* after Adolph Ochs rejuvenated it in 1896, took the path of factuality. I shall refer to these two models of journalism as the ideal of the "story" and the ideal of "information." When telling stories is taken to be the role of the newspaper, journalism is said to fulfill what George Herbert Mead described as an "aesthetic" function. Mead wrote that some parts of the news—the election results or stock market reports—emphasize exclusively "the truth value of news," but for most of the news in a paper, the "enjoyability" or "consummatory value" is more important. The news serves primarily to create, for readers, satisfying aesthetic experiences which help them to interpret their own lives and to relate them to the nation, town, or class to which they belong. Mead took this to be the actual, and the proper, function of a newspaper and observed that it is manifest in the fact that "the reporter is generally sent out to get a story, not the facts."[1] In this view, the newspaper acts as a guide to living not so much by providing facts as by selecting them and framing them.

An alternative model of the newspaper's role proposes that the newspaper is uniquely defined as a genre of literature precisely to the extent that the facts it provides are unframed, that it purveys pure "information." Walter Benjamin suggested that "information" is a novel form of communication, a product of fully developed capitalism, whose distinguishing characteristic is that it "lays claim to prompt verifiability." Its aim, above all, is to be "understandable in itself." While it may actually be no more exact than varieties of "intelligence" of the past, unlike earlier intelligence, which might be justified by reference to the miraculous, "it is indispensable for information to sound plausible." For this reason, in Benjamin's analysis, information "proves incompatible with the spirit of storytelling."[2] This view of the newspaper is echoed in the recent work of Alvin Gouldner, who refers to news as "decontextualized" communication. It is a form of what Basil Bernstein, on whose work Gouldner relies, calls an "elaborated code," in which all is spelled out, nothing left to implicit or tacit understanding.[3]

Rightly or wrongly, the informational ideal in journalism is associated with fairness, objectivity, scrupulous dispassion. Newspapers which stress information tend to be seen as more reliable than "story" papers. But who makes this judgment and on what grounds? Who regards the information model as more trustworthy than the story ideal, and what is meant, after all, by "reliable" or "trustworthy"? If journalists on the whole give credit to both ideas at once, how is it that different newspaper institutions come to stand for one or the other? And how is it that those which stand for the information model come to be regarded as the more responsible?

It is the unexceptional theme of this chapter that, in the most general terms, there is a connection between the educated middle class and information and a connection between the middle and working classes and the story ideal. The puzzle here, as in most other discussions of popular culture, is why this should be the case. What is it about information that seems to appeal to the educated middle class? What is it about the story that seems to attract the working-class reader? Is it right to associate the information model with the notion of objectivity? Should we regard it as a "higher" form of journalism than the story model? In the critical decades from 1883 to the first years of this century, when at the same moment yellow journalism was at its height and the *New York Times* established itself as the most reliable and respected newspaper in the country, why did wealthier people in New York read the *Times* and less wealthy people read the *World?* What is the meaning of the two journalisms of the 1890s?

JOURNALISM AS ENTERTAINMENT: JOSEPH PULITZER AND THE *NEW YORK WORLD*

Joseph Pulitzer began his newspaper career in St. Louis. Party papers prevailed there until the 1870s when "independent journalism" gained a foothold. A turning point for St. Louis journalism came in 1871 when the *Morning Globe* hired Chicago's Joseph McCullagh as editor. McCullagh stressed news, rather than opinion, and, on what was by then the increasingly familiar model of James Gordon Bennett, concentrated on local police, court, society, and street reporting.

Pulitzer was an Austrian Jewish immigrant who arrived in the United States in 1864, at the age of seventeen, to fight in the Civil War. In St. Louis, after the war, he studied law and was admitted to the bar, but, in part because of his limited facility in English, he did not practice law. Instead, he became a reporter for the city's German-language newspaper, the *Westliche Post.* Active and successful in journalism and in politics—first Republican, then Democratic—Pulitzer was able to buy the *St. Louis Post and Dispatch* in 1878. He served as its publisher, editor, and business manager. Under his guidance, the paper became more audacious in promoting the Democratic Party and turned much brighter in its style. It began to carry statistics of trade from the Merchants' Exchange, the produce markets, and the waterfront. In 1879 it

became the first St. Louis paper to publish quotations on stocks issued by local firms. Pulitzer repeatedly appealed to "the people," by which he meant, it seems, "the stable householder, of whatever class."[4] The *Post and Dispatch* was antagonistic to labor, and it held to the high price of five cents an issue. According to Julian Rammelkamp, historian of Pulitzer's years as St. Louis editor, "The fundamental aims of the paper were middle class—to foster the development of St. Louis as a business center and as an attractive place of residence for the average citizen."[5] Pulitzer's great innovation in his years in St. Louis was the development of the newspaper crusade. The crusade was by no means unknown elsewhere, especially in New York, but Pulitzer made startling headlines and political expos's a constant feature of his paper, stimulating circulation and presumably changing the city for the better.

In 1883 Pulitzer plugged his Western voice into the amplifier of the East, New York City. He bought the *New York World,* a paper of some reputation during the 1860s and 1870s which had fallen on hard times. When Pulitzer bought it, its circulation was about fifteen thousand. A year later it was sixty thousand. In another year it was one hundred thousand, and by the fall of 1886 it passed a quarter million. Pulitzer attributed this astonishingly rapid success to his editorial position. "We can conscientiously say," he wrote in an 1884 editorial, "that we believe the success of THE WORLD is largely due to the sound principles of the paper rather than to its news features or its price."[6]

There was a measure of truth in this. It is not an accident that the *World* and Hearst's *Journal,* the city's two most widely read papers at the turn of the century, were both Democratic. But this was not the mainspring, or mainstay, of Pulitzer's (or Hearst's) success. Pulitzer's energy and innovation in business practice played a larger role. Publishing the *World* at a penny a copy, he forced the *Times* to drop its price from four cents to two, the *Herald,* from three to two, and the *Tribune,* from four to three (the two-cent *Sun* stayed the same). He initiated the practice of selling advertising space on the basis of actual circulation and selling it at fixed prices; at the same time, he abandoned the traditional penalties for advertisers who used illustrations or broke column rules.[7] Pulitzer thus helped rationalize newspapers' business practice and the relations between newspapers and advertisers. . . .

Pulitzer's rationalization of the *World*'s advertising policies helped the *World* adapt to general changes in the social organization of business, but the innovation most responsible for the paper's rapidly growing circulation was, in a word, sensationalism. The sensationalism Pulitzer brought to New York was not altogether revolutionary. Its attention to local news, especially crime and scandal and high society, continued in the tradition of the penny press. Indeed, this subject-matter focus, which had scandalized the established press of the 1830s, was typical of most major papers by the 1880s in New York—with some variation, of course, and with the lagging and Olympian exception of the *Evening Post*. But what defined sensationalism in the 1880s was less substance than style: how extravagantly should the news be displayed? Sensationalism meant self-advertisement. If, as James Gordon Bennett recognized in the 1840s, everything, including advertising, could and should be news, the sensational papers of the 1880s and 1890s discovered that everything, including news, could and should be advertising for the newspapers. For instance, the *World* in the 1890s regularly took a column or two on the front page to boast of its high circulation. It regularly headlined the fact, in its advertising pages, that it printed more advertisements than any other paper in the country and included the facts and figures to prove it.

Self-advertisement, as I use the term, is anything about newspaper layout and newspaper policy, outside of basic news gathering, which is designed to attract the eye and small change of readers. One of the most important developments of self-advertising in this sense was the use of illustrations. Pulitzer, perhaps feeling that illustrations

lowered the dignity of a newspaper, intended at first to eliminate them from the *World*, but he found, as *The Journalist* wrote, that "the circulation of the paper went with the cuts."[8] Pulitzer reversed field and, within the first year of his *World* management, hired Valerian Gribayedoff, a portrait artist, and Walt McDougall, a cartoonist. Their efforts, according to Robert Taft's history of American photography, "mark the beginning of the modern era of newspaper illustration."[9] The *New York Daily Graphic*, in 1873, became the first American daily to regularly use illustrations—and it offered little except illustrations. At first, Pulitzer did not regard the *World* as competing with the *Daily Graphic*. By the summer of 1884, however, Pulitzer classified both papers as "illustrated daily journals"; by 1889, the *World*'s extravagant use of both political cartoons and, especially in the Sunday editions, "cuts whose only justification was the fun of looking at pictures" drove the *Daily Graphic* out of business.[10]

Another major development in self-advertisement was larger and darker headlines. Here Pulitzer remained conservative for years. Rather than introduce headlines spanning several columns, he emphasized important stories simply by adding more banks of headlines within the same column. Headlines, like advertisements, abided by column-rules. Not until 1889 did the *World* run a two-column headline, but by the late 1890s, especially through the competition with Hearst, large, screaming headlines were frequently a part of the *World*'s make-up.[11]

Hearst proudly proclaimed: "It is the *Journal*'s policy to engage brains as well as to get the news, for the public is even more fond of entertainment than it is of information."[12] Melville Stone, of the *Chicago Morning News* and *Daily News*, maintained that the newspaper had three functions: to inform, to interpret, and to entertain.[13]

Pulitzer did not talk up the idea of entertainment, but the *World* came to embody it. The importance of the entertaining function of the paper was marked especially by the growth of the Sunday *World* which, like Sunday newspapers still, was as close to an illustrated magazine as to a daily newspaper in style and content. Sunday papers had been rare early in the century. In 1842 only one New Yorker in twenty-six bought a Sunday paper, while one in seven bought a daily. In 1850, after heavy Irish immigration, one in nine New Yorkers bought a Sunday paper. The Irish and other later immigrants came to the country without the American conservatism about Sabbath observance. This, plus the practice newspapers developed during the Civil War of printing special Sunday editions with war news, made it easier for papers to take the plunge into Sunday journalism and to appeal directly to the interests of readers for diversion on the day of rest. By 1889, one New Yorker in two bought a Sunday paper, making more Sunday newspapers readers than daily readers that year.[14] Charles Dana, editor of the *Sun,* estimated in 1894 that a paper with a daily edition of 50,000, at two or three cents, would have a Sunday edition of 100,000 to 150,000, at five cents.[15] What readers found and liked in the Sunday papers, they began to find in the daily press, too. Pulitzer used the Sunday *World* "as a laboratory to test ideas that finally proved to be applicable throughout the week."[16] Illustrations and comic strips (the first color comic strips appeared in the Sunday *World* in 1894) spread from the Sunday paper to the daily editions. . . .

Newspapers, like the *World,* which sought a wide and general readership, responded to the changing experience, perceptions, and aspirations of urban dwellers. This meant, indeed, an enlargement of the "entertainment" function of the newspaper, but it also meant the expansion of what has recently been called the "use-paper" rather than the newspaper, the daily journal as a compendium of tips for urban survival. City living, by the 1880s, had become very different from what it had been in the 1830s. It was much more a mosaic of races and social types; it was much more a maelstrom of social and geographic movement. Geographic mobility for a growing middle class was something it had never

been before—it was a daily round of movement from home to work and back again. Improved urban transportation and the movement of the middle class into the suburbs meant that this daily movement could be considerable in terms of miles and time consumed. Horse-drawn omnibuses helped urban expansion away from a port-based locus beginning in the 1830s, but the growth of intracity transportation was even more dramatic in the last half of the century. The walking city of 1850 had become a riding city by 1900. The expansion of horse-drawn buses and railways (horse manure and urine had become a serious pollution problem in New York by 1890), and later cable lines and electric surface lines, elevated rapid transit and subways, made mass suburban living possible by 1900 and created a new segregation in the city: the poor lived near the city's center, while the middle class moved farther out.[17]

This had several consequences for the newspaper. Riding an omnibus or street railway was a novel experience. For the first time in human history, people other than the very wealthy could, as a part of their daily life, ride in vehicles they were not responsible for driving. Their eyes and their hands were free; they could read on the bus. George Juergens has suggested that the *World*'s change to a sensational style and layout was adapted to the needs of commuters: reading on the bus was difficult with the small print and large-sized pages of most papers. So the *World* reduced the size of the page, increased the size of headlines and the use of pictures, and developed the "lead" paragraph, in which all of the most vital information of a story would be concentrated.[18] From the 1840s, the "lead" had been pushed by the high cost of telegraphic transmission of news; now it was pulled by the abbreviated moments in which newspapers were being read. It is likely, then, that the growing use of illustration and large headlines in newspapers was as much an adaptation to the new habits of the middle class as to the new character of the immigrant working class. . . .

JOURNALISM AS INFORMATION: THE RISE OF THE *NEW YORK TIMES*

The *World* may have set the pace for modern mass-circulation journalism, but after 1896 the *New York Times* established the standard. *The Journalist,* in a 1902 editorial on "Standards in American Journalism," recalled Charles Dudley Warner's claim in 1881 that the successful newspaper of the future would be the best newspaper: ". . . only that type of newspaper can live which represents something, accurately and sufficiently, to command a growing and attached clientele." *The Journalist* took this to be a prophecy of the success of the *New York Times:* ". . . there is a clear recognition as the road to substantial success in the newspaper business of the course which the *New York Times* has aimed to follow. . . ."[19] Reporter and newspaper critic Will Irwin wrote in 1911 that the *Times* came "the nearest of any newspaper to presenting a truthful picture of life in New York and the world at large."[20] Melville Stone, writing in the *Times'* seventy-fifth anniversary issue (1926), praised publisher Adolph Ochs for having defied the view that only the sensational newspaper could be a successful newspaper: "He in the end taught them [his competitors] that decency meant dollars."[21] There would probably have been little dissent from Frank Presbrey's estimation of the *Times,* in his 1929 *History and Development of Advertising,* as "the world's most influential newspaper. . . ."[22]

George Jones, who had edited the *Times* from 1869 until his death in 1891, had boasted that no man had ever been asked to subscribe to, or advertise in, the *Times.*[23] Ochs had no such contempt for solicitation. He became the first publisher, in 1898, to solicit circulation by telephone. He offered a bicycle tour of France and England to the one hundred persons bringing in the most new subscribers. The former campaign, of course, reached only the relatively well-to-do who had telephones. The latter scheme focused on school and college teachers and stressed, in the contest advertising, that "To be seen reading *The New York Times* is a stamp of respectability."[24]

Two months after Ochs took over the paper, the famous motto, "All the News That's Fit to Print," first appeared on the editorial page. At the same time, Ochs started a circulation-building contest offering $100 for a better slogan. The winning entry was "All the World's News, but Not a School for Scandal." Still, the editors preferred their own invention, and by February, 1897, "All the News That's Fit to Print" was moved permanently to the front page.

The *Times'* slogan, like its general statement of policy, emphasized decency as much as accuracy. The *Times* could not, and did not, compete with the *World* and the *Journal* for circulation; advertising in *The Journalist* in 1902, the *Times* claimed the highest circulation of any newspaper in the city—and then, in smaller print, excepted the *World* and the *Journal,* as if they were in another category of publication altogether.[25] In a sense, they were, and the *Times* used them as a foil in promoting itself. The *Times* joined the *Sun* and *Press* and other papers in a new "moral war" in journalism. It pointedly advertised itself with the slogan, "It does not soil the breakfast cloth," as opposed to the "yellow" journals.[26] Some items from the *Times,* in the winter of 1897, are probably representative of its attitude toward the yellow press. In a story headed "The Modern Newspaper" on February 12, the *Times* covered a speech at the Press Club of Colgate University given by the city editor of the *Utica Observer* in which editor W. W. Canfield attacked papers which padded news, printed private matters, spread indecent literature, and proved themselves unreliable. He pleaded for more newspapers like the *Times.* "A newspaper," he said, "was declared to be a companion, and surely the intelligent would not accept as a companion the vicious and the depraved." On the same day, the *Times* editorialized on "Freak Journalism and the Ball." It attacked the *World's* extravagant coverage of the Bradley Martin ball at the Waldorf, suggesting that the *World*'s artists made their drawings of the festivities before the ball took place. (It should be observed that the *Times* did not skimp on its own coverage of the ball. It reported the gala affair in a page-one, column-one story on February 12 and devoted all of page two to detailing who the guests were, what they wore, and where they dined before the great event.) . . .

There is, then, a moral dimension to the reading of different kinds of newspapers; there is pride and shame in reading. This helps establish the plausibility of the hypothesis that the *Times*' readership was not won simply by the utility of the articles it printed for businessmen and lawyers or the resonance of its political outlook with the politics of affluent readers. The *Times* attracted readers among the wealthy and among those aspiring to wealth and status, in part, because it was socially approved. It was itself a badge of respectability.

But this only poses the question in a different way: what made the *Times* respectable? What made it seem morally superior? Was it deemed respectable because it appealed to the affluent? Or did it appeal to the affluent because it was respectable? And if the latter, is "respectability" to be understood as a moral ideal emerging from the life experience of a particular social group at a particular time or as a moral ideal with legitimate claims to wider allegiance or, perhaps, both?

This repeats, within the field of journalism, perennial questions about high culture and popular culture. What distinguishes them? Can we find any grounds for asserting that "art" is superior to popular culture? The question is of sociological interest because the taste for high culture is so regularly associated with educated and wealthy classes, the taste for popular culture, with lower classes. And yet, while the tastes of different classes remain different from one another in a given period, they change over time. Up until about the Civil War in the United States, the most sophisticated elements in the population preferred their literature, and even their journalism, flowery rather than plain, magniloquent rather

than straightforward.[27] By 1900, when "information" journalism was sponsored by an economic and social elite, it was prized, but in 1835, when the first steps toward an information model were taken by the penny press in challenge of the elite of the day, it was reviled. The moral war between information journalism and story journalism in New York in the 1890s was, like the moral wars of the 1830s, a cover for class conflict. . . .

The readers of the *World* were relatively dependent and nonparticipant. The experience engendered by affluence and education makes one comfortable with a certain journalistic orientation, one which may indeed be, in some respects, more mature, more encompassing, more differentiated, more integrated. It may also be, in its own ways, more limited; refinement in newspapers, people, and sugar, is bleaching. If the *World*'s readers might have longed for more control of their lives, the readers of the *Times* may have wished for more nutrients in theirs.

At the turn of the century and even as late as the 1920s, "objectivity" was not a term journalists or critics of journalism used. Newspapers were criticized for failing to stick to the facts, and the *Times* boasted that it printed "all the news"—by which it meant information. But this was not objectivity; the attachment to information did not betray much anxiety about the subjectivity of personal perspective. The *Times* in 1900 trusted to information, that body of knowledge understandable in itself without context (or with a context taken for granted). That was not to last. By the 1920s, journalists no longer believed that facts could be understood in themselves; they no longer held to the sufficiency of information; they no longer shared in the vanity of neutrality that had characterized the educated middle class of the Progressive era. In the twentieth century, the skepticism and suspicion which thinkers of the late nineteenth century, like Nietzsche, taught, became part of general education. People came to see even the findings of facts as interested, even memory and dreams as selective, even rationality itself a front for interest or will or prejudice. This influenced journalism in the 1920s and 1930s and gave rise to the ideal of objectivity as we know it.

NOTES

1. George Herbert Mead, "The Nature of Aesthetic Experience," *International Journal of Ethics* 36 (July 1926): 390. John Dewey made a similar point: ". . . the newspaper is the only genuinely popular form of literature we have achieved. The newspaper hasn't been ashamed of localism, it has revelled in it, perhaps wallowed is the word. I am not arguing that it is high-class literature, or for the most part good literature, even from its own standpoint. But it is per-manently successful romance and drama; and that much can hardly be said for anything else in our literary lines" ("Americanism and Localism," *The Dial* 68 [June 1920]: 686).

2. Walter Benjamin, *Illuminations* (New York: Schocken Books, 1969), pp. 88–89.

3. Alvin Gouldner, *The Dialectic of Ideology and Technology* (New York: Seabury Press, 1976); and Basil Bernstein, "Elaborated and Restricted Codes" in "The Ethnography of Communication," ed. John Gumperz and Dell Hymes, *American Anthropologist* 66, (1964), pt. 2: 55–69. See also Basil Bernstein, *Class, Codes, and Control* (New York: Schocken Books, 1974).

4. Julian S. Rammelkamp, *Pulitzer's Post-Dispatch 1878–1883* (Princeton: Princeton University Press, 1967), p. 109.

5. Ibid., p. 239.

6. *New York World*, September 30, 1884, quoted in Willard G. Bleyer, *Main Currents in the History of American Journalism* (Boston: Houghton Mifflin, 1927), p. 333.

7. Frank Presbrey, *The History and Development of Advertising* (Garden City, N.Y.: Doubleday, Doran, 1929), p. 356.

8. *The Journalist* (August 22, 1885); quoted in George Juergens, *Joseph Pulitzer and the New York World* (Princeton: Princeton University Press, 1966), p. 95.

9. Robert Taft, *Photography and the American Scene* (New York: Macmillan, 1942), p. 428.

10. Juergens, *Joseph Pulitzer*, pp. 98–105.

11. Ibid., p. 27. Juergens stresses the conservatism of *World* typography in Pulitzer's first years.

12. Quoted in W. A. Swanberg, *Citizen Hearst* (New York: Charles Scribner's, 1961), p. 90. The statement appeared in a *Journal* editorial on November 8, 1896.

13. Melville Stone, *Fifty Years a Journalist* (Garden City, N.Y.: Doubleday, Page, 1921), pp. 53, 107.

14. Juergens, *Joseph Pulitzer*, pp. 56–57.

15. Charles Dana, *The Art of Newspaper Making* (New York: D. Appleton, 1900), p. 84. From a lecture delivered at Cornell University, January 11, 1894.

16. Juergens, *Joseph Pulitzer*, p. 57.

17. See Theodore Hershberg et al., "The 'Journey-to-Work': An Empirical Investigation of Work, Residence and Transportation, Philadelphia, 1850 and 1880" in *Toward an Interdisciplinary History of the City: Work, Space, Family and Group Experience in Nineteenth-Century Philadelphia*, ed. Theodore Hershberg (New York: Oxford University Press, forthcoming).

18. Juergens, *Joseph Pulitzer*, pp. 39, 47.

19. *The Journalist* 32 (December 27, 1902).

20. Will Irwin, "The American Newspaper. VI: The Editor and the News," *Colliers* 47 (April 1, 1911).

21. *New York Times*, September 19, 1926.

22. Presbrey, *History and Development of Advertising*, p. 354.

23. Elmer Davis, *History of the* New York Times: *1851–1921* (New York: The New York Times, 1921), p. 218.

24. Meyer Berger, *The Story of the* New York Times *1851–1951* (New York: Simon and Schuster, 1951; reprint ed., New York: Arno Press, 1970), p. 124.

25. *The Journalist* 32 (December 20, 1902).

26. Davis, *History of the New York Times*, pp. 223–224.

27. Edmund Wilson, *Patriotic Gore* (London: Oxford University Press, 1962), pp. 635–669, discusses the shift in American tastes in prose and in oratory from the well-embroidered to the efficient and plain-spoken in the mid-nineteenth century.

CHAPTER 16

The Telephone Takes Command

Claude S. Fischer

Claude S. Fischer is professor of sociology at the University of California at Berkeley. He is the author of America Calling: A Social History of the Telephone to 1940.

FOUNDING THE TELEPHONE INDUSTRY

. . . Alexander Graham Bell had been trying to improve the telegraph when he constructed the first telephone in March of 1876. That month he filed his patent claim, later to be a matter of legal dispute, and in May he showed the primitive device at the Centennial Exposition in Philadelphia. Alexander Graham Bell and his associates spent much of the next year or so giving demonstrations around the country of this "wonder," sometimes borrowing telegraph wires for long-distance calls (and sometimes failing). Watson would, for example, sing over the telephone to an audience gathered elsewhere in town. In 1877 a New York poster announced "An Entertainment of the Sunday School of Old John St. M. E. Church," including recitations, singing, and an exhibition of "Prof. Bell's Speaking and Singing Telephone." Admission was 25 cents.[1] These stunts garnered considerable publicity and awe as journalists relayed the news around the world.

Making a business of what was a novelty was more difficult. The backers of Alexander Graham Bell's telegraph work were his father-in-law, Gardiner Hubbard, and the father of one of his speech students, Thomas Sanders. In July 1877 the three men reorganized as the Bell Telephone Company, with Hubbard as trustee, and began seriously marketing the device. Initially, they leased pairs of telephones for simple two-point communications, commonly between two buildings of a business or between a businessman's home and office. The opening of the first telephone exchange, or switchboard, in New Haven in January 1878 was a profound step. Any subscriber could now be connected to any other.

The key financial decision, one of great long-term import, was Hubbard's determination that the company, as the exclusive builder of telephones, would lease the instruments and license local providers of telephone service. Bell thus controlled both the service and the consumers' equipment. (It is as if gas companies exclusively leased stoves and furnaces or electric utilities were the sole lessors of lamps.[2]) In this way Hubbard attracted franchisees around the country who used their own capital to rent telephones, string wires, build switchboards, and sell interconnections. Bell provided the instruments and technical advice and, in turn, collected rental fees. Over the years the company used its leverage on license renewals to set rates and to dictate technical and other features of the service. This close supervision allowed the company to convert a confederation of local franchisees into a "system" of local "Bell Operating Companies" acting in concert. Eventually, AT&T replaced the rents it charged with stock ownership in the local companies and, using this leverage, set common nationwide policies. But in the earliest years perhaps dozens of entrepreneurs in towns across America—some rounded up by Watson himself on marketing trips—made individual licensing agreements with Hubbard.[3]

By mid-1878 the telephone business was in ferment. About 10,000 Bell instruments were in use throughout the nation, but Bell now had serious competition. Western Union, already located in telegraph offices almost everywhere, adopted telephones designed by Thomas Edison and Elisha Gray to offer a competing service. Bell sued Western Union for patent infringement and hurriedly founded exchanges around the country to preempt markets. At the end of 1879 the contestants settled: Western Union conceded Bell all patent rights and instruments. In return, Bell agreed to renounce telegraph service, to pay Western Union 20 percent of gross receipts for a time, and to grant the telegraph company partial interest in a few local Bell companies. The resolution left Bell in early 1880 with about 60,000 subscribers in exchanges scattered about the country and a monopoly on the telephone business. (About 30 years later, Bell briefly absorbed Western Union until pressured by the federal government to sell it off.)

THE ERA OF MONOPOLY: 1880–1893

The typical telephone system of the 1880s was a cumbersome affair. . . . The instrument itself was a set of three boxes. The top box held a magneto generator, a crank, and a bell. The middle box had a speaker tube protruding forward and a receiver tube hanging from the side. The third box contained a wet-cell battery that needed to be refilled periodically and occasionally leaked. A caller turned the crank to signal the switchboard operator; the signal mechanically released a shutter on the switchboard in the central office, showing the origin of the call. The operator plugged her headset into the designated socket and asked the caller whom he or she was seeking. Then the operator rang the desired party and connected the two by wires and plugs in the switchboard. The two parties talked, usually loudly and with accompanying static, and then hung up. In some systems the caller cranked again to signal the end of the conversation. In others the operator listened in periodically to find out when the conversation was over so that she could disconnect the plugs.

The race to build exchanges, rapid adoption by businessmen, and other changes raised some technical problems in the 1880s. Edward J. Hall, considered "the most far-seeing, all around competent and efficient telephone man of his day," complained from his franchise in Buffalo as early as February 1880 of too much business and too many calls to provide subscribers adequate service.[4] One consequence of growth was increasing congestion at the switchboards. Spaghetti-like masses of wires crisscrossed the boards, which in turn grew in number, size, and complexity beyond the capacities of the operators struggling to reach around one another. Temporary solutions did not solve the problem, especially in the large urban centers, until the late 1890s.[5] In some places new electric and streetcar power lines created intolerable interference on the adjacent telephone lines. Some observers believe that this problem stunted telephone development in the late 1880s. (This nuisance recurred in rural America with the construction of power lines by the Rural Electrification Administration in the 1930s.)

Bell responded to the challenges by rebuilding its hardware. It eventually replaced single iron or steel wires (a system in which the electrical circuit was completed through the ground) with pairs of copper wires that returned the current. Bell also replaced wet batteries with a common-system battery; the power for all telephones on a line now came from the central exchange. In addition, Bell eventually developed new switchboards and procedures to alleviate switchboard congestion. These and other technical developments completely revamped much of Bell's telephone system by the early 1900s. Company leaders sought to develop high-quality service—clear sound, instant access, and the like—for the urban business customers they courted. To this end they rounded up as many telephone patents as possible, sponsored further research, and pooled the practical experience of their franchisees.

Theodore N. Vail, as general manager and then president until 1887, used Bell's temporary patent monopoly to secure a technical and organizational edge over all future competitors, especially by developing long-distance service.

Although not favored, like Alexander Graham Bell, by a Hollywood biography, Theodore N. Vail is a figure of mythic stature in the telephone industry and in American corporate history. Beginning as a lowly telegrapher, Vail deployed his organizational skills and modern methods to rise to superintendent of the federal Railway Mail Service. Hubbard lured Vail, then 33, away to manage the fledgling Bell company in 1878. For several years Vail pressed aggressive expansion, patent protection, and business reorganization. In 1887, by then president, Vail resigned after conflicts with a more cautious board of financial officers. He succeeded in several

The early telephone call boxes were artful mixtures of wood, metal, and electrical components.
National Archives of Canada.

business ventures around the world, but kept abreast of the telephone industry. Vail would come back.[6]

Vail's policy of establishing high-quality service meant that costs were high, especially in the larger cities where the complexities of switching were most difficult. The minimum flat rate in central Los Angeles in 1888, for example, was $4 per month plus two cents a connection after the fortieth call. This rate equaled about 10 percent of the average nonfarm employee's wages. That same year Boston subscribers paid a minimum flat rate of $6 a month.[7] In addition, Bell's affiliates took every advantage of their monopoly to levy what the market could bear. For example, when the competing telephone exchange closed in San Francisco in 1880, the Bell local raised its charges from $40 to $60 a year. The local manager justified the move: "The increase was made because the public always expects to be 'cinched' when opposing corporations consolidate and it was too good an opportunity to lose. (Moreover, it would have been wrong to disappoint the confiding public.)"[8] Conflicts with irate customers arose, the most famous of which was an 18-month boycott of telephones organized in Rochester, New York, in 1886.[9] Bell's rates began to drop as 1894 approached, probably because of the competition it anticipated when its patents expired, although Bell claimed that improved technology explained the drop in charges. By 1895 the Los Angeles rate was down by 38 percent to $2.50 a month—7 percent of wages—plus two cents a call. Even then, telephone service remained expensive.[10]

The common practice during this era and beyond was to charge customers a flat-rate for the telephone service, allowing unlimited calls. During the 1880s local Bell companies repeatedly debated and experimented with a message-rate formula, charging by the call. One argument in favor of this approach was that it would permit the basic rental fee to be lowered and thereby encourage small users, such as families, to subscribe. Edward J. Hall was a leading proponent, labeled by some the "father of the message-rate system." Another reason for a pricing change, more favored by Vail and others, was that ending flat-rate service would discourage use, and thus "cut off all the superfluous business that tends to make the operation of the business so unremunerative." Existing customers, however, resisted the change by complaining, by petitioning the town officials who issued permits for telephone poles, or, as in Rochester, by boycotting the telephone service. Not until after the era of monopoly did message-rate service become common, although still not universal, in Bell's largest exchanges.[11]

Vail's agenda went beyond securing a technical monopoly. Through various devices he centralized control of the Bell System and its affiliates. Doing so was complex, since local situations varied widely. Each regional operating company had to deal with many governments to secure permits, to fend off complaints about the unsightliness of the wires, and sometimes to negotiate rates. Still, standardized policies, as well as a superior technology, helped brace the Bell system against challenge. Vail's successors after 1887 were, in retrospect, more interested in extracting monopoly profits from the system than in securing its future. That shift in priorities would become evident when the patents expired.

Strategic disagreements about pricing policy arose inside Bell, in part from different visions of the telephone's potential. It was not at all obvious whom the telephone would serve and how. As Sidney Aronson has noted, "[T]he inventor and his backers . . . faced the formidable task of inventing uses for the telephone and impressing them on others."[12] During the first few decades of telephony, industry marketers devised a variety of applications, including transmitting sermons, broadcasting news, providing wake-up calls, and many other experiments. As late as the 1910s, the trade journal *Telephony* had an index entry under "Telephone, novel uses of."* The industry spent

considerable time, especially in the nineteenth century, simply introducing the public to the instrument and dispelling suspicions about it. . . .

Industry leaders approached telephony from their experiences with telegraphy. Alexander Graham Bell and his backers were initially trying to improve the telegraph. Theodore Vail came from a family involved in telegraphy and had been a telegrapher. Many local telephone entrepreneurs had started out selling telegraph service. An important exception was Edward J. Hall, the message-rate enthusiast, who started in his family's brick business after earning a degree in metallurgy. Hall established the first Buffalo telephone exchange, left the telephone business a few years later, and was lured back by Vail to manage long-distance development in 1885 and then Southern Bell for over 10 years.[13] Because telegraphy defined the background of most executives,[14] and because Americans in the nineteenth century used the telegraph almost exclusively as a business tool, it was logical that Bell used the telegraphy model to define the telephone as a device for business as well.

Who were the first telephone subscribers? Physicians were notable among the early users. The telephone allowed them to hear of emergencies quickly and to check in at their offices when they were away. Druggists typically had telephones, as well.[15] But businessmen formed the primary market.

Bell found some businessmen hesitant to replace the telegraph with the telephone because they valued a written record. Nevertheless, some manufacturers, lawyers, bankers, and the like—and later small shopkeepers—adopted the technology. In 1891 the New York and New Jersey Telephone Company served 937 physicians and hospitals, 401 drug stores, 363 liquor stores, 315 livery stables, 162 metalworking plants, 146 lawyers, 126 contractors, 100 printing shops—7322 commercial customers all told—but only 1442 residences. Residences with telephones were typically those of doctors or of business owners or managers.[16]

One issue for Bell was whether it could fruitfully expand into the general residential market

---

*Included under that entry in volume 71, for example, are "degree conferred by telephone, dispatching tugs in harbor service, gauging water by telephone, telephoning in an aeroplane."

(that is, beyond the households of the business elite). In late 1883, noting that "the Telephone business has passed its experimental stage," Vail surveyed affiliates around the country, asking, among other questions: "Is it desirable and what would be the most practical way, to provide a service which would be in the reach of families, etc.?" His aide summarized the responses:

> There would seem to be but one opinion on this query and that is, that it is *most desirable*. The difficulty which presents itself is the manner in which the desired end should be reached. It is admitted that a great increase in the business would occur by the introduction of a rate and system, whereby the Telephone would be made universal so to speak, amongst families, and several modes [are] suggested . . . [including more pay-telephone stations, party lines, and lower residential rates]. It would appear from many of the answers to this query, "that a reduction in royalty" would be a necessity. . . .[17]

There was the rub: Locals would have to reduce their rates, and to ease that reduction Bell would have to lower its charges on the locals. Except for a handful of populists in this era—notably Edward Hall of Buffalo; John I. Sabin, later president of Pacific Telephone; and Angus Hibbard of Chicago—the consensus was that any increased business would not make up for the profits lost by reducing rates, even in a measured-rate system. At the time many also believed that operating costs per subscriber increased as the number of customers increased because of the technical complications of interconnection.[18] Only later

The early urban telephone system required large numbers of telephone operators whose job was to connect the sender and receiver of a call through exchanges like this one. *National Archives of Canada.*

did industry analysts appreciate that, as a network, telephones became more attractive as more people subscribed and that there might be economies of scale. George Ladd, president of Pacific Telephone in 1883, expressed the conservative position. He wrote to Vail that he opposed the reduction of residential rates because it could not pay and customers would not be grateful: "I am opposed to low rates unless made necessary by competition. . . . Cheaper service will simply multiply the nuisance of wires and poles and excite [political pressure to put wires underground], without materially improving profits or permanently improving relations with the public."[19] Residential service was therefore a stepchild in the system.

This attitude, later described even by Bell's friends as arrogant, predominated in the company. In 1906, for example, New England Bell commissioned an attorney to study telephone service in the Midwest. In its earlier history, he reported, "the public interest received scant attention" from Bell companies. They "were almost, if not quite, inexcusably slow in coming to an intelligent apprehension of the public need and desire for increased and improved telephone service."[20]

Bell managers were also skeptical about providing service in smaller communities. Businessmen in several small California towns, for example, appealed to Pacific Telephone for service but were turned away. In a few cases local entrepreneurs built bootleg systems, risking lawsuits.[21] AT&T focused on providing big-city businesses with high-quality service, including long-distance calling, at high prices. Its representatives later explained that the pressures of escalating demand and technical renovations prevented the company from pursuing wider markets until the mid-1890s.[22] Still, most Bell managers saw few possibilities for expansion, and nearly none for greater profit, in the general residential market or even the business market outside the major centers.

Between 1880 and 1893 the number of telephones in the United States grew from about 60,000—roughly one per thousand people—to about 260,000—or one per 250 people. The vast majority, more than two-thirds, were located in businesses.[23] This expansion, while dramatic in the early years, slowed after 1883, perhaps because of the technical problems or, just as likely, because of predatory monopoly pricing.

NOTES

1. Reproduced in AT&T, *A Capsule History of the Bell System* (New York: AT&T, 1979), 11.
2. Crandall, "Has the AT&T Break-up Raised Telephone Rates?" *The Brookings Review* 5 (Winter), 40–41.
3. On the early evolution of the Bell System, see especially Robert Garnett, *The Telephone Enterprise* (Baltimore: Johns Hopkins Press, 1985); Kenneth Lipartito, *The Bell System and Regional Business* (Baltimore: Johns Hopkins Press, 1989).
4. Letter of 2 February 1880, in "Measured Rate Service," Box 1127, AT&THA [American Telephone and Telegraph Historical Archives]. In 1884 Hall recalled the situation in 1879: "In Buffalo we had so many subscribers that the service became demoralized. Our switchboards were not equipped to handle the necessary amount of business . . . growing under the high pressure of competition" (Hall, "Notes on History of the Bell Telephone Co. of Buffalo, New York," [1884], 9). . . .
5. See Robert J. Chapius, *100 Years of Telephone Switching* (New York: Elsevier, 1982); Morton Mueller, "The Switchboard Problem," *Technology and Culture* 30 (July): 534–60.
6. See Albert Paine, *Theodore N. Vail* (New York: Harper, 1929). Accounts of Vail appear in most telephone histories.
7. Los Angeles: "Telephone on the Pacific Coast, 1878–1923," Box 1045, AT&THA; Boston: Moyer, "Urban Growth," 352.
8. Letter (no. 75968) to Vail, 13 February 1884, in "San Francisco Exchange," Box 1141, AT&THA.
9. Bell had planned to switch from flat-rate to measured-rate (per-call) charges. With the support of city hall, subscribers organized a boycott. Eventually, Bell agreed to delay measured service for five years, place its wires underground, and pay the legal costs. See H. B. MacMeal, *The Story of Independent Telephony* (Chicago: Independent Pioneer Telephony Assoc., 1934), 111.

10. Los Angeles rates: "Telephone on the Pacific Coast, 1878–1923," Box 1045, AT&THA. Wage data come from the United States Bureau of the Census, *Historical Statistics of the United States,* tables D735–38.

11. On the debate over rates, see "Measured Rate Service" and other files in Box 1127, AT&THA. The quotation about "superfluous business" is from a Vail letter to Hall dated 7 February 1880.

12. Sidney Aronson, "Bell's Electrical Toy," in *The Social Impact of the Telephone,* ed. Ithiel de Sola Paul (Cambridge, MA: MIT, 1977), 19.

13. Biographical notes on Hall were culled from press releases and clippings provided by Mildred Ettlinger at AT&THA. See also Lipartito, *The Bell System,* for an account of Hall's work in the South.

14. William Patten, *Pioneering the Telephone in Canada* (Montreal: Telephone Pioneers, 1926), 1ff, points out that Canadian telephone executives also had backgrounds in telegraphy.

15. On doctors and telephony, see Sidney Aronson, "*Lancet* on the Telephone," *Medical History* 21 (January): 69–87, and S. Aronson and R. Greenbaum, "Take Two Aspirin and Call Me in the Morning," Queens College, N.Y. Typescript courtesy of Sidney Aronson, 1985. Histories of telephony often note the early role of doctors. . . .

16. Letter to Thomas Sherwin, 11 July 1891, in "Classification of Subscribers," Box 1247, AT&THA.

17. Circular by Vail, 28 December 1883, and attachments, in Box 1080, AT&THA.

18. Mueller, "The Switchboard Problem."

19. Responses to 28 December 1883, circular by Vail, Box 1080, AT&THA.

20. G. W. Anderson, *Telephone Competition in the Middle West and Its Lesson in New England* (Boston: New England Telephone & Telegraph, 1906), 13–14.

21. The California cases are in "PT&T News Bureau Files," Telephone Pioneer Communications Museum of San Francisco, Archives and Historical Research Center. . . .

22. See, e.g., the rationale for not pursuing wider markets as expressed in the United States Bureau of the Census, *Special Reports: Telephones and Telegraphs 1902* (1906), chap. 10. The stress on high quality was indeed important. In the South, for example, local managers were discouraged from building simple, low-cost systems, because of the national company's insistence on maintaining quality levels needed for the long-distance network (Lipartito, *The Bell System*). . . .

23. In the New York–New Jersey data over 80 percent of telephones were located in businesses. In the same year, in Kingston, Ontario, about 70 percent of telephones were located in businesses, although many officially listed as residential were really used for business by people such as physicians [Robert M. Pike, "Kingston Adopts the Telephone," *Urban History Review* 18 (June): 32–47; Robert M. Pike and Vincent Mosco, "Canadian Consumers and Telephone Pricing," *Telecommunications Policy* 10 (March): 17–32].

CHAPTER 17

Time, Space, and the Telegraph

James W. Carey

The late James Carey was professor at the Columbia School of Journalism and a leading figure in advancing the study of communications history. His book, Communication as Culture, *which is the source of the present excerpt, develops a model for examining the implications of early media development in the United States.*

The simplest and most important point about the telegraph is that it marked the decisive separation of "transportation" and "communication." Until the telegraph these words were synonymous. The telegraph ended that identity and allowed symbols to move independently of geography and independently of and faster than transport. I say decisive separation because there were premonitions earlier of what was to come, and there was, after all, pre-electric telegraphy—line-of-sight signaling devices.

Virtually any American city of any vintage has a telegraph hill or a beacon hill reminding us of such devices. They relied on shutters, flaps, disks, or arms operating as for semaphoric signaling at sea. They were optical rather than "writing at a distance" systems and the forerunners of microwave networks, which rely on relay stations on geographic high points for aerial transmissions.

Line-of-sight telegraphy came into practical use at the end of the eighteenth century. Its principal architect was a Frenchman, Claude Chappe, who persuaded the Committee of Public Instruction in post-Revolutionary France to approve a trial. Joseph Lakanal, one of its members, reported back to the committee on the outcome: "What brilliant destiny do science and the arts not reserve for a republic which by its immense population and the genius of its inhabitants, is called to become the nation to instruct Europe" (Wilson, 1976: 122).

The National Convention approved the adoption of the telegraph as a national utility and instructed the Committee of Public Safety to map routes. The major impetus to its development in France was the same as the one that led to the wave of canal and railroad building in America. The pre-electric telegraph would provide an answer to Montesquieu and other political theorists who thought France or the United States too big to be a republic. But even more, it provided a means whereby the departments that had replaced the provinces after the Revolution could be tied to and coordinated with the central authority (Wilson, 1976: 123).

The pre-electric telegraph was also a subject of experimentation in America. In 1800, a line-of-sight system was opened between Martha's Vineyard and Boston (Wilson, 1976: 210). Between 1807 and 1812, plans were laid for a telegraph to stretch from Maine to New Orleans. The first practical use of line-of-sight telegraphy was for the transmission of news of arriving ships, a practice begun long before 1837 (Thompson, 1947: 11). But even before line-of-sight devices had been developed, alterations in shipping patterns had led to the separation of information from cargo, and that had important consequences for international trade. . . .

Despite these reservations and qualifications, the telegraph provided the decisive and cumulative break of the identity of communication and transportation. The great theoretical significance of the technology lay not merely in the separation but also in the use of the telegraph as both a model of and a mechanism for control of the physical movement of things, specifically for the railroad. That is the fundamental discovery: not only can information move independently of and faster than physical entities, but it also can be a simulation of and control mechanism for what has been left behind. The discovery was first exploited in railroad dispatching in England in 1844 and in the United States in 1849. It was of particular use on the long stretches of single-track road in the American West, where accidents were a serious problem. Before the use of the telegraph to control switching, the Boston and Worcester Railroad, for one example, kept horses every five miles along the line, and they raced up and down the track so that their riders could warn engineers of impending collisions (Thompson, 1947: 205–206). By moving information faster than the rolling stock, the telegraph allowed for centralized control along many miles of track. Indeed, the operation of the telegraph in conjunction with the railroad allowed for an integrated system of transport and communication. The same principle realized in these mundane circumstances governs the development of all modern processes in electrical transmission and control from guided gun sights to simple servo mechanisms that open doors. The relationship of the telegraph and the railroad illustrates the basic notion of systems theory and the catch phrase that the "system is the solution," in that the integrated switched system is more important than any of its components.

The telegraph permitted the development, in the favorite metaphor of the day, of a thoroughly encephalated social nervous system in which signaling was divorced from musculature. It was the telegraph and the railroad—the actual, painful construction of an integrated system—that provided the entrance gate for the organic metaphors that dominated nineteenth-century thought. Although German romanticism and idealism had their place, it is less to the world of ideas and more to the world of actual practice that we need to look when trying to figure out why the nineteenth century was obsessed with organicism.

The effect of the telegraph on ideology, on ordinary ideas, can be shown more graphically with two other examples drawn from the commodities markets and the development of standard time. The telegraph, like most innovations in communication down through the computer, had its first and most profound impact on the conduct of commerce, government, and the military. It was, in short, a producer good before it was a consumer good. The telegraph . . . was used in its early months for the long-distance playing of chess. Its commercial significance was slow to be realized. But once that significance was determined, it was used to reorganize commerce; and from the patterns of usage in commerce came many of the telegraph's most profound consequences for ordinary thought. Among its first effects was the reorganization of commodity markets.

It was the normal expectation of early nineteenth century Americans that the price of a commodity would diverge from city to city so that the cost of wheat, corn, or whatever would be radically different in, say, Pittsburgh, Cincinnati, and St. Louis. This belief reflected the fact that before the telegraph, markets were independent of one another, or, more accurately, that the effect of one market on another was so gradually manifested as to be virtually unnoticed. In short, the prices of commodities were largely determined by local conditions of supply and demand. One of the leading historians of the markets has commented, "To be sure in all articles of trade the conditions at all sources of supply had their ultimate effect on distant values and yet even in these the communication was so slow that the conditions might change entirely before their effect could be felt" (Emery, 1896: 106).

Under such circumstances, the principal method of trading is called arbitrage: buying cheap and selling dear by moving goods around in space. That is, if prices are higher in St. Louis than in Cincinnati, it makes sense to buy in Cincinnati and resell in St. Louis, as long as the price differential is greater than the cost of transportation between the two cities. If arbitrage is widely practiced between cities, prices should settle into an equilibrium whereby the difference in price is held to the difference in transportation cost. This result is, in turn, based on the assumption of classical economics of perfect information—that all buyers and sellers are aware of the options available in all relevant markets—a situation rarely approached in practice before the telegraph.

Throughout the United States, price divergence between markets declined during the nineteenth century. Arthur H. Cole computed the average annual and monthly price disparity for uniform groups of commodities during the period 1816–1842, that is, up to the eve of the telegraph. Over that period the average annual price disparity fell from 9.3 to 4.8; and the average monthly disparity, from 15.4 to 4.8 (Cole, 1938: 94–96, 103). The decline itself is testimony to improvements in communication brought about by canal and turnpike building. The steepness of the decline is probably masked somewhat because Cole grouped the prices for the periods 1816–1830 and 1830–1842, whereas it was late in the canal era and the beginnings of large-scale railroad building that the sharpest declines were felt.

Looked at from one side, the decline represents the gradual increase in the effective size of the market. Looked at from the other side, it represents a decline in spatially based speculative opportunities—opportunities, that is, to turn trade into profit by moving goods between distinct markets. In a sense the railroad and canal regionalized markets; the telegraph nationalized them.

The effect of the telegraph is a simple one: it evens out markets in space. The telegraph puts everyone in the same place for purposes of trade; it makes geography irrelevant. The telegraph brings the conditions of supply and demand in all markets to bear on the determination of a price. Except for the marginal exception here and there, it eliminates opportunities for arbitrage by realizing the classical assumption of perfect information.

But the significance of the telegraph does not lie solely in the decline of arbitrage; rather, the telegraph shifts speculation into another dimension. It shifts speculation from space to time, from arbitrage to futures. After the telegraph, commodity trading moved from trading between places to trading between times. The arbitrager trades Cincinnati for St. Louis; the futures trader sells August against October, this year against next. To put the matter somewhat differently, as the telegraph closed down spatial uncertainty in prices, it opened up, because of improvements in communication, the uncertainty of time. It was not, then, mere historic accident that the Chicago Commodity Exchange, to this day the principal American futures market, opened in 1848, the same year the telegraph reached that city. In a certain sense the telegraph invented the future as a new zone of uncertainty and a new region of practical action.

Let me make a retreat from that conclusion about the effects of the telegraph on time because I have overdrawn the case. First, the opportunities for arbitrage are never completely eliminated. There are always imperfections in market information, even on the floor of a stock exchange: buyers and sellers who do not know of one another and the prices at which the others are willing to trade. We know this as well from ordinary experience at auctions, where someone always knows a buyer who will pay more than the auctioned price. Second, there was a hiatus between arbitrage and the futures market when time contracts dominated, and this was a development of some importance. An approximation of futures trading occurred as early as 1733, when the East India Company initiated the practice of trading warrants. The function of a warrant was to transfer ownership of goods without consummating their physical transfer. The warrant did not represent, as such, particular warehoused goods; they were merely endorsed from person to person. The use of warrants or time contracts evolved rapidly in the United States in the trading of agricultural staples. They evolved there to meet new conditions of effective market size, and as importantly, their evolution was unrestrained by historic practice.

The critical condition governing the development of time contracts was also the separation of communication from transport. Increasingly, news of crop conditions reached the market before the commodity itself. For example, warrant trading advanced when cotton was shipped to England by sail while passengers and information moved by steamer. Based on news of the crop and on samples of the commodity, time contracts or "to-arrive" contracts were executed. These were used principally for transatlantic sales, but after the Mississippi Valley opened up to agricultural trade, they were widely used in Chicago in the 1840s (Baer and Woodruff, 1935: 3–5).

The telegraph started to change the use of time contracts, as well as arbitrage. By widely transmitting knowledge of prices and crop conditions, it drew markets and prices together. We do not have good before-and-after measures, but we do have evidence, cited earlier, for the long-run decline in price disparities among markets. Moreover, we have measures from Cincinnati in particular. In the 1820s Cincinnati lagged two years behind Eastern markets. That meant that it took two years for disturbances in the Eastern market structure to affect Cincinnati prices. By 1840 the lag was down to four months; and by 1857—and probably much earlier—the effect of Eastern markets on Cincinnati was instantaneous. But once space was, in the phrase of the day, annihilated, once everyone was in the same place for purposes of trade, time as a new region of experience, uncertainty, speculation, and exploration was opened up to the forces of commerce.

A back-door example of this inversion of space and time can be drawn from a later episode involving the effect of the telephone on the New York Stock Exchange. By 1894 the telephone had made information time identical in major cities. Buyers and sellers, wherever they were, knew current prices as quickly as traders did on the floor of the exchange. The information gap, then, between New York and Boston had been eliminated and business gravitated from New York to Boston brokerage firms. The New York exchange countered this movement by creating a thirty-second time advantage that ensured New York's superiority to Boston. The exchange ruled that telephones would not be allowed on the floor. Price information had to be relayed by messenger to an area off the floor of the exchange that had been set aside for telephones. This move destroyed the temporal identity of markets, and a thirty-second monopoly of knowledge was created that drew business back to New York (Emery, 1896: 139).

This movement of commodities out of space and into time had three other consequences of great importance in examining the effect of the telegraph. First, futures trading required the decontexualization of markets; or, to put it in a slightly different way, markets were made relatively unresponsive to local conditions of supply and demand. The telegraph removed markets from the particular context in which they were historically located and concentrated on them forces emanating from any place and any time. This was a redefinition from physical or geographic markets to spiritual ones. In a sense they

were made more mysterious; they became everywhere markets and everytime markets and thus less apprehensible at the very moment they became more powerful.

Second, not only were distant and amorphous forces brought to bear on markets, but the commodity was sundered from its representations; that is, the development of futures trading depended on the ability to trade or circulate negotiable instruments independently of the actual physical movement of goods. The representation of the commodity became the warehouse receipts from grain elevators along the railroad line. These instruments were then traded independently of any movement of the actual goods. The buyer of such receipts never expected to take delivery; the seller of such receipts never expected to make delivery. There is the old joke, which is also a cautionary tale, of the futures trader who forgot what he was up to and ended up with forty tons of wheat on his suburban lawn; but it is merely a joke and a tale. The futures trader often sells before he buys, or buys and sells simultaneously. But the buying and selling is not of goods but of receipts. What is being traded is not money for commodities but time against price. In short, the warehouse receipt, which stands as a representation of the product, has no intrinsic relation to the real product.

But in order to trade receipts rather than goods, a third change was necessary. In futures trading products are not bought or sold by inspection of the actual product or a sample thereof. Rather, they are sold through a grading system. In order to lend itself to futures trading, a product has to be mixed, standardized, diluted in order to be reduced to a specific, though abstract, grade. With the coming of the telegraph, products could no longer be shipped in separate units as numerous as there were owners of grain. "The high volume sales required impersonalized standards. Buyers were no longer able personally to check every lot" (Chandler, 1977: 211). Consequently, not all products are traded on the futures market because some resist the attempt to reduce them to standardized categories of quality.

The development of the futures markets, in summary, depended on a number of specific changes in markets and the commodity system. It required that information move independently of and faster than products. It required that prices be made uniform in space and that markets be decontextualized. It required, as well, that commodities be separated from the receipts that represent them and that commodities be reduced to uniform grades.

These were, it should be quickly added, the conditions that underlay Marx's analysis of the commodity fetish. That concept, now used widely and often indiscriminately, was developed in the *Grundrisse* and *Das Kapital* during the late 1850s, when futures trading became the dominant arena for the establishment of agricultural values. In particular, Marx made the key elements in the commodity fetish the decontextualization of markets, the separation of use value from exchange value brought about by the decline in the representative

function of the warehouse receipt, and the abstraction of the product out of real conditions of production by a grading system. In the *Grundrisse* he comments, "This locational movement—the bringing of the product to market which is a necessary condition of its circulation, except when the point of production is itself a market—could more precisely be regarded as the transformation of the product into a commodity" (Marx, 1973: 534).

Marx's reference is to what Walter Benjamin (1968) would later call the "loss of aura" in his parallel analysis of the effect of mechanical reproduction on the work of art. After the object is abstracted out of the real conditions of its production and use and is transported to distant markets, standardized and graded, and represented by fully contingent symbols, it is made available as a commodity. Its status as a commodity represents the sundering of a real, direct relationship between buyer and seller, separates use value from exchange value, deprives objects of any

The original bicycle courier in urban areas. *National Archives of Canada.*

uniqueness (which must then be returned to the object via advertising), and, most important, masks to the buyer the real conditions of production. Further, the process of divorcing the receipt from the product can be thought of as part of a general social process initiated by the use of money and widely written about in contemporary semiotics; the progressive divorce of the signifier from the signified, a process in which the world of signifiers progressively overwhelms and moves independently of real material objects.

To summarize, the growth of communications in the nineteenth century had the practical effect of diminishing space as a differentiating criterion in human affairs. What Harold Innis called the "penetrative powers of the price system" was, in effect, the spread of a uniform price system throughout space so that for purposes of trade everyone was in the same place. The telegraph was the critical instrument in this spread. In commerce this meant the decontextualization of markets so that prices no longer depended on local factors of supply and demand but responded to national and international forces. The spread of the price system was part of the attempt to colonize space. The correlative to the penetration of the price system was what the composer Igor Stravinsky called the "statisticalization of mind": the transformation of the entire mental world into quantity, and the distribution of quantities in space so that the relationship between things and people becomes solely one of numbers. Statistics widens the market for everything and makes it more uniform and interdependent. The telegraph worked this same effect on the practical consciousness of time through the construction of standard time zones.

BIBLIOGRAPHY

Baer, Julius B., and George P. Woodruff (1935). *Commodity Exchanges.* New York: Harper & Bros.

Benjamin, Walter (1968). *Illuminations.* New York: Harcourt, Brace and World.

Chandler, Alfred D. (1977). *The Visible Hand: The Managerial Revolution in American Business.* Cambridge, MA: Harvard University Press.

Cole, Arthur H. (1938). *Wholesale Commodity Prices in the United States, 1700–1861.* Cambridge, MA: Harvard University Press.

Emery, Henry Crosby (1896). *Speculation on the Stock and Produce Exchanges of the United States, Studies in History, Economics and Public Law* (332.6EM3STX.AGX). New York: Columbia University Press.

Marx, Karl (1973). *Grundrisse: Foundations of the Critique of Political Economy.* New York: Vintage.

Thompson, Robert L. (1947). *Wiring a Continent.* Princeton, NJ: Princeton University Press.

Wilson, Geoffrey (1976). *The Old Telegraph.* London: Phillimore.

PART FIVE

Image Technologies and the Emergence of Mass Society

Hindenburg crash. © *Bettmann / CORBIS All Rights Reserved.*

By the end of the nineteenth century, the "wired world", chiefly through the telephone and telegraph, had extended the scope of previous communication by distributing messages farther, faster, and with less effort. As a result, news was packaged differently and had a new emphasis, as did popular entertainment. Ways of reading also changed, along with the constitution of reading publics. These developments were paralleled and influenced by a century long transition to a predominantly industrial economy, with its accompanying urbanization. One result was the emergence of "consumer society". The local and regional lost its hold as new ideas, images and patterns of consumption ushered in the twentieth century.

The decades that marked the end of the nineteenth and beginning of the twentieth centuries were characterized by many developments in addition to those we have already considered and those to be taken up in the essays that follow. As background it might be useful to mention that this period saw the bicycle, automobile, and airplane emerge as significant modes of transportation. The sense of space they fostered, coupled with the increased speed of railway and steamship travel, led to World Standard Time via the creation of time zones. This further shifted cultural identification away from the immediate and local. In the sphere of art, Cubism and Futurism also responded to and celebrated changes in space and time. Cubism broke up and repositioned space by simultaneously putting several perspectives onto one plane. Futurism encouraged the accelerated pace of life propelled by the new technologies.

This was also a time of major public works, such as bridges, canals, and tunnels. Urban electrification integrated rail transportation into the city, as streetcar and subway lines took hold in major cities of the world. All this promoted further urban growth, permitting workers to live at increasing distances from their work place, creating thereby a commuter as well as consumer society.

The transition from the nineteenth century to the new patterns of consumption that would emerge so powerfully in the twentieth century is the subject of our first selection, "Dream Worlds of Consumption," by Rosalynd Williams. She begins with a discussion of universal expositions, later called World's Fairs. The one held at the Crystal Palace in London in 1851 is cited as the first of a series culminating with the turn of the century extravaganza in Paris in 1900. During the Paris celebration, notions of abstract technological progress, a central theme of previous exhibitions, were overshadowed by the possibilities of consumer goods—a new world of things which challenged art and religion as focal points of human aspiration. Underwriting this shift was the development of department stores. As disposable income increased in an expanding industrial economy, these giant commercial sites enabled at least part of the "dream world" to be experienced by the public at large.

One of the key elements prefacing the transition to twentieth century society and culture was a new awareness of people, places and things fostered by photography. Photography began in 1839 and during its first decades influenced illustrators working in a variety of disciplines, in time creating a new standard for the quality of information in pictures. It would also go on to change forever the way we view and relate to the world. By the time of the 1900 Paris exhibition photography has begun to affect the imagination of its visitors in other ways. It demonstrated the power of the motion picture. The motion picture would emerge into a mass medium between this time and World War I. Building on the reproductive powers of the photograph, the cinematic experience is one that we still struggle to explain. Williams discusses some early reactions to it.

What unleashed the influence of photography was its wide circulation. This happened in the final decades of the nineteenth century, when new techniques of lithography enabled photographic reproductions to be used in newspapers, books, and magazines. In our second excerpt Ulrich Keller examines this development by looking at some well known and not so well-known images from the early history of photojournalism.

With the recording of images through photography a regular occurrence, it seemed only a matter of time until sound, particularly the human voice and then music followed suit. Our next two entries, by Lisa Gitelman and Jonathan Sterne, explore the early history of sound recording which began with Thomas Edison's invention of the phonograph in 1877. Today we have become accustomed to rapid technological change in this area. When the first edition of this textbook was published just under twenty years ago, the Sony Walkman was all the rage. Today its is almost completely forgotten, as your i-pod might be in a few years. The situation was no less volatile at the end of the nineteenth century.

Gitelman points out how early sound recording was thought to be a boon to business, as it was thought to be something akin to a Dictaphone as well as being a way of recording for posterity voices that were either famous or familial. Since Edison's early phonograph was both a recording and a playback technology, families could self-record, as they do today with various video technologies. As Gitelman points out, Edison's exhibitions to promote his device included all manner of sound recording experiments while not realizing at the time that the future of this technology would reside in commercially produced musical recordings. A loose parallel can be drawn with early home computers, and the later realization that software would represent a major segment of the industries future. Can you think of any other technology in which the eventual use differs from what at the time was thought to be its primary application?

And just as in the world of computers today we have competing formats such as Mac and PC—humorously depicted in a series of popular television ads—so in the late nineteenth century, as Sterne points out, Edison's phonograph was challenged by Emile Berliner's gramophone. It was the tinfoil cylinder versus the wax disc. The advantages and disadvantages of each are noted by Sterne. Since the disc was easier to mass produce it lent itself more favorably to the marketing of recorded music. Eventually, by the turn of the twentieth century, Edison would begin to manufacture disc phonographs. Can you think of any recent example of competing formats in an entertainment driven technology?

In the following selection, Daniel Czitrom considers the cinematic experience by looking at the early history of movie theaters and their publics. Movie going as a collective public experience began, as he notes, with the nickelodeons that sprang up shortly after the turn of the century. These small makeshift venues can be compared physically to the box-like multiplexes we sometimes frequent today. Their appeal was mainly to working-class audiences, many of them immigrants whose lack of fluency in English posed no problem during the silent screen era—the occasional intertitles were often read aloud and translated by other members of the audience. The period following the one discussed by Czitrom, saw the emergence of grandiose movie palaces, especially during the 1920s. By that time all social classes had become enthralled by the movie going experience, which had dire consequences for vaudeville. This old and established form of live variety entertainment came to a virtual end by the late 1920s. However, some of its performers were able to make the leap to radio.

One of the issues we think readers should consider in conjunction with the emergence of motion pictures as a major form of popular culture is the transition from silent to sound films that occurred in the late 1920's. Silent films, of course, were not actually silent, since they usually featured live musical accompaniment. Just when the art of silent had reached extraordinary heights, early sound films of noticeably poorer quality began to displace them. However, as Scott Eyman notes in our next selection, when recorded dialogue was added—partly because of the influence of radio—peopled welcomed the opportunity to hear the actors talk on screen. He goes on to chronicle the enormous changes brought about by the coming of sound, arguing that it was the most far-reaching transformation in motion picture history since the advent of film projection itself.

In the early years of movie going, the novelty of seeing action on screen was sufficient to satisfy audiences. After 1910, however, certain genres of film and identifiable actors were preferred. The star system was born. In our next selection, Jib Fowles looks at this phenomenon. He links it to the changing social patterns that gave rise to less-rooted working and middle-class populations, who saw entertainment and sports personalities as the embodiment of many of their aspirations. As he notes, this transformation did not occur overnight; it had been building during the post–Civil War decades, as the telegraph, photograph, and improved transportation helped make entertainers and athletes more widely known. With the establishment of motion pictures, this tendency escalated tremendously. Actors became recognizable personalities who were often associated with particular roles.

In the twentieth century the popularity of image and sound technologies is closely linked with the idea of mass society and advertising. Beginning around 1900, advertisers conceived and then tried to create a mass audience, drawing upon in part the public appeal of image and sound technologies, the growing popularity of illustrated magazines and newspapers and the success of new venues for public performance, such as the cinema. As we shall see in the next section the rise of electronic media deepens both the capacity and the appeal of these new modalities for dissemination and for persuasion.

CHAPTER 18

Dream Worlds of Consumption

Rosalynd Williams

Rosalynd Williams is a cultural historian and professor at the Massachusetts Institute of Technology. In her books Dream Worlds, *from which this excerpt is taken, and* Notes on the Underground: An Essay on Technology, Society, and the Imagination, *she explores the relationship between the rapidly changing character of industrial production in the late nineteenth century and the rise of consumer culture.*

THE SCHOOL OF TROCADÉRO

The arrival of the twentieth century was celebrated in Paris by a universal exposition spread over 550 acres and visited by 50 million people from around the world. The 1900 exposition was the climax of a series of similar events that began with the Crystal Palace exposition in London in 1851 and continued to be held at regular intervals during the second half of the century (in 1855, 1867, 1878, and 1889) in Paris, the undisputed if unofficial capital of European civilization. The purpose of all expositions was, in the popular phrase of the time, to teach a "lesson of things." "Things" meant for the most part, the recent products of scientific knowledge and technical innovation that were revolutionizing daily life; the "lesson" was the social benefit of this unprecedented material and intellectual progress. The 1855 exposition featured a Palace of Industry filled with tools, machinery, and sequential exhibits of products in various stages of manufacture. The 1867 fair had an even more elaborately organized Palace of Industry (including the first displays of aluminum and of petroleum distillation), and a History of Labor exhibit showing tools from all eras. At the 1878 exposition the wonders of scientific discovery, especially electricity and photography, were stressed.

In 1889, at the exposition commemorating the outbreak of the French Revolution, the "lesson of things" was taught on a grand scale. The two focal points of the 1889 fair were the Gallery of Machines, a lone hall with a vault nearly 400 feet across where sightseers could gaze from a suspended walkway at a sea of spinning wheels, clanking hammers, and whirring gears, and the Eiffel Tower, a monument at once scientific, technological, and aesthetic, the architecture of which was derived from that of iron railroad bridges; at its summit was an assortment of apparatus for meteorological, aeronautical, and communications research.

Over the decades, the dominant tone of these expositions altered. The emphasis gradually changed from instructing the visitor in the wonders of modern science and technology to entertaining him. In 1889, for all their serious didactic intent, the Eiffel Tower and Gallery of Machines were popular above all because they provided such thrilling vistas. More and more, consumer merchandise rather than productive tools was displayed. The Crystal Palace exposition had been so innocent of commercial purpose that no selling prices were posted there, but at the Paris exposition in 1855 began the tradition of placing price tags on all objects, as well as of charging admission.[1] From then on the emphasis on selling, prizes, and advertising grew until one booster of the 1900 exposition enthused:

> Expositions secure for the manufacturer, for the businessman, the most striking publicity. In one day they bring before his machine, his display, his shop windows, more people than he would see in a lifetime in his factory or store. They seek out clients in all parts of the world, bring them at a set time, so that everything is ready to receive them and seduce them. That is why the number of exhibitors increases steadily.[2]

At the 1900 exposition the sensual pleasures of consumption clearly triumphed over the abstract, intellectual enjoyment of contemplating the progress of knowledge. This emphasis was evident the moment a visitor entered the grounds through the Monumental Gateway, which, according to one bemused contemporary, consisted of "two pale-blue, pierced minarets and polychrome statues surmounted by oriflammes and adorned with cabochons," terminating in "an immense flamboyant arch" above which, perched on a golden ball, "stood the flying figure of a siren in a tight skirt, the symbolic ship of the City of Paris on her head, throwing back an evening coat of imitation ermine—La Parisienne."[3] Whatever this chic madonna represented, it was certainly not science nor technology. Inside this gateway the sprawling exposition had no orderly arrangement or focal points such as previous ones had possessed. Machines were scattered throughout the grounds next to their products, an indication that tools of production now seemed hopelessly boring apart from the things they made. The vault of the Gallery of Machines had been cut up—desecrated like a "secularized temple," complained one admirer of the 1889 version[4]—and overrun by a display of food products:

> [Instead of] a universal workshop . . . a festival hall has invaded the center of the structure. The extremities are abandoned to the rustic charms of agriculture and to the fattening joys of eating. No more sharp whistles, trembling, clacking transmission belts; nothing being released except champagne corks.[5]

The Palace of Electricity at the Paris Exposition of 1900. *AKG-Images.*

Despite this confusion or, rather, because of it, thoughtful observers sensed that the 1900 exposition was particularly prophetic, that it was a microcosm of emerging France, a scale model of future Paris, that something rich and strange was happening there which broke decisively with the past and prefigured twentieth-century society. In 1889 and even more in 1900, the expositions attracted a host of journalists of a philosophical bent who provided not only descriptions of the various exhibits but also reflections on their significance. For the most part their sense of the exposition's prophetic value remained poorly articulated. While convinced that the fair revealed the shape of things to come, they were unsure of the contours and were vaguely apprehensive without knowing quite why. One exception was Maurice Talmeyr (1850–1933), a journalist who reported regularly on the 1900 exposition in a Catholic periodical. No less apprehensive than many of his colleagues, he was unusual in being able to explain why he found the fair so disturbing. He summarized his conclusions in his article "L'École du Trocadéro" ("The School of Trocadéro"), published in November, 1900, just as the exposition was drawing to a close, in the *Revue des deux mondes,* the most prestigious biweekly in France at that time.[6]

The Trocadéro was the section of the exposition on the Right Bank of the Seine, directly across the river from the Eiffel Tower, where all the colonial exhibits were gathered. It was in this "school," Talmeyr contended, that the true lesson of the exposition could be discerned. Exhibits of exotic places were not a new feature. As far back as 1867 expositions had included reproductions of an Egyptian temple and a Moroccan tent, and in 1889 one of the most popular attractions had been the notorious Rue du Caire ("Street of Cairo") where dark-eyed belly dancers performed seductive dances before patrons in "Oriental" cafés. In 1900, when imperial adventurism was at its height, the number of colonial exhibits expanded accordingly to become, in Talmeyr's

words, a gaudy and incoherent jumble of "Hindu temples, savage huts, pagodas, souks, Algerian alleys, Chineses, Japanese, Sudanese, Senegalese, Siamese, Cambodian quarters . . . a bazaar of climates, architectural styles, smells, colors, cuisine, music." Reproductions of the most disparate places were heaped together to "settle down together, as a Lap and a Moroccan, a Malgache and a Peruvian go to bed in the same sleeping car . . . the universe in a garden!" . . .

THE SIGNIFICANCE OF THE EXPOSITION

The exposition of 1900 provides a scale model of the consumer revolution. The cultural changes working gradually and diffusely throughout society were there made visible in a concrete and concentrated way. One change was the sheer emphasis on merchandising. Even more striking and disturbing, at least to observers like Talmeyr, was the change in how this merchandising was accomplished—by appealing to the fantasies of the consumer. The conjunction of banking and dreaming, of sales pitch and seduction, of publicity and pleasure, is far more unsettling than when each element is taken separately. As Talmeyr appreciates, the conjunction is inherently deceptive. Fantasy which openly presents itself as such keeps its integrity and may claim to point to truth beyond everyday experience, what the poet Keats called the "truth of the imagination." At the Trocadéro, on the contrary, reveries were passed off as reality, thereby losing their independent status to become the alluring handmaidens of commerce. When they assume concrete form and masquerade as objective fact, dreams lose their liberating possibilities as alternatives to daylight reality. What is involved here is not a casual level of fantasy, a kind of mild and transient wishful thinking, but a far more thoroughgoing substitution of subjective images for external reality. Talmeyr stresses the inevitable corruption that results when business exploits dreams. To him all advertising is false advertising. Blatant lies and subtle ones, lies of omission and of commission, lies in detail and in the ensemble, the exhibits claiming to represent the "real Java" or the "real China" or the real anything are not real at all. People are duped. Seeking a pleasurable escape from the workaday world, they find it in a deceptive dream world which is no dream at all but a sales pitch in disguise.

The 1900 exposition incarnates this new and decisive conjunction between imaginative desires and material ones, between dreams and commerce, between events of collective consciousness and of economic fact. It is obvious how economic goods satisfy physical needs such as those for food and shelter; less evident, but of overwhelming significance in understanding modern society, is how merchandise can fill needs of the imagination. The expression "the dream world of the consumer" refers to this non-material dimension. From earliest history we find indications that the human mind has transcended concerns of physical survival to imagine a finer, richer, more satisfying life. Through most of history, however, only a very few people ever thought of trying to approximate such dreams in daily life. Instead, art and religion provided ways to express these desires. But in the late nineteenth century, commodities that provided an approximation of these age-old longings began to be widely available. Consumer goods, rather than other facets of culture, became focal points for desire. The seemingly contrary activities of hard-headed accounting and dreamy-eyed fantasizing merged as business appealed to consumers by inviting them into a fabulous world of pleasure, comfort, and amusement. This was not at all the future that a conservative nationalist like Talmeyr wished; it was not the vision of a workers' society that socialists wanted; nor did it conform to traditional bourgeois virtues of sobriety and rationality. But welcome or not, the "lesson of things" taught by the make-believe city of the 1900 exposition was that a dream world of the consumer was emerging in real cities outside its gates.

EXOTICISM IN DEPARTMENT STORES

One obvious confirmation of this lesson was the emergence of department stores (in French *grands magasins*, "big" or "great" stores) in Paris. The emergence of these stores in late nineteenth-century France depended on the same growth of prosperity and transformation of merchandising techniques that lay behind the international expositions. Talmeyr was on the mark when he observed that the Indian exhibit at the Trocadéro reminded him of an Oriental Louvre or Bon Marché. The Bon Marché was the first department store, opening in Paris in 1852, the year after the Crystal Palace exposition, and the Louvre appeared just three years later. The objective advantages of somewhat lower prices and larger selection which these stores offered over traditional retail outlets were not the only reasons for their success. Even more significant factors were their practices of marking each item with a fixed price and of encouraging customers to inspect merchandise even if they did not make a purchase. Until then very different customs had prevailed in retail establishments. Prices had generally been subject to negotiation, and the buyer, once haggling began, was more or less obligated to buy.

The department store introduced an entirely new set of social interactions to shopping. In exchange for the freedom to browse, meaning the liberty to indulge in dreams without being obligated to buy in fact, the buyer gave up the freedom to participate actively in establishing prices and instead had to accept the price set by the seller.[7] Active verbal interchange between customer and retailer was replaced by the passive, mute response of consumer to things—a striking example of how "the civilizing process" tames aggressions and feelings toward people while encouraging desires and feelings directed toward things. Department stores were organized to inflame these material desires and feelings. Even if the consumer was free not to buy at that time, techniques of merchandising pushed him to want

Nightlife in cities was enhanced and encouraged by street and interior lighting, such as Friedrichstrasse in Berlin, Germany, depicted in this 1910 postcard. *AKG-Images.*

to buy *sometime*. As environments of mass consumption, department stores were, and still are, places where consumers are an audience to be entertained by commodities, where selling is mingled with amusement, where arousal of free-floating desire is as important as immediate purchase of particular items. Other examples of such environments are expositions, trade fairs, amusement parks, and (to cite more contemporary examples) shopping malls and large new airports or even subway stations. The numbed hypnosis induced by these places is a form of sociability as typical of modern mass consumption as the sociability of the salon was typical of prerevolutionary upper-class consumption. . . .

THE ELECTRICAL FAIRYLAND

By now it is becoming clear how momentous were the effects of nineteenth-century technological progress in altering the social universe of consumption. Besides being responsible for an increase in productivity which made possible a rise in real income; besides creating many new products and lowering the prices of traditional ones; besides all this, technology made possible the material realization of fantasies which had hitherto existed only in the realm of imagination. More than any other technological innovation of the late nineteenth century, even more than the development of cinematography, the advent of electrical power invested everyday life with fabulous qualities. The importance of an electrical power grid in transforming and diversifying production is obvious, as is its eventual effect in putting a whole new range of goods on the market. What is less appreciated, but what amounts to a cultural revolution, is the way electricity created a fairyland environment, the sense of being, not in a distant place, but in a make-believe place where obedient genies leap to their master's command, where miracles of speed and motion are wrought by the slightest gesture, where a landscape of glowing pleasure domes and twinkling lights stretches into infinity.

Above all, the advent of large-scale city lighting by electrical power nurtured a collective sense of life in a dream world. In the 1890s nocturnal lighting in urban areas was by no means novel, since gas had been used for this purpose for decades; however, gas illumination was pale and flickering compared to the powerful incandescent and arc lights which began to brighten the night sky in that decade. The expositions provided a preview of the transformation of nighttime Paris from somber semidarkness to a celestial landscape. At the 1878 exposition an electric light at a café near but not actually on the fairgrounds caused a sensation. In 1889 a nightly show of illuminated fountains entranced crowds with a spectacle of falling rainbows, cascading jewels, and flaming liquids, while spotlights placed on the top of the Eiffel Tower swept the darkening sky as the lights of the city were being turned on. At the 1900 exposition electrical lighting was used for the first time on a massive scale, to keep the fair open well into the night. Furthermore, the special lighting effects were stunning. In one of his articles for the *Revue de Paris,* Corday describes the nightly performance:

> A simple touch of the finger on a lever, and a wire as thick as a pencil throws upon the Monumental Gateway . . . the brilliance of three thousand incandescent lights which, under uncut gems of colored glass, become the sparkling soul of enormous jewels.
>
> Another touch of the finger: The banks of the Seine and the bridges are lighted with fires whose reflection prolongs the splendor. . . . The façade of the Palace of Electricity is embraced, a stained-glass window of light, where all these diverse splendors are assembled in apotheosis.[8]

Like the technological marvels already mentioned, this one was at once exploited for commercial purposes. As early as 1873 the writer Villiers de l'Isle-Adam (1838–1889) predicted in a short story, "L'Affichage céleste" (which might be loosely translated as "The Heavenly Billboard"), that the "seeming miracles" of electrical lights could be used to generate "an absolute Publicity" when advertising messages were projected upward to shine among the stars:

> •Wouldn't it be something to surprise the Great Bear himself if, suddenly, between his sublime paws, this disturbing message were to appear: *Are corsets necessary, yes or no?* . . . What emotion concerning dessert liqueurs . . . if one were to perceive, in the south of Regulus, this heart of the Lion, on the very tip of the ear of corn of the Virgin, an Angel holding a flask in hand, while from his mouth comes a small paper on which could be read these words: *My, it's good!*[9]

Thanks to this wonderful invention, concluded Villiers, the "sterile spaces" of heaven could be converted "into truly and fruitfully instructive spectacles. . . . It is not a question here of feelings. Business is business. . . . Heaven will finally make something of itself and acquire an intrinsic value." As with so many other writers of that era, Villiers's admiration of technological wonders is tempered by the ironic consideration of the banal commercial ends to which the marvelous means were directed. Unlike the wonders of nature, the wonders of technology could not give rise to unambiguous enthusiasm or unmixed awe, for they were obviously manipulated to arouse consumers' enthusiasm and awe.

The prophetic value of Villiers's story lies less in his descriptions of the physical appearance of the nocturnal sky with its stars obscured by neon lights, than in his forebodings of the moral consequences when commerce seizes all visions, even heavenly ones, to hawk its wares. Villiers's prophecies were borne out by the rapid application of electrical lighting to advertising. As he foresaw, electricity was used to spell out trade names, slogans, and movie titles. Even without being shaped into words, the unrelenting glare of the lights elevated ordinary merchandise to the level of the marvelous. Department-store windows were illuminated with spotlights bounced off mirrors. At the 1900 exposition, wax figurines modeling the latest fashions were displayed in glass cages under brilliant lights, a sight which attracted hordes of female spectators.

When electrical lighting was used to publicize another technical novelty, the automobile, the conjunction attracted mammoth crowds of both sexes.

Beginning in 1898, an annual Salon de l'Automobile was held in Paris to introduce the latest models to the public. It was one of the first trade shows; the French were pioneers in advertising the automobiles as well as in developing the product itself. This innovation in merchandising—like the universal expositions the Salon de l'Automobile resembles so closely—claimed the educational function of acquainting the public with recent technological advances, a goal, however, which was strictly subordinate to that of attracting present and future customers. The opening of the 1904 Salon de l'Automobile was attended by 40,000 people (compared to 10,000 who went to the opening of the annual painting salon), and 30,000 came each day for the first week. Each afternoon during the Salon, de l'Automobile, the Champs-Elysées was thronged with crowds making their way to the show, which was held in the Grand Palais, an imposing building constructed for the 1900 universal exposition. During the Salon the glass and steel domes of the Grand Palais were illuminated at dusk with 200,000 lights; the top of the building glowed in the gathering darkness like a stupendous lantern. People were enchanted: "a radiant jewel," they raved, "a colossal industrial fairyland," "a fairytale spectacle."[10]

NOTES

1. Many of these details are from Richard D. Mandell, *Paris 1900: The Great World's Fair* (n.p.: University of Toronto Press, 1967), chapter 1. For an excellent short summary of the French universal expositions, see Raymond Isay, *Panorama des expositions universelles* (3rd ed., Paris: Gallimard, 1937).

2. Henri Chardon, "L'Exposition de 1900," *Revue de Paris* 1 (February 1, 1896): 644. Chardon was participating in a debate as to whether another exposition should be held in 1900. Because of the commercialism of the 1889 event, there was strong opposition to the proposal. On the debate see Mandell, *Paris 1900*, pp. 25–51.

3. This description is from Paul Morand, *1900 A.D.*, trans. Mrs. Romilly Fedden (New York: William Farquhar Payson, 1931), p. 66. See also pp. 65–66 and the photograph facing p. 67.

4. Eugene-Melchior de Vogüé, "La Défunte Exposition," *Revue des deux mondes*, 4th per., 162 (November 15, 1900): 384–85.

5. Michel Corday (Louis-Léonard Pollet), "La Force à l'Exposition," *Revue de Paris* 1 (January 15, 1900): 439.

6. Maurice Talmeyr, "L'École du Trocadéro," *Revue des deux mondes*. All quotations from Talmeyr are from this article unless otherwise noted. He also wrote a series "Notes sur l'Exposition" that appeared in *Le Correspondant* between April 10, 1899, and April 25, 1900. Altogether the series included thirteen articles.

7. Richard D. Sennett, *The Fall of Public Man* (New York: Alfred A. Knopf, 1976), pp. 141–49.

8. Michel Corday, "A l'Exposition.—La Force a l'Exposition," *Revue de Paris* 1 (January 15, 1900): 438–39. See his note at the bottom of p. 438 regarding the number of kilowatts involved in this display.

9. In Villiers de l'Isle-Adam, *Oeuvres*, ed. Jacques-Henry Bornecque (n.p.: Le Club Français du Livre, 1957), p. 57. The short story was first republished in *La Renaissance littéraire et artistique* (November 30, 1873) and was republished in 1883 as part of Villiers's *Contes cruels*.

10. Robert de La Sizeranne, "La Beauté des machines, a propos du Salon de l'Automobile," *Revue des deux mondes*, 5th per., 42 (December 1, 1907): 657; Camille Mauclair, "La Decoration lumineuse," *Revue bleue* 8 (November 23, 1907): 656; and Emile Berr, "Une Exposition parisienne.—Le 'Salon' des chauffeurs," *Revue bleu* 11 (December 24, 1904): 829.

CHAPTER 19

Early Photojournalism

Ulrich Keller

Ulrich Keller is a professor in the department of art history at the University of California at Santa Barbara and an adjunct curator of photography at the University of California at Santa Barbara Art Museum.

More than half a century elapsed between Daguerre's epochal invention and the early 1890s when it finally became commercially feasible to reproduce photographs as photographs in large newspaper editions. Prior to this point, the continuous tones of the camera image had to be transcribed into line engraving—which meant that there was little incentive for newspapers to employ photographers on a regular or even just intermittent basis. The picture reporters on the payroll of *Harper's, L'Illustration, The Illustrated London News,* etc., were all draughtsmen whose sketches were produced at considerably lower cost than wet collodion glass negatives in big view cameras. Invariably representing battles, accidents, and ceremonial events at the peak moment—whether or not the artist had been there—the sketches also were more exciting than images out of the camera, which usually arrived too late and could not record fast action anyway. And while the drawings of the Special Artists were usually imprecise, if not altogether fictitious in character, this did not give an edge to the photographic images, because the latter lost their specific mark of authenticity when transferred to woodblocks.[1]

Thus it is no wonder that until ca. 1885 the history of photography does not know of a single photographer who specialized exclusively in news reporting, or worked solely for press organs for any length of time. Limited and instructive exceptions to the rule were prompted only by major wars, which held sufficient incentive to a few enterprising men such as Brady, Beato, and Fenton to embark on extended news photo campaigns. Even the longest of these, [Mathew] Brady's two-year campaign covering the Civil War with dozens of cameramen, was just that: a temporary effort, not a permanent news gathering machinery. Moreover, with his galleries in Washington and New York continuing to turn out a large volume of *cartes de visite,* portraiture still seems to have been Brady's mainstay product. And if his grand war reportage eventually ended in bankruptcy, it was precisely because no commercially viable link could be forged to the existing pictorial mass media. As it seems, Brady derived only publicity but no revenues from the publication of his images by *Leslie's* and *Harper's.* For profits he had to rely on the marketing of original prints through his galleries and perhaps a few book and stationery stores. The large potential audience of Brady's war documentation could not be reached in this haphazard way, and retail sales proved altogether inadequate to cover the enormous production costs of ca. $100,000.[2]

If the prehistory of photojournalism is therefore the story of an ideally indicated but practically unfeasible alliance between camera and printing press, we encounter a fundamentally different situation around the turn of the century. . . . The cameraman, while anonymous, can be identified as one of several photographers on the staff of the news agency Underwood & Underwood, which regularly furnished pictures to *Harper's Weekly*. He must have used a light, fast, hand-held camera fitted with a telephoto lens; most likely he operated from a privileged, cordoned-off press location, and it is entirely possible that Teddy Roosevelt's expressive performance was directly addressed to the press. We need not stress that the resulting photographs were reproduced *as* photographs on the magazine page. Furthermore, since the photographer submitted a whole series of images, an editor had to think about an effective layout strategy.

He found an intelligent, witty solution, indeed, foreshadowing the fact that photojournalism was going to be a matter of teamwork, with editors and art directors destined to add an important creative dimension to the photographer's basic camera work. The contrast to Lincoln's campaign photograph of 1860 is certainly striking. Under the pressure of corporate employers catering to mass audiences, news photography has developed a captivating, dynamic style. Instead of a posed portrait, we are presented with exciting closeups of a statesman in action. . . .

There can be no doubt, then, that the much-debated "birth" of photojournalism *pre*dates, rather than *post*dates, Theodore Roosevelt's presidency. The years from 1890 to the beginning of the First World War can indeed be identified as the formative period, one which was inaugurated but not wholly defined by the halftone innovation. It was at this time that photojournalism established itself technically and aesthetically, as a professional career and a social institution. The complexity of the phenomenon warrants a detailed analysis.

THE CONSTITUTIVE ELEMENTS OF PHOTOJOURNALISM

Somewhat crudely, and leaving aside for the moment all practical and ideological ramifications, it is possible to distinguish three basic ingredients in the organizational infrastructure of early photojournalism: a new brand of newspapers using halftone illustrations based on photographs in lieu of woodcuts based on drawings; a new type of news agency distributing photographs rather than texts; and a new generation of photographers equipped with small, fast, hand-held cameras instead of slow and big ones mounted on tripods. To begin with the first and most important (even if somewhat overrated) element, it was the advent of the halftone printing block that prompted the transition from pictorial to photographic journalism.

Portrait of President Abraham Lincoln. *Courtesy of the Library of Congress.*

Halftone Pictures

On an experimental basis, halftone reproductions were used since 1867 in weekly magazines and since 1880 in daily papers. But only after substantial improvements had been made by American inventors in 1889–1890 did it become feasible for large-circulation newspapers to print photographic halftone illustrations regularly in large quantities. The development was significant and amounted to a radical redefinition if not a second "invention" of picture journalism.[3] True, fifty years earlier the use of the illustrated weeklies had produced the eminent cultural phenomenon of a *permanent, institutionalized supply of news pictures to mass audiences.* The shockwaves of the event had been registered in Wordsworth's notorious attack on "Illustrated Books and Newspapers":

> Discourse was deemed Man's noblest attitude,
> And written words the glory of his hand. . . .
> Now prose and verse sunk into disrepute.
> Must laquey a dumb Art that best can suit
> The taste of this once-intellectual Land.
> A backward movement surely have we here.
> From manhood,—back to childhood. . . .
> Avaunt this vile abuse of pictured page!
> Must eyes be all in all, the tongue and ear
> Nothing? Heaven keep us from a lower stage![4]

In spite of the anxieties it spawned in some quarters, early picture journalism was a relatively modest affair in terms of the quantity of reproductions involved. Until 1873 not a single daily newspaper carried images regularly, and the illustrated weeklies devoted to the publication of news for the general public were few in number, perhaps less than two dozen in all of Europe and America. It can be estimated that the total volume of news pictures to which a given country's public was exposed rarely exceeded 100 per week. By 1910, after the fast, efficient halftone block had all but eliminated the older reproduction technologies, the statistics reveal a dramatic increase. Hundreds of illustrated dailies and weeklies were now published in every industrialized nation, and the total number of pictures published reached staggering proportions, at least by contemporary standards. Fourteen daily newspapers in New York City *alone,* for example, inundated their readers with an average of 903 pictures per week in 1910.[5] While the steep rise is attributable to a variety of factors, few experts will deny that the halftone block was the single most important of these. The permanent supply of news pictures to the urban mass audiences, at any rate, had established itself on a markedly higher level than in the woodcut era.

Significantly, it was no longer possible to launch a wholesale attack on the legitimacy of the pictorial press, as Wordsworth had done half a century earlier. Instead, the danger was now seen in the excessive quantity of reproductions. As *Harper's Weekly* declared in a 1911 editorial on "Over-Illustrations," "We can't see the ideas for the illustration. Our world is simply flooded with them."[6] Popular picture consumption had become a fact of life; only its extent and pervasiveness remained subject to debate.

Apart from quantities, there is a qualitative side to the halftone revolution. In a justly acclaimed analytical investigation of countless manual and photomechanical printing techniques of the late nineteenth century, Estelle Jussim claimed that the halftone picture creates "an optical illusion with surrogate power" where line engravings had rendered more subjective, less reliable images. While Jussim is only thinking of art reproductions, the intellectual historian Neil Harris has broadened her claim of the halftone's "illusionary" and at the same time "objective" powers to include all kinds of photomechanical imagery, especially in newspapers and magazines.[7] According to this view, the halftone process reproduces a given "reality" more "realistically" than ever; in a somewhat tautological manner, it is seen to simply repeat and confirm what exists already. However, if we take the position that is nowadays perhaps more tenable—that reality is not given but rather socially constructed through competing representations—a different conclusion suggests itself. The power of the halftone technology then arises precisely from the fact that it bestows the quality of authentic "reality" on constructed, in many cases biased and contrived scenes. Under this assumption our interest shifts automatically from the technical intricacies of line engravings and dot screens to the institutional framework behind and around them. It is this social instance that formulates the meanings and messages that photomechanical printing encodes "realistically" for mass consumption in a merely secondary operation. It is this social instance that must be analyzed.

Press Photographers

If the halftone block had made the newspapers accessible to photography around 1890, it was substantial improvements in emulsions and camera design that made photography attractive to the papers. The fast gelatin dry plates and roll films of the 1880s, coupled with the hand-held snapshot cameras made possible by them, opened up the realm of movement and action to photography.[8] Previously, the newspaper had relied on the camera for a very limited subject range, especially portraits and sites. Even with the halftone innovation the newspapers would have continued to make very broad use of hand art, had it not been for the new emulsions, which ensured that instead of a few selected subjects photography could now be used to cover practically the whole range of newsworthy subjects. Combined, the halftone block and the gelatin emulsion represented an irresistible force which proceeded with breathtaking speed to ban graphic imagery from the illustrated press. Within fifteen years, many daily and weekly newspapers replaced their draughtsmen with cameramen. By 1900 a large corps of press photographers existed in America, and with the steady increase in the volume of news imagery published, this corps kept growing until it spanned the world in an ever more finely woven capillary network.

Inevitably, the subject range covered by this press corps became almost limitless. From a war in

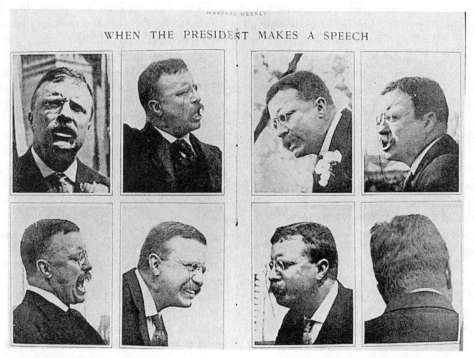

Underwood & Underwood, President Theodore Roosevelt speaking. *Underwood & Underwood. From Harper's Weekly January 26, 1907.*

Asia to a railway accident in Brazil, a presidential campaign stop in Little Rock, Arkansas, and the little girl feeding a pigeon in Central Park, everything could take the form of a news photograph. Especially the trivial phase of the expanding spectrum of news imagery deserves to be emphasized here. Important events had always been illustrated. Trivial incidents made an appearance in force only around 1900 and they have stayed with us ever since, underscoring once more that this is the period from which modern photojournalism should be dated.

In press archives, one can occasionally find visual evidence of the newly won importance of photojournalism. An Underwood & Underwood stereograph of President McKinley's funeral procession, to cite just one instance, features a wooden platform populated by a whole battalion of press photographers. . . . It is not a sensational picture, but it confirms that in a matter of a few years photojournalism had become a built-in feature of public life. A point is reached where no important event can take place without extensive photographic coverage. More than that, it is obvious that these newspaper representatives are highly privileged witnesses of the event in progress. Forty years earlier, only one photographer is known to have been present at the no-less-important event of Lincoln's inauguration, and he had to be content with a peripheral, impractical vantage point. In 1901, however, a large platform is expressly built to give the press photographers an optimal viewpoint: they now act as lieutenants of powerful news organizations and millions of readers. Clearly, the alliance of the press and photography has produced an institution of consequence.

The Spanish-American War appears to have been the first major armed conflict in history to be depicted primarily by photographers, as opposed to draughtsmen. It came too soon, however, to lead to any highly organized form of coverage. This distinction belongs to the Russo-Japanese War, which took place half a world away from the United States but nonetheless became subject to more massive photographic documentation than all previous wars together. *Collier's* alone employed six photographers on both sides of the front, not to mention a host of correspondents.[9] Again, no principal difference sets this monumental effort apart from the superbly organized photo campaigns of foreign wars and domestic pomp and circumstance that *Life* magazine was to stage a few decades later.

While the bulk of the growing army of press photographers consisted of lowly staffers careening about town on motorcycles in pursuit of accident victims and police interviews, a few specially talented photojournalists soon obtained high status as chroniclers of "big-time" news events. The heyday of star-photographers on the order of Erich Salomon and Margaret Bourke-White was to come later, but already in the early 1900s some press photographers began to circle the globe, accumulating large expense accounts and representing big-time publishers and millions of readers at the major events of the day. The days of intermittent, entrepreneurial news photography by men such as Fenton, Brady, and Gardner with their limited resources and distribution networks had definitely come to an end.

One man deserves to be singled out in the present context as the epitome of the species of the "big-time" news photographer, if not the emerging profession of photojournalism in general. Born in 1856 in England, Jimmy Hare became a photojournalist of the first hour when, after years of freelancing for illustrated magazines, he was hired as a full-time staff photographer by the *Illustrated American* in 1895. Three years later he switched to *Collier's*, a newly founded weekly destined to play a leading role in the early phase of photojournalism. Hare's first major assignment was the Spanish-American War; a few years later he was back in the camps and trenches as the most productive member of *Collier's* camera team covering the Russo-Japanese conflict. In the following years, Hare continued to document major domestic news stories, such as the sensational exploits of pioneer aviators from the Wright brothers to Bleriot. A last challenge was provided by the First World War, which Hare covered in the service of *Leslie's* magazine. When he retired he was a celebrity of sorts. Newspapers and press associations frequently paid homage to him with articles and honorary memberships, and shortly before he died, a colorful biography was published about "the man who never faked a picture nor ran from danger." True, the star photojournalists of the *Berliner Illustrierte Zeitung* and *Life* were to reap greater fame, but Jimmy came first.

All this said, the fact remains that, as a class, early photojournalists were still relatively unsophisticated in their use of aesthetic and discursive strategies. Even the best Hare photographs look plain and unexciting next to those of Felix Man, Henri Cartier-Bresson, and Margaret Bourke-White, who managed to impress recognizable "authorial," if not artistic, signatures on their work. Early photojournalism was marked by a clear aesthetic deficit, and the as yet very rudimentary editorial planning and processing procedures alone cannot account for this deficit. An additional factor comes into view when we remember that the pay scale and social prestige of any incipient profession tends to be too low to attract eminent talents. More importantly, it seems that in looking for inspiration from other branches of photography and the arts in general, early press photographers were not likely to be richly rewarded. Most of contemporary painting and all of "Art" or "Pictorial" photography were entrenched in elitist social rituals, lofty ideologies, and romantic to symbolist styles. A photojournalist could find precious little stimulation for his daily work here, which thus never escaped the narrow confines of a cut-and-dried routine operation. Only the 1920s brought a dramatic narrowing of the gap between art and industry, technology, mass communication. Formerly despised contexts of picture-making in science, industry, advertising, and press now came to be accepted as legitimate fields of aesthetic productivity, and steeply rising earnings lent these fields an additional lure. To put it in the form of a speculative example, if around 1900 someone wanted

to build an oeuvre and a reputation by means of camera work at all, he or she had hardly any choice but to join the Photo-Secession and to produce dream-like gum prints of languid females in symbolic guises. Only the functionalistic reorientation of the arts in the 1920s provided the context in which photojournalism could become a challenging aesthetic practice likely to attract individuals of talent and ambition.[10]

Photo Agencies

In addition to newspapers using halftone illustrations and a corps of press photographers using snapshot cameras, a third factor contributed essentially to the institutionalization of photojournalism: the emergence of agencies disseminating photographic news pictures. At the root of this latter development was the fact that not even the greatest newspapers with the most versatile staff photographers could cover every important news event, especially if it happened in an unpredictable moment and place. Therefore, a mechanism was needed which could supply a newspaper with pictures of noteworthy occurrences beyond the reach of its own investigative apparatus. This intermediary function was assumed by picture agencies, which made it their business to secure photographs of worthwhile subjects for sale to subscribing newspapers.

. . . It goes without saying that the sinking of the *Titanic* represented the type of unforeseeable and inaccessible event that must always elude planned, systematic news coverage. However, an anonymous amateur photographer was at hand on one of the rescue ships, and he found the opportunity for a snapshot as some survivors of the catastrophe approached the *Carpathia*. The resulting picture was aesthetically poor, but the subject matter made it sensational. The New York–based photo agency, Bain's News Picture Service, somehow got hold of the snapshot and distributed it to many newspapers that otherwise would have gone without illustration of the *Titanic* episode.

Bain News Picture Service, *Titanic*'s lifeboats on the way to the *Carpathia*, April 15, 1912. *Courtesy of the Library of Congress.*

Photo agencies not only bought pictures from outside sources, they also employed their own staff photographers, some of whom generated unprecedented in-depth reportages of the political scene. In 1899 George Grantham Bain, director and photographer of a fledgling picture agency, decided to attach himself to the office of the American president. Over an extended period of time, Bain accompanied McKinley on every trip and also gained frequent access to the White House for formal portrait sessions. The product of this sustained effort was a voluminous reference album containing hundreds of news pictures, meticulously numbered and captioned for commercial distribution.[11] . . . Naturally, an individual newspaper never could have afforded to devote so much attention to a single political figure. For picture agencies, on the other hand,

which catered to the American press as a whole, a profitable line of business opened up here.

As far as I can see, no similar undertaking had ever been carried out under earlier presidents. The Bain album marks the historically significant transition from the intermittent pictorial news recording method of the nineteenth century to the permanent, institutionalized mode of coverage made possible by the increasingly complex machinery of photojournalism at the beginning of our own century. It is a mode of operation that has been perfected ever since. When President Lyndon B. Johnson woke up at 6:30 A.M. in his White House living quarters, he pressed two buttons: that of his body guard and that of Yoichi Okamoto, his personal photographer. Okamoto was one of two persons permitted to enter the Oval Office without knocking, and within the first three months of Johnson's term he took 11,000 pictures.[12] Bain was more conservative in his use of film, but he set the basic pattern for a long line of White House photographers.

Historically, it is worth pointing out that *verbal* news reportages became subject to distribution by commercial agencies already during the 1830s, i.e., as soon as a host of mass circulation newspapers emerged in Paris and other metropolitan centers. Given the fact that the big picture magazines made their appearance soon thereafter, one might expect to see the establishment of *pictorial* news agencies during the 1850s and 1860s, but no such development occurred. For one thing, there was only a small number of news-oriented illustrated weeklies, just one or two per country, and since each of these pursued limited national interests, few picture topics would have been in sufficiently broad demand to warrant commercial distribution. Furthermore, as long as most news images took the form of drawings, quick forwarding to a multitude of subscribing papers would have been difficult because of duplication problems. Photographic copying of drawings, for example, would have involved a considerable loss of time and graphic quality. . . .

NOTES

1. For pre-photographic picture journalism see: M. Jackson, *The Pictorial Press: Its Origins and Progress* (London: Hurst & Blackett, 1885); C. Thomas, "Illustrated Journalism," in *Journal of the Society of Arts*, vol. 39 (30 January 1891), pp. 173ff.; and P. Hodgson, *The War Illustrators* (New York: Macmillan, 1977).

2. D. M. Kunhardt and P. B. Kunhardt, *Mathew Brady and His World* (Alexandria, VA: Time-Life, 1977), pp. 56ff.; J. D. Horan, *Mathew Brady, Historian with a Camera* (New York: Bonanza, 1955), pp. 35ff.; R. Meredith, *Mr. Lincoln's Cameraman, Mathew B. Brady*, 2nd rev. ed. (New York: Dover, 1974), pp. 88ff.

3. . . . See H. and A. Gernsheim, *The History of Photography From the Camera Obscura to the Beginning of the Modern Era* (New York: McGraw-Hill, 1969), pp. 539ff.; E. Ostroff, "Etching, Engraving and Photography: History of Photomechanical Reproduction," and "Photography and Photogravure: History of Photomechanical Reproduction," in *Journal of Photographic Science*, vol. 27 (1969), pp. 65ff. and 101ff.

4. W. Knight, ed., *The Poetical Works by William Wordsworth*, vol. 8 (Edinburgh: Paterson, 1886), p. 172.

5. R. S. Schunemann, *The Photograph in Print: An Examination of New York Daily Newspapers, 1890–1937* (University of Minnesota, 1966), pp. 102ff. In the picture magazines, halftone photographs outnumbered engravings by the late 1890s (C. K. Shorter, "Illustrated Journalism: Its Past and Its Future," *The Contemporary Review*, vol. 75, 1899, pp. 481 ff.).

6. *Harper's Weekly*, vol. 55 (29 July 1911), p. 6.

7. E. Jussim, *Visual Communication and the Graphic Arts: Photographic Technologies in the Nineteenth Century* (New York: Bowker, 1974, 1983), p. 288; Neil Harris, "Iconography and Intellectual History: The Half-Tone Effect," in J. Higham and P. K. Conklin, eds., *New Directions in American Intellectual History* (Baltimore: Johns Hopkins University Press, 1979), pp. 198ff. Jussim clearly states that she is primarily interested in the modalities of transmission. "The meanings transmitted do not concern us here" (p. 12); that's exactly the problem.

8. Compare Gernsheim (1969), pp. 397ff.

9. L. L. Gould, R. Greffe, *Photojournalist: The Career of Jimmy Hare* (Austin: Univ. of Texas, 1977), pp. 31ff.; C. Carnes, *Jimmy Hare, News Photographer: Half a Century with a Camera* (New York: Macmillan, 1940), pp. 152ff.; *The Russo-Japanese War: A Photographic and Descriptive Review* (New York: Collier, 1905).

10. For Art Photography, see U. Keller, "The Myth of Art Photography: A Sociological Analysis," and "The Myth of Art Photography: An Iconographic Analysis," in *History of Photography*, vol. 8 (October–December 1984), pp. 249ff.; and vol. 9 (January–March 1985), pp. 1ff. For the changing concerns of the 1920s, especially in Germany, see D. Mellor, ed., *Germany: The New Photography, 1927–33* (London: Arts Council of Great Britain, 1978).

11. The anonymous album is part of the legacy of Underwood & Underwood. Since this firm did not enter the field of news photography until 1901 and Bain is the only photographer known to have accompanied President McKinley in 1899, it seems likely, though not certain, that the anonymous album is Bain's. J. Price, "Press Pictures Have Come Far in Half a Century," in *Editor and Publisher*, vol. 71 (February 19, 1938), p. 7.

12. Y. Okamoto, "Photographing President LBJ," in R. S. Schunemann, ed., *Photographic Communication: Principles, Problems and Challenges of Photojournalism* (New York: Hastings, 1972), pp. 194ff.

CHAPTER **20**

Inscribing Sound

Lisa Gitelman

Lisa Gitelman is a professor with the Department of Media Studies at Catholic University in Washington, DC. She is author most recently of Always Already New: Media, History, and the Data of Culture

Thomas Edison was the first to demonstrate the phonograph in public, when he took his prototype to the New York City offices of the *Scientific American* magazine in 1877. There, witnesses reported, the phonograph greeted them and inquired after their health. They were fascinated by the apparent simplicity of the device; it was "a little affair of a few pieces of metal," not a complicated machine with "rubber larynx and lips." Wrapped around a cylinder rotated by hand, the tinfoil recording surface was impressed with indentations that formed "an exact record of the sound that produced them" and comprised what was termed "the writing of the machine." These words or "remarks" could then be "translated" or played back. Observers seemed for a time to believe that they themselves might translate, using a magnifying glass painstakingly to discern phonetic dots and dashes. But the really remarkable aspect of the device arose, one onlooker marveled, in "literally making it read itself." It was as if "instead of perusing a book ourselves, we drop it into a machine, set the latter in motion, and behold! The voice of the author is heard repeating his own composition.[1] Edison and his appreciative audience clearly assumed that his invention would soon provide a better, more immediate means of stenography. Machinery, accurate and impartial, would objectively and materially realize the author's voice.

In statements to the press and later in his own article in the *North American Review*, Edison enumerated the use of phonographs for writing letters and taking dictation of many sorts, as well as for things like talking clocks, talking dolls, and recorded novels. Music was mentioned, but usually as a form of dictation: You could send love songs to a friend, sing your child a lullaby, and then, if it worked, save up the same rendition for bedtime tomorrow. In keeping with the important public uses of shorthand for court and legislative reports, the phonograph would also provide a cultural repository, a library for sounds. The British critic Matthew Arnold had only recently defined culture as "the best that has been thought and said in the world," and now the phonograph could save up the voices and sayings, Edison noted, of "our Washingtons, our Lincolns, our Gladstones." And there was plenty more to save. The American Philological Society, Edison reported to the *New York Times,* had requested a phonograph "to preserve the accents of the Onondagas and Tuscaroras, who are dying out." According to the newspaper, only "one old man speaks the language fluently and correctly, and he is afraid that he will die.[2]

The contrast between *our* statesmen and the dwindling Onondaga hints that the phonograph was immediately an instrument of Anglo-American cultural hierarchy. It became party to habitual and manifold distinctions between an "us" and a "them." Drawing a similar distinction, *Punch* magazine satirized in 1878 that the work of "our best poets" could be publicly disseminated by young women using phonographs, taking the place of the "hirsute Italian organ-grinders" who walked about the streets of London. The phonograph became at once instrumental to expressions of difference like these and suggestive of a strictly (because mechanically) nonhierarchical vox populi. One enthusiast proposed half seriously that a phonograph could be installed in the new Statue of Liberty, then under construction in New York Harbor, so it could make democratic announcements to passing ships. Reality seemed hardly less fanciful. With this remarkable device, published accounts made clear, women could read while sewing. Students could read in the dark. The blind could read. And the dead could speak.[3]

In January 1878 Edison signed contracts assigning the rights to exhibit the phonograph, while reserving for himself the right to exploit its primary dictation function at a later time. Exhibition rights went to a small group of investors, most of them involved already in the financial progress of Alexander Graham Bell's telephone. Together they formed the Edison Speaking Phonograph Company and hired James Redpath as their general manager. A former abolitionist, Redpath had done the most to transform the localized adult-education lecture series of the early American lyceums into more formal, national "circuits" administered by centralized speakers' bureaus. He had just sold his lyceum bureau, and he came to the phonograph company with a name for promoting "merit" rather than what his biographer later dismissed as "mere newspaper reputation."[4] The distinction was blurred, however, throughout the ensuing year of phonograph exhibitions. With so much distance separating the primitive phonograph's technological abilities from the ecstatic hyperbole that surrounded the invention in the press, phonograph exhibitors relied upon novelty in their appeals to audiences. Novelty, of course, would wear off, although it would take well into the summer of the following year to "[milk] the Exhibition cow pretty dry," as one of the company directors put it privately in a letter to Edison.[5]

The Edison Speaking Phonograph Company functioned by granting regional demonstration rights to exhibitors; individuals **purchased** the right to exhibit a phonograph within a protected territory. They were trained to use the machine, which required a certain knack, and agreed to pay the company 25 percent of their gross receipts. This was less of a lecture circuit, then, than a bureaucracy. For the most part, phonograph exhibitors worked locally; whatever sense they had of belonging to a national enterprise came from corporate coordination and a good deal of petty accountancy. Paper circulated around the country—correspondence, bank drafts, letters of receipt—but the men and their machines remained more local in their peregrinations, covered in the local press, supported (or not) by local audiences and institutions in their contractually specified state or area. The company set admission at twenty-five cents, although some exhibitors soon cut the price down to a dime. Ironically, no *phonographically* recorded version of a phonograph exhibition survives; the tinfoil records did not last long. Instead, the character of these demonstrations can be pieced together from accounts published in newspapers, letters mailed to Redpath and the company, and a variety of other sources, which include a burlesque of the exhibitions entitled *Prof. Black's Phunnygraph or Talking Machine.*

While the Edison Speaking Phonograph Company was getting on its feet, several of Edison's friends and associates held public exhibitions that paired demonstrations of the telephone with the phonograph and raised the expectations of company insiders. Charging theater managers $100 a night for this double bill, Edward Johnson toured upstate New York at the end of January, Not all of his performances recouped the hundred dollars, but in Elmira and Courtland, "It was a decided success," he claimed, and the climax of the evening was "always reached when the Phonograph first speaks." "Everybody talks Phonograph," Johnson reported, on "the day after the concert and all agree that a 2nd concert would be more successful than the first."

Johnson's plan was simple. He categorized the fare as "Recitations, Conversational remarks, Songs (with words), Cornet Solos, Animal Mimicry, Laughter, Coughing, etc., etc.," which would be "delivered into the mouth of the machine, and subsequently reproduced." He described getting a lot of laughs by trying to sing himself, but he also tried to entice volunteers from the audience or otherwise to take advantage of local talent.[6] Another Edison associate, Professor J. W. S. Arnold, filled half of Chickering Hall in New York City, where his phonograph "told the story of Mary's little lamb" and then, like Johnson's phonograph, rendered a medley of speaking, shouting, and singing. At the end of the evening Arnold distributed strips of used tinfoil, and there was reportedly "a wild scramble for these keepsakes."[7]

These early exhibitions helped establish a formula for Redpath's agents to follow. Redpath himself managed a short season at Irving Hall in New York City, but the typical exhibition was more provincial. In nearby Jersey City, New Jersey, for instance, demonstration rights were owned by Frank Lundy, a journalist, who displayed little polish during exhibitions and who complained bitterly to the company that his territory was always being invaded by others or usurped by Edison's own open-door policy at the Menlo Park laboratory, a short train ride away. Lundy came through Jersey City in mid-June. He gave one exhibition at a Methodist Episcopal church ("admission 25 cents"), and another at Library Hall as part of a concert given by "the ladies of Christ Church." Both programs featured musical performances by community groups as well as explanations and demonstrations of the phonograph. Lundy reportedly "recited to" the machine, various "selections from Shakespeare and Mother Goose's melodies, laughed and sung, and registered the notes of [a] cornet, all of which were faithfully reproduced, to the great delight of the audience, who received pieces of the tin-foil as mementos." But poor Lundy's show on June 20th had been upstaged the day before by a meeting of the Jersey City "Aesthetic Society," which convened to wish one of its members bon voyage. Members of the "best families in Jersey City" as well as "many of the stars of New York literary society" were reportedly received at Mrs. Smith's residence on the eve of her departure for the Continent. For the occasion, one New York journalist brought along a phonograph and occupied part of the evening recording and reproducing laughter and song, as well as a farewell message to Smith, and a certain Miss Groesbeck's "inimitable representation" of a baby crying. Of these recorded cries, "the effect was very amusing," and the journalist "preserved the strip" of foil, saving the material impressions of Groesbeck's "mouth" impressions.[8]

Phonograph exhibitions such as these relied upon a familiar rhetoric of educational merit. Lecturers introduced Edison's machine as an important scientific discovery by giving an explanation of how the phonograph worked and then enacting this explanation with demonstrations of recording and playback.[9] Audiences were edified, and they were entertained. They learned and they enjoyed. Phonograph exhibitions thus reinforced the double message of the lyceum movement in

America, sugarcoating education as part of an elaborate ethos of social improvement.

Phonograph exhibitions flirted with the improvement of their audiences in three distinct yet interrelated ways. First, they offered all in attendance the opportunity to participate, at least tacitly, in the progress of technology. Audiences could be up to the minute, apprised of the latest scientific discovery, party to the success of the inventor whom the newspapers were calling the "Wizard of Menlo Park." They were also exposed—playfully and again tacitly—to "good taste." In making their selections for recording and playback, exhibitors made incongruous associations between well-known lines from Shakespeare and well-known lines from Mother Goose, between talented musicians and men like Edward Johnson, between inarticulate animal and baby noises and the articulate sounds of speech. Audiences could draw and maintain their own distinctions, laugh at the appropriate moments, recognize impressions, be "in" on the joke. In the process, they participated in the enactment of cultural hierarchy alluded to above. Finally, the exhibitions elevated the local experience to something much larger and more important. Local audiences heard and saw themselves materially preserved on bumpy strips of tinfoil. Those that met in the meanest church basements were recorded just like audiences in the grand concert halls of New York, Chicago, and New Orleans. Audience members could therefore imagine themselves as part of a modern, educated, tasteful, and recordable community, an "us" (as opposed to "them"), formed with similarly modern, educated, tasteful, and recordable people across the United States. The phonograph exhibition, in other words, offered a democratic vision of "us" and "our" sounds, available to the imagination in some measure because they must have hinted at their opposite: "them" and "theirs."

Of course, this vision came notably vested with cultural hierarchies and a local/global matrix—region/nation, here/elsewhere, local beat/wire story. The familiar practices of public lectures and amusements, the varied contexts within which public speech acts made sense as cultural productions, the enormous, framing tide of newsprint all informed the phonograph's reception. If phonographs were "speaking," their functional subjects remained importantly diffuse among available spoken forms: lectures and orations as well as "remarks," "sayings," recitations, declamations, mimicry, hawking, barking, and so on. The sheer heterogeneity of public speech acts should not be overlooked any more than the diversity of the speakers whose words more and less articulated an American public sphere. The nation that had been declared or voiced into being a century before remained a noisy place.[10]

Actual audience response to the phonograph exhibitions is difficult to judge. Some parts of the country simply were not interested. Mississippi and parts of the South, for example, were far more concerned with the yellow fever epidemic that plagued the region in 1878. Audiences in New Orleans were reportedly disappointed that the machine had to be yelled into in order to reproduce well, and there were other quibbles with the technology once the newspapers had raised expectations to an unrealistic level. Out in rural Louisiana, one exhibitor found that his demonstrations fell flat unless the audience heard all recordings as they were made. Record quality was still so poor that knowing what had been recorded was often necessary for playback to be intelligible. James Redpath spent a good deal of energy consoling exhibitors who failed to make a return on their investments, but he also fielded questions from individuals who, after witnessing exhibitions, wrote to ask if they could secure exhibition rights themselves. To one exhibitor in Brattleboro, Vermont, Redpath wrote sympathetically that "other intelligent districts" had proved as poor a field as Brattleboro, but that great success was to be had in districts where "the population is not more than ordinarily intelligent," Some parts of the country remained untried, while others were pretty well saturated, like parts of Pennsylvania, Wisconsin, and Illinois.[11]

Exhibitors everywhere wrote back to the company for more of the tinfoil that they purchased by the pound. The company kept a "Foil" account open on its books to enter these transactions. Pounds of tinfoil sheets entered into national circulation, arriving in the possession of exhibitors only to be publicly consumed, indented, divided, distributed, collected into private hands, and saved.

NOTES

1. *Scientific American* 37 (December 1877): 384.
2. "The Edison Speaking Machine, Exhibition Before Members of Congress," *New York Times* (April 20, 1878), 1:1.
3. This from a pamphlet by Frederick F. Garbit, *The Phonograph and Its Inventor, Thomas Alvah [sic] Edison.* Boston, 1878.
4. Charles F. Horner, *The Life of James Redpath and the Development of the Modern Lyceum* (New York: Barse & Hopkins, 1926), 227, 185.
5. Records of the Edison Speaking Phonograph Company exist at the Edison National Historic Site in West Orange, N. J., and at the Historical Society of Pennsylvania in Philadelphia. Documents from West Orange have been microfilmed and form part of the ongoing *Thomas A. Edison Papers, A Selective Microfilm Edition,* ed. Thomas E. Jeffery et al., 4 parts to date (Bethesda, Md.: University Publications of America). These items are also available as part of the ongoing electronic edition of the Edison Papers; see *http://edison.rutgers.edu.* For the items cited here, like Uriah Painter to Thomas Edison of August 2, 1879 ("milked the cow"), microfilm reel and frame numbers are given in the following form: TAEM 49:316. Documents from Philadelphia form part of the Painter Papers collection and have been cited as such. The company's incorporation papers are TAEM 51:771, The history of the company may be gleaned from volume 4 of *The Papers of Thomas A, Edison, The Wizard of Menlo Park,* ed. Paul B. Israel, Keith A. Nier, and Louis Carlat (Baltimore: Johns Hopkins University Press, 1998). Also see Paul Israel's "The Unknown History of the Tinfoil Phonograph," *NARAS Journal* 8 (1997–1998): 29–42.
6. Johnson to U. H. Painter of January 27th, 1878, in the Painter Papers; Johnson prospectus of February 18, 1878, TAEM 97:623. Both are transcribed and published in volume 4 of the *Papers of Thomas A. Edison.* I am grateful to Paul Israel and the other editors of the Edison Papers for sharing their work in manuscript and for sharing their knowledge of the Painter Papers.
7. "The Phonograph Exhibited: Prof. Arnold's Description of the Machine in Chickering Hall—Various Experiments, with Remarkable Results," *New York Times* (March 24, 1878), 2:5.
8. Lundy's complaint of August 31, 1878, TAEM 19:109; accounts of Jersey City are reported in the *Jersey Journal,* June 13th, 14th, and 21st, and the *Argus,* June 20th.
9. For a discussion of this improving ethos at later demonstrations see Charles Musser, "Photographers of Sound: Howe and the Phonograph, 1890–1896," chapter 3 in *High Class Moving Picture's: Lyman H. Howe and the Forgotten Era of Traveling Exhibitions, 1880–1920* (Princeton: Princeton University Press, 1991).
10. I am thinking here of Benedict Anderson, as well as Chris Looby, Jay Fliegelman, and Christopher Grasso, respectively *Voicing America: Language, Literary Form, and the Origins of the United States* (Chicago: University of Chicago Press, 1996); and *Declaring Independence: Jefferson, Natural Language, and the Culture of Performance* (Stanford: Stanford University Press, 1993); *A Speaking Aristocracy: Transforming Public Discourse in Eighteenth-Century Connecticut* (Chapel Hill: University of North Carolina Press, 1999). All of these discussions notably address an earlier period, as does Michael Warner's *The Letters of the Republic: Publication and the Public Sphere in Eighteenth-Century America* (Cambridge: Harvard University Press, 1990). For catalyzing imaginaries (above) Anderson has "the fatality of human linguistic diversity" (p. 43).
11. These details from the Painter Papers, Letter books and Treasurer's books of the Edison Speaking Phonograph Company, including Smith to Hubbard of November 23, 1878; Mason to Redpath of November 1, 1878; Cushing to Redpath of July 16, 1878; Redpath to Mason, July 10, 1878.

CHAPTER 21

The Making of the Phonograph

Jonathan Sterne

Jonathan Sterne is an associate professor and Chair of the Department of Art History and Communication Studies at McGill University in Montreal, Canada.

PLASTICITY, DOMESTICITY, AND PUBLICITY

Already in 1890, frustrated phonograph merchants were turning away from business uses and toward the growing coin-in-the-slot business. By the mid-1890s, this was one of the main areas in which money could be made. David Nasaw locates the boom in the coin-in-the-slot business as part of a larger, emergent, middle-class culture of public and semipublic entertainments. Coin-in-the-slot machines, where a user could hear a song for a fee, were located in hotel lobbies, train stations, and arcades. As cities grew more spread out, a well-placed arcade could entertain commuters with a few minutes to kill and a few cents in their pockets. The boom period for this business lasted only a few years. Between the erosion of phonography's novelty to coin-in-the-slot users and a bottleneck in the manufacture and distribution of new recordings, the potential of arcade-style listening to support the industry died off in the first decade of the twentieth century.[1] Coin-in-the-slot machines persisted into the 1910s and 1920s, when new developments allowed the invention of the first machine that would be called a *jukebox* in 1927.[2]

The industry's changing attitude toward marketing the **phonograph** could perhaps be best illusrtated by the shift in content among three major publications, the *Phonogram* (1891–93), the *Phonoscope* (1896–1900), and a second *Phonogram* (1900–1902). While the first *Phonogram* focused almost exclusively on business use, the *Phonoscope* focused on entertainment uses in public places, and the second *Phonogram* treated the phonograph largely as a means of domestic entertainment. Concurrent changes in middle-class domestic life during this period help set in relief the changes in the shape of phonography.

Since a medium is a configuration of a variety of social forces, we would expect that, as the social field changes, the possibilities for the medium change as well. The phonograph's history illustrates this quite well; the varying uses highlighted in the industry literature correspond to changes in middle-class sociability. Any discussion of the phonograph's possibilities would be incomplete without the list of potential applications offered by Edison in an early publication on the potential of the phonograph. Edison's list is a central facet of almost every history of sound recording, although there is no clear consensus on what conclusion to draw from it. Read on its own terms, it appears as nothing more than the product of brainstorming; potential uses appear in no particular order and with no relation to one another. Edison's list:

1. Letter writing and dictation without the aid of a stenographer.
2. Phonographic books for the blind.
3. The teaching of elocution.
4. Reproduction of music.
5. The "family record"—a registry of sayings, reminiscences, etc., by members of a family in their own voices, and the last words of dying persons.
6. Music boxes and toys.
7. Clocks that should announce in an articulate voice the time for going home, going to meals, etc.
8. The preservation of languages by exact reproduction of the manner of pronouncing.
9. Educational purposes such as preserving the explanations made by a teacher, so that the pupil can refer to them at any moment, and spelling or other lessons placed upon the phonograph for convenience in committing to memory.
10. Connection with the telephone, so as to make that instrument an auxiliary in the transmission of permanent and invaluable records, instead of being the recipient of momentary and fleeting communications.[3]

This list is usually cited by phonograph historians to suggest one of two things: that Edison was brilliant (or at least prophetic) because all of the uses on the list eventually came to pass; or, that nobody had any idea what to do with the technology when it was invented and, therefore, needed to be told. Neither reading is terribly compelling when set against the actual history of the machine—most of these uses came to pass, but the specific form that they ultimately took was determined by the changing world of their users. It was a matter not of fulfillment of prophesy, but of the changing ground on which the possibilities for phonography could be shaped.

Consider the uses numbered 4 and 5, the reproduction of music and the family record; a common and greatly oversimplified narrative of the phonograph's development has the early cylinder machines at a great disadvantage to the later disk machines because of how they worked. But this narrative works only insofar as historians privilege the mass reproduction of music—the "eventual" use—over a possible and immediately plausible use when the machine was first marketed: the production of the aural family album. Although the latter function is still present today in photographic practice, it had a much greater significance for the Victorian middle-class parlor culture than it did for the emergent consumer class.[4] Technological change is shaped by cultural change. If we consider early sound-recording devices in their contemporary milieu, the telos toward mass production of prepackaged recordings appears as only one of many possible futures.

Phonographs and graphophones commercially available in the late 1880s and the 1890s used wax cylinders as their medium. Prerecorded cylinders could not be easily mass produced for commercial sale: since each machine could record onto only a single cylinder at a time, performers would have to repeat a performance several times, even when several machines were employed during a recording session. In retrospect, we can say that Emile Berliner's gramophone, made public in 1888 and first marketed in 1895, changed all this. The gramophone is the direct ancestor of the phonographs most commonly used in the twentieth century: it uses a rotating flat disk on a horizontal plane. Berliner's machine was considerably louder than its immediate predecessors, but one of its most important differences was that its disks were reproduced through a "stamping" process and, therefore, easily mass produced.[5] The making of a master disk for stamping, however, was somewhat complicated and labor-intensive, it involved etching and acid baths for the first copy and the matrix that would be used to stamp subsequent copies. As a result, gramophone records were easier to mass produce but much harder for people to make in their own homes.

The common narrative derived from these basic facts argues that the disk machines caught on *because* of the possibility for mass-producing content: essentially, that it was a better way to make money off phonography, from the family record to the musical record. Yet this is precisely where the changing status of the middle class comes into play. The domestic and social life of the emerging professional-managerial class was moving away from parlor culture by the 1890s. Whereas the parlor was a room in Victorian middle-class homes for formal presentation and the maintenance of family identity, where family albums and artwork would be combined with various styles of furniture and art to convey a certain identity to visitors and to family members themselves, the emergent consumerist middle class began in the 1890s to look on these practices as old-fashioned and sterile. Parlors largely populated with hand-crafted goods and family-specific cultural productions gave way in the early twentieth century to living rooms, which were considerably more informal in decor and arrangement and admitted more and more mass-produced goods.[6] The marketing of prerecorded music should be understood in this context. As phonographs became more widely available to a middle-class market, that market itself was changing. The middle-class consumer culture that would provide the cultural, economic, and affective basis for building collections of recordings and extensive listening to prerecorded music was only just emerging as these machines became available. As a result, both inventors and marketers hedged their bets, promoting phonographs as both machines with which a family could produce its own culture and mass-produced commodities that would put their users in touch with a larger public.

If the triumphalist narratives are to be believed, we would expect to find a sort of "Aha, now we can finally do it!" attitude toward the mass production of recordings once this was possible. But Emile Berliner's remarks in his first public presentation of the gramophone show precisely the opposite. He remains unsure as to how to think about the production of recordings: Who would record, under what conditions, and for what purpose? In his address to the Franklin Institute announcing the gramophone in 1888, Berliner moved freely among different notions of content—from the reproduction of mass-produced music, to an institutionalized variation on home recording, to an unrealized form of broadcasting, and back again:

> Those having one [a gramophone], may then buy an assortment of phonautograms, to be increased occasionally, comprising recitations, songs, and instrumental solos or orchestral pieces of every variety.
>
> In each city there will be at least one office having a gramophone recorder with all the necessary outfits. There will be an acoustic cabinet, or acousticon, containing a very large funnel, or other sound concentrator, the narrow end of which ends in a tube leading to the recording diaphragm. At the wide opening of the funnel will be placed a piano, and back of it a semicircular wall for reflecting the sound into the funnel. Persons desirous of having their voices "taken" will step before the funnel, and, upon a given signal, sing or speak, or they may perform upon an instrument. While they are waiting the plate will be developed, and, when it is satisfactory, it is turned over to the electrotyper, or to the glass moulder in charge, who will make as many copies as desired.
>
> . . . There is another process which may be employed. Supposing his Holiness, the Pope, should desire to send broadcast a pontifical blessing to his millions of believers, he may speak into the recorder, and the plate then, after his words are etched, is turned over to a plate-printer, who may, within a few hours, print thousands of phonautograms on translucent tracing paper. The printed phonauto-grams are then sent to the principal cities in the world, and upon arrival they are photo-engraved by simply using them as photograph positives. The resultant engraved plate is then copied, *ad infinitum*, by electrotyping, or glass moulding, and sold to those having standard reproducers.

Prominent singers, speakers, or performers, may derive an income from royalties on the sale of their phonautograms, and valuable plates may be printed and registered ro protect against unauthorized publication.[7]

Berliner's uncertain futurology offered a rich brew of potential media systems for the gramophone. While mass production was certainly an idea that seemed—and, indeed, proved to be—promising, it appeared alongside the idea of the local gramophone office, where people could go to make their own recordings. The gramophone office, essentially envisioned as a local, for-rent recording studio, suggests a system where home listening would mix original creations with mass-produced entertainment. Berliner's gramophone office nicely hybridizes Victorian domesticity with the new culture of "going out," to use David Nasaw's phrase.[8]

The appearance of the term *broadcast* as an adverb is also interesting here since we have since come to think of the mass production of recordings and broadcasting as two different things. Berliner's use of the term was probably closer to the agricultural sense of the word than to the sense that we would now associate with radio or television. Yet it suggests an interesting connection among the possibilities of dissemination that our current conventions of use do not emphasize. Berliner's *broadcast* indicated the dispersal of sound events over time *and* space. When we refer to radio or telephone broadcasting, we think only of dispersal over space. We can read into Berliner's usage, then, a sense of the plasticity of the sound event over time *and* space so central to modern sound culture. This potential for dissemination was perhaps the most salient quality of new sound technologies as they were being shaped into media.[9] This is one possible explanation for the relatively fluid boundaries among the point-to-point, broadcast, and archival functions in the minds of late-nineteenth-century inventors, promoters, and users.

NOTES

1. See Nasaw, *Going Out,* 120–14.
2. Read and Welch, *From Tin Foil to Stereos,* 269.
3. Paraphrasing Edison as quoted in Roland Gelatt, *The Fabulous Phonograph, 1877–1977* (New York: Appleton-Century, 1977), 29; Attali, *Noise, 93;* and Chanan, *Repeated Takes,* 4.
4. "*The Phonogram . . .* has suggested to the manufacturers that albums be constructed, varying in size to suit purchasers, so that they may hold two, four, six, eight or even a hundred cylinders, and that these be prepared artistically, to resemble, as much as possible, in form, a photograph album, yet possessing the conveniences for holding the wax phonograms and keeping them intact" ("'Being Dead, He Yet Speaketh,'" *Phonogram I 2,* no. II [November 1892]: 249).
5. Cylinders, too, could be mass produced (at least in theory), but no such scheme caught on between 1888 and 1895, when the gramophone was first being marketed.
6. Ohmann, *Selling Culture,* 140–49.
7. Emile Berliner, "The Gramophone: Etching the Human Voice," *Journal of the Franklin Institute* 75, no. 6 (June 1888): 445–46.
8. Nasaw, *Going Out.*
9. Jacques Derrida, Briankle Chang, and John Peters all argue in their own way that this potential for dissemination is, in fact, the defining characteristic of all communication. While this may be the case, modern sound culture explicitly "problematized" (i.e., made a theoretical and practical issue of) both the sound event itself and the conditions under which it could become mobile. Dissemination became an explicitly social, economic, and cultural problem. See Jacques Derrida, *The Postcard: From Socrates to Freud and Beyond,* trans. Alan Bass (Chicago: University of Chicago Press, 1987); Briankle Chang, *Deconstructing Communication: Representation, Subject, and Economies of Discourse* (Minneapolis: University of Minnesota Press, 1996), esp, 171–221; and John Durham Peters, *Speaking into the Air: A History of the Idea of Communication* (Chicago: University of Chicago Press, 1999), 33–62.

CHAPTER 22

Early Motion Pictures

Daniel Czitrom

Daniel Czitrom is a professor of history at Mount Holyoke College. He is the author of the highly influential Media and the American Mind: From Morse to McLuhan.

Projected motion picture photography became a reality in the 1890s, but the dream of throwing moving pictures on a screen stretched back at least three centuries. Various European inventors described and created "magic lanterns" (primitive slide projectors) as early as the mid-seventeenth century. But not until the early nineteenth century did Peter Mark Roget and others seriously consider the principle of persistence of vision, a concept fundamental to all moving pictures, drawn or photographed.

In the 1870s and 1880s several scientists engaged in the investigation of animal and human movement turned to photography as a research tool. The most important of these, Etienne Jules Marey of France and Eadweard Muybridge, an Englishman living in America, created varieties of protocinema that greatly advanced visual time-and-motion study. They also inspired inventors around the world to try their hand at constructing devices capable of producing the illusion of motion photography. Most of these inventors, including Thomas Edison, took up motion picture work for quite a different reason than Marey and Muybridge: the lure of a profit-making commercial amusement.[1]

Early film historians and journalists chose to perpetuate and embellish the legend of Edison's preeminence in the development of motion pictures. In fact, as the painstaking and voluminous research of Gordon Hendricks has shown, the true credit for the creation of the first motion picture camera (*kinetograph*) and viewing machine (*kinetoscope*) belongs to Edison's employee, W. K. L. Dickson. Between 1888 and 1896, Dickson was "the center of all Edison's motion picture work during the crucial period of its technical perfection, and when others were led to the commercial use of the new medium, he was the instrument by which the others brought it into function." Edison himself admitted in 1895 that his reason for toying with motion pictures was "to devise an instrument which should do for the eye what the phonograph does for the ear"; however, his interest in motion pictures always remained subordinate to his passion for the phonograph.[2]

With the perfection of a moving picture camera in 1892, and the subsequent invention of the peep hole kinetoscope in 1893, the stage was set for the modern film industry. Previewed at the Columbian Exposition in Chicago during the summer of 1893, the kinetoscope could handle only one customer at a time. For a penny or a nickel in the slot, one could watch brief, unenlarged 35-mm black-and-white motion pictures. The kinetoscope provided a source of inspiration to other inventors; and, more importantly, its successful commercial exploitation convinced investors that motion pictures had a solid financial future. Kinetoscope parlors had opened in New York, Chicago, San Francisco, and scores of other cities all over the country by the end of 1894. The kinetoscope spread quickly to Europe as well, where Edison, revealing his minimal commitment to motion pictures, never even bothered to take out patents.[3]

At this time the Dickson-Edison kinetograph was the sole source of film subjects for the kinetoscopes. These early films were only fifty feet long, lasting only fifteen seconds or so. Beginning in 1893 dozens of dancers, acrobats, animal acts, lasso throwers, prize fighters, and assorted vaudevillians traveled to the Edison compound in West Orange, New Jersey. There they posed for the kinetograph, an immobile camera housed in a tarpaper shack dubbed the "Black Maria," the world's first studio built specifically for making movies.[4]

Although it virtually disappeared by 1900, the kinetoscope provided a critical catalyst to further invention and investment. With its diffusion all over America and Europe, the competitive pressure to create a viable motion picture projector, as well as other cameras, intensified. During the middle 1890s various people worked furiously at the task. By 1895, in Washington, D.C., C. Francis Jenkins and Thomas Armat had discovered the basic principle of the projector: intermittent motion for the film with a period of rest and illumination in excess of the period of movement from frame to frame. In New York, Major Woodville Latham and his two sons, along with Enoch Rector and Eugene Lauste, contributed the famous *Latham loop,* which allowed the use of longer lengths of film. William Paul successfully demonstrated his *animatograph* projector in London in early 1896. The Frenchmen Auguste and Louis Lumiere opened a commercial showing of their *cinematograph* in Paris in late 1895—a remarkable combination of camera, projector, and developer all in one. W. K. L. Dickson and Herman Casler perfected their *biograph* in 1896, clearly the superior projector of its day and the foundation for the American Mutoscope and Biograph Company.[5]

Once again, the name of Edison is most closely associated in the popular mind with the invention of the first projection machine. Actually, the basis of the *Edison Vitascope,* first publicly displayed in New York on 24 April 1896, was essentially the projector created by Thomas Armat. The Edison interests persuaded Armat "that in order to secure the largest profit in the shortest time it is necessary that we attach Mr. Edison's name in some prominent capacity to this new machine. . . . We should not of course misrepresent the facts to any inquirer, but we think we can use Mr. Edison's name in such a manner as to keep with the actual truth and yet get the benefit of his prestige."[6]

With the technology for the projection of motion pictures a reality, where were they to be shown? Between 1895 and 1905, prior to the nickelodeon boom, films were presented mainly in vaudeville performances, traveling shows, and penny arcades. Movies fit naturally into vaudeville; at first they were merely another novelty act. Audiences literally cheered the first exhibitions of the vitascope, biograph, and cinematograph in the years 1895 to 1897. But the triteness and poor quality of these early films soon dimmed the novelty and by 1900 or so vaudeville shows used films mainly as chasers that were calculated to clear the house for the next performance. Itinerant film exhibitors also became active in these years, as different inventors leased the territorial rights to projectors or sold them outright to enterprising showmen. From rural New England and upstate New York to Louisiana and Alaska, numerous visitors made movies a profitable attraction in theaters and tent shows. Finally, the penny arcades provided the third means of exposure for the infant cinema. Aside from their use of kinetoscopes, arcade owners quickly seized on other possibilities. Arcade patrons included a hard core of devoted movie fans, who wandered from place to place in search of films they had not seen yet. Some arcade owners bought, rented, or built their own projectors; they then partitioned off part of the arcade for screening movies. They acquired films from vaudeville managers who discarded them.[7]

The combination of the new audience and a growing class of profit-minded small entrepreneurs resulted in the explosion of store theaters (nick-elodeons) after 1905. A supply of film subjects and equipment was necessary to meet the demand, and the first of several periods of wildcat development ran from 1896 to 1909. The three pioneer companies of Edison, Vitagraph, and Biograph in effect controlled the production of motion picture equipment, but a black market quickly developed. Each company that sprang up in these years became a manufacturer of instruments in addition to producing films. Many firms had long lists of patent claims, each arguing that it had a legal right to do business. Aside from the few real inventors and holders of legitimate patents, a good deal of stealing and copying of equipment took place. Lawsuits ran a close second to movies in production priorities. In 1909 the ten major manufacturers finally achieved a temporary peace with the formation of the Motion Picture Patents Company, a patent pooling and licensing organization. In addition to granting only ten licenses to use equipment and produce films, the Patents Company created the General Film Exchange to distribute films only to licensed exhibitors, who were forced to pay a two dollar weekly fee. The immediate impetus for this agreement, aside from the desire to rationalize profits, offers one clue as to how early motion pictures became a big business. Edison and Biograph had been the main rivals in the patents struggle, and the Empire Trust Company, holder of two hundred thousand dollars in Biograph mortgage bonds, sent J. J. Kennedy (an executive and efficiency expert) to hammer out an agreement and save their investment.[8]

By 1909 motion pictures had clearly become a large industry, with three distinct phases of production, exhibition, and distribution; in addition, directing, acting, photography, writing, and lab work emerged as separate crafts. The agreement of 1909, however, rather than establishing peace, touched off another round of intense speculative development, because numerous independent producers and exhibitors openly and vigorously challenged the licensing of the Patent Company.

In 1914, after five years of guerrilla warfare with the independents, the trust lay dormant; the courts declared it legally dead in 1917. Several momentous results accrued from the intense battle won by the innovative and adventurous independents. They produced a higher quality of pictures and pioneered the multi reel feature film. Under their leadership Hollywood replaced New York as the center of production, and the star system was born. At the close of the world war, they controlled the movie industry not only in America, but all over the globe.[9]

Of all the facets of motion picture history, none is so stunning as the extraordinarily rapid growth in the audience during the brief period between 1905 and 1918. Two key factors, closely connected, made this boom possible. First, the introduction and refinement of the story film liberated the moving picture from its previous length of a minute or two, allowing exhibitors to present a longer program of films. One-reel westerns, comedies, melodramas, and travelogues, lasting ten to fifteen minutes each, became the staple of film programs until they were replaced by feature pictures around World War I. George Melies, Edwin S. Porter (*The Great Train Robbery*, 1903), and D. W. Griffith, in his early work with Biograph (1908 to 1913), all set the pace for transforming the motion picture from a novelty into an art.

Secondly, the emergence of the nickelodeon as a place devoted to screening motion pictures meant that movies could now stand on their own as an entertainment. These store theaters, presenting a continuous show of moving pictures, may have begun as early as 1896 in New Orleans and Chicago. In 1902 Thomas Tally closed down his penny arcade in Los Angeles and opened the Electric Theater, charging ten cents for "Up to Date High Class Moving Picture Entertainment, Especially for Ladies and Children." But the first to use the term *nickelodeon* were John P. Harris and Harry Davis, who converted a vacant store front in Pittsburgh in late 1905.[10]

News of their success spread quickly and spawned imitators everywhere. All over America adventurous exhibitors converted penny arcades, empty store rooms, tenement lofts, and almost any available space into movie theaters. Because no official statistics remain from those years, we must rely on contemporary estimates. By 1907 between three and five thousand nickelodeons had been established, with over two million admissions a day. In 1911 the Patents Company reported 11,500 theaters across America devoted solely to showing motion pictures, with hundreds more showing them occasionally; daily attendance that year probably reached five million. By 1914 the figures reached about 18,000 theaters, with more than seven million daily admissions totaling about $300 million.[11]

All of the surveys of motion picture popularity, and indeed a large fraction of all discussions of the new medium, placed movies in a larger context of urban commercial amusements. Movies represented "the most spectacular single feature of the amusement situation in recent years," a situation that included penny arcades, dance academies and dance halls, vaudeville and burlesque theaters, poolrooms, amusement parks, and even saloons. Motion pictures inhabited the physical and psychic space of the urban street life. Standing opposite these commercial amusements, in the minds of the cultural traditionalists, were municipal parks, playgrounds, libraries, museums, school recreation centers, YMCAs, and church-sponsored recreation. The competition between the two sides, noted sociologist Edward A. Ross, was nothing less than a battle between "warring sides of human nature—appetite and will, impulse and reason, inclination and ideal." The mushrooming growth of movies and other commercial amusements thus signaled a weakness and perhaps a fundamental shift in the values of American civilization. "Why has the love of spontaneous play," wondered Reverend Richard H. Edwards, "given way so largely to the love of merely being amused?"

For those who spoke about "the moral significance of play" and preferred the literal meaning of the term *recreation*, the flood of commercial amusements posed a grave cultural threat. Most identified the amusement situation as inseparable from the expansion of the city and factory labor. Referring to the enormous vogue of the movies in Providence, Rhode Island before World War I, Francis R. North noted the "great alluring power in an amusement which for a few cents . . . can make a humdrum mill hand become an absorbed witness of stirring scenes otherwise unattainable, a quick transference from the real to the unreal."

Commercial amusements tempted rural folk as well, and some writers argued that "the young people coming from the country form the mainstay of the amusement resorts." Frederick C. Howe warned in 1914 that "commercialized leisure is moulding our civilization—not as it should be moulded but as commerce dictates. . . . And leisure must be controlled by the community, if it is to become an agency of civilization rather than the reverse."

A scientific assessment of the situation, as attempted by the myriad of recreation and amusement surveys of the early twentieth century, seemed a logical first step. Beyond this, the drive for municipal supervision of public recreation and commercial amusements fit comfortably into the Progressive ethos of philanthropists, social workers, and urban reformers all over America. "In a word," asserted Michael M. Davis of the Russell Sage Foundation in 1912, "recreation within the modern city has become a matter of public concern; laissez faire, in recreation as in industry, can no longer be the policy of the state."[12]

What actually transpired in and around the early nickelodeons varied from theater to theater and city to city. On the whole they do not seem to have been an especially pleasant place to watch a show. A 1911 report made on moving picture shows by New York City authorities disclosed that "the conditions found to exist are such as to attach to cheap and impermanent places of amusement, to wit: poor sanitation, dangerous overcrowding, and inadequate protection from fire or panic." Despite the foul smells, poor ventilation, and frequent breakdowns in projection, investigators found overflow crowds in a majority of theaters. Managers scurried around their halls, halfheartedly spraying the fetid air with deodorizers and vainly trying to calm the quarrels and shoving matches that commonly broke out over attempts to better one's view. The overall atmosphere was perhaps no more rowdy or squalid than the tenement home life endured by much of the audience; but the nickelodeons offered a place of escape for its eager patrons.[13]

The darkness of the nickelodeon theater, argued some doctors and social workers, caused eye strain and related disorders: "Intense ocular and cerebral weariness, a sort of dazed 'good-for-nothing' feeling, lack of energy, or appetite, etc.," as one physician put it. The health problem melted into a moral one, as critics condemned the darkness. Declared John Collier at a child welfare conference, "It is an evil pure and simple, destructive of social interchange, and of artistic effect." Jane Addams observed that "the very darkness of the theater is an added attraction to many young people, for whom the space is filled with the glamour of love-making." Darkness in the nickelodeon reinforced old fears of theaters as havens for prostitutes and places where innocent girls could be taken advantage of. John Collier asked: "Must moving picture shows be given in a dark auditorium, with all the lack of social spirit and the tendency to careless conduct which a dark auditorium leads to?"[14]

If the inside of the theaters was seamy, the immediate space outside could be severely jolting. Gaudy architecture and lurid, exaggerated posters were literally "a psychological blow in the face," as one writer put it. Sensational handbills, passed out among school children, vividly described movies such as *Temptations of a Great City:* "Wine women and gayety encompass his downfall. Sowing wild oats. See the great cafe scene, trap infested road to youth, and the gilded spider webs that are set in a great city after dark." Phonographs or live barkers would often be placed just outside the theater, exhorting passers-by to come in. Inside, the nickelodeon program varied from

theater to theater. An hour-long show might include illustrated song slides accompanying a singer, one or more vaudeville acts, and an illustrated lecture, in addition to several one-reelers. But movies were the prime attraction.[15]

In the summer of 1909, while strolling in a provincial New England town, economist Simon Patten found the library, church, and schools, "the conserving moral agencies of a respectable town," all closed. In contrast to this literally dark side of town, Patten described the brighter side where all the people were. Alongside candy shops, fruit and nut stands, and ice cream parlors, Patten noted the throngs at the nickel theater:

> Opposite the barren school yard was the arcaded entrance to the Nickelodeon, finished in white stucco, with the ticket seller throned in a chariot drawn by an elephant trimmed with red, white and blue lights. A phonograph was going over and over its lingo, and a few machines were free to the absorbed crowd which circulated through the arcade as through the street. Here were groups of working girls—now happy "summer girls"—because they had left the grime, ugliness, and dejection of their factories behind them, and were freshened and revived by doing what they liked to do.[16]

Here the contrast was more than symbolic. Like many others, Patten warned that the traditional cultural institutions needed to adapt quickly in the face of movies and other commercial amusements. They could compete only by transforming themselves into active and "concrete expressions of happiness, security, and pleasure in life."[17]

As for the nickelodeon program itself, everyone concurred that vaudeville was "by far the most pernicious element in the whole motion picture situation." Early projected motion pictures had found their first home in vaudeville houses during the 1890s. But with the rise of theaters devoted to motion pictures, the situation reversed itself. Exhibitors across the nation added vaudeville acts to their film shows as a novelty for attracting patronage in a highly competitive business. Not all movie houses included vaudeville acts on the bill; local demand, availability of talent, and other conditions dictated the exact format of the show. But vaudeville became enough of a commonplace in American nickelodeons for observers to agree that it was the most objectionable feature of them. Particularly in immigrant ghettos, where ethnic vaudeville remained popular until the 1920s, reformers feared the uncontrolled (and uncensorable) quality of the live performance. The singers, dancers, and dialect comics of vaudeville appalled and frustrated those who were struggling to regulate the burgeoning nickelodeon movement.

The mayor's committee in Portland, Oregon complained in 1914, for example, about the numerous shows "where decent and altogether harmless films are combined with the rankest sort of vaudeville. There is a censorship upon the films, but none at all on male and female performers, who in dialog, joke, and song give out as much filth as the audience will stand for." In 1910 an Indianapolis civic committee denounced the vaudeville performances in local movie theaters as unfit for any stage: "Almost without exception the songs were silly and sentimental and often sung suggestively." Robert O. Bartholomew, the Cleveland censor of motion pictures, could not believe some of the things he witnessed in that city's nickelodeons in 1913:

> Many verses of different songs have been gathered which would not bear printing in this report. Dancers were often seen who endeavored to arouse interest and applause by going through vulgar movements of the body. . . . A young woman after dancing in such a manner as to set off all the young men and boys in the audience in a state of pandemonium brought onto the stage a large python snake about ten feet long. The snake was first wrapped about the body, then caressed and finally kissed in its mouth.[18]

Nickelodeon vaudeville was usually cheap, almost impossible to regulate, and socially objectionable—to the authorities, if not to the audience. As a result, police harassment and stricter theater regulations were employed all over the country to exclude vaudeville from movie houses. By 1918 nearly all movie exhibitors had responded to external pressure and internal trade opinion by eliminating vaudeville. They were forced to concede what one exhibitor had written in a trade paper in 1909, that "a properly managed exclusive picture show is in a higher class than a show comprised partly of vaudeville."[19]

In every town and city the place of exhibition proved the most vulnerable point of the industry, a soft underbelly for critics to attack. New York's experience between 1908 and 1913 provides a rough historical model for what transpired all over the country as cultural traditionalists sought to control the sphere of exhibition. By 1908 over five hundred nickelodeons had appeared in New York, a large proportion of them in tenement districts. A city ordinance required only a twenty-five dollar license for theaters with common shows (movies were so designated) that had a capacity below three hundred; the regular theater license of five hundred dollars was well above the means of average exhibitors, so they made certain that their number of seats remained below three hundred. At a stormy public meeting on 23 December 1908, prominent clergymen and laymen urged Mayor George McClellan to close the nickelodeons for a variety of reasons. These included violation of Sunday blue laws (the busiest day for the nickelodeon trade), safety hazards, and degradation of community morals. "Is a man at liberty," demanded Reverend J. M. Foster, "to make money from the morals of people? Is he to profit from the corruption of the minds of children?" The next day Mayor McClellan revoked the licenses of every movie show in the city, some 550 in all.

On Christmas day, exhibitors, film producers, and distributors responded by meeting and forming the Moving Picture Exhibitors Association, with William Fox as their leader. The movie men successfully fought the order with injunctions, but the message was clear: some form of regulation was necessary. Marcus Loew began to ask various civic bodies for names of potential inspectors to investigate the theaters. It took several years, however, for New York to enact the first comprehensive law in the United States regulating movie theaters. The 1913 legislation included provisions for fire protection, ventilation, sanitation, exits, and structural requirements. Seating limits increased from three hundred to six hundred to provide exhibitors more funds for making improvements. Significantly, all vaudeville acts were banned from movie houses unless they met the stiffer requirements of regular stage theaters.[20]

NOTES

1. The best account of the prehistory of the motion picture is in Kenneth MacGowan, *Behind the Screen: The History and Techniques of the Motion Picture* (New York: Delacorte Press, 1965), pp. 25–84. Also useful are Kurt W. Marek, *Archaeology of the Cinema* (London: Thames and Hudson, 1965); and Frederick A. Talbot, *Moving Pictures: How They Are Made and Worked* (Philadelphia: J. B. Lippincott, 1912), pp. 1–29. On the specific contributions of Marey, Muybridge, and others, see Robert Sklar, *Movie-Made America* (New York: Random House, 1975), pp. 5–9; Mac-Gowan, *Behind the Screen,* pp. 45–64.

2. Gordon Hendricks, *The Edison Motion Picture Myth* (Berkeley: University of California Press, 1961), p. 142. The Edison quotation is taken from his preface to W. K. L. Dickson and Antonia Dickson, *History of the Kinetograph, Kinetoscope, and Kinetophonograph* (New York: n.p., 1895), the Dicksons' own history of the inventions.

3. On the success and wide geographical dispersion of kinetoscopes, see Gordon Hendricks, *The Kinetoscope* (New York: Beginnings of the American Film, 1966), pp. 64–69. These parlors often contained phonographs and other machine novelties. On the kinetoscope at the Chicago fair, see Robert Grau, *The Theater of Science: A Volume of Progress and Achievement in the Motion Picture Industry* (New York: Broadway Publishing Co., 1914), pp. 3–4; and Hendricks, *Kinetoscope,* pp. 40–45.

4. For descriptions of these early films and how they were made, see Dickson and Dickson, *History,* pp. 23–40; Hendricks, *Kinetoscope,* pp. 21–28,

70–97; Joseph H. North, *The Early Development of the Motion Picture, 1887–1900* (New York: Arno Press, 1973), pp. 1–26.

5. Gordon Hendricks, *Beginnings of the Biograph* (New York: Beginnings of the American Film, 1964); MacGowan, *Behind the Screen,* pp. 75–84; North, *Early Development,* pp. 23–33; Terry Ramsaye, "The Motion Picture," *Annals of the American Academy of Political and Social Science* 128 (November 1926): 1–19.

6. Norman C. Raff and Frank R. Gammon, two of Edison's business partners, to Thomas Armat, 5 March 1896, in Terry Ramsaye, *A Million and One Nights: A History of the Motion Picture* (New York: Simon and Schuster, 1926), p. 224.

7. FILMS IN VAUDEVILLE: "Edison Vitascope Cheered," *New York Times,* 24 April 1896; Grau, *Theater of Science,* pp. 11–12; Benjamin B. Hampton, *History of the American Film Industry* (1931; reprint ed., New York: Dover Publications, 1971), pp. 12–14. ITINERANT EXHIBITORS: Grau, *Theater of Science,* pp. 28–33; North, *Early Development,* pp. 55–56; George Pratt, "No Magic, No Mystery, No Sleight of Hand," *Image* 8 (December 1959): 192–211. PENNY ARCADES: Lewis Jacobs, *The Rise of the American Film* (New York: Harcourt, Brace and Co., 1939), pp. 5–8; Grau, *Theater of Science,* pp. 11–16; Hampton, *History,* pp. 12–14.

8. Jacobs, *Rise,* pp. 52–66, 81–85; Hampton, *History,* pp. 64–82; Ramsaye, *Million and One Nights,* pp. 59–72. An important review of the activities of the Motion Picture Patents Company is Ralph Cassady, Jr., "Monopoly in Motion Picture Production and Distribution: 1908–1915," *Southern California Law Review* 32 (Summer 1959): 325–90.

9. The rise of the independents and their contributions to both film industry and film art is a whole story in itself. See Jacobs, *Rise,* pp. 51–94; Hampton, *History,* pp. 83–145; Anthony Slide, *Early American Cinema* (New York: A. S. Barnes, 1970), pp. 102–35.

10. Tally's advertisement reproduced in MacGowan, *Behind the Screen,* p. 128; Hampton, *History,* pp. 44–46; Jacobs, *Rise,* pp. 52–63.

11. I have compiled these figures from several sources, using the more conservative estimates where there is conflict. 1907: Joseph M. Patterson, "The Nickelodeon," *Saturday Evening Post* 180 (23 November 1907): 10; "The Nickelodeon," *Moving*

Picture World 1 (4 May 1907): 140. 1911: Patents Company figures are in Cassady, "Monopoly in Motion Picture Production and Distribution," p. 363 (a little over half of these were licensed by the trust, paying the weekly two-dollar fee); William Inglis, "Morals and Moving Pictures," *Harper's Weekly* 54 (30 July 1910): 12–13. 1914: Frederic C. Howe, "What to do With the Motion Picture Show," *Outlook* 107 (20 June 1914): 412–16. Howe, chairman of the National Board of Censorship of Moving Pictures, estimated a daily attendance of between seven and twelve million; W. P. Lawson, "The Miracle of the Movie," *Harper's Weekly* 60 (2 January 1915): 7–9.

12. Statistics gathered from the following sources: U.S. Department of Commerce, *Thirty-eighth Statistical Abstract of the United States* (Washington, D.C.: Government Printing Office, 1915). NEW YORK: Michael M. Davis, *The Exploitation of Pleasure: A Study of Commercial Recreation in New York* (New York: Russell Sage Foundation, 1911). Davis's careful study of the attendance at New York City theaters estimated 900,000 for Manhattan movie houses alone. Three years later the National Board of Censorship placed the New York daily attendance between 850,000 and 900,000, so the 1.5 million weekly figure for 1911 is probably low. CLEVELAND: Robert O. Bartholomew, *Report of Censorship of Motion Pictures* (Cleveland: n.p., 1913). DETROIT: Rowland Haynes, "Detroit Recreation Survey" (1912), cited in Richard H. Edwards, *Popular Amusements* (New York: Association Press, 1915), pp. 50–51. SAN FRANCISCO: "Public Recreation," *Transactions of the Commonwealth Club of California* (1913), cited in Edwards, *Popular Amusements*, pp. 16, 51. MILWAUKEE: Rowland Haynes, "Recreation Survey, Milwaukee, Wisconsin," *Playground* 6 (May 1912): 38–66. KANSAS CITY: Rowland Haynes and Fred F. McClure, *Second Annual Report of the Recreation Department of the Board of Public Welfare* (Kansas City: n.p., 1912). INDIANAPOLIS: F. R. North, "Indianapolis Recreation Survey" (1914), cited in Edwards, *Popular Amusements*, p. 33. TOLEDO: J. J. Phelan, *Motion Pictures as a Phase of Commercialized Amusements in Toledo, Ohio* (Toledo: Little Book Press, 1919).

13. Edward A. Ross, Introduction to Richard H. Edwards, *Popular Amusements* (New York: Association Press, 1915), p. 5; Edwards, *Popular Amusements*, pp. 20–21, 133; Francis R. North, *A Recreation Survey of the City of Providence* (Providence: Providence Playground Association, 1912), p. 58; Belle L. Israels, "Recreation in Rural Communities," *Proceedings of the International Conference of Charities and Correction* (Fort Wayne: n.p., 1911), p. 105; Frederic C. Howe, "Leisure," *Survey* 31 (3 January 1914): 415–16; Davis, *Exploitation of Pleasure*, p. 4.

14. Raymond Fosdick, *A Report on the Condition of Moving Picture Shows in New York* (New York: n.p., 1911), p. 11. See also Charles de Young Elkus, "Report on Motion Pictures," *Transactions of the Commonwealth Club of California* 8 (1914): 251–72, a report on fifty-eight motion picture houses in San Francisco.

15. Dr. George M. Gould in the *Journal of the American Medical Association,* quoted in "Health," *Survey* 29 (15 February 1913): 677; John Collier, *The Problem of Motion Pictures* (New York: National Board of Censorship, 1910), p. 5; Jane Addams, *The Spirit of Youth and the City Streets* (New York: Macmillan Co., 1910), p. 86; John Collier, "Light on Moving Pictures," *Survey* 25 (1 October 1910): 801. See also Vice Commission of Chicago, *The Social Evil in Chicago* (Chicago: Gunthrop Warner, 1911), p. 247, for claims that "children have been influenced for evil by the conditions surrounding some of these shows."

16. Davis, *Exploitation of Pleasure,* p. 54; Haynes and McClure, *Recreation Survey of Kansas City,* p. 78, quotes examples of the handbills. For further descriptions of what went on inside the nickelodeons, as well as the reasons for their rapid spread across the country, see the trade papers, for example: "Trade Notes," *Moving Picture World* 1 (30 March 1907): 57–58; Melville C. Rice, "The Penny Arcade as a Side Show," *The Nickelodeon* 1 (January 1909): 23; "Vaudeville in Picture Theaters," *The Nickelodeon* 1 (March 1909): 85–86. See also Edward Wagenknecht, *Movies in the Age of Innocence* (Norman: University of Oklahoma Press, 1962), Introduction.

17. Ibid., p. 28.

18. Collier, *The Problem of Motion Pictures,* p. 5; Grau, *Theater of Science,* pp. 19–20; Marcus Loew, "The Motion Picture and Vaudeville," in Joseph P. Kennedy, ed., *The Story of the Films* (Chicago: A. W. Shaw, 1927), pp. 285–300; William T. Foster, *Vaudeville and Motion Picture Shows: A Study of*

Theaters in Portland, Oregon (Portland: Reed College, 1914), pp. 12–13; "Moving Pictures in Indianapolis," Survey 24 (23 July 1910): 614; Bartholomew, Report of Censorship of Motion Pictures, p. 14.

19. "Vaudeville or Not?" The Nickelodeon 1 (November 1909): 134. For an example of provaudevillian sentiment in the trade, see "The Elevation of Vaudeville," Moving Picture World 1 (18 May 1907): 164. See also Boyd Fisher, "The Regulation of Motion Picture Theaters," American City 7 (September 1912): 520–22; John Collier, " 'Movies' and the Law," Survey 27 (20 January 1912): 1628–29.

20. "Say Picture Shows Corrupt Children," New York Times, 24 December 1908; "Picture Shows All Put Out of Business," New York Times, 25 December 1908; "Picture Show Men Organize to Fight," New York Times, 26 December 1908; "Mayor Makes War on Sunday Vaudeville," New York Times, 29 December 1908; Sonya Levien, "New York's Motion Picture Law," American City 9 (October 1913): 319–21. See also Sklar, Movie-Made America, pp. 30–31.

CHAPTER **23**

Movies Talk

Scott Eyman

Scott Eyman is the book editor of the Palm Beach Post and the author of five books of film scholarship, including biographies of Mary Pickford, Ernest Lubitsch, and Louis B. Mayer.

It is the muggy afternoon of August 30, 1927. On the newly constructed soundstage of the Warner Bros. Studio on Sunset Boulevard, Al Jolson is industriously, unwittingly, engaged in the destruction of one great art and the creation of another.

The scene: a son's homecoming. The man universally recognized as the greatest entertainer of his day is singing Irving Berlin's "Blue Skies" to Eugénie Besserer, playing his mother. After an initial chorus sung with Jolson's usual nervy bravura, he suddenly stops. He asks his mother if she likes the song, tells her he'd rather please her than anybody. The floodgates open and the hilarious babbling begins:

"Mama, darlin', if I'm a success in this show, well, we're gonna move from here. Oh yes, we're gonna move up in the Bronx. A lot of nice green grass up there and a whole lot of people you know. There's the Ginsbergs, the Guttenbergs, and the Goldbergs. Oh, a whole lotta Bergs, I don't know 'em all.

"And I'm gonna buy you a nice black silk dress, Mama. You see Mrs. Friedman, the butcher's wife, she'll be jealous of you . . . Yes, she will. You see if she isn't. And I'm gonna get you a nice pink dress that'll go with your brown eyes . . ."

While the crew stands transfixed, Jolson keeps talking, a torrent of unaccustomed words in the midst of a predominantly silent film, a medium that has proudly subsisted on pantomime or, at the most, synchronized underscoring, sound effects, and a laconic word or two.

But now every word that Jolson says is being recorded by a single large, black, cylindrical microphone a foot above his head, which transmits the sound to a 16-inch wax disc spinning at 33 1/3 revolutions a minute.

Singing has never been a trial for Al Jolson; it is life that is difficult, and carrying a picture, a family drama mixed with a rough approximation of a backstage musical before backstage musicals are invented, has been causing him enormous anxiety. Only four years before, he walked out on a silent film for D. W. Griffith because of nerves, and the desperate volubility with which Jolson is haranguing Besserer may well be the result of an adrenaline rush of pure fear.

Certainly, costar May McAvoy has observed a much quieter, needier man than will ever be on public view in later years. "Act like he knew it all?" asked McAvoy. "Oh no. Never! He was the most cooperative person, and just darling." Jolson leans on McAvoy, an experienced actress who has worked for leading directors such as Ernst Lubitsch. After most scenes, he asks "How'd I do? Was I all right? Please tell me. Let me know. Let's do it over again if it wasn't good."

Production of *The Jazz Singer* had actually begun two months earlier. While Jolson is out of town fulfilling a nightclub engagement, Warners begins production with location scenes in New York that don't require his presence. Meanwhile, the Warner studio on Sunset Boulevard gears up for sound with difficulty, for the studio is stretched thin financially.

"I ordered $40 worth of parts to build a sound-mixing panel," Warner Bros. technician William Mueller will remember years later, "but the man wouldn't leave [the parts] until he got his money. I paid him out of my own pocket only to be told by the studio purchasing agent, Jack Warner's brother-in-law, that I probably wouldn't get my money back. They also demanded that I return what I had left from a $500 cash advance so they could meet the payroll that week."

Likewise, Mueller and Nathan Levinson, Western Electric's man in Hollywood, knew they needed $10,000 to build proper sound facilities and had taken an entire morning to convince Jack Warner to spend the money. He finally agreed, then left for lunch. Knowing their man, Levinson and Mueller got the studio superintendent to clear the necessary area and began construction. "When Jack came back two hours later, he told us he'd changed his mind, but by that time it was too late."

The "Blue Skies" sequence is business as usual for *The Jazz Singer*. All the sound scenes are being made as separate little films, after the surrounding silent footage has been shot. With one exception, the sound sequences are shot within nine consecutive days beginning August 17, and each of them is given its own production code number on the schedule sheets. (Warners might be thinking about eventually releasing them separately as short subjects should Sam Warner's crazy advocacy of feature-length sound films not work out. It is also possible that this is simply because Vitaphone, the name of their sound system, is a separate production entity.)

The sound scenes are usually shot in the afternoon, from 1 to 5 P.M., with three cameras. Work throughout the rest of the studio is suspended while the production staff gathers to listen to Jolson give what amounts to free concerts.

Shooting of the sound sequences begins with "It All Depends on You," completed in seven takes; "Mother of Mine," shot on August 18, in only two; "Mammy," shot that same day in three takes; and so on. The last number is "Blue Skies," which replaces "It All Depends on You." It is the only scene with any meaningful dialogue beyond Jolson's catchphrase "You ain't heard nothin' yet!" Aside from its comfortable position in the arsenal of Jolson hits, "Blue Skies" is a favorite of the Warners; it has already been performed twice in their Vitaphone sound shorts within the last year.

In later years, sound engineer George Groves asserts that Jolson's cheerful speech to his movie mother is "*purely* ad-lib . . . without any rehearsal. Everybody just held their breath." Likewise, head engineer Stanley Watkins says that "Jolson was to sing, but there was to be no dialogue . . . when the picture was being made he insisted on ad-libbing in a couple of places. Sam Warner managed to persuade his brothers to leave the scenes in. 'It won't do any harm,' [Sam said.] In my opinion it was a put-up job between Sam Warner and Jolson."

Yet, technician William Mueller will have a diametrically opposed recollection and spins a remarkably involved conspiratorial tale: "When the songs went well, someone—I don't remember who—decided to have a talking sequence as well. Jolson absolutely would not do it. He said he was a singer and not an actor. He thought it would ruin his career and even offered to pay Warners the money they had already spent to get out of it.

"Finally, they got him to make a test. Then they framed him. While the director and assistant director went to his house to tell him how wonderful it was, they had the prop man view the dailies . . . . He rushed out to Jolson's house, burst in, and raved about the films. Then he said that [George] Jessel had sneaked in to watch and was very excited about it. He said that Jessel, knowing that Jolson wanted out, also had gone to Jack Warner and offered to do the film for nothing. That did it. Jolson couldn't stand that, so he agreed to do [the scene] himself."

The Jazz Singer offers not just music but an effervescent personality projecting itself in words, bursting through the screen to wrap the audience in an exuberant embrace. The picture is a gamble, of course—the brothers have spent $500,000 on a film that can be shown in precisely two theaters in the United States—but, as Sam, Jack, and Harry Warner look at it for the first time, it must seem like the gamble has paid off: the first feature starring the world's most popular entertainer—and in synchronized sound. Surely, triumph is only a month away.

Within three weeks, Sam Warner, who has ramrodded sound past his obstinate brothers, will be suddenly, incomprehensibly dead. *The Jazz Singer,* his best testament, will be acclaimed and settle in for long, successful runs everywhere in the world. Warner Bros. will begin a sudden ascent from a position in the lower third of the industry to highly competitive jostling with MGM and Paramount.

Because of this single scene, made as a flier on a hot summer afternoon, a modest story about a cantor's son who would rather sing Irving Berlin than "Kol Nidre" fires the starting pistol for an unparalleled industrial and aesthetic revolution.

Hollywood, 1927.

Silent films—an art impassioned by music, focused by darkness, pure emotion transmitted through light—were at the height of their aesthetic and commercial success.

In the late summer of that last tranquil year, *Beau Geste* and *Seventh Heaven* were finishing up their successful roadshow engagements. *Wings,* William Wellman's World War I epic, was opening, as was Josef von Sternberg's *Underworld.* Paramount announced that they were going to take the mass of footage Erich von Stroheim had shot for *The Wedding March* and make two separate movies out of it. *Variety's* headline for Dorothy Arzner's new assignment was GIRL DIRECTING CLARA BOW. Mary Pickford was thinking of playing Joan of Arc, and 2,000 girls were vying for the part of Lorelei Lee in *Gentlemen Prefer Blondes.* New York's Cameo Theater was advertising "Emit Jannings in *Passion.* Cooled by Refrigeration."

On La Brea Avenue, the Chaplin studio was just days away from resuming production on *The Circus,* a tortured film that had been on hiatus since December 1926, when Chaplin's wife served him with divorce papers and attached the studio. In Culver City, Ramon Novarro announced that he was quitting movies and entering a monastery. MGM didn't renew Lillian Gish's contract; but, in a not entirely unrelated event, the studio signed Louis B. Mayer to a new five-year deal that could bring him as much as $800,000 annually, making him the highest-paid production head in Hollywood.

And, in a small item, *Variety* reported that Warner Bros. might have as many as eleven theaters equipped to show Vitaphone in another month.

Eight hundred feature films a year were being turned out for an audience of 100 million people who attended 25,000 movie theaters every week. Three-quarters of those theaters were located in small towns, but they took in less than a quarter of the box-office receipts, which amounted to between $1 billion and $1.2 billion a year.

Some 42,000 people were employed in Hollywood. The American film industry accounted for 82 percent of the world's movies, while the foreign market accounted for 40 percent of Hollywood's total business. The American studios, exclusive of their attached theater chains, were valued at about $65 million.

Despite the presence of big money, Hollywood had retained its alfresco, bucolic atmosphere. Sets for silent films were constructed next to each other, and the photographing of a scene would be punctuated by hammering and sawing going on just out of camera range. The atmosphere tended strongly toward the informal. "When I first came out to Hollywood in 1919," said the cameraman Karl Struss, "I was walking down Hollywood Boulevard and here come Doug [Fairbanks] and Charlie Chaplin, one riding a donkey, the other a horse. They stopped near Highland Avenue—this is around eleven at night—got off the horses and went in. They were having a good time; nothing alcoholic, just fooling around."

Stars and directors were well-paid and well-treated, but otherwise the men who ran the studios could do what they pleased with their employees. While the American Federation of Labor had tried to unionize the studio crafts as early as 1916, and there had been a labor strike in 1918, Hollywood would remain a nonunion town until the Depression.

Within the studios, there was an element of personal pride in making pictures that relied on the visuals rather than the titles. SAY IT WITH PROPS—SAY IT WITH ACTION were signs that hung over scenario writers' desks. Speech was indicated by printed titles that interrupted the picture itself, always an irritant to creative directors. The ideal, of course, was the picture without titles, which was accomplished a few times, once by a director named Joseph De Grasse in a film called *The Old Swimming Hole,* and once by the great F. W. Murnau in his fabled *The Last Laugh.* Further than that, they could not go. Or so they thought.

Even though there were no microphones, actors were not free to mouth any clownish thing that came to mind. "In the silent days, you did learn the lines that you were supposed to speak," said the actor William Bakewell. "But technique-wise, before you spoke an important line, it was important that you register the expression, the thought . . . because the cutter then could have a clean cut there in which to inject the subtitle. In other words, you had to time it, to register enough ahead before you spoke, so that [the title] would fit."

Some actors were less painstaking than others. The child star Frank "Junior" Coghlan remembered making a silent film called *Rubber Tires,* which had a scene where the leading man [Harrison Ford, emphatically not the Harrison Ford of the present day] stops his car and runs across the road to see if he can be of any help to a car that's broken down. Ford walked up to the other actors and said, "Geef geef geef. Geef geef geef. Geef geef geef." Since it was a long shot, not even the director, let alone the audience, could tell the difference, but Ford's lack of participatory spirit startled the other actors.

Even modestly budgeted films provided musical ensembles of two or three pieces on the set—a typical grouping would be organ, violin, and cello. The mood music helped the actors express the emotion of a given scene . . . and helped them block out the construction sounds from nearby sets. For heavily emotional moments, actors would request their favorite lachrymose ballads or tragic arias from opera; for comedies, sprightly, up-tempo jazz numbers.

"I used to have the little orchestra play from *Samson and Delilah,*" remembered the MGM star

Anita Page. "The music was one of the reasons that I loved silent pictures much better than talkies. You acted better in silents—talkies had so many more things to worry about. But in silents, you could just float. You moved to the music and you lived the part. You just did it!"

How the director talked the actors through the scene varied with the personality. Madge Bellamy, the star of John Ford's *The Iron Horse,* recalled that "[Allan] Dwan used sarcasm. He would say, for instance, 'To the left, you see your love approaching. You believe that he doesn't love you anymore. He comes up and kisses you tenderly. You burst into tears of happiness and relief—if you can manage it.'

"[Thomas] Ince would have yelled, 'You see him coming. You love him. God, how you love him! What pain you feel—you are in an agony of suspense! He kisses you! What happiness! Cut! Let's do it again!'

"[Frank] Borzage was just as emotional, but quieter. He would weep as he directed. He would say, 'You see him. He means everything to you. He may not love you anymore! He is your whole life! Doesn't he care for you now?' By this time, Borzage would be in tears. 'He kisses you! Oh, what joy!' Frank would be too choked up to go on."

On Tuesday nights around town, the place to be seen was The Coconut Grove, the nightclub at the Ambassador Hotel. The promenading of the stars was the main attraction, despite the ostensible presence of Gus Arnheim's orchestra. Another popular nightspot was The Biltmore Hotel in downtown Los Angeles, where the second Saturday of the month was the occasion for The Mayfair Club. It was a dinner dance, with speakers. "Jack Warner would get up and make his usual wisecracks," recalled Evelyn Brent. "it was a small industry . . . (and) everybody in the business was at those Mayfair dances."

For kicks, people would pile into their cars and head down to Venice to ride the roller coaster. The entertainment at parties was usually a buffet supper, unless it was at Pickfair, in which case it was a formal sit-down dinner. For after-dinner,

there was often a screening of a movie, or a new game called charades that swept through the community. Paramount's leading lady Esther Ralston traditionally gave a New Year's Eve party for about 100 people. One year, there was a prize for whoever dressed the youngest. Director Frank Tuttle won the prize when he arrived dressed as an unborn child, complete with umbilical cord.

In Hollywood itself, the Montmartre was the favorite place for lunch, while Musso & Frank's was already in place on Hollywood Boulevard, one door north of where it is now (it would relocate in 1936). Musso's had stiff competition from Henry's, also on Hollywood Boulevard, five doors east of Vine Street. Although the restaurant was named after and run by Henry Bergman, a rotund member of Charlie Chaplin's repertory company, it was common knowledge that Chaplin had financed the establishment. The great comedian would eat there at least one night a week. In keeping with his own culinary tastes, the bill of fare was basic, steaks and chops, immaculately prepared. And, Henry's delivered.

Although the factory town that turned out the movies was largely unpretentious in matters of style, the theaters in which the movies were shown were palaces, baroque fantasies on Moorish/Byzantine/Oriental themes. The carpeting was plush, the orchestra in the pit superb. The audience walked to their seats through air scented with incense to worship at the cathedral of light, part of a congregation composed of all members of society, in all parts of the world. Silent movies were more than an accomplished popular art; as Lillian Gish often insisted, they were a universal language.

Because of the immensely seductive atmospherics of the overall experience, the silent film had an unparalleled capacity to draw an audience inside it, probably because it demanded the audience use its imagination. Viewers had to supply the voices and sound effects; in so doing, they made the final creative contribution to the filmmaking process. Silent film was about more than a movie; it was about an experience.

The joining together of a movie with live music and the audience's participation created something that was more than the sum of its parts; in Kevin Brownlow's metaphor, the effect was that of cultural carbons joined in an arc lamp, creating light of extraordinary intensity.

Sound changed *everything*.

It changed how movies were made, of course, but more importantly, it changed what movies *were*.

To take just one example, sound permanently altered the nature of screen comedy: the fizzy surrealism of Mack Sennett, the incredibly expressive pantomime of Chaplin, gave way to the racy cross-talk of Ben Hecht and his confrères. The primarily visual was supplanted by the primarily verbal.

Sound standardized movies, made them less malleable, less open to individual interpretation. Allusion and metaphor were the bedrocks of the silent medium, but dialogue literalized every moment, converted it from subjective to objective.

Sound also changed the character of the men and women who made the movies. Sound demanded writers of dialogue, and it seemed as if anyone with the most modest theatrical or journalistic credentials was imported to Hollywood. Paramount went in so heavily for journalists that their hiring strategy was informally but widely known as the Paramount Fresh Air Fund for New York Newspapermen. Lightweight New York literati became West Coast wage slaves and hated themselves for abandoning what they imagined would have been glorious literary careers. While $50-a-week journalists became grudgingly affluent, veteran actors, writers, and directors used to making $100,000 a year suddenly had their credentials called into question.

And, sound brought the unions to Hollywood, for, along with New York journalists, it brought a mass importation of New York actors and playwrights, all of them members of one union or another who saw no reason why Hollywood should be exempt from the same nominal bargaining agents as New York.

And all of it happened within four short years.

There is no aspect of film history that has been so slighted. After noting the extermination of an art form at the height of its power—something unprecedented in history—the conventional volume gives us a nudge of Jolson, a touch of Lubitsch and Mamoulian, a mention of *All Quiet on the Western Front*, a sorrowing comment on Chaplin's Luddite tendencies, and suddenly it's 1935 and Victor McLaglen is staggering through the fog-shrouded streets of *The Informer*. As a result, most people assume the delightful, if broadly exaggerated, satire of *Singin' in the Rain* is more or less the whole story.

To examine this period of unparalleled industrial change, it is necessary to reverse the perspective, to give a fair, detailed idea of what silents were like to the people who made and watched them, and how talkies permanently changed the creative and personal equations.

As if the art form had an independent consciousness and was determined to flaunt its attributes in the face of imminent extinction, in 1927 and 1928 silent movies exploded in a riot of style, dramatic intensity, and thematic complexity. There were accomplished works of art such as King Vidor's *The Crowd* and von Sternberg's *The Last Command*, eye-popping entertainments like *The Beloved Rogue* and *The Gaucho*, the intense lyrical romanticism of Borzage's *Seventh Heaven* and *Street Angel*.

In most respects, late silent pictures seem more complete than early talkies, so painfully landlocked, so eerily styleless. With few exceptions, we see early talkies as grotesque curios; beginning in 1926, with the first Vitaphone films, audiences saw them as miracles. It is impossible to re-create the sense of wonder that made the public eager to abandon the visual and gestural dynamism of silent film, made them so eager to overlook the crudity of the technology and the stiffness of the first wave of sound films. For audiences of 1926–1930, talkies were what the Lumière films had been for audiences of 1895—the recording function was paramount; that what was being recorded was of no real dramatic interest was irrelevant.

The conventional wisdom has always been that talkies evolved out of silent films, but sound actually grew up alongside silents. The initially half-witted hybrid thrived in spite of itself, expanding voraciously and choking off the more fragile strain. Talkies were not an evolution, but a mutation, a different art form entirely; as a result, an art form was eliminated and hundreds of careers were extinguished. Major directors were ruined, great stars plummeted.

It is an epic story, full of bewildered losers who exceeded the abilities of their primitive technology and ran out of capital, counter-pointed by the triumph of the flamboyant Warner Bros. and of William Fox, whose tremendous commercial success was purchased with full shares of the hubris that eventually destroyed him.

So Hollywood was nudged, however unwillingly, into its corporate and creative future. Victims retired, victors took their place. In the early 1930s, the deco designs of Hans Dreier and Van Nest Polglase replaced the stuffy English furniture that was *de rigueur* at most studios in the silent days; short, stylish hair was adopted by women stars. The industry had been turned upside down, but had righted itself with considerable dispatch.

The fact that sound wasn't accepted until thirty years after it was first (roughly) devised was due in great part to factors both sociological and human: the immaculate presentation of silent films, and the reactionary attitudes of producers and exhibitors. Then there were two secondary technical factors: amplification (had that been available, talkies might have arrived in the 1900s) and electrical recording (acoustic recording lacked the necessary clarity).

Sound gave us the artistry of Astaire, the shattering screech of Kane's cockatoo, the wrenching anguish of Brando's "I coulda been a contender." It gave movies a more comprehensive form and smoothed out their dramatic flow. But the transition to sound was no gentle grafting, but a brutal, crude transplantation. As a result, many of cinema's roots withered and died, and much native strength was lost. The culture of Hollywood itself grew harsher, more Darwinian.

"The fun, easy, relaxed days of the motion picture were over the minute dialogue came in," asserted Charles "Buddy" Rogers. "Not only did the director want the dialogue his way, but the dialogue director, the soundman—we had to cope with about six or seven different technicians, and it was quite different."

CHAPTER **24**

Mass Media and the Star System

Jib Fowles

Jib Fowles was professor of media studies at the University of Houston—Clear Lake. His articles have appeared in numerous popular as well as scholarly journals. He is also the author of several books on media and popular culture.

In the period between 1870 and 1920, first slowly and then with quickening ardor, Americans had become fascinated with entertainers. This fascination grew so intense that a group of performers obtained a historically unique degree of conspicuousness. Why did it happen? What was going on in the United States that can account for the phenomenal birth of the star role?

The social changes that followed the Civil War can be encapsulated in a word: cities. According to the Bureau of the Census, the U.S. population was 20 percent urban and 80 percent rural in 1860; by 1880 it was 28 percent urban, and by 1900 40 percent urban.[1] The pace of urbanization continued steadily in the twentieth century, and in the second decade the United States crossed the line separating a chiefly rural society from a chiefly urban one. This decade can be seen as the hinge of U.S. history; it is no coincidence that the star role materialized then.

There were two wellsprings of the large numbers congregating in towns and cities. Many were Americans who had been raised on small farms or in villages only to turn their backs on that way of life. Other millions were migrants from Europe and elsewhere. In 1862 less than 100,000 immigrants were counted, but over 400,000 arrived in 1872, and 800,000 in 1882. Immigration peaked in 1914 when 1,218,000 new citizens entered, the majority taking up residence in urban settings. Whether their previous experiences had been rural or not, once they reached this country they tended to stay in metropolitan areas.

What these droves of new arrivals sought and found in the exploding cities and towns was employment. The fertility of the newly opened Great Plains, together with the increasing mechanization of farming, meant that less labor was required to feed the nation efficiently. Correspondingly, after the Civil War the manufacturing sector of the economy began to grow by leaps and bounds. Individuals found that their best employment opportunities lay in the new urban factories, foundries, plants, and mills. Situated at these transportation hubs, other business enterprises grew in size and complexity, creating more jobs. This was the period when the large business organization became increasingly prevalent, eventually dominating the economic landscape. Over several decades of pell-mell change, America was transformed from a nation of self-sufficient small farmers to a nation of urbanized wage earners.

Although these changes were uneven and at times bitterly conflictful, it is clear from the present vantage point that in the long haul the people caught up in the transformation materially benefited and had steadily more wealth at their disposal, at least up to the onslaught of the Great Depression. Census Bureau data reveal that in constant (1914) dollars the average annual income for a non farm employee was $375 in 1870, $395 in 1880, $519 in 1890, and $573 in 1900.[2] This climb continued, reaching $607 in 1910, $672 in 1920, and $834 in 1930. As wages rose, the average hours of weekly work in manufacturing industries dropped slowly but steadily: in 1890, the first year for which government data on this topic were reported, the average was sixty hours; this figure fell to fifty-one in 1920 and forty-two in 1930.

Increasingly, then, city dwellers were people with coins in their pockets and time on their hands. The majority of the population enjoyed a modicum of leisure. James A. Garfield, in his 1880 presidential campaign, declaimed, "We may divide the whole struggle of the human race into two chapters: first the fight to get leisure; and then the second fight of civilization—what shall we do with our leisure when we get it?"

Some of the development of leisure activities occurred in the public domain, such as city parks and libraries. But much of it beckoned entrepreneurs. Entertainment and amusements of every sort and for every price sprang up. Much free time and loose change were absorbed by the budding saloon industry. Besides the combination companies, vaudeville shows, and eventually moving pictures, there were also circuses and Wild West extravaganzas, "museums" (collections of oddities) and minstrel shows, amusement parks, and horse races. In contrast to the austerity of the preceding two centuries of American history, the variety of diversions was astounding.

Baseball as a spectator sport also came into its own after the Civil War. Originally a village pastime, baseball was brought to urban centers by the new arrivals. As cities prospered and began to rival each other, they started to contest on the baseball diamond. At first the teams were composed of amateurs, but when the Cincinnati Red Stockings were humiliated by the touring Washington Nationals in 1867, local partisans resolved it would not happen again. The Red Stockings were reconstituted the following year as the first team with salaried players. In the 1869 season they competed without defeat, winning fifty-six games and tying one. Other municipalities began to follow suit, and soon interurban leagues were forming. In cities nationwide an increasing number of enthusiasts began to troop out to the ballpark in fair weather to cheer their local team.

If this growing urban population was gaining more per capita wealth, more free time, and more engaging diversions, then what might it have been losing? This, it turns out, is the key question.

In moving from farms and small villages to towns and cities, individuals were undertaking a radical shift from one kind of social existence to another. The lower the human density had been in rural areas, the stronger the social emphasis had been upon conventionality, fellow feeling, and cohesion. But in cities, the higher the density became, the greater was the extent of impersonality and normlessness. The social sanctions prevailing in rural areas or back in home countries may have imposed uncomfortable strictures upon the individual, but they had also brought personal definition. Religious and community pressures had lent sure guidelines to beliefs and behavior. But once individuals had joined the urban throng, they were stripped of these supporting prescriptions and left to their own devices. For the new urbanites the abiding question became one of self-definition.

City folk were alone in ways more profound than country folk had ever experienced. Urban

individuals had to determine their own economic locus; no longer did one follow in the footsteps of a parent, or search through just a handful of potential occupations. Employment options proliferated. One's private life was also increasingly of one's own making, rather than being handed to a person. If marriages had previously been arranged or at least guided, now everyone was on his or her own. Gone were the rigid behavioral precepts of rural Protestant creeds. Gone was any single, uncontested set of standards. As people flowed into metropolises from all walks of life and all corners of the globe, the chances of any one ethos prevailing could only decline.

Previous to this period, a premium upon the individual had received much philosophical endorsement in Western civilization, especially in the United States and particularly at the time of the American Revolution. In those feisty days, the Founding Fathers advocated a faith in the stalwart independent figure who bowed to no external authority. Visiting the country early in the nineteenth century, the French nobleman Alexis de Tocqueville observed that " 'individualism' is a word recently coined to express a new idea." That new idea took on a hard edge in Ralph Waldo Emerson's 1841 essay "Self-Reliance": "Society everywhere is in conspiracy against the manhood of every one of its members," he wrote, and "Who so would be a man, must be a nonconformist." When the poet Walt Whitman later published his famous volume *Leaves of Grass,* the first line was "I celebrate myself."

It was one thing for social philosophers and poets to uphold the ideal of the autonomous individual, but it was quite another for that ideal to become an actuality in the lives of numerous disconnected city dwellers in the last third of the nineteenth and first third of the twentieth centuries. The reality was not half so pleasant as the concept. A new peril had emerged: to be lost in the crowd, to forfeit emotional grounding. One outcome of the transformation from the close-knit human fabric of the countryside to the loose-knit one of the city was a general manifestation of anxiety and mental distress. This development had been foreseen by James Bruce, a British lord and historian who visited the United States in 1876. He noted that "the urban type of mind and life" was coming to predominate, and predicted that "it will tend to increase that nervous strain, that sense of tension, which Americans are already doomed to show as compared with the more sluggish races of Europe."[3]

As individuals left behind the highly prescriptive Protestant ideology of rural America, historian Jackson Lears relates, they left behind a sturdy framework of purpose, sliding into anomie and psychic discomfort. He traces the rise of what was variously called the "American nervousness," "nervous prostration," and "neurasthenia," and observes, "By the early twentieth century, the problem seemed general; references to 'our neurasthenia epidemic' proliferated in the established press."[4]

Among the many antidotes for the widespread malaise of anxiety and depression was a growing number of self-help manuals and behavioral guides. Until the turn of the century, the majority of these exhorted individuals to strengthen their "character"—to bolster their resoluteness and inner strength. Devoid of meaningful support, individuals had to tighten the screws on their resolve. At a certain point, however, this kind of self-help book began to lose favor, and a second brand with a different emphasis started to catch on. According to Warren Susman's scholarly scrutiny of these manuals, instead of emphasizing "character" the replacements explained how to develop "personality."[5] The individual, in the face of a strident and traceless urban environment, had temporized. Rather than forcing his or her will upon this new world, and perhaps battering one-self senseless in the process, a person was now to take a more accommodating path, one that emphasized personal charm. Honey was to be used instead of vinegar as the social lubricant; the goal was to attract. In order to endure and find purpose, the individual needed to develop his personality and get others to like him.

Personality was never an issue until the sense of identity was called into question. Previous to the urban explosion, Americans had little difficulty in knowing who they were; the very dilemma would have seemed absurd to most of them. Within the confines of cultural heritage, family tradition, community, church, political persuasion, and profession, they were sharply defined. But shorn of these supports and isolated in the new urban milieu, their identities had to derive from inside, not outside. To establish the self called for establishing one's personality.

The stream of humans leaving old modes of existence and pouring into a new one needed models of personality—models of worldly, successful, attractive people free of "neurasthenia." Where were such models who could help in defining the individual against the backdrop of urban anonymity?

They were—it was increasingly if unreflectingly felt—on stage, on screen, and on the playing fields. Stars seemed to exude the perfected, confident behavior that unanchored city dwellers coveted. As performers acted and reacted in emotionally charged dramas, as they became decisive or adorable, their performances seemed to reveal purified feelings within, and to issue from harmonious personalities. How to be a whole and resolved person, what the peerless male or ideal female was like: this is what spectators thought they were viewing. Performers offered various models of the well-integrated self, at a time of excruciating need, and when other well-wrought exemplars were not forthcoming. In a most revealing word choice, celebrated actors came to be called "personalities."

Chaplin once tried to describe why his early comedies had so decisively surpassed the Keystone reels in popularity. He explained that the Keystone films always built to an extended chase scene, and that "personally I hated a chase. It dissipates one's personality; little as I knew about the movies, I knew that nothing transcended personality."

Chaplin, Pickford, and Fairbanks were the particular personalities most generally appreciated, for good reason. Despite their differences, there was much they had in common. All three were slight of stature and brimming with a compacted, radiant energy. Their slightness emphasized their youthfulness—an important empathetic feature for an audience of newcomers to a new culture. The stars' small bodies, moving with practiced grace, suggested uncorrupted souls. All three demonstrated tenacity and pluck in their roles; they were never undone for long. They would overcome the forces of evil, authority, and tedium, and would venture forward as intact, happy individuals. They were resolute but never stiff; a liberal dose of comedy made their roles delectable—more so in the case of Chaplin, but humor was never absent for Fairbanks or for Pickford, who once commented, "I always tried to get laughter into my pictures." As well as beating the opposition, these idols pursued love and were sure to end up in exalting unions. For a moment, unsure urban viewers could experience exaltation, too. Here, in these three protostars, they found their inspiration for coping with a strange new world.

The star role thus arrived at the time when ancient institutions—ones that had helped lend each individual a sense of personal identity—were slackening. While the changing nature of social organization after the Civil War accounts in a general way for the unprecedented interest in performing artists, the actual delivery of stars to the American public has to be seen as a technological achievement, or a series of such achievements. Without these technologies the star role would never have taken shape. Technologies fulfilled the culture's mandate for stars.

What this sequence of technical advances accomplished was the circulation of performers' images to an ever-widening audience. By allowing a large number of people to focus on a small number of performers, these technologies fashioned the crucible of extensive public attention from which issued the star role.

The technological side to the story of the star role actually began before images could be easily circulated. Immediately after the Civil War it was the performers themselves who were circulated; the technologies responsible were the newly developed railroad and telegraph systems. Absent these transportation and communication lines, organized baseball with its star players would never have come into existence. To set up a season's schedule, make travel arrangements, keep in touch with touring teams, and relay messages back to the home stand, the telegraph was indispensable. (The telephone was largely restricted to local calls until the turn of the century.) The telegraph was also an important implement of the growing clan of sportswriters, who were spinning out column after column of baseball stories for a fascinated readership. "Box scores, betting odds, and all kinds of messages were relayed from one city to another; and by 1870 daily reports were published in many metropolitan newspapers," states historian John Betts. "Sport had emerged into such a popular topic of conversation that newspapers rapidly expanded their coverage in the 1880s and 1890s, relying in great part on messages sent over the lines from distant points."[6]

What the readers of the sports pages principally wanted to learn about were the achievements of the starring players. Conveyed to a national audience by the railroad and the telegraph, certain players began to stand out from the rest. One of those was Cap Anson, who played for eight years before becoming manager of the Chicago White Sox in 1880, and then continued both to play and manage for another nineteen. Writing about Anson's long career, baseball historian Harold Seymour states, "During that time, his name became a household word—better known, it was said, than that of any statesman or soldier of his time. The fans in Chicago flocked to cheer him. On the road they came out in equally large numbers to jeer."[7]

Just as the railroad and telegraph helped to create a following for baseball players, they also built a national audience for certain actors and actresses. Without these technologies the combination companies could not have toured so readily, and vaudeville acts could not have been booked and been transported so efficiently. Events would have proceeded at the horse-and-buggy pace of earlier times; schedules would not have been half so tight; and the extent of the players' exposure would never have been sufficient to create celebrities. With the railroad and telegraph systems in place, performers could be rotated rapidly through the populace, and some of them would catch and hold the regard of a large audience. Telegraphed accounts of new performers, which appeared in journals and newspapers, produced initial familiarity, and publicity wired ahead brought out ticket-buying customers.

Although the railroad and telegraph initiated the closer relationship of player and public, they were quickly proven less than adequate. The audience's need for stars was deeper than the ability of these technologies to satisfy. The stars could not be in all places at all times, but suddenly their images could. As the technologies of photography and photographic reproduction advanced, they were swiftly put to the purpose of disseminating stars' pictures, particularly of their faces. Photographs of baseball players and other sports figures were circulated widely in the 1880s and 1890s. Pictures of stage performers, especially actresses like Maude Adams and Ethel Barrymore, came into vogue at the same time. The public wanted to get closer to the players they had seen in the theater or on the playing field; they wanted to hold their likenesses in their hands.

Then something cataclysmic happened: the pace of the technologized distribution of star images turned furious with the advent of motion pictures. It was this technology, above all others, that ushered in the age of the star. When Thomas Edison combined several existing and arriving inventions to construct the system of movie camera, film stock, and projector, it was an epochal advance. Photography's advantage for the wide and rapid distribution of the star's image was combined with the theater's advantage at presenting the star in performance.

The ability to provide people across the nation with virtually simultaneous exposure to a star was an important feature of the movies. No longer did years have to pass before a performer and a sizable audience got to know each other. Because many prints would be made and distributed, the star could be seen by millions of people within months or even weeks. When Americans left farm and village life, they had sacrificed a commonality of experience; now here was something new to be shared by all: the celebrity performer whose image was flushed through the culture upon a movie's release.

Beyond distribution, the other star-creating feature of film technology was that audiences could now see not a static image of a performer, as in a photograph, but the performer in motion. The star's behavior could now be observed. Behavior defines a social entity and reveals the person within, and it was the person within that Americans were most curious about and most receptive to.

Above all, the technology of the cinema permitted audiences to concentrate on the faces of the performers. The close-up shot, conveying visages and excluding all else, eradicated the distance between viewer and actor, and so represented a great improvement over traditional proscenium theater. It was even an improvement over real life: moviegoers could stare at those famous faces unabashedly and study every feature, every tic of feeling.

The close-up shot, so simple in its execution and so profound in its consequences, was the greatest gift of the new entertainment form. There is no exaggerating the importance of this cinematic technique in providing the audience with what it desired. Although probably apocryphal, the tale goes that when early directors like D. W. Griffith were first experimenting with the close-up, some theater-trained producers scoffed, arguing that patrons expected to see the entire performer top to bottom, not just the head. In any case, it quickly became clear that a camera shot tightly framed around the face had majestic properties and captured attention as nothing else. It was not long before leading performers were fighting for close-ups and demanding the camera operators, lighting specialists, and makeup experts who were gifted at them. These masters could create close-ups of bewitching brilliance and appeal.

Of all portions of the human body, the face is the primary one to go unclothed, unshielded. It is via the face that privacy is broached and humans enter into contact with each other. Behavioral science research has demonstrated that in face-to-face communication, words count for less than 10 percent of what is exchanged. The real messages are carried in the tone of voice (38 percent) and in facial expressions (55 percent).[8] The face discloses the fundamentals of affect; the close-up enthrones this primal language and prohibits irrelevant clues.

The face in a close-up may be emoting or it may be responding. But whether it is acting or reacting, it is still the avenue to the soul, the inner personality of the star. Everything else about the movies of the early twentieth century—the plots, the dialogue, the direction, the cinematography, the supporting characters—existed to highlight these luminous personalities. While closeness to others was diminishing in urbanized life, here was first-rate intimacy. If identity was in question, here were personalities to try on.

The proximity of star and spectator was further narrowed by the advent of sound reproduction, coming to movies late in the 1920s. Now the audience knew leading performers through their voices as well as their images. Studios responded to the new familiarity by providing publicity of a less fantastic nature; stars were now represented as being similar to other mortals. They were shown as domesticated, with spouses and children. Kitchens cropped up in publicity stills.

The arrival of sound precipitated pronounced changes in the movie industry and in the way stars were delivered to Americans. Sound movies cost over twice as much to produce as silent films, so the industry was required to recapitalize. Financial resources did come to Hollywood's aid, but with them arrived a new breed of movie executives who realized that the likelihood

of a proper return on investment could be improved only by controlling what everyone recognized was the central element of movie production: the stars. Stars could no longer be permitted to ride roughshod, their inflated egos wrecking production schedules. The need to exert control was hastened by the onset of the Great Depression. As the economic straits worsened, the volume of ticket sales entered its first major reversal. When unemployment climbed to one-third of the labor force, many Americans had to forgo their weekly visits with their star friends. At home a competing new medium was waiting to take up some of the slack. Radio might not have had pictures, but it offered everything else: it delivered comedy and sports stars for free, at a click of the knob. All these factors increased the pressure for the close corporate rule of the movie business.

The upshot was the "star system," by which a degree of orderliness and predictability was brought to the rambunctious film industry. Since stars were what the movies were selling, stars would have to be carefully cultivated and regulated. Only in this way could the eight major studios meet their annual combined production quota of three to four hundred films. The development of stars was systematized to the extent possible: each studio would present a crop of new aspirants to the public, largely in B movies; the less successful would be weeded out, and the more successful would be put to work on a regular basis. Seven-year contracts became standard throughout the industry. By regularizing the process of star selection and use, studios diligently worked to stabilize themselves in turbulent times.

From the celebrity actor's point of view, the star system brought both advantages and disadvantages. The pressures for regularity steered most stars into stereotyped molds. There was little leeway for experimentation in roles. Some, like Bette Davis, chafed against this restrictiveness, but most accepted it without comment, if not willingly. The standardizing of their image brought them steady work, and indeed longer careers than stars had previously enjoyed. Once a studio had gone to the expense of developing a star, it had every inclination to employ the person as long as possible. The average star career in the silent movie period has been estimated at three to five years; under the star system it could be six to eight times longer.

As the 1930s wore on and movie attendance continued to drop, cost-cutting measures became prevalent in Hollywood. Popular but expensive performers were released by studios like Paramount and Universal in an attempt to reduce burdensome financial commitments. As Leo Rosten explains the results of this maneuver "The 'sensible' businessmen did cut their movie costs by letting high-priced stars go—but they cut their profits (or increased their lack of profits) even more. And the stars which Paramount and Universal dropped—or who were lured away by Warner Brothers or MGM—kept bringing the big money into the coffers of the studios for which they worked."[9] Again it was demonstrated that, above all, stars were what the public wanted. Even in times of extreme exigency, when studios cut stars they hurt themselves.

It was not until the Depression and World War II were over that the 1929 high of 90 million tickets sold weekly was again reached. But even though attendance had slumped, Americans had not been losing their commitment to stars. Other indicators suggest that fan devotion remained high over the 1930s. People who could not afford ticket prices were buying postage stamps and mailing in their pledges of adoration. It has been estimated that at the beginning of the 1930s more than 30 million letters were sent to stars each year. The studios were in danger of being swamped by this outpouring. Moviegoers organized themselves into fan clubs to more powerfully display their affection. In 1934 there were 535 recognized clubs,

with a combined membership of 750,000—a horde of devotees. According to Alexander Walker's tally, Joan Crawford and Jean Harlow each had about fifty clubs, and Clark Gable had over seventy.[10] The burden on the studios to handle this star worship became onerous, and new clubs had to be discouraged.

Matters continued in this vein until mid-century, when a new technology arrived that did yet better at distributing star images. This was accomplished by delivering the imagery directly into homes.

NOTES

1. U.S. Department of Commerce, Bureau of the Census, *Historical Statistics of the United States: Colonial Times to 1970* (Washington, D.C.: U.S. Government Printing Office, 1975), 11–12.
2. Ibid., 165.
3. Quoted in Russell Lynes, *The Lively Audience: A Social History of the Visual and Performing Arts in America, 1890–1950* (New York: Harper and Row, 1985), 2.
4. T. J. Jackson Lears, *No Place of Grace: Antimodernism and the Transformation of American Culture, 1880–1920* (New York: Pantheon, 1984), 280.
5. Warren I. Susman, *Culture as History: The Transformation of American Society in the Twentieth Century* (New York: Pantheon, 1984), 280.
6. John Richards Betts, "The Technological Revolution and the Rise of Sport, 1850–1900," *Mississippi Valley Historical Review* 40 (1953): 240.
7. Harold Seymour, *Baseball: The Early Years* (New York: Oxford University Press, 1960), 173.
8. Albert Mehrabian, *Silent Messages* (Belmont, Calif.: Wadsworth, 1971), 44.
9. Leo C. Rosten, *Hollywood: The Movie Colony, The Movie Makers* (New York: Harcourt Brace, 1941), 143.
10. Alexander Walker, *Stardom* (New York: Stein and Day, 1970), 251.

PART SIX

Radio Days

Front page of the *New York Times* the day following the *Titanic* tragedy, based largely on wireless reports from the North Atlantic, 1912. *Reprinted by permission of The New York Times Company.*

The transition to "consumer society" was further accelerated through the birth of broadcast radio during the 1920s. Radio was an outgrowth of the "wireless," sometimes referred to as "radiotelegraphy," invented by Marconi shortly before the turn of the century. Marconi's goal was to successfully transmit Morse-coded messages from point-to-point without the use of wires. Transatlantic communication in this manner was regarded as a major achievement by almost everyone, except the telegraph cable companies! Marconi, however, had little interest in the wireless as a medium for voice transmission. Others, most notably the Canadian experimenter Reginald Fessenden, worked on this problem. Considerable strides were made until World War I impeded further research.

After the end of the war a number of amateur stations began "broadcasting" voice, together with live and recorded music. Enthusiastic hobbyists listened in on earphones using inexpensive crystal sets. Initially they were students of the new technology, versed in Morse code and keen to decipher military, civilian and maritime messages. But as voice and music broadcasts increased, other family members donned the earphones. They created a scenario reminiscent of "proto-broadcasting" over the telephone. What began as a hobby became an entertainment experience, greatly facilitated in the early 1920s by the emergence of an increasing number of corporate stations that broadcasted on a regular basis. The end of this decade saw the creation of the vacuum tube radio with loud speakers. Within a half dozen years, despite economic hard times during the depression, many families owned a set. Radio had become a true mass medium. The glow of the dial in the dark of the evening, as voices from afar entered the living room, recalled storytelling around a primeval campfire.

Radio, no matter how it developed as a mass medium, through private ownership in the United States, government sponsorship in Europe, or in both ways as in Canada, captivated a generation. Looking back at the 1930s we can see several parallels between attitudes toward, and the influence of, radio and what would occur in the 1950s during the golden age of television. Woody Allen gives us a vivid commentary on this in his excellent film *Radio Days*, from which we have drawn the title of this part. It is well worth considering in conjunction with the chapters that follow, as well as records, tapes, CDs, and websites containing broadcasts from radio's golden age.

In the decade prior to World War I, as wireless use expanded, most people thought radio telegraphy was novel and useful. The attitude changed to indispensable following the sinking of the Titanic in 1912. The communications implications of this disaster are discussed by Stephen Kern in our first essay. He argues that the wireless, and a number other electric technologies deriving from what we have called the "wired world," expanded the way the present was regarded. It enabled people to experience distant events as they occurred. He shows how this capacity was foreshadowed in a more limited way, from station-to-station by the telegraph, and at the interpersonal level (as well as through "proto-broadcasting") by the telephone. We should add that disasters such as the Titanic's sinking, which highlighted the potential of wireless, are sometimes vivid illustrations of how the dominant medium of a period operates. In the early years of radio broadcasting, the crash of the Hindenberg and Orson Welles' broadcast of H.G. Well's War of the Worlds attest to this. During the television era the Kennedy assassination (1963), the NASA Challenger explosion (1986), and the tragic events of September 11th 2001 are further examples.

One of the key questions surrounding wireless (Morse coded transmissions) and early radio (voice) was whether or not they should be regarded as media for point-to-point communication, like the telegraph or telephone, or as something different. The something different, was the term "broadcasting," whose etymology (word history) and application to the future of radio is discussed in our next entry by John Durham Peters. As he shows, it took almost 25 years to go from Marconi's invention of wireless to a full grasp of radio as a medium that was not a "common carrier," what Peters likens to a "postal envelope," but as a medium for public communication necessitating a very different kind of regulatory governance. What was initially construed as a limitation in using the airwaves for communication multiple receivers could access a message that might be intended for only one station turned out to be the factor that gave rise to the dominant mass medium of the first half of the twentieth century: broadcast radio.

The remarkable, though often overlooked, transition radio underwent during the 1920s, from popular hobby to major mass medium, is discussed by Susan J. Douglas in our next selection. She presents a range of perceptions that existed toward the new medium on the eve of its "Golden Age." Also commented on, and still an issue today with television and the use of VCRs, DVDs and the internet, was the convenience of radio in accessing entertainment. Often people preferred to stay at home and listen, rather than go to hear live music or a play. As a result certain forms of popular culture began a shift to broadcasting to maintain and eventually increase their audiences. Debates about programming resulted. They are still with us, as is an ongoing critique of the way the medium, radio then, television now, has presented politics and religion.

No look at radio's golden age would be complete without a sample of the various programs that filled the airwaves. The excerpt by Christopher Sterling and John Kittross provides us with a representative glimpse of what was available. Their survey includes musical variety, comedy, drama, sports, and political programming. One very popular but controversial program not mentioned by Sterling and Kittross was Amos 'n' Andy. Wildly entertaining, this attempt by two white performers to create stories based around southern black characters who relocated to the north is an example of the controversial role that radio would play in the cause of race relations.

The programming that people would come to enjoy during the Golden Age of Radio came at a price. That price was sponsorship, as Michele Hilmes points out in our next entry. Advertising agencies brokered deals between sponsors and networks to support specific programs. The agencies, using various methods of audience research, such as surveys, in turn influenced the very programs that were being sponsored. As a result the network's control over its own agenda was often compromised. Hilmes uses the example of the J. Walter Thompson Agency and how it managed to transfer the influence it had achieved in print advertising to the airwaves. She also discusses something worth noting with respect to the next section of this book. The control that commercial sponsorship had over radio programing was eventually extended to network television, until it came under severe sanctions as a result of the rigged quiz show scandals of the late 1950s.

Despite the rich culture auditory information and entertainment radio created during its Golden Age in the 1930s and 1940s, many observers predicted that the medium would disappear in the 1950s with the rapid rise of television. Clearly, this did not happen. In our next selection, Peter Fornatale and Joshua Mills show us why. Where previously live music had dominated national network based radio, during the 1950s a post-war resurgence in the recording industry coincided with the emergence an influential youth culture and the shift from national network to local radio programming. "Deejays" attained celebrity status and popular music proliferated as never before.

Adult programing during this time became diversified to appeal to niche audiences, especially during the 1970s with the rise of FM broadcasting. As Fornatale and Mills point out, following from the observations of Marshall McLuhan, inexpensive portable radios could be taken almost anywhere and, unlike television, radio does not have to be looked at to be enjoyed. Just as we recommended Woody Allen's film *Radio Days* for an entertaining glimpse into radio's Golden Age, George Lucas's film, *American Graffiti*, provides a humorous window on the importance of radio to the post-war baby boomer generation.

CHAPTER 25

Wireless World

Stephen Kern

Stephen Kern is professor of history at The Ohio State University. He is the author of a major and widely influential work in cultural history, The Culture of Time and Space: 1880–1918.

On the night of April 14, 1912, the largest moving structure ever built, the *Titanic*, steamed at a recklessly high speed into an ice field in the North Atlantic. The first officer recalled that the sea was especially calm and so that night there were no "ice blinks"—flashes of light given off when waves splash against icebergs and illuminate their crystallized surfaces. Visibility was further reduced by fog. At 11:40 P.M. a lookout suddenly spotted an iceberg dead ahead. The ship turned sharply and, as it scraped by, was opened up like a tin can with a gash below the water line three hundred feet long. The captain determined that they were going to sink fast and at 12:15 A.M. ordered his wireless operator to send the distress call. Within a few minutes the airwaves were rippling with signals as over a dozen ships became aware of the disaster. This was simultaneous drama on the high seas, driven by steam power and choreographed by the magic of wireless telegraphy.

Ten ships heard the call from over a hundred miles away and remained in contact but were too distant to help, as were also the *Hellig Olav* at 90 miles and the *Niagara* at 75 miles. The *Mount Temple* was 50 miles away but had to move slowly through ice fields. The *Carpathia* at 58 miles was the first to arrive, but not until almost two hours after the *Titanic* went down with 1,522 passengers. Another ship, close enough to have saved all the passengers, was not in wireless contact. The *Californian* was approximately 19 miles away, but its wireless operator had hung up his earphones

for the night about ten minutes before the *Titanic* sent out its first CQD. Two watchmen on the deck of the *Californian* saw the rockets that the *Titanic* fired but could not figure out what they meant or convince their captain to pull anchor and find out. What the eyes and ears of man could not perceive the wireless could receive over vast distances and through darkness and fog.

The operator on the *Carpathia* got the call for help when he put on his earphones to verify a "time rush" (an exchange of time signals with a neighboring ship to see if their clocks agree). At 1:06 A.M. he heard the *Titanic* tell another ship coming to help, "Get your boats ready; going down fast on the head." The world began to get news of the disaster at 1:20 A.M., when a wireless station in Newfoundland picked up the message that the *Titanic* was sinking and was putting women off in boats. Shortly after that hundreds of wireless instruments along the Atlantic coast began to transmit and the airways became jumbled in confusion. The *Titanic*'s wireless had a range of only 1,500 miles, so signals to Europe had to go first to New York and then across the ocean by cable; still, by early morning the entire world was privy to news of the disaster.[1]

To one of the survivors in a life boat it seemed as if the stars above saw the ship in distress and "had awakened to flash messages across the black dome of the sky to each other."[2] The communication that he imagined between stars was accomplished on a lesser scale between the ships at sea by wireless. On April 21, the *New York Times* commented on its magical power.

> Night and day all the year round the millions upon the earth and the thousands upon the sea now reach out and grasp the thin air and use it as a thing more potent for human aid than any strand of wire or cable that was ever spun or woven. Last week 745 [*sic*] human lives were saved from perishing by the wireless. But for the almost magic use of the air the *Titanic* tragedy would have been shrouded in the secrecy that not so long ago was the power of the sea. . . . Few New Yorkers realize that all through the roar of the big city there are constantly speeding messages between people separated by vast distances, and that over housetops and even through the walls of buildings and in the very air one breathes are words written by electricity.

An editorial in the *London Times* of April 16 noted the expanded range of experience made possible by the wireless. "The wounded monster's distress sounded through the latitudes and longitudes of the Atlantic, and from all sides her sisters great and small hastened to her succor. . . . We recognize with a sense near to awe that we have been almost witness of a great ship in her death agonies." An officer of the American Telephone and Telegraph Company praised the communication that made it possible to follow the rescue. The telephone and wireless, he wrote, "enabled the peoples of many lands to stand together in sympathetic union, to share a common grief." William Alden Smith, the Michigan senator who chaired an exhaustive inquiry into the sinking, as part of his summary of those hearings before the United States Senate on May 18, 1912, referred to the new sense of world unity that required worldwide safety regulations. "When the world weeps together over a common loss," he said, "when nature moves in the same directions in all spheres, why should not the nations clear the sea of its conflicting idioms and wisely regulate this new servant of humanity?"[3] Although the wireless had been used before to save lives at sea, this rescue effort was particularly highlighted because so many were aware of the tragedy: the survivors watching from life boats, the wireless operators in

distant places, and the frustrated seamen in the rescue ships.

The ability to experience many distant events at the same time, made possible by the wireless and dramatized by the sinking of the *Titanic,* was part of a major change in the experience of the present. Thinking on the subject was divided over two basic issues: whether the present is a sequence of single local events or a simultaneity of multiple distant events, and whether the present is an infinitesimal slice of time between past and future or of more extended duration. The latter debate was limited largely to philosophers, but the issue of sequence versus simultaneity was expressed by numerous artists, poets, and novelists and was concretely manifested in some new technology in addition to the wireless—the telephone, the high-speed rotary press, and the cinema.

Already in 1889 Lord Salisbury commented on the simultaneity of experience made possible by the telegraph, which had "combined together almost at one moment . . . the opinions of the whole intelligent world with respect to everything that is passing at that time upon the face of the globe."[4] The telegraph had been in operation since the 1830s, but its use was limited to trained operators and confined to transmitting stations. The wireless proliferated source points of electronic communication, and the telephone brought it to the masses.

The history of wireless telegraphy begins with a paper by James Clerk Maxwell in 1864, which argued that electromagnetic waves must exist and should be able to be propagated through space. In 1887 Heinrich Hertz produced those waves in a laboratory, and in 1894 Guglielmo Marconi devised an apparatus to transmit and receive them. In 1897 Marconi went to England and established the first coast station on the Isle of Wight for communication with ships at sea. In 1901 a message was sent across the Atlantic from a special high-power transmitter in England, and two years later King Edward VII and President Theodore Roosevelt exchanged messages over it. As wireless instruments proliferated, an International Congress on Wireless Telegraphy was held at Berlin in 1903 to regulate their use. The Marconi Company established the first wireless news service in 1904 with nightly transmissions from Cornwall and Cape Cod. The first distress signal from a ship at sea was sent in 1899, and in 1909, following a collision between two ships, a wireless call saved 1,700 lives. The technology got some sensational publicity in 1910 when a wireless message led to the arrest of an American physician in London, who murdered and buried his wife and attempted to escape aboard a ship with his secretary dressed as a boy. The captain became suspicious of the two, wired Scotland Yard, and arranged to have a detective arrest the couple at sea before they arrived in port. By 1912 the wireless was an essential part of international communication linking land stations and ships at sea in an instantaneous, worldwide network.[5]

The telephone had an even broader impact and made it possible, in a sense, to be in two places at the same time. It allowed people to talk to one another across great distances, to think about what others were feeling and to respond at once without the time to reflect afforded by written communication. Business and personal exchanges suddenly became instantaneous instead of protracted and sequential. Party lines created another kind of simultaneous experience, because in the early systems bells rang along the entire line and everyone who was interested could listen in. One imaginative journalist envisioned the simultaneity of telephone communication as a fabric made from the fibers of telephone lines, switchboard cables, and speech: "Before the great switchboard the girls seem like weavers at some gigantic loom, the numerous cords crossing and recrossing as if in the execution of some wondrous fabric. Indeed, a wondrous fabric of speech is here woven into the record of each day."[6]

Within a few years of its invention in 1876 the telephone was used for public "broadcasts." In 1879 sermons were broadcast over telephone lines in the United States, and in 1880 a concert in Zurich was sent over telephone lines fifty miles to Basel. The following year an opera in Berlin and a [string] quartet in Manchester were transmitted to neighboring cities. The Belgians began such transmissions in 1884: the telephone company of Charleroi gave a concert which could be heard by all of the subscribers, an opera in Monnaie was heard 250 kilometers away at the royal palace at Ostend, and the North Railroad Station in Brussels piped in music from the Vaux-Hall in what was perhaps the first experiment with Muzak.[7]

Jules Verne envisioned "telephonic journalism" in a science fiction story of 1888.[8] Five years later it became a reality when a Hungarian engineer started such a news service in Budapest and expanded it into a comprehensive entertainment service with outlets in the homes of its 6,000 subscribers, each of whom had a timetable of programs including concerts, lectures, dramatic readings, newspaper reviews, stock market reports, and direct transmissions of speeches by members of Parliament. It focused the attention of the inhabitants of an entire city on a single experience, regulated their lives according to the program schedules, and invaded their privacy with an emergency signal that enabled the station to ring every subscriber when special news broke. An English journalist imagined that this service, if introduced in England, would "democratize" many luxuries of the rich as the "humblest cottage would be in immediate contact with the city, and the 'private wire' would make all classes kin."[9] At the same time it would diminish the isolation of individuals in cities and make it possible for one voice to be heard simultaneously by the six million people of London. In the United States in 1896, telephones were used to report presidential election returns, and, according to a contemporary report, "thousands sat with their ear glued to the receiver the whole night long, hypnotized by the possibilities unfolded to them for the first time."[10]

There was diverse critical response to the simultaneity of experience created by modern journalism. Already in 1892 the indefatigable alarmist Max Nordau complained that the simplest village inhabitant has a wider geographical horizon than the prime minister of a century ago. If the villager reads a paper he "interests himself simultaneously in the issue of a revolution in Chile, a bush-war in East Africa, a massacre in North China, a famine in

Russia."[11] Nordau anticipated that it would take a century for people to be able "to read a dozen square yards of newspapers daily, to be constantly called to the telephone, to be thinking simultaneously of the five continents of the world" without injury to the nerves. Paul Claudel reacted more positively in 1904 when he wrote that the morning newspaper gives us a sense of "the present in its totality,"[12] and an editorial in *Paris-Midi* of February 23, 1914, characterized the headlines of one daily paper as "simultaneous poetry."

NOTES

1. Walter Lord, *A Night to Remember* (New York, 1955); Richard O'Connor, *Down to Eternity* (New York, 1956); Peter Padfield, *The Titanic and the Californian* (London, 1965); Geoffrey Marcus, *The Maiden Voyage* (New York, 1969).

2. Lawrence Beesley, *The Loss of the SS Titanic* (New York, 1912), 101.

3. U. N. Bethell, *The Transmission of Intelligence by Electricity* (New York, 1912), 6; Smith quote cited by Wyn Craig Wade, *The Titanic: End of a Dream* (New York, 1979), 399–400.

4. Lord Salisbury's speech was printed in *The Electrician*, November 8, 1889, and cited by Asa Briggs, "The Pleasure Telephone: A Chapter in the Prehistory of the Media," in *The Social Impact of the Telephone*, ed. Ithiel Pool (Cambridge, 1977), 41.

5. G. E. C. Wedlake, *SOS: The Story of Radio-Communication* (London, 1973), 18–74.

6. Sylvester Baxter, "The Telephone Girl," *The Outlook* (May 26, 1906): 235.

7. Julien Brault, *Histoire du téléphone* (Paris, 1888), 90–95.

8. Jules Verne, "In the Year 2889," *The Forum*, 6 (1888): 664.

9. "The Telephone Newspaper," *Scientific American* (October 26, 1896); Arthur Mee, "The Pleasure Telephone," *The Strand Magazine*, 16 (1898): 34; and Asa Briggs, "The Pleasure Telephone," 41.

10. "The Telephone and Election Returns," *Electrical Review* (December 16, 1896): 298.

11. Max Nordau, *Degeneration* (1892; rpt. New York, 1968), 39.

12. Paul Claudel, "Connaissance du temps," in *Fou-Tcheou* (1904), quoted in Pär Bergman, *"Modernolatria" et "Simultaneità": Recherches sur deux tendances dans l'avant-garde littéraire en Italie et en France à la veille de la première guerre mondiale* (Uppsala, Sweden, 1962), 23.

CHAPTER

The Public Voice of Radio

John Durham Peters

John Durham Peters is the F. Wendell Miller professor of Communication at the University of Iowa. He is the author of Speaking into the Air: A History of the Idea of Communication *and* Courting the Abyss: Free Speech and the Liberal Tradition.

In the 1920s and 1930s the radio was undoubtedly a leading source of unmitigated bleat. Radio's early history stages, with some starkness, all the issues facing communication in our time: the longing for an assured delivery and the desire to touch over long distances.

The radio signal is surely one of the strangest things we know; little wonder its ability to spirit intelligence through space elicited immediate comparisons to telepathy, séances, and angelic visitations. At any point on the earth's surface in the twentieth century, silent streams of radio voices, music, sound effects, and distress signals fill every corner of space. In any place you are reading this, messages surround and fly past you, infinitely inconspicuous, like the cicadas in the *Phaedrus,* who sing of things we cannot hear with our unaided ears. The remarkable property of the radio signal (discovered in the 1890s, the same decade when Warren and Brandeis wrote of privacy) is its inherent publicity. Electromagnetic signals radiate "to whom it may concern"; they are no respecters of persons, and they rain on the just and the unjust.

Early developers found the omnipresent quality of the radio signal a defect, seeing only dialogue as a legitimate form of communication. Like the phonograph, radio technology was first conceived as a means of point-to-point communication. Marconi was characteristic of his generation in thinking of the new technology as a wireless telegraph. But the telegraph had single termini; the airwaves did not. The looming obstacle, as with the mails before envelopes and anonymous sending and with the party line years of the telephone, was the lack of confidentiality. Anyone with a receiver set potentially had, as the parable of the sower put it, "ears to hear." Reception of the signal was inherently open-ended. As the adman Bruce Barton wrote in 1922, "Radio telephone messages can never be secret. They go out in all directions; and anyone with a machine tuned to the proper wave length can hear what you are saying to your partner in New Orleans or your sweetheart in Kenosha."[1] The inability to bar unintended recipients was a major hindrance to the profitability of wireless telegraphy and, after the audion tube in 1907, wireless telephony as well. The quest for a confidential channel, sometimes called "syntony" or "selectivity," was a preoccupation of early radio engineers.[2] Wanted was person-to-person connection, not a party line.[3]

The quest for "private service on a party line" was an aim for both telephone and radio in this period.[4] Sought was the electromagnetic equivalent of the postal envelope. The term "listening in," the eventual verb for describing audience behavior in commercial radio, even borrowed the notion of eavesdropping on party lines, as if radio audiences were overhearing messages not originally intended for their ears.[5]

An exhibit of the principle that cultural preconception shapes the uses of technology as much as its internal properties do, radio "broadcasting" was not embraced until wireless technology had been in use for a quarter of a century.[6] The origins of the term are obscure, but all fingers point to an agricultural use not far from the *Phaedrus,* the parable of the sower, and the nervous metaphors of Comstock and Warren and Brandeis: the scattering of seeds. In nineteenth-century American literature, "broadcast" was most often used as an adjective meaning scattered. In *Tom Sawyer,* "A sweep of chilly air passed by, rustling all the leaves and snowing the flaky ashes broadcast about the fire." Thoreau wrote that "Nature strews her nuts and flowers broadcast, and never collects them into heaps" (*A Week on the Concord and Merrimack Rivers*). Whitman's *Leaves of Grass* praises the United States for being "essentially the greatest poem. In the history of the earth hitherto the largest and most stirring appear tame and orderly to their ampler largeness and stir. Here at last is something in the doings of man that corresponds with the broadcast doings of the day and night." The term *broadcasting* did not at first refer to any organized social practice. The free character of things broadcast naturally fit the radio signal's tendency to stray.

The discovery of radio as an agency of broadcasting is often attributed to David Sarnoff, future head of the National Broadcasting Company. In a now famous 1915–16 memo Sarnoff described the wireless as a household music box.[7] The "ether" would be filled not with the cacophony of amateur operators making point-to-point transmissions, but with music "broadcast" to a nation of listeners—who would then want to purchase

Westinghouse radio sets. One obstacle, of course, to the development of radio as pure broadcasting was the question of how to make money from a communication circuit that seemed to be a continuous potlatch or gift to the public.[8] Sarnoff lit on the idea that desirable programming would fuel acquisition of radio hardware; he had not yet discovered the eventually victorious, lamentable practice of advertiser support for programs. Sarnoff saw the ether's lack of privacy as an opportunity rather than an obstacle. The lack of a specific addressee, he thought, would be the specialty rather than a defect of radio, speaking to the great audience invisible.[9] Sarnoff's memo was a dead letter in its impact on his Westinghouse superiors, though in retrospect it seems prophetic. Maybe, like Socrates, they were suspicious of forms of communication whose reception was open-ended and whose addressees were anonymous.

World War I saw power wrested from radio amateurs by the military, the state, and large corporations. The amateur vision of the ether as a cacophonous public forum in which anyone could take part was losing ground by the 1920s and was preserved largely in the efforts of noncommercial broadcasters, themselves pushed decisively aside by the early 1930s.[10] Herbert Hoover, who as secretary of commerce was probably the chief agent in making American radio a corporate, federally regulated entity, spoke in 1922 against the wireless as a means of person-to-person contact: "The use of the radio telephone for communication between single individuals, as in the case of the ordinary telephone, is a perfectly hopeless notion. Obviously, if ten million subscribers are crying through the air for their mates they will never make a junction."[11] 'Like Socrates' concerns about writing, Hoover was worried about the inability of "broadcasting" to achieve "junction." The Iowa-born, Stanford-trained engineer is not usually thought of as a particularly erotic thinker, but here eros looms, trying as ever to "bridge the chasm." Imagine the myriad crisscrossing of radio telephone voices crying for their loves, lost in transit,

incomplete passes, the very air full of undelivered longings. Ah, Bartleby! Ah, humanity! Saint Paul's warning to the Corinthians who practiced glossolalia without interpreters could be motto of every broadcaster: You will be speaking into the air (1 Cor. 14:9). Like Paul, Hoover wanted to control the confusion of tongues.

Eventually radio became officially defined as an agent of public communication. The key question in the 1920s and early 1930s was its regulatory status: Was radio a common carrier or something else? This question involved the old couplet of dialogue and dissemination. "Common carriage" was a nineteenth-century category that included shipping lines, elevators, and above all railroads. The Interstate Commerce Act (1887) gave the Interstate Commerce Commission (ICC) jurisdiction over "common carriers," which were ceded a "natural monopoly" in return for which they had to offer all comers equal service and submit their rates to the ICC for approval. The Mann-Elkins Act (1910) and the Transportation Act (1920) expanded the definition of "common carrier" to include "transmission of intelligence by wire or wireless," thus placing the telegraph and telephone under ICC jurisdiction.[12]

But radio had difficulty fitting the point-to-point model. Heather Wessely captures the contrast well: "Rail transport is not a service designed with a potential terminus in every household."[13] Radio spoke into the blue yonder. A key case before the ICC, *Sta-Shine Products Co. v. Station WGBB* (1932), raised the question whether radio broadcasts entailed a "transmission of intelligence." Should the ICC treat radio stations as common carriers, thus regulating advertising rates? The decision declared radio outside the ICC's jurisdiction, since "no service is performed at the receiving end by the broadcasting company, similar to the service performed by common carriers." Broadcasting lacked "the boy in the blue uniform who rings the door bell and who brings the message itself," Common carriers saw to it that people receive their cargoes or messages, but broadcasting made no effort to ensure delivery. "Unless one has a radio receiving set properly attuned, he will never get and is not expected to get the intelligence, whether it be instruction, entertainment, or advertising, sent out from the broadcasting station,"[14] By the standards of common carriage, broadcasting was a deformed communication circuit, since the "transmission of intelligence" was left to chance.

The conclusive definition of broadcasting was left to the jurisdiction of a New Deal agency, the Federal Communications Commission (FCC). The contrast between broadcasting and common carriage became a cornerstone of United States broadcasting policy in the Communications Act of 1934. According to section 3(h) of the act, "A person engaged in radio broadcasting shall not, insofar as such person is so engaged, be deemed a common carrier."[15] Common carriers operate point-to-point, deliver their goods to a definite address, and must be accessible to anyone and accountable for the tariffs they charge. A common carrier is characterized by "the separation of the content from the conduit" and lacks editorial discretion over the messages private people send.[16] Thus, if you shout obscenities into a phone, the phone company is exempt from prosecution; if you do so into a radio microphone, the station may have to answer to the FCC. Common carriers must be message blind and sender blind, but never receiver blind. Broadcasters, if not quite audience blind, see their audiences through a glass darkly.[17] Broadcasting, as legally defined, involves privately controlled transmission but public reception, whereas common carriage involves publicly controlled transmission but private reception. The two models possess striking symmetry. A common carrier offers universal access to transmission and restricted access to reception, whereas broadcasting offers restricted access to transmission and universal access to reception. Like Socrates in the *Phaedrus,* common carriage seeks to guarantee the delivery of the seed; like Jesus in the parable of the sower, broadcasting focuses on scattering the message to all (even if the actual reception is spotty).

The Communications Act of 1934 thus installed the ancient notion of dissemination in the heart of a modern technology in the guise of "broadcasting." As it developed, however, the term acquired a double sense. In its generic use, it refers to transmission over the air, but "broadcasting" as a legal term refers not to the diverse practices of the airwaves but to an idealized configuration among speakers and audiences. It conjures visions of the agora, the town meeting, or the "public sphere"; broadcasting is supposed to be more a town crier summoning citizens to assembly than a midway barker inviting the curious to spend their nickels on the freak show. By defining broadcasting in terms of the public interest, the 1934 Communications Act articulated a vision of the audience—a civic one, the audience as disinterested public—that fit the technology's lack of confidentiality and gave a lofty lineage to a set of practices that owed as much to the circus as to the polis.

In fact, by the 1930s, commercial broadcasters had developed a number of techniques for routing audiences and managing the junction. The brief shining moment of dissemination was washed over by a flood of dialogism.

NOTES

1. Bruce Barton. "This Magic Called Radio: What Will It Mean in Your Home in the Next Ten Years?" *American Magazine,* June 1922, 11–13, 70–71 at 70.
2. Hugh G. J. Aitken, *Syntony and Spark: The Origins of Radio* (New York: Wiley. 1976), and "Radio Wave Band for Every Country," *New York Times,* 23 August 1921, 4.
3. The development of cryptography before and during World War If made it technically possible to destine messages for a specific address via the airwaves. Alan Turing played a key role in this in Great Britain, as did Claude Shannon in the United States.

4. Phrase taken from "To Stop Telephone-Eavesdropping," *Literary Digest*, 17 October 1914, 733.

5. Covert, "'We May Hear Too Much,'" 203.

6. See Susan J. Douglas, *Inventing American Broadcasting* (Baltimore: Johns Hopkins University Press, 1987), and Susan Smulyan, *Selling Radio: The Commercialization of American Broadcasting, 1920–1934* (Washington, D.C.: Smithsonian Institution Press, 1994).

7. David Sarnoff, "Memorandum to E. J. Naily," in *Documents of American Broadcasting*, ed. Frank J. Kahn (Englewood Cliffs, N.J.: Prentice-Hall, 1984), 23–25.

8. Smulyan, *Selling Radio.*

9. Daniel J. Boorstin, *The Americans: The Democratic Experience* (New York: Vintage, 1973), 391.

10. Robert W. McChesney, *Telecommunications, Mass Media, and Democracy: The Battle for the Control of U.S. Broadcasting, 1928–1935* (New York: Oxford Univetsity Press, 1993).

11. Quoted in Richard A. Schwarzlose, "Technology and the Individual: The Impact of Innovation on Communication," in *Mass Media between the Wars, 1918–1941*, ed. Catherine l. Covert and John D. Stevens (Syracuse: Syracuse University Press, 1984), 100.

12. The relevant documents can be found in Bernard Schwartz, *The Economic Regulation of Business and Industry: A Legislative History of U.S. Regulatory Agencies,* 5 vols. (New York: Chelsea House, 1973). Congressman James R. Mann also wrote the Mann Act of 1910, prohibiting "the transportation of women across state lines for immoral purposes." His legislation dealt with all sorts of common carriers.

13. Heather A. Wessely, "Culture, History and the Public Interest; Developing a Broadcasting Service for the United States" (manuscript, Department of Communication Studies, University of Iowa, 1993), 54.

14. *Sta-Shine Products Company, Inc. V. Station WGBB of Freeport NY* 188 ICC 271 (1932); quotations from 276, 277–78.

15. As justice White put in 1979: "The language of § 3 (h) is unequivocal; it stipulates that broadcaters shall not be treated as common carriers." *FCC v. Midwest Video Corporation*, in *Documents of American Broadcasting*, ed. Frank J. Kahn (Englewood Cliffs, N.J.: Prentice-Hall, 1984), 364.

16. T. Barton Carter, Marc A. Franklin, and Jay B. Wright, *The First Amendment and the Fifth Estate: Regulation of Electronic Mass Media* (Mineola, N.Y.: Foundation, 1986), 395.

17. This legal distinction may in part be a post hoc version of the division of labor agreed upon in 1926 between RCA and AT&T, leaving the former with the air/broadcasting and the latter with wires/telephony. See Noobar R. Danielian, *AT&T: The Story of Industrial Conquest* (New York: Vanguard, 1939).

CHAPTER 27

Early Radio

Susan J. Douglas

Susan J. Douglas is professor of communication studies at the University of Michigan. Her book Inventing American Broadcasting: 1912–1922 *deserves serious attention from students of communication for its close reading of the early, formative period of broadcasting in the United States. The present excerpt is taken from her newest work,* Listening In.

It was the early 1920s, nighttime, and around the country, especially in the Northeast and Upper Midwest, American boys and men (and, to a much lesser extent, women and girls) connected themselves umbilically by headphones to small black boxes powered by sets of batteries. They led the way in a cultural revolution: the turn to listening in the 1920s. Painstakingly moving a thin wire known as the cat whisker around a hunk of crystal, they heard a blend of talk, music, and static as their heads became filled with the voices and sounds of nearby and far-off places. Others, usually those with more money, had sets with tuning dials—five of them—all of which had to be perfectly calibrated to reel in particular stations. This was an exploration, and as such it was thrilling and often maddeningly frustrating.

As with the spread of home computing in the late 1980s and 1990s, often it was boys who embraced this device and introduced the rest of the family to it.[1] This was an exploratory listening, predicated on technical expertise and patience, in which people listened not for continuity but for change; not for one message or program from New York but for many messages from all over the place; to see how far they could get, not which celebrity they could hear; and to hear the eerie, supernatural mixture of natural static and man-made voices. They listened to get a more immediate sense of their nation as it was living, breathing, and talking right then and there. They were lured by the prospect of witnessing entirely new auditory spectacles, the aural equivalents of lightning and fireworks. Turning to listening, entering the realm of listening for so many hours each night, was an entirely new cognitive, emotional, and cultural experience and one we still have an only rudimentary understanding of today.

These were the frothy "boom" years of radio, when virtually nothing was fixed—not the frequencies of stations (although at first everyone was supposed to broadcast on the same wavelength), not the method of financial support, not government regulations, and not the design or domestic location of the radio itself. There were no networks—known in the late 1920s as the chains—and there was very little advertising on the air. With a few exceptions, like the Sunday broadcasts of church services, there was not a predictable program schedule. Instead, stories geared for children might be followed by a lecture on "hygiene of the mouth" or "how to make a house a home," which would in turn be followed by phonograph music or "Madame Burumowska, formerly of the Moscow Opera" singing Rimsky-Korsakov's "Hymn to the Sun."[2] Department stores, newspapers, the manufacturers of radio equipment, colleges and universities, labor unions, socialists, and ham operators all joined the rush to start stations.

. Today we take it for granted, often wearily, that broadcasting is supported by advertising, that its mission is to promote compulsive consumerism, that most broadcast stations are affiliated with national networks or owned by broadcasting chains, and that broadcasting is regulated by the Federal Communications Commission, all too often in ways that benefit corporate consolidation and greed at the expense of real diversity on, and access to, the airwaves. It seems fixed, as if this system was and is the only one imaginable. It seems so hopelessly and relentlessly top-down.

Many of these precedents got set in the mid- and late 1920s—some of them even earlier—when none of this was taken for granted. In fact, we have had advertising-supported broadcasting for so long—seventy years—that it is easy to forget that this was extremely controversial and hotly debated in the 1920s, condemned as a crass invasion of people's private lives. (We can thank AT&T for pioneering the use of radio advertising in 1922 on its station WEAF.) Susan Smulyan and Bob McChesney, in their excellent books on early radio, remind us that there was nothing inevitable about the way radio came to be financed and regulated.[3] This was a contested process, with educators and labor organizers, corporate interests, amateur operators, and the government all advancing their very different visions for the future.

Because this decade was so formative, radio historians have especially focused on the 1920s and done a fine job chronicling the rise of radio advertising, the emergence of the networks, the establishment of radio regulation, and the evolution of programming from impromptu speeches and soprano solos to regularly scheduled shows like *Amos 'n' Andy.*[4]

I want to explore something else here: what did it mean, amidst the visual onslaught of billboards, magazines, movies, spectator sports, and newspapers, to retreat to your home and turn to listening? I want to get back into the garage, the attic, and the living room—despite the fragmentary nature of the historical record here—to speculate on this new phenomenology of listening and to lay out what was involved in bringing radio into everyday life. People didn't just walk into a shop in 1922, buy a radio, bring it home, plug it in, and hear orchestral music. That wouldn't be possible until the late 1920s at the earliest. Everyday people had to assemble the device (which included stringing up an antenna), had to learn how to listen, how they wanted to listen, and what they wanted to listen to at the same time that stations, and then networks, were deciding what was best to broadcast. So I want to explore how the terms of radio listening itself were constructed, contested, and thus invented in the 1920s, by programmers and by listeners.

I also want to consider how this major perceptual shift in our culture, a concentrated and dedicated turn to listening, inflected evolving and uncertain notions of manhood and nationhood in the early 1920s. It was men and boys who brought this device into the home, and tinkering with it allowed them to assert new forms of masculine mastery while entering a realm of invisibility where certain pressures about manhood could be avoided. At the same time a quest for nationhood and a reversion to its opposite, tribalism—most of which was white tribalism—characterized the 1920s.

This technologically produced aurality allowed listeners to reformulate their identities as individuals and as members of a nation by listening in to signs of unity and signs of difference. By the late 1920s "chain broadcasting" was centralizing radio programming in New York and standardizing the broadcast day so that listeners tuning between stations at night often heard the same chain program. Meanwhile, independent stations featured locally produced programs with local talent. Listeners could tune in to either or both, and tie in, imaginatively, with shows that sought to capture and represent a "national" culture and those that sought to defend regional and local cultural authority. And in the debate about what kinds of shows and stations were better, which often dominated the letters-to-the-editor pages of the popular *Radio Digest,* we see enormous tensions surrounding network radio's role as a culturally nationalizing force.

It is important to emphasize here that what quickly got coined as listening in went through three distinct but overlapping stages in the 1920s, and that shifts in modes of listening were tied to technical changes in radio apparatus. The first stage, roughly between 1920 (although with the hams this had started much earlier) and 1924, was characterized by the phenomenon called DXing: trying to tune in as many faraway stations as possible. Most DXers started with crystal sets, often moved on to tube sets, and listened at first on headphones, the surrounding sounds of home shut out by the black disks on their ears. And while we don't have the kind of detailed surveys of listeners that historians long for, the journalistic record contains various romantic accounts by middle-class "distance fiends" who gushed about the pleasures of DXing. What is especially striking about these accounts is the way they describe using radio listening to imagine America as a nation more harmonious than it was yet simultaneously reveling in and embracing its differences—what divided it, what rebelled against "America" as a homogenizing notion.

The second stage was music listening, which began, of course, at the same time as DXing, since most of what stations played was music, but became more possible and popular with the introduction in 1925 of improved loudspeakers. The third stage, which crystallized with the extraordinary success of *Amos 'n' Andy* in 1929 as a network program, was story listening, in which people sat down at the same time each day or each week to listen to the same characters enact comedic or dramatic performances.

The rapid explosion of exploratory listening would not have occurred without that fraternity called the amateur operators and later known as ham operators.[5] They constituted the very first radio audience in the first decade of the century, and through their technical innovations as well as their social uses of wireless telegraphy, they paved the way for radio broadcasting in the 1920s. But they also extended the nature of such listening. In the 1920s, while most listeners were trying to tune in broadcast stations, the amateurs—who had not only received but also broadcast wherever and whenever they wanted before 1912—were forbidden from transmitting in the broadcast band and were relegated to an etheric reservation then thought of as pretty worthless: waves 200 meters and down, or shortwaves. Shortwaves, it was thought at the time, wouldn't travel any distance at all; longer waves did that. If the amateurs were going to continue as active agents in the spectrum, they had no choice but to figure out whether they could get anything out of the shortwaves. And figure it out they did, long before Marconi or any corporation.

The amateur fraternity in America began to take shape between 1906 and 1907, after the discovery that certain crystals, like silicon or Carborundum, were excellent detectors of radio waves. More to the point, unlike the prototype vacuum tubes new to the market in 1907, crystals were cheap, durable, and reliable. The events at a receiving station were the same as those at the transmitting end but in reverse sequence. At the transmitting end, inventors had to devise the most efficient method of generating very-high-frequency alternating current from a direct current source. At the receiving end, the problem was "rectifying" these oscillations: translating high-frequency alternating current back to a unidirectional pulsating current that could flow through a telephone receiver. Radio waves are of such a high frequency that the telephone diaphragm alone could not handle their speed or rapid reversal. By 1906 the Fleming "valve" and De Forest "audion"—precursors to the vacuum tube—

had been developed, and while they allowed the current to run in one direction only, they were very expensive, highly temperamental, and short-lived. Crystals rectified radio signals in the same way, but no one at the time knew how or why.

The discovery of the crystal detector opened up radio—then still called wireless telegraphy and still quite in its infancy—to legions of boys and men who were, basically, hobbyists. They were primarily white and middle-class, located predominantly in urban areas, especially ports, and they built their own stations in their bedrooms, attics, or garages. They became known for their ingenuity in assembling a motley array of electrical and metal castoffs—from curtain rods and bedposts to Model T ignition coils—into highly effective homemade sets. The one component that was often too complicated for most amateurs to duplicate, and too expensive to buy, was the headphone set. Coincidentally, telephones began vanishing from public booths across America as amateurs lifted them for their own stations. By 1910 the amateurs outnumbered everyone else—private wireless companies and the military—on the air.

Popular culture at this time—from the Boy Scout manual and *Tom Swift and His Wireless Message* to articles in *The New York Times*—celebrated amateur radio as an example of "the ambition and really great inventive genius of American boys." These accounts gained force as real-life dramas made heroes of professional operators. On January 23, 1909, two ships, the *Republic* and the *Florida*, collided twenty-six miles southeast of Nantucket in a heavy fog. The *Republic*'s wireless operator, Jack Binns, sent distress signals for both ships, and because of his work nearly all of the twelve hundred passengers of both ships were saved. The story was front-page news for four straight days. By the time he got back to New York, Binns was a celebrity, sought after by reporters and autograph hounds, and offered one thousand dollars a week for ten weeks to appear on the vaudeville stage. Amateurs who listened in on Binns's distress calls became heroes by association and brought more converts to the hobby.

Boy fixing a radio. *The Advertising Archives*

At the same time it was becoming clear that not all amateurs were such upstanding Boy Scout types. There were some who deliberately sent false or obscene messages, and their favorite target was the U.S. Navy, the major military user of wireless. The temptation to indulge in such practical joking was enhanced by the fact that detection was virtually impossible. Fights ensued on the air when hams, posing as admirals, sent ships on wild goose chases, and when naval operators couldn't get a message through because local amateurs were comparing the answers to their arithmetic homework and refused to pipe down.[6]

The navy sought, unsuccessfully at first, to get the amateurs banished from the airwaves. The *Titanic* disaster, however, moved public and congressional opinion against the amateurs' unrestricted access to transmitting. The loss of so many lives, when there were ships near enough to rescue the survivors had they only had wireless onboard, drove home the need to require wireless equipment and at least two operators on all ships.

But few aspects of the tragedy outraged people more than the ceaseless interference, cruel rumors, and utter misinformation that dominated the airwaves in the aftermath of the disaster. Immediately after the *Titanic*'s wireless operator, Harold Bride, notified stations that the ship had hit an iceberg, wireless stations all along the northeast coast of North America clogged the airwaves with inquiries and messages. Out of this cacophony emerged a message picked up by both sides of the Atlantic and reprinted in the major papers: "All Titanic passengers safe; towing to Halifax." Editors of the London *Times* and *The New York Times* were appalled to learn the next day that the message was false, and they blamed the amateurs for manufacturing such a cruel hoax.

The etheric congestion that persisted as the survivors made their way to New York further cemented the amateurs' fate. Passed just four months later, the Radio Act of 1912 required that all amateurs be licensed, and it forbade them from transmitting on the main commercial and military wavelengths. They could listen in, but for transmitting they were banished to an area of the spectrum regarded as useless: the shortwaves of 200 meters and less. The power of their sets was restricted to 1,000 watts.

Despite this, the number of amateurs increased in the 1910s, and they improved their image by providing impromptu communications networks when windstorms or other disasters crippled telephone and telegraph lines. In 1914 Hiram Percy Maxim, the inventor and radio enthusiast, organized the American Radio Relay League to establish a formal relay system or network among amateurs that could step in on a regular basis during natural disasters. Now there was a grassroots, coast-to-coast communications network that made it possible, according to *Popular Mechanics*, "for the private citizen to

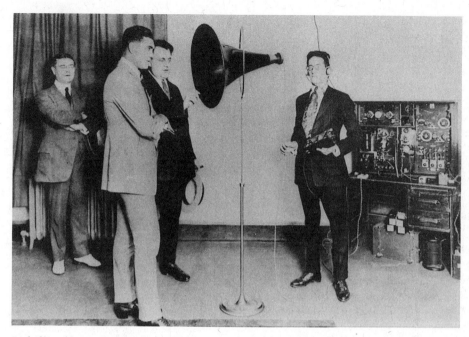

Early broadcasters began to piggyback on the *star system*. Heavyweight boxing champion Jack Dempsey does a studio interview at a local station in 1922. *National Archives of Canada.*

communicate across great distances without the aid of either the government or a corporation."[7]

During World War I the federal government banned all amateur activity and closed all amateur stations to prevent any interference with government transmissions. But by June of 1920 there were already fifteen times as many amateur stations in America as there were other types of stations combined, and the next year there were 10,809 licensed amateurs (many more, with smaller receiving sets, were unlicensed).[8] This was the incipient broadcast audience who would form the core of DXers, whose excited talk about listening in would bring converts to the pastime and who helped their friends and neighbors set up their own receiving sets.

As these boys and men clamped on their headphones in the early 1920s, they were working their way through various cultural changes that required everyone to navigate between the powerful tides of tradition and modernity. The 1920s seemed, both then and now, a time of cultural extremes, of opposites. And one thing is clear: most Americans were deeply ambivalent about being poised between these poles. The proliferation of new technologies, the shortening of hemlines and bobbing of hair, the spread of modernism in art, literature, and music, and the census report which claimed that, for the first time in history, half of Americans lived in cities (although a city was preposterously defined as 2,500 people or more), all insisted that modernity had arrived, that Victorian culture had been overthrown. In many of those cities, like New York, Chicago, and San Francisco, the combined population of those born in foreign countries and those born here of foreign parents was sometimes double or triple the population of native-born Americans with native-born parents.

Speed and difference seemed to define the culture that radio entered. Although wireless telegraphy had been around, and widely praised in the popular press, since the 1890s, people perceived the rapidity with which radio listening redefined everyday life as unprecedented. "Never in the history of electricity has an invention so gripped the popular fancy," claimed the *Review of Reviews*. "Its rapid growth has no parallel in industrial history," echoed *The Nation's Business*.[9] This perception that Americans were feverishly overthrowing the past—its pace and its substance—was embodied in the radio boom.

Not surprisingly, many Americans wanted to cling to, even restore, life as it had been in the allegedly "Gay Nineties," before cars, movies, the second wave of immigration, women's suffrage, and the Harlem Renaissance. So the 1920s were also characterized by reaction, some of it vicious. Violent race riots in East St. Louis, Chicago, and Washington, D.C., between 1917 and 1919, and the subsequent epidemic of lynchings and the rise of the Ku Klux Klan, revealed pathological racial fissures in the culture. The spread of religious fundamentalism, especially in the South, seemed a direct repudiation of the speakeasies and secularism of the ever-growing big cities. Prohibition was "an ethnic conflict . . . an attempt to promote Protestant middle-class culture as a means of imposing order on a disorderly world." The National Origins Act of 1924 severely restricted immigration, especially from southern and eastern European countries. What the Berkeley historian Lawrence Levine has called "Anglo-conformity"—the nativist insistence that immigrants abandon their past and embrace Anglo-American appearances and behaviors—clashed with a refusal by many to assimilate, become homogenized, disappear.[10]

So radio, which historians agree played a central role in delivering and forging a national culture in the 1930s and '40s, did not do so the instant the radio boom started. It couldn't. Rather, in this environment people used radio both to celebrate and strengthen local, ethnic, religious, and class-based communities and to participate in national spectacles, like election returns, the Dempsey-Carpentier boxing match in July 1921, or the World Series.

NOTES

1. "Astonishing Growth of the Radiotelephone," *Literary Digest*, April 15, 1922, p. 28.
2. Ibid.; Waldemar Kaempffert, "Radio Broadcasting," *Review of Reviews*, April 1922, p. 399.
3. See Susan Douglas, *Inventing American Broadcasting, 1899–1922* (Baltimore: Johns Hopkins University Press, 1987); Susan Smulyan, *Selling Radio: The Commercialization of American Broadcasting, 1920–1934* (Washington, D.C.: Smithsonian Institution Press, 1994); Robert W. McChesney, *Telecommunications, Mass Media, and Democracy: The Battle for Control of U.S. Broadcasting, 1928–1935* (New York: Oxford University Press, 1993).
4. The real pioneer was Erik Barnouw, whose three-volume *History of Broadcasting in the United States* has remained the standard for decades. For the 1920s, see his *Tower in Babel* (New York: Oxford University Press, 1966). Other fine works include Philip T. Rosen, *The Modern Stentors: Radio Broadcasters and the Federal Government, 1920–1934* (Westport, Conn.: Greenwood Press, 1980), and Smulyan's book, which is especially good on the emergence of the networks and broadcast advertising. See also Michele Hilmes, *Radio Voices: American Broadcasting, 1922–1952* (Minneapolis: University of Minnesota Press, 1997).
5. For more detail on the amateurs, see S. Douglas, *Inventing American Broadcasting*, chaps. 6 and 9.
6. Robert A. Morton, "The Amateur Wireless Operator," *Outlook*, January 15, 1910, pp. 132–33.
7. Cited in Clinton B. DeSoto, *Two Hundred Meters and Down: The Story of Amateur Radio* (West Hartford, Conn.: ARRL, 1936), p. 40.
8. S. Douglas, *Inventing American Broadcasting*, p. 299.
9. Kaempffert, "Radio Broadcasting," p. 398; cited in "The Radio Business," *Literary Digest*, May 5, 1923, p. 28.
10. Lynn Dumenil, *Modern Temper: American Culture and Society in the 1920s* (New York: Hill & Wang, 1995), pp. 224, 226–27; John Mack Faragher et al., *Out of Many: A History of the American People* (Upper Saddle River, N.J.: Prentice Hall, 1997), p. 742; Lawrence Levine, *The Opening of the American Mind* (Boston: Beacon Press, 1996), pp. 106–14.

CHAPTER 28

The Golden Age of Programming

Christopher Sterling and John M. Kittross

Christopher Sterling is a professor at George Washington University in Washington, D.C. John M. Kittross is a professor at Emerson College, Boston.

In the last half of the 1930s, most full-time radio stations broadcast at least 12 hours a day, and many for 18 hours or more. Generally stations filled the expanded air time with variations of program types already developed. Three departures from this pattern were news and commentary, the daytime serial drama, and quiz and audience-participation programs.

The FCC's March 1938 survey of programming showed that 53 percent was devoted to music, 11 percent to talks and dialogues, 9 percent to drama, 9 percent to variety, 9 percent to news (which would not have been measurable a few years earlier), 5 percent to religion and devotion, 2 percent to special events, and 2 percent to miscellaneous. While network affiliates got from 50 percent to 70 percent of programming from their network, they also increased the time devoted to local and live programming. Of all radio programming in the survey period, 64 percent was live—roughly half network and half local—while 21 percent was from electrical transcriptions and 12 percent was from phonograph records—a definite increase in non live programming on the typical station. . . .

Music remained the staple of most radio schedules. Several transcription companies, operated both by networks and some independents, offered local stations prerecorded music, sometimes assembled into programs. By early 1939 more than 575 stations subscribed to at least one transcription service, and nearly half of them used two or more. RCA's transcription operation probably accounted for 35 percent of the industry's business, although 25 to 30 companies had combined annual revenues of $5 million in the late 1930s.

A station usually signed a contract with a transcription firm to deliver several hundred recorded musical selections—usually on 16-inch discs, running at $33\frac{1}{3}$ rpm, with approximately 15 minutes per side—to start, and then perhaps 15 additional selections a month. The transcription firm usually dealt with only one station in a particular market to avoid program duplication, and payment by the station was either a percentage of its gross revenues or a flat sum. While such material averaged only 10–15 percent of time on network-affiliated stations, nonaffiliated local stations used it much more, some for 80 percent of their schedules. Popular songs and instrumentals predominated, but all kinds of music were offered.

Although the use of music increased locally, classical musical programs declined in importance on the networks after the early 1930s. A notable exception was the NBC Symphony Orchestra, one of the outstanding cultural creations of radio in America. The orchestra was founded when David Sarnoff helped persuade Arturo Toscanini, the just retired conductor of the New York Philharmonic, to return from Italy to conduct ten concerts, the first one on Christmas night 1937. NBC hired the best musicians possible to work in the new symphony orchestra. Three months later the network announced that Toscanini would lead the orchestra for another three years; but, as it turned out, the NBC Symphony continued for nearly 17 years until Toscanini's final retirement, well into his eighties, in 1954. The broadcasts normally originated from specially built Studio 8H, then the largest in the world, in the RCA Building in Rockefeller Center, and were broadcast on NBC-Blue on a sustaining basis, at the conductor's insistence. From 1948 the NBC Symphony was seen on television as well. After the NBC Symphony formally disbanded, the orchestra continued to play independently as the "Symphony of the Air."

Large dance bands were increasingly heard on both national and local programs. The 1930s were the "big band era," and many famous orchestras were heard first locally and then on the networks. Both industries benefited from such broadcasts, since the publicity of a major radio appearance attracted more people to the band's concerts. By 1937 the bands of Benny Goodman, Ozzie Nelson, Russ Morgan, Sammy Kaye, and Tommy Dorsey had played on network radio. *Your Hit Parade,* one of the top long-running radio programs, presented the most popular songs of the previous week, as determined by a national "survey" of record and sheet music sales, performed live by major singers and orchestras. The show began in fall 1935 and was sponsored on radio until 1953, and from 1951 until 1959 on television, by the American, Tobacco Company's Lucky Strike (and, toward the very end, Hit Parade) cigarettes.

Local stations presented a wide range of live music, some stations supporting a full orchestra, and an increasing amount of recorded music. The conflict between broadcasters and ASCAP . . . had a substantial effect on radio music in 1940–1941.

Compared to the highly professional variety programs, local or national *amateur hour* broadcasts presented unknowns who would

sing, tap dance, or do imitations in the hope of making a career. Such programs were used as fillers for years. Although the quality was uneven, the audiences that had cheered hometown talent supported contestants from all over the country. The most famous amateur variety show, *Major Bowes and His Original Amateur Hour,* began on New York station WHN in 1934 and moved to NBC-Red in March 1935. Within a few months, it was the most popular program on radio—at one time reaching a near-unbelievable rating of 45 when 20 was more typical! It presented amateurs who went on to fame—including Frank Sinatra, who made his radio debut in this program's first year—and others who went down to defeat and anonymity. Bowes became known by his catch-phrases and for his abrupt, even brutal manner with a gong as an aural equivalent of the "hook" used to remove inept or stage-frightened performers. The program continued on radio until 1952 and went on television from 1949 to the late 1960s, with Ted Mack serving as MC after Bowes's death—and bears a family resemblance to the *Gong Show* of the mid-1970s.

Many other national and local programs were built around a single performer, almost always a male singer or comic, usually backed by a musical group and supplemented by weekly guest performers. Most of these variety stars were products of vaudeville, burlesque, legitimate theater, or music halls. One was Bob Hope, who began his weekly show on CBS in 1935.

Such variety programming remained a network favorite, with little change, until inauguration of the army draft just before World War II gave a military slant to programs of the early 1940s. The *Army Show* (later the *Army Hour*), on NBC-Blue, *This Is Fort Dix* over Mutual, the Navy Band hour, and *Wings over America* were typical. The formats resembled earlier radio variety shows, with bits of song, humor, and chatter, but the participants frequently were military personnel, and the programs often originated from military camps and bases.

DRAMA

By far the most important network dramatic programming, in hours broadcast per week, was the woman's serial drama, or soap opera. Starting in 1935, the weekly hours of such fare increased sharply until, in 1940, the four networks combined devoted 75 hours a week to such programs, nine of every ten sponsored daytime network hours. These programs lasted 15 minutes, came on at the same time each weekday, and had soap and food manufacturers as sponsors. Typical of the longer running programs were *Back Stage Wife* ("what it means to be the wife of a famous Broadway star—dream sweetheart of a million other women"), which began in 1935; *The Guiding Light* (about a kindly cleric); *Lorenzo Jones* (inventor of useless gadgets); *Our Gal Sunday* ("Can this girl from a mining town in the West find happiness as the wife of a wealthy and titled Englishman?"); and *Road of Life* (doctors and nurses, although it began as the tale of an Irish-American mother's attempt to raise her children). In each case, domestic life was emphasized with its ups, and more usually, downs. Many of the actors and actresses played the same parts for decades. For a portion of each day, they performed a live, convincing, emotion-filled episode with little rehearsal, but their evenings were free for the stage or other professional activities. Behind many of the serials was the husband and wife team of Frank and Anne Hummert, who originally wrote all their own work but eventually employed dialogue writers to work within their character development and story lines. Elaine Carrington and Irna Phillips also wrote "soapers"— sometimes several at the same time.

The typical serial format was wonderfully simple: a brief musical introduction played on the studio organ, a narrator opening the day's episode with a recap of what had happened before, two segments of action separated by a commercial break, and a closing word from the narrator suggesting the problems ahead. Dialogue and organ music were somber and simple; story progress

was very slow, giving time for character development and allowing a listener to miss an episode or two painlessly. Audiences were loyal, and many programs lasted 15 or more seasons, until radio's programming character changed in the 1950s. Listeners to soap operas were among the first studied by social psychologists, and much criticism was levied at the genre in 1940 and 1941, as it was nearly impossible to schedule anything else between 10 A.M. and 5 P.M. These complaints dropped off as the number of serials decreased during the war years.

"Prestige" drama increased in the 1930s. These programs usually were "anthologies" offering different stories with new casts each week, sometimes adaptations from other media, but often original radio plays. Writers such as poet Archibald MacLeish, later Librarian of Congress, and unknown authors such as Norman Corwin and Arch Oboler gained recognition almost overnight. Prestige series included the *Columbia Workshop* of experimental drama on CBS, started late in 1936 and the more conventional *Lux Radio Theater,* which presented such stars as Helen Hayes, Leslie Howard, and an unknown player named Orson Welles in hour-long versions of current films.

Welles at twenty-three was the guiding light behind a new CBS series in fall 1938, the *Mercury Theater on the Air.* As writer, director, and star, he built up a company of actors whose names were famous for decades: Joseph Cotten, Agnes Moorehead, Everett Sloane, Ray Collins. His Sunday evening, October 30, 1938, Halloween program probably ranks as the most famous single radio show ever presented. It was an adaptation by Welles and Howard Koch of H. G. Wells's science fiction story "War of the Worlds." The location was changed to northern New Jersey, the time was moved to the present, and, even more important, the narrative was changed to reflect radio's format. Listeners who tuned in to the program's beginning, or who listened carefully to the between-acts announcements, understood these circumstances. But those who tuned in late—and many had a habit of listening to the first few minutes of ventriloquist Edgar Bergen and his dummy Charlie McCarthy on NBC before tuning over to CBS for the play—were due for a surprise. The program in progress seemed to feature a band performing in a hotel. A few moments later, an announcer broke in with a "news bulletin" saying that a gas cloud had been observed on the planet Mars. Then back to the music; another interruption, asking observatories to keep watch; more music; an interview with a "noted astronomer" on the possibility of life on Mars (unlikely); more music—and, suddenly, a bulletin saying that a large meteorite had fallen in the vicinity of Grovers Mill, New Jersey. The pace built in a series of news bulletins and on-the-spot reports of the opening of the cylindrical "meteorite," the emergence of the Martians, the assembly of Martian war machines, the rout of U.S. military forces, and government reaction. Reports of casualties, traffic jams, transmissions from hapless military pilots, ominous breaking off of on-the-spot reports, the later report of the "death" of the field reporter, and use of familiar names and places—all gave it reality. As the Martian war machines headed toward New York to discharge their poison gas over the city—to the sounds of fleeing ocean liners, the last gasps of a newsman atop the broadcasting studio, and the cracked voice of a solitary ham radio operator calling "Isn't anybody there? Isn't anybody?"—many listeners did not wait to hear the mid-program announcement that it was all a hoax. By 8:30, thousands of people were praying, preparing for the end, and fleeing the Martians.

These reactions were not silly, although it may look that way today. The pacing of the program undermined critical faculties. It convinced the listener that a reporter had traveled the miles from Grovers Mill "in ten minutes," when less than three minutes actually had elapsed. Already sure that mobs were fleeing, listeners who looked out their windows and saw lots of people going about normal pursuits assumed that everyone was trying to get away from the Martians, just as the radio said. If no one was in sight, they assumed

that everyone else had fled and left them behind. Few heard the three announcements of the program's fictional nature or the last half-hour, which was mostly a monologue by Welles, as a scientist who believes that he is one of the few survivors and who observes the demise of the Martians from the effects of earthly germs and bacteria. If they had heard this obviously dramatic material, many persons might have caught on. In the East, especially near the "landing site," thousands of people—a small proportion of the population but a large number nevertheless—called police, fled their homes, or otherwise reacted as though the invasion were real.

This panic had a number of causes, notably the way the program's "Halloween prank" nature was glossed over in the introduction. Afterwards researchers learned that many listeners did not try to double-check the "news" on another station or telephone friends; and that others, who found normal programming elsewhere on the dial, decided that these stations had not yet received the word. The panic was also a reaction to the "Munich Crisis" just one month before, when Americans had been glued to their radios expecting the world to go to war. . . .

Welles was amazed but only slightly abashed at the program's impact. The FCC let it be known that it would not consider such "scare" programs and formats as broadcasting in the public interest. Although "War of the Worlds" was rebroadcast recently in the United States as a "period piece" without much effect, its original adaptation broadcast in other countries brought the same sort of panic. Several persons were killed in a riot in South America, when resentment over having been fooled boiled over. This drama showed better than any other program or episode the impact of radio on society—"if it was on the radio, then it must be true."

Thrillers and situation comedies filled more network time per week than any other form of drama. Adventure programs, starting in the early 1930s . . . were heard both in the evenings, as crime-detective shows for adults, and in the late afternoons, as action-adventure serials for children. These live, mostly network shows could be technically complicated, with large casts, sound effects, and split-second timing. Programs included the true story–recreating *Gangbusters* starting in 1935, whose loud opening of sirens, machine-gun fire, and marching feet gave rise to the phrase "coming on like Gangbusters"; *Mr. Keen, Tracer of Lost Persons;* and *I Love a Mystery,* which had one of radio's most loyal audiences. The last was written by Carlton E. Morse, writer of the enduringly popular *One Man's Family. Mr. District Attorney,* a program starting in 1939 which opened with the DA reciting his oath of office, provided a generation with the concept of the law as protector as well as prosecutor.

Programs aimed at children included *Jack Armstrong—The All-American Boy; Tom Mix,* a cowboy-adventure program; *Captain Midnight* and *Hop Harrigan,* both with pilot-heroes; *Terry and the Pirates,* based on the Milton Caniff comic strip; and a number of other serials that made the American "children's hour" far different from the period of silence that the British offered for several decades. Two of the most important children's adventure programs were not serials. *The Lone Ranger* and *The Green Hornet,* which began over Mutual in 1938, were written and acted by the team at WXYZ, Detroit. . . . Indeed, the publisher-hero Green Hornet was identified as the Lone Ranger's grandnephew! *The Green Hornet* used a classical music theme and a hard-punching opening: "He hunts the biggest of all game! Public enemies who try to destroy our America. . . . With his faithful valet, Kato, Britt Reid, daring young publisher, matches wits with the underworld, risking his life that criminals and racketeers, within the law, may feel its weight by the sting of—the Green Hornet!" Until FBI chief Hoover objected, the Green Hornet's targets were "public enemies that even the G-Men cannot catch." When the United States entered World War II, the faithful valet-chauffeur Kato was quickly changed from Japanese to Filipino.

Radio's half-hour situation comedies were a staple for years. *Li'l Abner* began over NBC in 1939,

originating in Chicago as many programs then did; Fanny Brice, about whom the musical *Funny Girl* was written, created her immortal *Baby Snooks,* the child demon who created crisis after crisis for her father, and her baby brother Robespierre; *Blondie,* a 1939 CBS entry based on the Chic Young comic strip, featured the tribulations of Dagwood and Blondie Bumstead—another example of broadcasting's penchant for weak father figures; and *Henry Aldrich*—the misadventures of a crack-voiced adolescent—after appearing for some years as a segment on other programs, aired on its own over NBC-Blue in 1939.

Except for daytime serials and thriller programs, most network drama—anthology, or serial like *One Man's Family* and *Those We Love*—occurred in the evening. Only the largest stations produced their own dramatic programs regularly, most being content with network offerings, although many stations supplied dramatic or sound effects for commercials and special programs.

To an audience reared largely on movies, amateur theatricals, and traveling companies, radio provided something new and fascinating. The resulting loyal audience was very attractive to advertisers. Since it could perceive radio only by ear, the audience had to use its imagination to fill in the setting and the action. This it did well with the help of numerous musical and sound-effect conventions. Everyone understood transitions of time and space; the absence of carpet in radioland homes told the listener when somebody was entering or leaving a room. A filter that removed some of the audio frequencies placed a voice on the telephone; a bit more filter and some reverberation or "echo" would transport a ghost to fantasyland. But without the audience's imagination, radio drama never would have succeeded. . . .

POLITICAL BROADCASTING

Radio as a political instrument in the United States came into its own with the first administration of Franklin D. Roosevelt. Taking with him a habit from his New York governorship, F.D.R. began a series of "Fireside Chats" with the American public on the problems of Depression-hit America. There were 28 such broadcasts—8 in each of his first two terms, and 12 in the third, wartime term, nearly all of them half-hour programs broadcast in prime time—and they generally received ratings near the top. Roosevelt had a natural approach to radio, and his words came across more as a conversation between friends than a political speech. In the third "chat," when he stopped for a moment and drank from a glass of water, it seemed perfectly natural and correct.

In the 1936 presidential election campaign, a desperate Republican party tried a number of innovative uses of radio. The GOP nominee, Kansas governor Alfred Landon, submitted to a lengthy radio interview just prior to his nomination. More than 200 stations carried the convention in Cleveland, and the convention floor bristled with microphones. Once the campaign got underway, frequent spot radio commercials emphasized aspects of the GOP platform. In October, Senator Arthur Vandenberg presented a "debate" on CBS in which he asked questions of an absent President Roosevelt and then played carefully selected recordings of earlier F.D.R. speeches and promises. The program violated CBS policy against recordings, and many of the network's affiliates either refused to carry it or cut out during the program when they realized its unfair approach. Finally, when the networks refused to sell the Republicans time after the convention, the GOP used Chicago station WGN to present an allegorical play depicting its campaign promises.

On the other hand, the Democrats used nothing special—only F.D.R. That consummate political speaker had huge audiences listening to his broadcast speeches. On election night, the networks initially interrupted regular programs with ballot bulletins from time to time, supplementing with commentary. CBS went full-time to election results at 10:30 P.M., while Mutual reported its first election that year.

The second Roosevelt administration showed increasing use of radio, not just by the President and his cabinet but by numerous federal agencies as well. The Office of Education, for example, produced 11 educational network programs; the Federal Theater Program—part of the Depression-spawned Works Progress Administration—produced more radio programming in its short life than any other agency; the departments of Agriculture and Interior supplied recorded programs to individual stations. Many local stations also benefited from the forecasting services of the U.S. Weather Bureau, and produced local programs featuring county agricultural agents.

The 1940 election campaign saw F.D.R. run again, this time against Republican Wendell Willkie, a little-known utilities executive before a whirlwind public relations campaign had propelled him into the limelight. Willkie pushed himself so hard that his voice weakened during the campaign—perhaps one of the reasons why Roosevelt consistently got higher ratings. Surveys conducted during this campaign suggested that most voters now considered radio more important than newspapers as a source of political news and tended to listen most to the candidate they favored; in other words, radio strengthened voters' predispositions. On election eve the Democrats mounted a special radio program of speeches, party propaganda, and entertainment by stage, screen, and radio stars. Full-time election coverage, as in 1936, came after the regular prime-time entertainment, although bulletins were provided throughout the evening. Human interest pieces and voter interviews were more common than in previous years.

Political broadcasting was not limited to the presidential campaign. Louisiana Senator Huey Long made anti–F.D.R. populist speeches until his 1935 assassination. Like Roosevelt, he had an informal approach, inviting listeners to call a friend or two and tell them Huey Long was on the air, and then delaying the meat of his address for the next several minutes. Catholic radio priest Coughlin . . . after promising to leave the air in

1936 if his third-party candidate got less than nine million votes—he got less than one million—came back to rail against the New Deal. He became increasingly rightist, criticizing Jews and defending many of the tenets of Nazism, until pressure from the church hierarchy and other sources forced him off the air. . . .

CHAPTER **29**

Radio Voices

Michele Hilmes

Michele Hilmes is professor of communication arts at the University of Wisconsin, Madison. In addition to Radio Voices, *from which this excerpt comes, she is the author of* Hollywood and Broadcasting: From Radio to Cable.

One of the largest and most "radio active" advertising agencies in the United States during this period [the 1920s] was the J. Walter Thompson Company. The story of this agency's entry into broadcasting, and its relationship to the dominant network at the time, NBC, provides a glimpse into the machinations behind the stars and programs soon to become so familiar to the American public, and reveals some of the terms on which the negotiation of cultural standards and traditions took place. . . .

Though, according to Roland Marchand, advertising agencies were slow to see the possibilities in radio for product promotion, this attitude varied greatly from agency to agency.[1] There did indeed exist opposition to radio in agencies in the early 1920s—hardly surprising, considering the tight connection between ad agencies and the print media, who did indeed have something to fear from competition with radio. Marchand and many other writers cite articles that appeared in the print trade publication *Printers' Ink* from 1922 through 1926, objecting to the use of radio as an advertising medium. These, however, hardly represent the interests of the entire advertising field, many members of which may have been cognizant of a need not to offend the print media but demonstrated a growing awareness of the possibilities the new medium presented.

The full chronology of advertising agency involvement in radio does indeed deserve a history in itself, not least because it is virtually coterminous with commercial radio broadcasting. One or two examples of programs and experimental broadcasts made by advertising agencies in the 1920s may be helpful. As already noted, the N. W. Ayer agency was responsible for what was arguably the most influential show on radio in the early 1920s, *The Eveready Hour,* sponsored by the National Carbon Company, a maker of batteries (a product of obvious relevance to radio listeners). Having organized a radio department as early as 1923 and participated in the earliest experimentation in network broadcasting through AT&T's limited distribution of *The Eveready Hour,* N. W. Ayer continued to experiment actively during the mid-1920s, turning to dramatic fictional programs, literary adaptations, and variety show formats.[2] Another example is the William H. Rankin Agency, one of the heaviest early users of station WEAF's toll service beginning in 1922, which provided one of the earliest examples of Hollywood-agency-radio interaction by inviting actress Marion Davies to give a talk on "How I Make Up for Movies" for its client Mineralava.[3] By most accounts this was the first time a premium was offered—an autographed picture of the actress herself—to all those who would write in to say they heard the broadcast, and the "thousands" of requests that poured in helped to establish radio as an effective medium for reaching a consuming public.[4]

At J. Walter Thompson, it appears, the agency was led into radio by a few of its more adventurous clients. Though obviously interested in the medium—and refusing to join in a 1924 protest by a print-dominated committee opposed to radio advertising—a rather wistfully titled article in the J. Walter Thompson *Newletter* from February 1925 sums up activity to date: "Why Don't We Use the Radio?" The article summarized activity by radio stations and WEAF advertisers but still concluded, "This is a questionable medium for us to use at present." Primary objections concerned the "unsettled state" of broadcasting in 1925, the possibilities for misinterpretation of the spoken word, the impossibility of ascertaining circulation, and a concern that radio's more "indirect" selling might not be as effective as print.[5] But another article two weeks later acknowledged that two JWT clients had gone on the air regionally, both broadcasting "household talks" for women, both written in connection with JWT's "women's division" of the Chicago office.[6] One of them, Mary Hale Martin, previously the featured print service columnist for the Libby canned goods company, would continue with her Friday-morning *Mary Hale Martin's Household Hour* well into the 1930s.

Not until 1927, however; would JWT form its first official Radio Department, under the direction of William H. Ensign—formerly of N. W. Ayer and musical director for *Roxy and His Gang*.

By May 1928, according to Ensign's departmental progress report, two new employees had been added, and by July JWT's radio clients included Goodrich Tire Company, Shell Oil, the Isuan Corporation, Certo Gelatin, and Maxwell House Coffee, with proposals out to six other clients, most of whom would go on the air that year. Also in Ensign's report were the number of agencies that had organized radio departments in the preceding year—fifteen major firms, including Young & Rubicam; Barton, Durstine and Osborne; Lord, Thomas and Logan; and Lerman and Mitchell. It is interesting to note that talk of television's imminent arrival occurred at this early date.[7] Over the next year, use and acceptance of radio continued to build at JWT, and by 1929 the department was ripe for a takeover.

. . . The struggle for power between JWT's men's and women's groups . . . occurred in 1929, during the course of which Aminta Casseres of the New York Women's Division lost her bid to be head of the Radio Department to John U. Reber, previously an account executive and head of new business. "The Grim Reber," as he was known around the JWT offices, became director of the Radio Department in May 1929, and he very quickly grew disenchanted with the limited role envisioned for agencies by the radio networks, particularly NBC. A longtime colleague, Calvin Kuhl, who worked closely with Reber during most of his career at JWT, recalled him to be "the first to dismiss the 'radio experts' (producers, writers, directors) furnished by NBC, and use agency people to direct and write the show." Kuhl goes on to describe Reber's programming philosophy as it developed in the late 1920s and early 1930s:

> At the beginning NBC naturally turned to Broadway and Vaudeville for writing and directing experience. . . . These people were hidebound in their thinking and techniques. . . . They thought of the audience as so many tuxedo clad and evening gowned bodies in rows of seats before a stage. . . . In the late 20s and early 30s an advertising agency on behalf of a client might approach NBC with a tentative interest in "buying" a show, and NBC would then dream up a show via its culls from

Broadway and Vaudeville. . . . Well, almost immediately after persuading a J. W. Thompson client to buy a half hour of such NBC produced twaddle, John, complaining to NBC of the mediocrity and unimaginativeness of their fare, said "Hell, if that's the best you can do, we can do better, with our own writers and directors," which he then proceeded to do.[8]

Reber himself began sounding this note soon after his ascendancy as chief of radio. In a representatives' meeting in April 1930, by which time JWT had more than thirty-three shows on the air amounting to sixty hours a week, Reber claimed bluntly, "Our Radio Department can do a better radio program than the National Broadcasting Company," citing client testimonials.[9]

The term most frequently used to explain JWT's proficiency was "showmanship": JWT had it, NBC didn't. Most specifically, "showmanship" resulted from knowledge of the audience and its tastes.[10] Unlike NBC, with its dual agenda of at once profiting from commercial programs and upholding and maintaining cultural standards before the public, advertising agencies such as JWT had realized some time previously that it was mass sales that produced advertising profit, and mass sales resulted from attention to the "tabloid mind."

As early as 1923, the JWT *News Bulletin,* an in-house newletter of campaigns and ideas, reveals a concern with the habits and emotions of the "common" reader. In "Mrs. Wilkins Reads the Ladies Home Journal," JWT copywriter Dorothy Dwight Townsend evokes the world of those recently arrived in the middle class, looking to the mass media for ways to assimilate and "improve" themselves:

She looked in at homes she would never dare to enter; studied the get-up of women she never dared stare at in the city. Such smart women—in such beautiful homes—they did things with such an air! She studied the woman showing her friend the waists washed in Lux. The next morning when she washed out Helen's party stockings she would think of them. Unconsciously she had found herself holding up dainty things with two fingers— her other fingers crooked and outstretched as the

Lux women always did it. . . . She would have told you her mother taught her all she knew about housekeeping but she had learned more from this magazine than her mother ever knew.[11]

By 1927, JWT had recognized not only the existence but the value of "these vast new layers of people who have money to spend and who have very few media to reach them excepting the tabloids and confession magazines" and had begun to advocate a new "lowbrow" approach to advertising.[12] Here we see not only the acknowledgment and market empowerment of a previously unrecognized social group, but the beginnings of the identification of the media's role in reaching them—particularly radio, in which the terms *mass* and *culture* would come together in a powerful new combination.

This approach culminated in JWT's famous Lux Hollywood star endorsement campaign, not surprisingly spearheaded for the company by the eastern advertising manager of *Photoplay* magazine, acting as an intermediary in signing up stars for endorsements. By 1928, JWT claimed that "it was impossible to wash your hands in Hollywood unless you used Lux Toilet Soap," and numerous effusive—but never paid—endorsements began to appear in mass-circulation magazines.[13] These efforts were much aided by the flamboyant personality of JWT's Los Angeles agent, Danny Danker, who by all accounts succeeded in ingratiating himself with the upper levels of Hollywood stardom by living the Hollywood life, to the chagrin of stuffier New York JWT personnel, including John Reber. According to one anonymous "ex-employee (female)" on record in the JWT files (and marked "obviously unquotable"): "Danny Danker was THE POWER in Hollywood and was said to operate very much like dear Louella, getting any talent he wanted through blackmail. He also ran a procuring service for visiting executives and had a stable of starlets handy at all times."[14] It is generally agreed that John Reber "was perhaps the first to realize that the star system, the lifeblood of motion pictures, could revolutionize radio,"[15] and he is widely credited with leading the movement of radio production to Hollywood. To accomplish this he had to rely on the network of contacts and endorsements that Danker had established, though it was not a comfortable relationship. According to longtime JWT Hollywood writer Carroll Carroll:

> Mr. Reber did not want Danny to have anything to do with "his" department. But Danny's power was such in Hollywood that—as our needs for guest stars grew—Danny became more and more essential to the operation. . . . Naturally as Danny's power grew the seething feud between him and Reber boiled harder. Who would have won is anybody's guess. Danny died first.[16]

Reber sent a young and inexperienced Calvin Kuhl out to Los Angeles in March 1934 to serve as the nominal head of JWT radio operations there, but it seems mostly to keep an eye on Danker and report back. However strained their relations, the combined efforts of Reber and Danker ushered in what has been called "the Hollywood era of radio," which was also the era of agency dominance. By the mid-1930s, JWT was producing at least five shows in each year's top ten, all from Hollywood, using its unparalleled access to Hollywood talent procured, by whatever means, by Danker and his associates. Soon other agencies rushed to start Los Angeles offices as well. By 1942, JWT could claim to have developed more radio stars than any other organization, including Rudy Vallee, Burns and Allen, Al Jolson, Walter Winchell, Eddie Cantor, Major Bowes, Fanny Brice, and Edgar Bergen and Charlie McCarthy. In pioneering both the big-name variety show and the film adaptation program, most notably *The Lux Radio Theatre,* JWT also brought established Hollywood stars to the radio in increasing numbers.

By the mid-1930s, not only prime time but most of the daytime schedule as well was occupied by programs supplied by agencies on behalf of sponsors, especially the extremely popular daytime serials. Though the networks continued in their program-building efforts, establishing talent bureaus in New York, Chicago, and eventually Los Angeles, in an effort to stabilize the

situation, and often coming up with successful formats, their main objective remained to sell these programs to clients. These clients' agencies would then take over the programs' production, contracting with the NBC Talent Bureau for writers, stars, and so on, and using NBC facilities only for rehearsal space and actual broadcast. Many agencies declined even this small amount of dependence on the networks—and CBS never attempted to initiate programming or control talent to NBC's extent—so that the daytime hours in particular became sponsor franchises.

Large companies such as Procter & Gamble bought time in one- to two-hour blocks and programmed them with shows produced either in-house or by agencies hired for the purpose. Blackett-Sample-Hummert, home of Frank and Anne Hummert's "soap opera factory," operated almost totally outside of the networks' supervision, as will be seen in the controversy over "tasteless and inappropriate" content discussed below. Indeed, the late 1920s move away from musical variety programs toward fictional drama and serial narrative was driven almost entirely by the agencies, displacing the more educational, "tasteful," and derivative forms encouraged by early network practices. Production sites such as Chicago, further away from network headquarter operations and historically more amenable to the interests of their commercial clients led the way in network adoption of these forms, often resisted at first by NBC and CBS as disreputable and lax in their standards. In addition, it was agencies that first began to push for the use of recorded programs, called transcriptions, for clients who wished to avoid network costs and reach regional audiences for more effective advertising. This early form of syndication was much resisted by the networks, because it cut them directly out of the business in favor of the other main opposing interest in radio, powerful stations, who could program transcriptions at their own discretion and retain all profits.[17]

NETWORK WOES

It did not take long for this kind of challenge to network authority, and the disdainful attitude that went with it, to have an effect on NBC operations. Though sale of as much time as possible to sponsors remained from the beginning the primary goal of both networks, the control exercised by the increasingly powerful agencies began to undermine the networks' control over their own business. When sponsors or agencies created and owned their own programs, they could jump from network to network when more favorable time slots opened, leaving a network without the property its distribution system had helped to build up. Even more saliently, networks were placed in the awkward position of having to defend themselves to the FCC, to their affiliated stations, and to the public when criticism of programming practices arose, in order to sustain the idea that they were in fact operating as trustees of the public interest, without being able to wield much actual power over what went on during those programs. Despite such controlling policies as required submission of scripts before broadcast to the Continuity Acceptance Department, the presence on each set of an NBC director, and the continuing existence of commercial program departments and talent bureaus, agency productions increasingly eluded network control. A plaintive note crept into NBC interdepartmental correspondence.

In June 1932, John F. Royal complained to Roy Witmer, head of sales at NBC, about the agencies' failure to submit their scripts, called continuities, in sufficient time before broadcast:

> In my opinion the agencies take advantage of us, not only in the matter of late copy, but in many other things. . . . The clients, through their agencies, talk about cooperation, but they seldom give any. The trouble is that each agency thinks only of its own programs. They are selfish and inconsiderate. . . . If the agencies found that it was necessary that their continuities be a part of their general merchandising plan, they would have them ready, but inasmuch as it only means cooperating with

the broadcasting company, that is the last thing on their minds.[18]

NBC attempted to crack down on this procedure, but by May 1933, the agencies had devised another way around network censors. Bertha Brainard, head of commercial programming, described a new problem:

> Agencies and clients have been in the habit of sending to Continuity a skeletonized script which they do not believe will be used on the air. This is read carefully by the Continuity Department, stamped as the master, and sent through to the Production Department. Not infrequently on the day of the rehearsal an entirely new script is brought to the Production man for his use. He then endeavors, if the material seems to be objectionable, to reach anyone in authority for approval on the script. This is an entirely unsatisfactory method, particularly on the week-ends.[19]

Brainard outlined a new policy, by which only a script stamped "master" and so approved would be allowed to be broadcast, under any circumstances. Unfortunately, even this process could not contain the danger seemingly inherent in commercial production. The infamous Mae West episode of 1937 demonstrated that even a preapproved script could be *read* differently over the air from how it might be read in a continuity office, undermining the power of the written word.[20] Even worse, some entire genres of programming in their essence seemed to subvert institutional and social control. Three types of programs were especially problematic: the stand-up comedian on nighttime variety, children's adventure programs, and women's daytime serials. All of these genres had been developed by advertising agencies.

The big-name variety shows pioneered by JWT, including *The Fleischmann's Yeast Hour* (Rudy Vallee), *The Chase and Sanborn Hour* (Eddie Cantor/Bergen and McCarthy), *The Shell Chateau* (Al Jolson), and *The Kraft Music Hall* (Al Jolson/Bing Crosby), provided high-profile entertainment on NBC, attracted large audiences, and generally boosted the reputation of the network— but at a cost. Though anchored by recurring casts of hosts and orchestras, and a few established cast members who supported the hosts, most functioned by inviting stars from the movies, vaudeville, and other venues to perform on a nightly or multinight basis. This provided ample opportunity for surprises, as witnessed by an October 1935 memo from Roy Witmer to a member of the production department, D. S. Shaw:

> The Program Department complains that on Fleischmann-Rudy Vallee programs, Shell, and Kraft, they are often not informed concerning guest artists, and that the only way they know what's on the show is when they hear about it on the next day. It seems that the same is true on A&P, Lucky Strike, and Vicks . . . Won't you please see that a particular effort is made to keep the Program Department informed well in advance about all guest appearances?[21]

This problem was exacerbated when the so inconsiderately invited guests resorted to humor unacceptable to the network. Despite the policy of preclearance of scripts by the Continuity Acceptance Department, comedians in particular were notorious for changing their routines on the air, or inflecting even previously approved material with different meanings. . . .

With the advent of television, this same structuring tension would be put to new uses, culminating in the changes brought about ostensibly by the quiz show scandals but, as several historians have pointed out, actually arising out of the networks' increasing impatience with dependence on sponsors and agencies.[22] This rising friction could take on strange and petty forms, as perhaps best exemplified in one of Fred Allen's better-known scrapes in 1947. Allen had already gained a reputation as radio's bad boy, and he was frequently censored for taking on the network itself as the butt of his jokes. On April 20, 1947, his show included a routine that referred to the previous week's show being cut off abruptly by NBC, having run over its time limit. The next week, Allen's script included the following lines:

Portland: What happens to all the time they save cutting off the ends of programs?

Allen: Well, there is a big executive in radio. He sits in a little glass closet with his mother of pearl gong. When your program runs overtime he thumps his gong—Bong!—you're off the air. Then he marks down how much time he's saved.

Portland: What does he do with all this time?

Allen: He adds it all up—ten seconds here—twenty seconds there—when the big executive has saved up enough seconds, minutes and hours to make two weeks, he uses the two weeks of *your* time for *his* vacation.

NBC found this characterization of the "big radio executive" offensive and threatened to fade out the exchange if the script was not revised. Their suggested alternative: change it to "There is an advertising agency executive who sits over there. . . ." When Allen refused this change, his program was faded to a hush for twenty-five seconds.[23] NBC had clearly had enough. Though it would take the networks until the late 1950s to vanquish their longtime rivals and take back the dominant position they had lost in the 1930s, it is no coincidence that the networks' most influential early president, Pat Weaver, began immediately to undercut the power of the agencies with shared sponsorship and network-produced spectaculars.

But until that happy day, radio networks of the 1930s responded to the pressures of social negotiation in two ways: first, by creating a separate daytime sphere in which the worst offenders of official taste could be contained . . . ; and second, by encouraging a type of domestic drama that avoided the pitfalls of race, ethnicity, and troublesome gender-related and sexual material, along with overstimulating adventure, by focusing on the "average American family." Carefully white, middle-class, and small-town, confining its interests to the everyday doings of noncontroversial folks in America's heartland, such programs often achieved very high standards of writing, acting, and empathy with a popular way of life and were faithfully followed by large audiences. Among the best known and most loved of these were *Vic and Sade,* Paul Rhymer's [paean] to simple family life; *One Man's Family,* written by Carlton E. Morse, really a serial but adhering to nighttime standards; and *The Aldrich Family,* a show that developed into more what we would now call the domestic sitcom, combining drama and comedy. Another strand of this emergent format consists of the husband-and-wife comedy, exemplified by *Fibber McGee and Molly* but also by such shows as *Easy Aces,* written by Goodman Ace and starring himself and his wife, Jane; *The George Burns and Gracie Allen Show,* which started out on the JWT produced *Fleischmann's Yeast Hour* (Rudy Vallee); and many more.

Though not particularly prevalent until the late 1940s, this format led to many of the sitcoms carried over onto early television, such as those starring Joan Davis, Lucille Ball, and Burns and Allen, as well as *Life with Luigi, The Life of Riley, The Honeymooners*—the list goes on. Though sitcoms of the 1950s have received an increasing amount of critical attention, few scholars have made use of the story of their roots in radio, to the detriment of many very revealing sources of social and cultural context. However, other forms and controversies dominated the decades of radio. The story of women in the daytime, prestige drama in the nighttime, and the transformation of both during the war years must be added to our history.

NOTES

1. Roland Marchand, *Advertising the American Dream: Making Way for Modernity 1920–1940* (Berkeley: University of California Press, 1985), 88–94.
2. H. A. Batten, speech transcript, January 5, 1938, N.W. Ayer, 9.
3. William Peck Banning, *Commercial Broadcasting Pioneer: The WEAF Experiment, 1922–1926* (Cambridge: Harvard University Press, 1946), 103.
4. "How Advertising Came to Radio—and Television, 1900–1932," from "History of Radio" file, N. W Ayer archive, 31–32.
5. "Why Don't We Use the Radio?" *J. Walter Thompson Newsletter,* February 5, 1925, 4–7. Box 7, JWT.
6. "Two J.W.T. Clients Use Radio Advertisements," *J. Walter Thompson Newsletter,* February 19, 1925, 5. Box 7, JWT.
7. Minutes of representatives meeting—Wednesday, July 11, 1928, box 1, folder 5, JWT.
8. H. Calvin Kuhl, "The Grim Reber," Writings and Speeches, JWT, 25–27.
9. Minutes of group meeting, Assembly Hall, April 16, 1930, JWT.
10. For a rather disdainfully critical acknowledgment of this claim, see Ben Bodec, "Ad Agencies and Radio Theories," *Variety,* January 3, 1933, 62.
11. Dorothy Dwight Townsend, "Mrs. Wilkins Reads the Ladies Home Journal," *JWT News Bulletin,* June 1923, 1–5. JWT.
12. Minutes of representatives meeting, September 8, 1927, box 1, folder 4, JWT, 6.
13. Minutes of representatives meetings, April 9, 1929, JWT, 6–7.
14. JWT Officers and Staff—Sidney Bernstein—JWT Personnel Information—Daniel Danker, RG3, JWT.
15. Robert T. Colwell, "Theme Song Days," RG3, box 3, folder 9, Sidney Bernstein papers, Officers and Staff, JWT Personnel Information: Robert Talcott Colwell, JWT, 3.
16. JWT Officers and Staff—Sidney Bernstein—JWT Personnel Information—Daniel Danker, RG3, JWT.
17. Susan Smulyan, *Selling Radio: The Commercialization of American Broadcasting 1920–1934* (Washington, D.C.: Smithsonian Institution Press, 1994).
18. John F. Royal to Roy C. Witmer, June 15, 1932, Correspondence files, 1932, NBC.
19. Bertha Brainard to Roy C. Witmer, May 16, 1933, Program—Commercial, 1933, NBC.
20. Matthew Murray, "Television Wipes Its Feet: The Commercial and Ethical Considerations behind the Adoption of the Televison Code," *Journal of Popular Film and Television* 21 (Fall 1993).
21. Witmer to Shaw, October 23, 1935, box 92, folder 11, NBC.
22. William Boddy, *Fifties Television: The Industry and Its Critics* (Urbana: University of Illinois Press, 1990); Christopher Anderson, *Hollywood TV: The Studio Systems in the Fifties* (Austin: University of Texas Press, 1994).
23. "Operations Report for Studio and Office Sections," April 20, 1947, box 355, folder 59, NBC.

CHAPTER 30

Radio in the Television Age

Peter Fornatale and Joshua E. Mills

Pete Fornatale was a pioneer in classic rock radio in New York City for more than three decades. Joshua Mills is director of the master's program in business journalism at the City University of New York.

Radio jokes abounded in the early 1950s: one cartoon showed a young boy dusting off a radio in the attic and asking his dad, "What's that?" Americans had seen icemen put out of work, ice chests discarded for refrigerators, and silent pictures give way to talkies. It was against memories like these—recent memories—that many people gauged radio's chances against television. Radio was rapidly becoming something else, but what that was, no one could say. It is no wonder that so many people, in discussing radio's imminent death, confused the networks with the industry as a whole. The networks were certainly crippled, but independent radio thrived; the little talking box was a long way from being ready for the attic. At first, the young pioneers of radio's second coming did not attract as much publicity as the network moguls. Many of the most innovative labored in the Midwest, far from the media capitals. Because they often worked by trial-and-error, they could not always articulate their plans and strategies. But they were succeeding.

Even in the winter of radio's greatest discontent, 1954, when total advertising revenues dipped for the first time since 1938, industry revenues still grossed more than $450 million. Television had given radio a chill and a bad case of the shakes—but there never was any stoppage of vital signs. Station owners, investors, manufacturers, and all their employees had a vested interest in finding a new way to make radio work. What these people had to do was to determine how to change, and then explain to their audiences how they were changing.

There were several crucial components to local radio's success. One was the widespread reliance on records, and on the disc jockey (or deejay), the announcer who played the records, read the advertisements, did promotion for the station, and sometimes read the news as well. (The term "disc jockey" first appeared in the July 23, 1941, issue of *Variety*, replacing an earlier term, "record jockey.") Disc jockeys had their antecedent in early announcers like Reginald Fessenden, the distinguished inventor and pioneer, who on Christmas Eve 1906 broadcast a reading of passages from Luke (astonishing and startling a great number of wireless operators accustomed to hearing only Morse code and static on their sets; some undoubtedly thought the Lord had come calling for them this Christmas). Frank Conrad, who produced informal broadcasts of news, weather, and recordings from his garage in Pittsburgh in 1920, was another hero. But the modern disc jockey did not emerge until the playing of records on radio became widespread and that practice was frowned on for many years.

Because the custom in radio had been to broadcast live performances of music, the conventional wisdom in the industry was that it was demeaning for a station to play recordings. There were legal obstacles as well. It was common practice during the 1930s for record companies to stamp on their releases "not licensed for radio broadcast." They feared that airplay would cut into record sales and the concert fees of performers (a view that is the exact opposite of current theory, which holds that airplay is critical to promoting sales). And the FCC insisted that stations playing records remind their listeners constantly that they were not hearing live performances. Nonetheless, some announcers experimented with recordings.

An early pioneer was Al Jarvis, who thought he could use records to offer listeners a more diverse program, a panorama of stars, night after night. He went on the air at KFWB, Los Angeles, in 1932 with a program called "The World's Largest Make-Believe Ballroom." Although the show was locally successful, it did not attract any attention outside its listening area. Los Angeles at the time was not yet a major market in the eyes of network leaders and owners of major East Coast stations. But Jarvis's program came under close scrutiny by a KFWB newsman, Martin Block. Block moved to New York City and joined WNEW, an independent station, where he gained prominence by playing records in between news reports on the trial of Bruno Hauptmann, who was convicted in 1935 of kidnapping the Lindbergh child. Block eventually broadcast a show he called "Make Believe Ballroom" and earned his reputation as the first modern disc jockey.

In 1940 the age of the deejay won legal relief; the courts ruled that broadcasters, once they had purchased a record, could play it on the air as they liked. And the FCC eased its requirements for identifying recorded material to once every half-hour. Legal skirmishing persisted on another front, however, in negotiations with the American Society of Composers, Authors and Publishers (ASCAP) over royalties. Broadcasters were sufficiently dissatisfied with ASCAP to fund the development of a second licensing organization,

Broadcast Music, Inc. (BMI), in 1939. The ASCAP-BMI disputes would have a significant impact on radio in the 1950s. . . .

It is easy to appreciate the bonanza that disc jockeys proved to be for local stations. Deejay shows required no orchestras and no writers. Gone were actors and actresses, directors, and most of the support staff. One critic contemptuously labeled the deejays' product "gypsy radio" and noted: "It is ludicrously cheap . . . only a license, a transmitter, and a subscription to *Billboard* [for its charts of best-selling records] are essential." With deejays at the microphones, station managers developed a new strategy that became a major component of local radio. It originally was known as "formula radio," and later as "format radio." The most familiar type is Top 40—which means playing only songs drawn from the 40 best-selling records. But Top 40 is only one formula. The concept, as it emerged in the late 1940s and early 1950s, involved methodology rather than content. Stations no longer left things to chance, nor to the disc jockey's whims. They developed rules that would give each station a definable personality to its listeners. These rules might include playing X number of songs an hour, identifying the station X number of times by its call letters, and specifying where to do the commercials. What formula radio postulated was that listeners appreciate consistency: no matter who the deejay or what the time of day, the station would be recognizable among its competitors. This was a radical bit of thinking.

The goal became to hold the audience. Broadcasters believed that listeners drawn to a station wouldn't turn the dial as long as the station's "sound" remained consistent. Thus radio's eclectic programming gave way to formulas.

The networks eventually began experimenting with stars as disc jockeys. Their reputations, personalities, and patter were supposed to draw an audience. But records and deejays worked better on local radio for several reasons. Stations could play songs that were regional hits, if they conscientiously surveyed shops to see what people were buying. They could offer deejays who were familiar with the community—and who worked, through live appearances, at meeting their listeners.

This local emphasis, of which the deejay was only one facet, became the single most important element in radio's success during the television era. By accepting that it would not be prime-time entertainment, radio was free to offer different things to different people. A network— radio or television—could bring the world into your home, but it couldn't tell you which roads had flooded on your way to work. Local radio could not only play regionally popular music, it could provide more local news than the networks, public service announcements (vaccination programs, church bazaars, school closings), hometown sports results, and, through advertisements, news about local merchants. It sounds so simple and obvious, it's hard to imagine that anyone ever thought that radio could die. But operators had to learn to provide this new material, and the public needed to learn that it would be there.

In 1954 the National Association of Radio and Television Broadcasters issued a report that noted, "Stations are participating more and more in community activities. They originate campaigns for new libraries and better highways. They make their microphones available to clubs, schools, church groups, business associations. The report of local news and doings has assumed major proportions and now makes up about 40 percent of all news broadcasts on the average station." New technology helped: with tape recorders and editing equipment, local stations were able to provide in-depth coverage that national networks had no time to duplicate.

On the heels of localization came specialization: seeking out and catering to special interest audiences. If television, like radio of the Golden Age, sought to provide its advertisers with the largest audience possible, radio was now able to fill the cracks and find the people not watching television or not served by television. Where only a few years before radio had offered a standardized,

coast-to-coast sound, it now spoke in a variety of voices to specialized audiences. This breakthrough in radio programming had been suggested as early as 1947 by an FCC report, "An Economic Study of Standard Broadcasting." The FCC suggested that "a small segment of the listening audience carefully selected as a minority group, may, if it is loyally attached to the station, give it a unique fascination for advertisers."

Even before television flourished, independent stations, especially those competing with network affiliates, had begun to carve out specialized audiences because they couldn't compete with the networks' high-priced star system. One of the earliest studies of targeting a special audience was conducted by the NBC Radio Network in 1948. The project examined teenagers' listening habits in New York City, Philadelphia, Pittsburgh, and Chicago, and found that 64 percent of the adolescents had their own radios. NBC released the report, "Urban Teen-Agers as Radio Listeners and Customers" the following year, and noted that this audience had a buying power of $6 billion. The report found that "Your Hit Parade" was the favorite show among 18- and 19-year-olds, and that it also did well among younger teens. It is ironic that NBC could have commissioned this study, and then could ignore its findings while independent stations trampled its affiliates by going after the teen market.

The FCC report on specialized audiences had suggested cultivation of "minority groups" for *expansion*. With television's arrival, the motivation became *survival*. One of the first groups so cultivated was the black audience. Television, like the radio networks before it, provided no material specifically for blacks. "Amos 'n' Andy," a long-running and immensely popular radio show, had made a successful transition to television in 1951. For many years it was the only television show, however misinformed and prejudiced its stereotypes, about black family life. (In the early 1960s, the growing power of civil rights groups convinced broadcasters to take the show off the air.) Television not only failed to reach out to black audiences, but because blacks had a lower median income than whites and purchased fewer televisions in the early 1950s, they were a natural target for radio. Studies in city after city showed that a majority of the black population listened to the radio station that seemed most aware of black interests.

Some radio stations responded by designing shows for black audiences, with encouraging results. Albert Abarbanel and Alex Haley discussed the phenomenon of "Negro radio" in *Harper's* magazine in 1956 and suggested that it served several functions by:

- helping black businessmen, and whites serving black areas, to target their audiences.
- helping listeners discern through the ads where they were welcome to shop (particularly useful in segregated areas).
- providing highly visible, prestigious jobs within the community for blacks.
- providing community service announcements about black civic groups, church groups, and recreational facilities.

Most of the stations were white-owned. And they drew white audiences as well, particularly because the music, whether gospel, rhythm 'n' blues, or jazz, was more interesting than most music available on other radio stations. Negro radio, Abarbanel and Haley concluded, "seems to have satisfied almost everybody. It has brought American businessmen enormous, previously untapped profits. It has rejuvenated small radio stations and added new income to large ones. . . ."

"Negro radio" had other ramifications for the radio industry; if other special interest groups could be identified, they too could be serviced by radio. Programming spread that was directed at teenagers, farmers, ethnic groups, religious denominations. Most of these groups found little programming of special interest to them on television. Between localization and specialization, radio escaped direct competition with television and found it could profit without the evening audiences.

In *Understanding Media* Marshall McLuhan observed: "With TV accepting the central network burden derived from our centralized industrial organization, radio was free to diversify, and to begin a regional and local community service that it had not known, even in the earliest days of radio 'hams.' Since TV, radio has turned to the individual needs of people at different times of the day, a fact that goes with the multiplicity of receiving sets in bedrooms, bathrooms, kitchens, cars and now in people's pockets. Different programs are provided for those engaged in diverse activities."

It seems so obvious: People could be doing something else and still listen to radio. The status of the radio in the Golden Age—and its position in the living room—must be recalled to appreciate how innovative this concept was. Radio became liberated from the living room. It was free to penetrate other rooms of the house, seeking those not watching television. It moved to the kitchen, out to the patio, into the car, and its programming reflected that change. Radio offered service, entertainment, and companionship; it became an omnipresent medium.

Radio's penetration into American life was enhanced by new technology: the discovery of the transistor, the development of more sophisticated car radios, and the invention and marketing of the clock radio.

The vacuum tube had served the industry well from its refinement by Lee DeForest in 1907 through World War II, but it was relatively inefficient. Large and fragile, it had a high power consumption and limited life expectancy. As early as 1924, researchers sought an alternate method of power amplification. Not until after World War II did they find it. On December 23, 1947, Drs. John Bardeen, Walter H. Brattain, and William B. Shockley, working at Bell Laboratories in Murray Hill, New Jersey, found a key that unlocked radio's future. They called it the transistor, a contraction of *transfer resistor*. Like the vacuum tube it could conduct, modulate, and amplify electrical signals. But it moved electrons through a solid, not a vacuum. The transistor had many advantages over the vacuum tube: it used less power and created less heat; it was durable and had a longer life; it was less expensive; and it was miniscule. The transistor made possible the miniaturization of electronic devices and became a major weapon in radio's struggle against television.

While military applications of the transistor were examined, news of the breakthrough was suppressed until June 30, 1948. It was refined for several years and then tested in consumer equipment. The first commercial transistor radio, the Regency, made by Texas Instruments and priced at $40, went on sale in 1953. At first it was marketed—and perceived by the public—as a novelty. "The world's smallest radio—small enough to fit in the palm of the hand—was demonstrated yesterday afternoon in Times Square," Jack Gould wrote in *The New York Times.* "The populace took the coming of the 'Dick Tracy Age' with disconcerting calmness." But consumers quickly grew excited about the transistor radio, and sales took off. Between 1953 and 1956 the number of portable radios sold annually doubled to 3.1 million. By 1965 more than 12 million transistor radios a year were being sold.

PART SEVEN

TV Times

Television promoted itself to audiences by incorporating aspects of earlier media: highlighting the star system, publicizing scheduled programs in newspapers and magazines, and through television watching guides, such as *TV Times*, for viewers in the United Kingdom in the 1950s. *The Advertising Archive.*

The first television broadcasts in North America began in 1939. Radio, at the height of its golden age, had its pre-eminence challenged. However, just as World War I put the development of broadcast radio on hold, so World War II delayed for almost a decade the dream of television as the new mass medium. By the early 1950s television was in the throws of a remarkable growth. Sales of television receivers boomed. Radio would never be the same again. Given what we have already discussed regarding the relationship between new media and old, it should come as no surprise to learn that the early content of television drew from both the motion pictures and radio. Distinct directions soon followed, most notably the filming of comedy and adventure series. "*I Love Lucy*" was one of the first programs to follow this convention, and, with the help of "canned laughter," it broke the format of the live broadcast that was the staple of "radio days."

The mass audience that was enamored with radio in the 1930s adapted with enthusiasm to television. Following the war, production and consumption increased and along with it, as William Boddy shows in our first selection, a television culture emerged. As people became more mobile, a variety of new job opportunities opened up. Yet family life remained strongly "home centered," especially on evenings and week-ends, when, thanks to a shorter work week there was increased leisure time, and more money to spend on it. Television, with its affordability, mix of national and local programs, and panoramic view of the new consumer culture via advertising, became as Boddy demonstrates a technology central to social life.

Although television during the 1950s managed to draw people always from radio sets and movie theaters, it was not always technologically reliable. Snowy pictures, sound problems, and interrupted signals were often a problem, especially in areas at the periphery of major cities—the expanding suburbs. However, the next several decades saw improved signal delivery systems; the transistor replacing the older vacuum tube, followed by integrated circuits (during the 1950s set breakdowns resulting from tube failure were a regular occurrence and every neighborhood had its TV repair shop); the emergence of reliable affordable color sets; and the introduction of cable transmission and satellite links. As of this writing, we are witnessing yet another transformation, the wide-spread adoption of digital high-definition television. Digital cable dramatically increases screen resolution, potentially providing viewers with a visual experience comparable to 35mm and 70mm films. As television standardizes production around digital technology significant shifts in programming and patterns of viewing may result. We leave it to readers informed by the essays that follow to speculate on what this might entail.

The unique aspect of television is a concern of Edmund Carpenter, an anthropologist who during the 1950s collaborated with Marshall McLuhan on a major research project and on a journal dealing with human communication, entitled *Explorations*. Like McLuhan, Carpenter argues that a medium constructs its messages as much through its form as through specific content. ("The medium is the message" was McLuhan's provocative maxim for overstating this notion.) Media therefore are never neutral. They impart what Harold Innis—who also influenced Carpenter—called a "bias" to communication. In his essay, Carpenter likens media, especially television, to languages. Television is contrasted with radio, film, theater, and the book, particularly through a consideration of the way each medium gives a distinct shape to what appears to be the same story. His analysis of *The Caine Mutiny* in this respect is revealing. It should encourage readers to think of books they have read that were made into movies or television programs, and to think about how viewing films in the theater compares with viewing them on television.

The social impact of television during the 1950s is the subject of our next excerpt. Lynn Spigel explores the way television, suburban life, and the new post-war patterns of consumption developed in concert. As she notes, the resulting shift in domestic space and the aspirations of a newly emerging middle-class were often mirrored in the programs. Since a number of the programs she mentions are available via syndicated reruns, video or DVD we urge readers to "have a look." In what ways do they reflect a social world quite different from today? What themes are still relevant and consistent with a 1990s sensibility?

Our next selection deals with television news. In it, Mitchell Stephens shows us how radio, then television, imitated and eventually altered the news-gathering roles of other media. Radio news originally adopted the reporting style of newspapers. However, the sometimes complex sentences of newspaper reporting had to be reduced to make reading "on the air" effective. World War II was a major arena for this evolution. It created enormous audiences for broadcast news. Stephens argues that the Vietnam War played a similar role in giving television news its distinct format of almost instant televisual reporting and as a consequence pushed radio further into the background of local broadcasting and music formats.

Television news has led to certain expectations and dependencies for viewers. Stephens argues that this is not all to the good. He challenges McLuhan's optimistic view that television extends our eyes and ears into a greater awareness of events in the "global village." He warns of the dangers and limitations of linking news to newscaster celebrities and formulaic visual presentations.

Our next selection is rather unusual: a dinner conversation between two renowned and controversial commentators of media and popular culture: Neil Postman and Camille Paglia. Postman champions the book and the sense of culture he associates with it. Paglia argues that television—and the image culture it creates—dominates our era. However, they concur on the need for a critical literacy in both media. An interesting class project might be to continue their debate, adding examples from your own experience as well as from other essays in this book.

Television today is not what it once was, either in terms of program formats or the way we watch. Henry Jenkins' essay uses the example of *American Idol* to highlight this shift. What do you think of his categories of viewership? Are you a "zapper," a "casual," or a "loyal"? Talent competitions have been on television before, but *American Idol's* serialized format, following from other reality shows such as *Survivor* (a trend that began with soap operas, then entered the realm of television dramas in the latter years of the last century, and now is a staple of recent contemporary programs such as *Lost*), encourages a diverse viewership that is sustained and inter generational. The MIT (Massachusetts Institute of Technology) study of *Idol* cited by Jenkins is worth understanding, not just for its results, but also for its inclusivity in assessing the intermediality and role the audience plays in a commercially successful aspect of the popular culture of our time.

In scale, television far surpasses what was possible during the newspaper and radio eras. Each medium, however, built on its precursors and tried to bypass their inherent limitations. Today, television still provides a compelling demonstration of "simultaneity" and "co-presence," which began almost 150 years ago with the telegraph. The moon landing, the Olympics, and the fall of the Berlin Wall, the events of 9/11 all provide instances of shared global experience, which should be continually reflected upon in light of the history and nature of a medium whose influence on our lives continues to deepen.

CHAPTER **31**

Television Begins

William Boddy

William Boddy teaches in the Department of Speech at Baruch College, City University of New York.

The first decade of commercial television in the United States set in place the major economic actors, programme forms, and regulatory structures of the vast American TV industry of the next thirty years. Moreover, the flood of exported American TV shows that began in the 1950s provided models of programme styles and popular taste for producers around the world.

The early regulatory decisions that established U.S. standards for such matters as broadcast spectrum allocation, image quality, and colour versus monochrome service substantially govern American television today. The impact of these decisions on the competing private interests inside and outside the broadcast industry was to create a small group of extremely profitable station and network operators who quickly became powerful figures on the political and regulatory scene. Both federal regulators and industry interests were well aware from the 1930s that approval for commercial television operation under a given set of standards might influence investment in a way that would preclude a later shift to higher technical standards. Another legacy of these early regulatory decisions is the fact that U.S. television operates under an inferior standard of image resolution and colour quality, part of a pattern of incoherence and duplicity in federal broadcast regulation. This regulatory background, and other ideological and economic constraints during television's early growth had influenced the

commercial structures and programme forms of the medium in America, as well as the relation of U.S. television to the rest of the world.

Broadcast regulation in the United States has been founded upon two opposing principles: that the federal licence confers a privilege, not a right, to the broadcaster to operate in "the public interest" using public airwaves, and that the licence establishes and protects the broad *de facto* property rights of private operators of television and radio stations under restricted oversight of network operations and programme content. Economic concentration within the burgeoning U.S. television industry was early and pronounced. In 1954, the two major television networks and their twelve owned-and-operated stations took in over half of the total profits of a TV industry which included two other network operators and hundreds of local stations.

The chief cause of this concentration (which had its effects in the industry's internal practices, programme forms, and export policies) was the decision of the Federal Communications Commission (FCC) to locate television service in the VHF (very high frequency) portion of the electromagnetic spectrum which could support only twelve channels nationwide and three or fewer stations in most large cities. This quickly created a relatively small group of extremely profitable large-market station operators served by two dominant network firms, NBC and CBS, with the American Broadcasting Company (ABC) and DuMont television networks as also-rans in a two-and-a-half network economy. The DuMont network went out of business in 1955 while the ABC network struggled through TV's first decade to achieve a weaker, though competitive position by 1960.

THE MANUFACTURING INDUSTRY

The direction of the American television industry in its first decade was largely charted by leaders of the radio broadcasting and set manufacture businesses, in particular TV's dominant firm, NBC-RCA. Emerging from the late 1930s and World War II, radio broadcasting found itself in a curiously ambivalent position of strength and defensiveness. Network economic strength derived from a decade of rising profits from network radio, reflected in advertising billings, stock prices, and ambitious plans for post war spending in multi million dollar broadcast talent contracts, facsimile broadcasting, international commercial radio networks, and in television itself. Simultaneously with the first round of the Justice Department's efforts to divest the Hollywood studios of their theatre chains and outlaw established distribution practices in 1938, the two broadcast networks faced a period of unsettling antitrust and regulatory scrutiny. An NBC executive in 1940 worried that "the New Deal at last has come to the world of radio communications," and warned that the network was vulnerable to the same antitrust charges and legal remedies of dismemberment that the beleaguered Hollywood studios were currently undergoing. A new reform-minded FCC in Roosevelt's second term did challenge network radio practices, forcing NBC to divest itself of its smaller network (thereby creating ABC) and producing the infamous "Blue Book" outlining the public service responsibilities of broadcast licensees.

THE DEFENCE OF COMMERCIAL TELEVISION

Faced with possible New Deal–inspired antitrust and regulatory reforms aimed at the broadcast industry, the networks emerged from the war with a broad public relations strategy, emphasizing both their patriotic role in developing wartime military electronics and the philosophical defence of commercial broadcasting. While the television industry prospered tremendously from World War II defence contracts, an April 1942 NBC memorandum indicates the company's efforts to keep key technical personnel out of the war effort, "to resist attacks made upon television engineers by other NDRC Labs as it is anticipated that we will need all the men we now have to carry forward the television development projects which are contemplated." Despite such behind-the-scenes efforts, the electronics and broadcast industries emerged from the war in high public esteem and unquestionable wealth.

The second post war network public relations strategy involved a new militant defense of the principles of commercial broadcasting, including a widely reported speech by CBS head William S. Paley to an industry group in 1946, which identified the recent public criticism of commercially supported radio programming as "the most urgent single problem of our industry." In terms which anticipate countless network defences of their television programme policies of the next decade, Paley explained:

> First we have an obligation to give most of the people what they want most of the time. Second, our clients, as advertisers, need to reach most of the people most of the time. This is not perverted or inverted cause and effect, as our attackers claim. It is one of the great strengths of our kind of broadcasting that the advertiser's desire to sell his product to the largest cross section of the public coincides with our obligation to serve the largest cross section of our audience.

In response to those worried about the deadening hand of the broadcast sponsor, Paley told broadcast critics that "the advertiser buys freedom for the listener at the same time he buys time and talent. For it is an historic fact that the only other kind of radio is government radio." It was on precisely such polarized terms that the networks successfully defended their commercial television practices and privileges over the next decade.

Despite its wealth and political confidence, U.S. commercial television did not immediately take off at the end of the war. There existed a bitter dispute between groups aligned with NBC-RCA who favoured immediate development on the VHF spectrum and those aligned with CBS, which wanted a delay in order to establish colour TV service on the wider ultra-high frequency (UHF) band. All the major actors, including the FCC, recognized the anti-competitive nature of the VHF allocations of the early 1940s, but the FCC was under considerable pressure to relaunch a commercial television service. RCA had not only a cumulative investment of 10 million dollars in television by the end of the war, but its formidable patent position in television was strongest in the VHF band. Political fears of being seen as holding up television and the need to stimulate new employment in post war electronics persuaded the FCC to ratify the restricted VHF frequencies in 1945, while at the same time admitting that "the development of the upper portion of the spectrum is necessary for the establishment of a truly nationwide and competitive television system."

The qualified decision discouraged investment by potential VHF set owners and station operators, and their caution was fuelled by a series of regulatory petitions from CBS on behalf of UHF colour television. Some within and outside CBS at the time saw the network motivated less by concern for colour UHF television than by a desire to protect its network radio interests by delaying television altogether; unlike NBC-RCA, CBS had no patent or manufacturing stakes in television equipment, and both CBS and NBC were predicting a decade-long wait before the business of network television became profitable. CBS was therefore torn between a defensive involvement with VHF broadcasting as the only commercial TV system approved by the FCC and a desire to thwart or delay its rival NBC-RCA's interests in VHF television. CBS's ambivalence led to the unlikely spectacle of a broadcast disclaimer at thirty-minute intervals during all CBS telecasts: "We hope that you will enjoy our programs. The Columbia Broadcasting System, however, is not engaged in the manufacture of television receiving sets and does not want you to consider these broadcasts as inducements to purchase television sets at this time. Because of a number of conditions which are not within our control, we cannot foresee how long this television broadcasting schedule will continue."

Furthermore, in support of its position before the FCC that VHF television standards were inadequate, CBS closed its New York City TV studios, refrained from applying for additional VHF broadcast licences, and warned other prospective VHF station owners that "the sensible broadcaster who has not yet entered television might logically conserve his capital—might prefer to stay out of the field—until the new standards arrive and better pictures are at hand." The regulatory uncertainty and anti-VHF campaign by CBS, what its annual report for 1945 called the "militant CBS sponsorship of color television in the ultra-high frequencies," led to precisely the television industry stagnation that RCA had warned would be ruinous to the American economy.

As CBS pursued a revised UHF colour television petition at the FCC into the spring of 1947, it began to look as if post war television would be a major industrial failure. By August 1946, eighty applications for TV station licences had been withdrawn at the FCC as Americans showed little interest in set ownership under the unsettled industry conditions and only 8,000 sets were sold by the end of 1946. But the April 1947 FCC denial of the CBS UHF petition, ratifying the existing VHF standards, marked the real starting-point of U.S. commercial television; within two months, sixty new station applicants had petitioned the FCC, and TV set sales finally moved upward. As a writer in the *Nation's Business* noted in July 1947, "Television . . . is something the average American family has just about decided it can't do without." By March 1948 *Newsweek* reported that TV was "catching on like a case of high-toned scarlet fever." Despite its first real growth in the second half of 1947, the early television industry faced a number of hurdles.

TRAINING THE TELEVISION AUDIENCE

Many commentators on early television suggested that the near-total attention the medium was expected to demand from viewers would preclude viewing periods of more than an hour or two a day, relegating the new medium to a decidedly secondary service to established radio. Television, one 1940 book argued, "requires concentrated attention and cannot serve as a background for such activities as bridge playing or conversation. It is on this difference that many broadcasters base their belief that television will never replace sound broadcasting, but will supplement the present art with a more specialized service." Other commentators pointed to the financial and personnel costs of supplying the vast programming hours of the television schedule. A 1940 *New Yorker* magazine writer offered a fantastical look back at "The Age of Television" from the projected vantage-point of 1960, recalling that following commercial TV's launch in 1945, the huge advertising revenues demanded by TV's enormous station operating and networking costs caused the prices of advertised goods to soar, provoking bread riots in 1947. On the other hand, the author suggested, the prodigious personnel demands of the medium had abolished adult unemployment and guaranteed that any child passing a simple literacy test could become a TV writer and discontinue further education. Such satiric projections were based on the widespread industry admission

that the costs of a full television programme schedule in the model of network radio might well be beyond the means of broadcast sponsors.

There were also early fears about the disruptive effects of television on the American home and family; a 1947 trade press observer worried that since television would demand complete attention, "the housewife who is accustomed to listen to soap operas while she washes, irons, and does the housework, cannot watch a visual program while she does her chores." The *New York Times* TV critic complained in 1948 that "the American household is on the threshold of a revolution. The wife scarcely knows where the kitchen is, let alone her place in it. Junior scorns the late-afternoon sunlight for the glamour of the darkened living room. Father's briefcase lies unopened in the foyer. The reason is television." A writer in *Parent's Magazine* in 1948 described her family's successful adjustment of daily routines to accommodate television, though she complained of adult neighbours "who insist on conversing" during the evening's television entertainment. Many early commentators worried about eye-strain produced by prolonged TV viewing, and as late as 1951 *Parent's Magazine* found it necessary to alert readers that "it is not advisable to wear sun glasses to view television." Such complaints and anxieties point to the complex adjustments that early commercial television provoked in U.S. domestic life.

THE SEARCH FOR A NATIONAL SIGNAL

There were also early doubts about the possibility of bringing television signals to virtually every American home as network radio had done in the mid-1930s. Because of TV's limitation to line-of-sight transmission and uncertainty over the economic viability of coaxial cable and microwave relay networks of scattered stations, the 1940s saw a number of exotic proposals to compensate for the expected limitations in TV networking, including the construction of a 300-mile-high transmitter in Kansas to cover the entire nation; "Stratovision," a system of thirty-three airplanes flying in constant 20-mile circles 20,000–25,000 feet above the earth to cover the entire U.S.A., and the revival of road companies of travelling actors to service disparate stations. Other critics of commercial broadcasting forecast that the geographical limitations of a commercially backed television system and the inability of sponsors to support anything like a full programme schedule would persist for five or ten years, arguing that the inevitable chicken-and-egg problem of small audiences and meagre programme budgets revealed the advantages of a BBC-style licence fee system for television support, and that the public interest would not be served by the expected decade-or-two wait before increased audiences could support full nationwide service. Thus, an important dissenting argument against the model of commercial network television was quickly silenced by the speed with which the commercial medium reached undisputed viability and economic power.

By the autumn of 1947 there were still only 60,000 TV sets in the entire country, two-thirds of them in New York City, the result of set manufacturers' sales allocations to retailers in the nation's media and advertising capital and TV programme makers faced an unusual, if transient, audience demographic problem. In September 1947, 3,000 of 47,000 sets in New York City were operating in bars; the rest were located in homes of high-income families; however, because the TV sets in bars attracted many more viewers per set than those in private homes, the overall audiences were roughly equal. *Business Week* worried that "satisfying them both means a big problem for televisors"; the television audience in bars preferred sports and news, industry observers believed, and programming intended for the higher-income home audience left them cold; moreover, there was insufficient sports and news material to fill the programme schedule. An observer in the summer of 1947 noted the programming slant: "So far it's a man's world in the programme department, with sports and news events hogging the average station's 20 hour-a-week showbill." The programme emphasis highlights earlier predictions of post-war television programming along lines thought to appeal particularly to men. An FCC commissioner wrote in 1941 that TV would offer remote coverage of sports "and current disasters such as fires, disasters and floods, as well as many other interesting events." Similarly, a 1943 *Newsweek* article, "What Will Postwar Television Be Like?", predicted TV programming of two types: "those which transport the viewer from his home to a place or an event, and those which bring someone or something into his living room"; the former would include "fires, train wrecks, and political meetings" as well as sporting events. The problem of programming to the gender- and class-distinct audiences in and out of the home in early television was quickly "solved" by the explosion in set sales by 1950.

THE AMERICAN FAMILY TAKES TO TELEVISION

The change in TV audiences from high-income to middle- and low-income households has been offered by some industry historians as the motivation for a number of programming shifts of the mid-1950s, including the rise of the filmed situation comedy, the decline of live anthology drama, and the move from urban-based to suburban-based sitcoms. However, while this demographic shift in TV set buyers and viewers did occur, it happened much earlier than its commonly supposed programming effects. In fact, the speed with which families with low and moderate incomes took up television surprised many contemporary industry observers. While *Business Week* in January 1948 cited an audience survey describing the typical New York City television family headed by an executive, professional, or small business owner: a journalist writing in 1949 argued that predictions of the previous year that TV set sales would remain restricted to upper-income groups were no longer valid: "TV is becoming the poor man's theater," he noted. By January 1950 one observer pointed to "the almost reckless abandon with which money has been invested in television by the public even where ready cash was not available. . . . Television is the poor man's latest and most prized luxury." More than 3 million television sets were sold in the first six months of 1950, 60 percent of them on credit, "with the poor crowding the rich away from the counters," according to *Business Week*. An economist's study of 1950 TV set owners showed ownership declined with incomes and educational levels beyond moderate levels, while suburban and smaller-city households were much more likely to buy sets than big-city households, even though such viewers had more TV channels available. *Fortune* magazine saw a tribute to "the resilience of the U.S. economy" in the continued boom in set sales in the face of tightening consumer credit, the imposition of a 10 percent excise tax, and continued regulatory uncertainty over colour television.

As early as 1948, many trade observers saw a lucrative future for VHF television operators; in January *Business Week* proclaimed 1948 "Television Year," and proclaimed that "to the tele-caster, the possibilities are immediate and unlimited." Later that year, the magazine reported that "television people are gambling that once the black ink starts to flow it will write big profit figures. They are rushing into television as fast as they can." The continuing substantial post war radio revenues subsidized early television development, as CBS and NBC slashed cultural and educational programming; moreover, an estimated 75 percent of freeze-era local TV stations were owned by radio broadcasters who likewise pared costs and shifted revenues from the older medium. Also significant for NBC were the enormous profits generated for RCA from sales and royalty revenues from TV sets; in 1948 there were already sixty-six manufacturers of sets, with 75 percent of the set market controlled by RCA, DuMont, and Philco. The high profits in early TV set manufacturing are reflected in the wild run-up in stock prices of TV manufacturing firms in 1949, with RCA's stock up 134 percent that year; for one week in the spring of 1950, trading in the seven largest set manufacturers amounted to 10 percent of total Wall Street trading.

There were undoubtedly some lean years for television programming despite the medium's steady growth in the late 1940s. In July 1947 the business press noted that television networks were "no more than a gleam in a broadcaster's eye," and complained that "the programs coming out of television's studios at present are reminiscent of 'The Great Train Robbery' stage of movie progress." The *New York Times* TV columnist wrote that "thoughtful retailers note that there are not enough programs telecast even to demonstrate sets properly in a store." With CBS caught flatfooted by its deliberate go-slow policy in VHF television production and networking facilities, *Life* magazine at the end of 1947 could point out that "there is still only one network of consequence," complaining that television "has disinterred some of the hoariest acts in vaudeville . . . [and] worst aspects of radio. . . . Only occasionally . . . does the entertainment seem almost mediocre." Another journalist in 1948 complained that much TV programming "is reminiscent of a junior high school graduation play," and *Fortune* in mid-1950 complained of "programme drivel that makes the worst movies and soap operas seem highbrow." As early as 1949 critic Gilbert Seldes, who had served as director of CBS television between 1939 and 1945, was already lamenting what he saw as a decline in the programme quality since the earlier days when minuscule audiences freed program-makers from the relentless need to address the widest public tastes: "We seem to be watching, for the hundredth time, the traditional development of an American art-enterprise: an incredible ingenuity in the mechanism, great skill in the production techniques—and stale, unrewarding, contrived, and imitative banality for the total result." Observers frequently expressed puzzlement at Americans' appetite for TV in the face of poor-quality programming in the late 1940s.

One factor behind this appetite was the enormous demographic changes brought on by suburbanization and the baby boom. Writing on the "Possible Social Effects of Television" in 1941, RCA Chairman David Sarnoff predicted that America's large cities would lose population to the new automobile suburbs between 1945 and 1960, arguing that television would provide a good fit with the new suburban households, linking them much like new high-speed roadways. As *Business Week* explained in 1956: "Video dropped into the middle of a new social revolution: the mass exodus to the suburbs, new realms of leisure, rising incomes, and a tremendous demand both for things and for entertainment that had been pent up by war and depression." The speed with which post war commercial television gained economic ascendancy provided critics and policymakers with a formidable *fait accompli* and discouraged commercial challengers and reformers.

THE SOCIAL IMPACT

The new suburban home as imagined arena for television programme had profound implications for freedom of expression in the medium, as a 1945 NBC executive suggested:

> Television comes directly into the home. All the precautions that have been thrown around sound broadcasting to render it domestically acceptable may be automatically assumed to be essential for television. Furthermore, because the visual impression is apt to be more vivid and detailed and because to be understood it requires less imaginative response on the part of the observer than does an auditory impression television must be much more carefully supervised if it is to avoid giving offense. This means that vulgarity, profanity, the sacrilegious in every form, and immorality of every kind will have no place in television. All programs must be in good taste, unprejudiced, and impartial.

Following complaints about New York–originated network programme containing comic routines, actress necklines, and suspense and horror material thought unsuitable to domestic audiences in the nation's hinterlands, the TV industry quickly moved to establish industry-wide programme censorship. With prodding by Catholic pressure groups, FCC commissioners, and Congressional investigators, the networks in 1951 enacted a Television Code closely modelled on the Hollywood Production Code.

POLITICAL PRESSURES IN THE TELEVISION INDUSTRY

Also echoing contemporary events in Hollywood were the successful efforts of the anti-communist Right to shape the personnel and program content of 1950s television. The 1950 publication *Red Channels: The Report on the Communist Influence in Radio and Television*, consisting largely of a list of over 150 actors and other television personnel with purported left-wing ties, quickly led to a decade-long pervasive political blacklist in network television. That year Jean Muir was removed from General Food's situation comedy *The Aldrich Family;* 1951 saw the resignation of playwright Elmer Rice in protest against the blacklist, and 1952 saw the firing of Philip Loeb from the popular sitcom *The Goldbergs,* despite the efforts of the show's powerful star Molly Goldberg. In 1951 *Life* magazine wrote approvingly that the openly operating blacklist "has served the good purpose of making 'gulliberals' think twice before lending their names and talents to causes which are often Communist-inspired," although the magazine lamented the fact that the anti-communist crusade had smeared innocents and "cast a mantle of fear over a normally sunny profession." Lauding the admittedly extra-legal vigilantism of networks and sponsors, *Life* argued: "In refusing to outlaw Communism . . . Congress really passed the buck of fighting Communists to the American people. It is a tough and tricky task, in which each individual with any power in the matter—and sponsors have a great deal—must be his own general." The anti-communist Right kept up the alarm in the early 1950s; Martin Berkeley, in a 1953 article, "Reds in Your Living Room," warned that after being crushed in Hollywood by the House UnAmerican Activities Committee, the "communist movement . . . then made calculated plans to seize the air waves of America." Berkeley warned his readers that if such plans succeeded "the Communist Party—through its secret members, its fellow-travelers, its dupes and sympathizers—will have control of *every word* that goes out over the air waves." In the spring of 1954 another conservative writer warned that TV's powers for persuasion had attracted "change-the-worlders" and "uplifters," but noted with satisfaction both the plethora of right-wing commentators and personalities on the air and a TV sponsor's recent dropping of a commentator who had challenged Senator Joseph McCarthy. Independent TV production companies and New York advertising agencies followed the networks' lead in full cooperation with the self-appointed anti-communist leaders, with pervasive and long-lasting effects on television program content.

Thus, under these conditions of rising prosperity and ideological conservatism many of the persistent aesthetic features of American television programming were established and defended by the powerful economic interests in the early television industry. For example, one insight into what some contemporary critics see as U.S. TV programming's dependence upon the soundtrack in a purported visual medium is the rationale offered by one 1948 advertising agency executive: "I want those words to follow the set-owner in case he takes a notion to get up and go out to the bathroom while the commercial is running on the screen." Similarly self-serving, if more fanciful, was CBS head Frank Stanton's 1951 argument on behalf of colour TV that "color television wholly eliminates the interval in which your mind must take a black and white image into the darkroom of your brain and print it on the intellect, as the true colored picture which the eye actually sees in nature. Thus, colour television adds speed and clarity—greater impact and more information to each image and every sequence." As we shall see, powerful private interests in commercial television were eager to

seize upon, and echo aesthetic claims if they served their strategic purposes in early television.

Many early TV critics in the U.S.A. attempted to deduce the aesthetic peculiarities of the dramatic medium from its technical limitations and its conditions of reception. Observers often lamented the tendency of TV to recycle talent and material from radio, movies, and the stage; they particularly cited TV's revival of vaudeville in the form of comedy-variety programmes, among television's most popular in the 1948–53 period. Early attempts to capture conventional theatre productions mid-proscenium were, the *New York Times* critic complained, "not unlike seeing a series of picture postcards, with rather serious consequences to the play's fluidity and continuity." Privileged by most critics were attempts to stage original drama for the medium; early television drama-makers faced constraints both financial (writers were offered only $25–200 for original TV scripts) and production-related and such constraints often were translated by critics into the essential conditions of the art of television. One production executive advised would-be writers in 1947 to consider the limitations of cramped studios, low budgets, and small TV screens and to "write around living rooms, kitchens, offices, schoolrooms, etc.," for no more than three or four characters, and urged TV directors to limit themselves to close-ups to convey the circumscribed action.

Many TV critics deduced an essentialist aesthetic mission for the medium, based on its reception in the domestic livingroom; Gilbert Seldes wrote in 1950: "The style of acting in television is determined by the conditions of reception; there is simply no place for the florid gesture, the overprojection of emotion, the exaggeration of voice or grimace or movement, inside the average American living room." Seldes also argued that television possessed "the capacity to transmit and deliver a rounded human character more completely than either radio or the movies. This is the source of its special power; this is what it must exploit to become totally successful." He saw "the sense of existing in the present" to be TV's essential trademark, upon which "a good director in television will base his entire style, the rhythm of movement, the frequency of close-up shots, the intensity of facial expression, the level of projection for the voice; on it the sponsor will build his advertising."

Commercial television was growing despite the restrictive conditions of the VHF spectrum which caused competitive distortions in the television industry. The FCC froze station construction permits between the autumn of 1948 and the spring of 1952, but by the end of the freeze the number of TV stations on the air had risen to 108, many of them extremely profitable. By the mid-1950s the commercial structures of network television which would endure for decades were firmly in place. The networks used their profits and negotiating power arising from the scarcity of VHF licences simultaneously to effect a network seller's market in national TV advertising and a network buyer's market in the prime-time programming market. Faced with rising time and production costs, television advertisers moved away from single sponsorship of programmes to various forms of joint sponsorship, ceding programme licensing to the networks while retaining a censorship control over program content in the form of informal or codified lists of proscribed subjects, characters, incidents, and language. At the same time, network licensing of prime-time programming reduced the market for independent programme producers to three network firms and allowed networks to demand ownership and syndication rights to their shows in exchange for a network time slot.

This financial model for the filmed programmes that would come to dominate network prime time and international programme markets was established as early as 1950 through network deals with a number of independent production companies, with Columbia Pictures' telefilm subsidiary Screen Gems making an early major Hollywood studio deal in 1952. The model typically involved network rights for two broadcasts of a typical thirty-nine episode annual season; the network licence fee would pay less than the full production costs of the programme, and to recoup the deficit, the production company would hope to resell the episodes to the domestic and foreign syndication markets. The 1952 ratings success of the thirty-minute filmed series *I Love Lucy* and *Dragnet* encouraged other production firms to enter the telefilm market and the growing syndication revenues for network reruns in the U.S.A. and abroad in the mid-1950s led to the near extinction of live drama in network prime time by 1957. Furthermore; the rising programme license fees by the mid-1950s attracted the major Hollywood studios into telefilm production, forming the industry relationships between programme producers and TV networks which largely endure today in American television.

In the midst of these programming shifts, the networks seized on the assertion by many early TV critics that the medium's capacity for the live transmission of dramatic or unstaged events defined its unique nature and mission as a rationale for network control of prime-time programming. Since only the networks could, by definition, provide interconnected live service to disparate stations, the networks defended their guardianship of the ontological essence of TV against those who "would destroy the very lifeblood and magic of television," as CBS President Frank Stanton told a meeting of CBS affiliates in 1956. Ironically, the network privileging of live TV came at the very moment when the three networks moved irrevocably into filmed programming in prime time in pursuit of booming syndication revenues which live programmes could not attain.

Such stirring network defences of television's aesthetic mission and dire warnings against tampering with network power, often mobilized around Cold War or nationalistic themes, became commonplaces by the mid-1950s. In 1956 CBS President Frank Stanton told one group that the age of intercontinental nuclear missiles ("perhaps the most perilous time in our history") demanded an instantaneous civilian mobilization in the form of a divinely inspired network television system, arguing that "it seems to be providential that we are thus able—at this pivotal point in world history—to reach into nearly every home in America simultaneously and at a moment's notice." Stanton told a Congressional committee that year that nothing less than America's national unity was at stake: "To curtail or destroy the networks' unique quality of instantaneous national interconnection would be a colossal backward step. It would make the United States much more like Europe than America. In fact, it would be a step in the direction of the *Balkanization,* the fragmentation, of the United States." Arguing the political legitimation of the commercial use of the television airwaves, Stanton told another Congressional committee in 1956 that "a network draws its validity in precisely the same fashion as an elected official of government—from election by and of the people." As contemporary media economists have noted, the peculiar combination of concentrated private economic power and ostensible public interest standard in American network television led to sometimes tortuous justifications of oligopolistic privilege.

There were two major challenges to network sovereignty in the early television industry in the United States the first from broadcasting's economic rivals in Hollywood and the second from philosophical nay-sayers and would-be reformers in the public realm. Contrary to some subsequent historical accounts, the Hollywood studios did not ignore television or limit their responses to CinemaScope, 3-D movies, and other theatrical gimmicks. For example, a single major studio, Paramount, had interests in four of the nation's first nine TV stations in 1947, as well as stakes in significant television patents and in the DuMont television network. However, Paramount and the other major studios were also involved in a decade-long losing battle with the U.S. Department of justice over their distribution practices and ownership of movie theatres; they also faced a steep drop in the post-war theatrical box office unrelated to television, disruptions in post-war foreign markets, and an internecine political blacklists. The efforts of the studios to build a major presence in TV station ownership and network operation were consistently thwarted by the hostile actions of the FCC. Their efforts to develop an alternative to broadcast television in the form of large-screen TV in movie theatres were frustrated by FCC refusals of broadcast frequency allocations and coaxial cable rate regulation reform, as well as by public indifference and the costs of theatre renovation. Despite many ambitious Hollywood announcements of prospective theatre-TV plans between 1948 and 1951, fewer than 100 theatres across the country were ever equipped for its use, and theatre television dwindled into a series of infrequent and *ad hoc* offerings of prize fights and business conferences.

CHAPTER **32**

The New Languages

Edmund Carpenter

Edmund Carpenter is an anthropologist known for his diverse and lively studies of the impact of media on societies, primitive and modern. He is a former collaborator with Marshall McLuhan on the Explorations project and journal (1953–1959), a major interdisciplinary forum devoted to the study of human communication.

Brain of the New World,
What a task is thine
to formulate the modern
. . . to recast poems, churches, art

—WHITMAN

English is a mass medium. All languages are mass media. The new mass media—film, radio, TV—are new languages their grammars as yet unknown. Each codifies reality differently; each conceals a unique metaphysics. Linguists tell us it's possible to say anything in any language if you use enough words or images, but there's rarely time; the natural course is for a culture to exploit its media biases.

The same is true of the other new languages. Both radio and TV offer short, unrelated programs, interrupted between and within by commercials. I say "interrupted," being myself an anachronism of book culture, but my children don't regard them as interruptions, as breaking continuity. Rather, they regard them as part of a whole, and their reaction is neither one of annoyance nor one of indifference. The ideal news broadcast has half a dozen speakers from as many parts of the world on as many subjects. The London correspondent doesn't comment on what the Washington correspondent has just said; he hasn't even heard him.

The child is right in not regarding commercials as interruptions. For the only time anyone smiles on TV is in commercials. The rest of life, in news broadcasts and soap operas, is presented as so horrible that the only way to get through life is to buy this product: then you'll smile. Aesop never wrote a clearer fable. It's heaven and hell brought up to date: Hell in the headline, Heaven in the ad. Without the other, neither has meaning.

Of the new languages, TV comes closest to drama and ritual. It combines music and art, language and gesture, rhetoric and color. It favors simultaneity of visual and auditory images. Cameras focus not on speakers but on persons spoken to or about; the audience *hears* the accuser but *watches* the accused. In a single impression it hears the prosecutor, watches the trembling hands of the big-town crook, and sees the look of moral

indignation on Senator Tobey's face. This is real drama, in process, with the outcome uncertain. Print can't do this; it has a different bias.

Books and movies only pretend uncertainty, but live TV retains this vital aspect of life. Seen on TV, the fire in the 1952 Democratic Convention threatened briefly to become a conflagration; seen on newsreel, it was history, without potentiality.

The absence of uncertainty is no handicap to other media, if they are properly used, for their biases are different. Thus it's clear from the beginning that Hamlet is a doomed man, but, far from detracting in interest, this heightens the sense of tragedy.

Now, one of the results of the time-space duality that developed in Western culture, principally from the Renaissance on, was a separation within the arts. Music, which created symbols in time, and graphic art, which created symbols in space, became separate pursuits, and men gifted in one rarely pursued the other. Dance and ritual, which inherently combined them, fell in popularity. Only in drama did they remain united.

It is significant that of the four new media, the three most recent are dramatic media, particularly TV, which combines language, music, art, dance. They don't however, exercise the same freedom with time that the stage dares practice. An intricate plot, employing flash backs, multiple time perspectives and overlays, intelligible on the stage, would mystify on the screen. The audience has no time to think back, to establish relations between early hints and subsequent discoveries. The picture passes before the eyes too quickly; there are no intervals in which to take stock of what has happened and make conjectures of what is going to happen. The observer is in a more passive state, less interested in subtleties. Both TV and film are nearer to narrative and depend much more upon the episodic. An intricate time construction can be done in film, but in fact rarely is. The soliloquies of *Richard III* belong on the stage; the film audience was unprepared for them. On stage Ophelia's death was described by three separate groups: one hears the announcement and watches the reactions simultaneously. On film the camera flatly shows her drowned where "a willow lies aslant a brook."

Media differences such as these mean that it's not simply a question of communicating a single idea in different ways but that a given idea or insight belongs primarily, though not exclusively, to one medium, and can be gained or communicated best through that medium.

Each medium selects its ideas. TV is a tiny box into which people are crowded and must live; film gives us the wide world. With its huge screen, film is perfectly suited for social drama, Civil War panoramas, the sea, land erosion, Cecil B. DeMille spectaculars. In contrast, the TV screen has room for two, at the most three, faces, comfortably. TV is closer to stage, yet different. Paddy Chayefsky writes:

> The theatre audience is far away from the actual action of the drama. They cannot see the silent reactions of the players. They must be told in a loud voice what is going on. The plot movement from one scene to another must be marked, rather than gently shaded as is required in television. In television, however, you can dig into the most humble, ordinary relationships; the relationship of bourgeois children to their mother, of middle-class husband to his wife, of white-collar father to his secretary—in short, the relationships of the people. We relate to each other in an incredibly complicated manner. There is far more exciting drama in the reasons why a man gets married than in why he murders someone. The man who is unhappy in his job, the wife who thinks of a lover, the girl who wants to get into television, your father, your mother, sister, brothers, cousins, friends—all these are better subjects for drama than Iago. What makes a man ambitious? Why does a girl always try to steal her kid sister's boy friends? Why does your uncle attend his annual class reunion faithfully every year? Why do you always find it depressing to visit your father? These are the substances of good television drama; and the deeper you probe into and examine the twisted, semi-formed complexes of emotional entanglements, the more exciting your writing becomes.[1]

The gestures of visual man are not intended to convey concepts that can be expressed in words, but inner experiences, nonrational emotions, which would still remain unexpressed when everything that can be told has been told. Such emotions lie in the deepest levels. They cannot be approached by words that are mere reflections of concepts, any more than musical experiences can be expressed in rational concepts. Facial expression is a human experience rendered immediately visible without the intermediary of word. It is Turgenev's "living truth of the human face."

Printing rendered illegible the faces of men. So much could be read from paper that the method of conveying meaning by facial expression fell into desuetude. The press grew to be the main bridge over which the more remote interhuman spiritual exchanges took place; the immediate, the personal, the inner, died. There was no longer need for the subtler means of expression provided by the body. The face became immobile; the inner life, still. Wells that dry up are wells from which no water is dipped.

Just as radio helped bring back inflection in speech, so film and TV are aiding us in the recovery of gesture and facial awareness—a rich, colorful language, conveying moods and emotions, happenings and characters, even thoughts, none of which could be properly packaged in words. If film had remained silent for another decade, how much faster this change might have been!

Feeding the product of one medium through another medium creates a new product. When Hollywood buys a novel, it buys a title and the publicity associated with it: nothing more. Nor should it.

Each of the four versions of the *Caine Mutiny*—book, play, movie, TV—had a different hero: Willie Keith, the lawyer Greenwald, the United States Navy, and Captain Queeg, respectively. Media and audience biases were clear. Thus the book told, in lengthy detail, of the growth and making of Ensign William Keith, American man, while the movie camera with its colorful shots of ships and sea, unconsciously favored the Navy as hero, a bias supported by the fact the Navy cooperated with the movie makers. Because of stage limitations, the play was confined, except for the last scene, to the courtroom, and favored the defense counsel as hero. The TV show, aimed at a mass audience, emphasized patriotism, authority, allegiance. More important, the cast was reduced to the principals and the plot to its principles; the real moral problem—the refusal of subordinates to assist an incompetent, unpopular superior—was clear, whereas in the book it was lost under detail, in the film under scenery. Finally, the New York play, with its audience slanted toward Expense Account patronage—Mr. Sampson, Western Sales Manager for the Cavity Drill Company—became a morality play with Willie Keith, innocent American youth, torn between two influences: Keefer, clever author but moral cripple, and Greenwald, equally brilliant but reliable, a businessman's intellectual. Greenwald saves Willie's soul.

This is why the preservation of book culture is as important as the development of TV. This is why new languages, instead of destroying old ones, serve as a stimulant to them. Only monopoly is destroyed. When actor-collector Edward G. Robinson was battling actor-collector Vincent Price on art on TV's *$64,000 Challenge,* he was asked how the quiz had affected his life; he answered petulantly, "Instead of looking at the pictures in my art books, I now have to read them." Print, along with all old languages, including speech, has profited enormously from the development of the new media. "The more the arts develop," writes E. M. Forster, "the more they depend on each other for definition. We will borrow from painting first and call it pattern. Later we will borrow from music and call it rhythm."

The appearance of a new medium often frees older media for creative effort. They no longer have to serve the interests of power and profit. Elia Kazan, discussing the American theatre, says:

> Take 1900–1920. The theatre flourished all over the country. It had no competition. The box office boomed. The top original fare it had to offer was *The Girl of the Golden West.* Its bow to culture was fusty productions of Shakespeare. . . . [Then] came the moving pictures. The theatre had to be better or go under. It got better. It got so spectacularly better

so fast that in 1920–1930 you wouldn't have recognized it. Perhaps it was an accident that Eugene O'Neill appeared at that moment—but it was no accident that in that moment of strange competition, the theatre had room for him. Because it was disrupted and hard pressed, it made room for his experiments, his unheard-of subjects, his passion, his power. There was room for him to grow to his full stature. And there was freedom for the talents that came after his.[2]

Yet a new language is rarely welcomed by the old. The oral tradition distrusted writing, manuscript culture was contemptuous of printing, book culture hated the press, that "slagheap of hellish passions," as one 19th-century scholar called it. A father, protesting to a Boston newspaper about crime and scandal, said he would rather see his children "in their graves while pure in innocence, than dwelling with pleasure upon these reports, which have grown so bold."

What really disturbed book-oriented people wasn't the sensationalism of the newspaper, but its nonlineal format, its nonlineal codifications of experience. The motto of conservative academicians became: *Hold that line!*

A new language lets us see with the fresh, sharp eyes of the child; it offers the pure joy of discovery. I was recently told a story about a Polish couple who, though long resident in Toronto, retained many of the customs of their homeland. Their son despaired of ever getting his father to buy a suit cut in style or getting his mother to take an interest in Canadian life. Then he bought them a TV set, and in a matter of months a major change took place. One evening the mother remarked that "Edith Piaf is the latest thing on Broadway," and the father appeared in "the kind of suit executives wear on TV." For years the father had passed this same suit in store windows and seen it both in advertisements and on living men, but not until he saw it on TV did it become meaningful. This same statement goes for all media: each offers a unique presentation of reality, which when new has a freshness and clarity that is extraordinarily powerful.

This is especially true of TV. We say, "We have a radio" but "We have television"—as if something had happened to us. It's no longer "The skin you love to touch" but "The Nylon that loves to touch you." We don't watch TV; it watches us: it guides us. Magazines and newspapers no longer convey "information" but offer ways of seeing things. They have abandoned realism as too easy: they substitute themselves for realism. *Life* is totally advertisements: its articles package and sell emotions and ideas just as its paid ads sell commodities.

Several years ago, a group of us at the University of Toronto undertook the following experiment: 136 students were divided, on the basis of their over-all academic standing of the previous year, into four equal groups who either (1) heard and saw a lecture delivered in a TV studio, (2) heard and saw this same lecture on a TV screen, (3) heard it over the radio, or (4) read it in manuscript. Thus there were, in the CBC studios, four controlled groups who simultaneously received a single lecture and then immediately wrote an identical examination to test both understanding and retention of content. Later the experiment was repeated, using three similar groups; this time the same lecture was (1) delivered in a classroom, (2) presented as a film (using the kinescope) in a small theatre, and (3) again read in print. The actual mechanics of the experiment were relatively simple, but the problem of writing the script for the lecture led to a consideration of the resources and limitations of the dramatic forms involved.

It immediately became apparent that no matter how the script was written and the show produced, it would be slanted in various ways for and against each of the media involved; no show could be produced that did not contain these biases, and the only real common denominator was the simultaneity of presentation. For each communication channel codifies reality differently and thus influences, to a surprising degree, the content of the message communicated. A medium is not simply an envelope that carries any

letter; it is itself a major part of that message. We therefore decided not to exploit the full resources of any one medium, but to try to chart a middle-of-the-road course between all of them.

The lecture that was finally produced dealt with linguistic codifications of reality and metaphysical concepts underlying grammatical systems. It was chosen because it concerned a field in which few students could be expected to have prior knowledge; moreover, it offered opportunities for the use of gesture. The cameras moved throughout the lecture, and took close-ups where relevant. No other visual aids were used, nor were shots taken of the audience while the lecture was in progress. Instead, the cameras simply focused on the speaker for 27 minutes.

The first difference we found between a classroom and a TV lecture was the brevity of the latter. The classroom lecture, if not ideally, at least in practice, sets a slower pace. It's verbose, repetitive. It allows for greater elaboration and permits the lecturer to take up several *related* points. TV, however, is stripped right down; there's less time for qualifications or alternative interpretations and only time enough for *one* point. (Into 27 minutes we put the meat of a two-hour classroom lecture.) The ideal TV speaker states his point and then brings out different facets of it by a variety of illustrations. But the classroom lecturer is less subtle and, to the agony of the better students, repeats and repeats his identical points in the hope, perhaps, that ultimately no student will miss them, or perhaps simply because he is dull. Teachers have had captive audiences for so long that few are equipped to compete for attention via the news media.

The next major difference noted was the abstracting role of each medium, beginning with print. Edmund M. Morgan, Harvard Law Professor, writes:

> One who forms his opinion from the reading of any record alone is prone to err, because the printed page fails to produce the impression or convey the idea which the spoken word produced or conveyed. The writer has read charges to the

jury which he had previously heard delivered, and has been amazed to see an oral deliverance which indicated a strong bias appear on the printed page as an ideally impartial exposition. He has seen an appellate court solemnly declare the testimony of a witness to be especially clear and convincing which the trial judge had orally characterized as the most abject perjury.[3]

Selectivity of print and radio are perhaps obvious enough, but we are less conscious of it in TV, partly because we have already been conditioned to it by the shorthand of film. Balázs writes:

> A man hurries to a railway station to take leave of his beloved. We see him on the platform. We cannot see the train, but the questing eyes of the man show us that his beloved is already seated in the train. We see only a close-up of the man's face, we see it twitch as if startled and then strips of light and shadow, light and shadow flit across it in quickening rhythm. Then tears gather in the eyes and that ends the scene. We are expected to know what happened and today we do know, but when I first saw this film in Berlin, I did not at once understand the end of this scene. Soon, however, everyone knew what had happened: the train had started and it was the lamps in its compartment which had thrown their light on the man's face as they glided past ever faster and faster.[4]

As in a movie theatre, only the screen is illuminated, and, on it, only points of immediate relevance are portrayed; everything else is eliminated. This explicitness makes TV not only personal but forceful. That's why stage hands in a TV studio watch the show over floor monitors, rather than watch the actual performance before their eyes.

The script of the lecture, timed for radio, proved too long for TV. Visual aids and gestures on TV not only allow the elimination of certain words, but require a unique script. The ideal radio delivery stresses pitch and intonation to make up for the absence of the visual. That flat, broken speech in "sidewalk interviews" is the speech of a person untrained in radio delivery.

The results of the examination showed that TV had won, followed by lecture, film, radio, and finally print. Eight months later the test was readministered to the bulk of the students who had taken it the first time. Again it was found that there were significant differences between the groups exposed to different media, and these differences were the same as those on the first test, save for the studio group, an uncertain group because of the chaos of the lecture conditions, which had moved from last to second place. Finally, two years later, the experiment was repeated, with major modifications, using students at Ryerson Institute. Marshall McLuhan reports:

> In this repeat performance, pains were taken to allow each medium full play of its possibilities with reference to the subject, just as in the earlier experiment each medium was neutralized as much as possible. Only the mimeograph form remained the same in each experiment. Here we added a printed form in which an imaginative typographical layout was followed. The lecturer used the blackboard and permitted discussion. Radio and TV employed dramatization, sound effects and graphics. In the examination, radio easily topped TV. Yet, as in the first experiment, both radio and TV manifested a decisive advantage over the lecture and written forms. As a conveyor both of ideas and information, TV was, in this second experiment, apparently enfeebled by the deployment of its dramatic resources, whereas radio benefited from such lavishness. "Technology is explicitness," writes Lyman Bryson. Are both radio and TV more explicit than writing or lecture? Would a greater explicitness, if inherent in these media, account for the ease with which they top other modes of performance?[5]

Announcement of the results of the first experiment evoked considerable interest. Advertising agencies circulated the results with the comment that here, at last, was scientific proof of the superiority of TV. This was unfortunate and missed the main point, for the results didn't indicate the superiority of one medium over others. They merely directed attention toward differences between them, differences so great as to be of kind rather than degree. Some CBC officials were furious, not because TV won, but because print lost.

The problem has been falsely seen as democracy vs. the mass media. But the mass media are democracy. The book itself was the first mechanical mass medium. What is really being asked, of course, is: can books' monopoly of knowledge survive the challenge of the new languages? The answer is: no. What should be asked is: what can print do better than any other medium and is that worth doing?

NOTES

1. *Television Plays.* New York: Simon and Schuster, 1955, pp. 176–178.
2. "Writers and Motion Pictures," *The Atlantic Monthly,* 199, 1957, p. 69.
3. G. Louis Joughin and Edmund M. Morgan, *The Legacy of Sacco and Vanzetti,* New York, Harcourt, Brace & Co., 1948, p. 34.
4. Béla Balázs, *Theory of Film,* New York, Roy Publishers, 1953, pp. 35–36.
5. From a personal communication to the author.

CHAPTER **33**

Making Room for TV

Lynn Spigel

Lynn Spigel is associate professor in the Department of Critical Studies, School of Cinema-Television, University of Southern California, and the author of several studies of television, including Make Room for TV.

Nicholas Ray's 1955 film, *Rebel without a Cause,* contains a highly melodramatic moment in which family members are unable to patch together the rift among them. The teenage son, Jim, returns home after the famous sequence in which he races his car to the edge of a cliff, only to witness the death of his competitor. Jim looks at his father asleep in front of the television set, and then he lies down on a sofa. From Jim's upside-down point of view on the sofa, the camera cuts to his shrewish mother who appears at the top of the stairwell. In a 180-degree spin, the camera flip-flops on the image of the mother, mimicking the way Jim sees her descending the stairs. This highly stylized shot jolts us out of the illusory realism of the scene, a disruption that continues as the camera reveals a television screen emitting a menacing blue static. As the camera lingers on the TV set, Jim confesses his guilt. Moments later, when his mother demands that he not go to the police, Jim begs his henpecked father to take his side. Finally, with seemingly murderous intentions, Jim chokes him. The camera pans across the TV set, its bluish static heightening the sense of family discord. With its "bad reception," television serves as a rhetorical figure for the loss of communication between family members. In fact, as Jim's father admits early in the scene, he was not even aware of his son's whereabouts during this fateful night, but instead had learned of the incident through an outside authority, the television newscast.

As this classic scene illustrates, in postwar years the television set became a central figure in representations of family relationships. The introduction of the machine into the home meant that family members needed to come to terms with the presence of a communication medium that might transform older modes of family interaction. The popular media published reports and advice from social critics and social scientists who were studying the effects of television on family relationships. The media also published pictorial representations of domestic life that showed people how television might—or might not—fit into the dynamics of their own domestic lives. Most significantly, like the scene from *Rebel without a Cause,* the media discourses were organized around ideas of family harmony and discord.

Indeed, contradictions between unity and division were central to representations of television during the period of its installation. Television was the great family minstrel that promised to bring Mom, Dad, and the kids together; at the same time, it had to be carefully controlled so that it harmonized with the separate gender roles and social functions of individual family members. This meant that the contradiction between unity and division was not a simple binary opposition; it was not a matter of either/or but rather both at once. Television was supposed to bring the family together but still allow for social and sexual divisions in the home. In fact, the attempt to maintain a balance between these two ideals was a central tension at work in popular discourses on television and the family.

THE FAMILY UNITED

In 1954, *McCall's* magazine coined the term "togetherness." The appearance of this term between the covers of a woman's magazine is significant not only because it shows the importance attached to family unity during the postwar years, but also because this phrase is symptomatic of discourses aimed at the housewife. Home magazines primarily discussed family life in language organized around spatial imagery of proximity, distance, isolation, and integration. In fact, the spatial organization of the home was presented as a set of scientific laws through which family relationships could be calculated and controlled. Topics ranging from childrearing to sexuality were discussed in spatial terms, and solutions to domestic problems were overwhelmingly spatial: if you are nervous, make yourself a quiet sitting corner far away from the central living area of the home. If your children are cranky, let them play in the yard. If your husband is bored at the office, turn your garage into a workshop where he'll recall the joys of his boyhood. It was primarily within the context of this spatial problem that television was discussed. The central question was, "Where should you put the television set?" This problem was tackled throughout the period, formulated and reformulated, solved and recast. In the process the television set became an integral part of the domestic environment depicted in the magazines.

At the simplest level, there was the question of the proper room for television. In 1949, *Better Homes and Gardens* asked, "Where does the receiver go?" It listed options including the living room, game room, or "some strategic spot where you can see it from the living room, dining room and kitchen."[1] At this point, however, the photographs of model rooms usually did not include television sets as part of the interior decor. On the few occasions when sets did appear, they were placed either in the basement or in the living room. By 1951, the television set traveled more freely through the household spaces depicted in the magazines. It appeared in the basement, living room, bedroom, kitchen, fun room, converted garage, sitting-sleeping room, music room, and even the "TV room." Furthermore, not only the room, but the exact location in the room, had to be considered for its possible use as a TV zone.

As the television set moved into the center of family life, other household fixtures traditionally associated with domestic bliss had to make room for it. Typically, the magazines presented the television set as the new family hearth through which love and affection might be rekindled.[2] In 1951, when *American Home* first displayed a television set on its cover photograph, it employed the conventionalized iconography of a model living room organized around the fireplace, but this time a television set was built into the mantelpiece. Even more radically, the television was shown to replace the fireplace altogether, as the magazines showed readers how television could function as the center of family attention. So common had this substitution become that by 1954 *House Beautiful* was presenting its readers with "another example of how the TV set is taking the place of the fireplace as the focal point around which to arrange the seating in the room."[3] Perhaps the most extreme example of this kind of substitution is the tradition at some broadcast stations of burning Yule logs on the television screen each Christmas Eve, a practice that originated in the 1950s.

More typically, the television set took the place of the piano.[4] In *American Home,* for instance, the appearance of the television set correlates significantly with the vanishing piano. While in 1948 the baby grand piano typically held a dominant place in model living rooms, over the years it gradually receded to the point where it was usually shown to be an upright model located in marginal areas such as basements. Meanwhile, the television set moved into the primary living spaces of model rooms where its stylish cabinets meshed with and enhanced the interior decor. The new "entertainment centers," comprised of a radio, television, and phonograph, often made the piano entirely obsolete. In 1953, *Better Homes and Gardens* suggested as much when it displayed a television set in a "built-in music corner" that "replaces the piano," now moved into the basement.[5] In that same year, in a special issue entitled "Music and Home Entertainment," *House Beautiful* focused on radio, television, and phonographs, asking readers, "Do You Really Need a Piano?"[6] One woman,

writing to *TV World* columnist Kathi Norris, answered the question in no uncertain terms:

> Dear Kathi:
>
> Since we got our television set, we've had to change the arrangement of furniture in our living room, and we just can't keep the piano. I need new pictures, but can't afford to buy them with the expense of television, so I was wondering if I might somehow find somebody who would trade me a picture or two for a perfectly good piano.[7]

This woman and, I suspect, others like her were beginning to think of television as a replacement for the traditional fixtures of family life.[8]

As the magazines continued to depict the set in the center of family activity, television seemed to become a natural part of domestic space. By the early 1940s, floor plans included a space for television in the home's structural layout, and television sets were increasingly depicted as everyday, commonplace objects that any family might hope to own. Indeed, the magazines included television as a staple home fixture before most Americans could even receive a television signal, much less consider purchasing the expensive item. The media discourses did not so much reflect social reality; instead, they preceded it. The home magazines helped to construct television as a household object, one that belonged in the family space. More surprisingly, however, in the span of roughly four years, television itself became *the* central figure in images of the American home; it became the cultural symbol par excellence of family life.

Television, it was said, would bring the family ever closer, an expression which, in itself a spatial metaphor, was continually repeated in a wide range of popular media—not only women's magazines, but also general magazines, men's magazines, and on the airwaves. In its capacity as unifying agent, television fit well with the more general postwar hopes for a return to family values. It was seen as a kind of household cement that promised to reassemble the splintered lives of families who had been separated during the war.

It was also meant to reinforce the new suburban family unit, which had left most of its extended family and friends behind in the city.

The emergence of the term "family room" in the postwar period is a perfect example of the importance attached to organizing household spaces around ideals of family togetherness. First coined in George Nelson and Henry Wright's *Tomorrow's House: A Complete Guide for the Home-Builder* (1946), the family room encapsulated a popular ideal throughout the period. Nelson and Wright, who alternatively called the family room "the room without a name," suggested the possible social functions of this new household space:

> Could the room without a name be evidence of a growing desire to provide a framework within which the members of a family will be better equipped to enjoy each other on the basis of mutual respect and affection? Might it thus indicate a deep-seated urge to reassert the validity of the family by providing a better design for living? We should very much like to think so, and if there is any truth in this assumption, our search for a name is ended—we shall simply call it the "family room."[9]

This notion of domestic cohesion was integral to the design for living put forward in the home magazines that popularized the family room in the years to come. It was also integral to the role of the television set, which was often pictured in the family rooms of the magazines' model homes. In 1950, *Better Homes and Gardens* literally merged television with the family room, telling readers to design a new double-purpose area, the "family-television room."[10]

But one needn't build a new room in order to bring the family together around the television set; kitchens, living rooms, and dining rooms would do just as well. What was needed was a particular attitude, a sense of closeness that permeated the room. Photographs, particularly in advertisements, graphically depicted the idea of the family circle with television viewers grouped around the television set in semicircle patterns.

As Roland Marchand has shown with respect to advertising in the 1920s and 1930s, the family circle was a prominent pictorial strategy for the promotion of household goods. The pictures always suggested that all members of the family were present, and since they were often shot in soft-focus or contained dreamy mists, there was a romantic haze around the family unit. Sometimes artists even drew concentric circles around the family, or else an arc of light evoked the theme. According to Marchand, the visual cliché of the family circle referred back to Victorian notions about domestic havens, implying that the home was secure and stable. The advertisements suggested a democratic model of family life, one in which all members shared in consumer decisions—although, as Marchand suggests, to some extent the father remained a dominant figure in the pictorial composition. In this romanticized imagery, modern fixtures were easily assimilated into the family space:

> The products of modern technology, including radios and phonographs, were comfortably accommodated within the hallowed circle. Whatever pressures and complexities modernity might bring, these images implied, the family at home would preserve an undaunted harmony and security. In an age of anxieties about family relationships and centrifugal social forces, this visual cliché was no social mirror; rather, it was a reassuring pictorial convention.[11]

Much like the advertisements for radio and the phonograph, advertisements for television made ample use of this reassuring pictorial convention—especially in the years immediately following the war when advertisers were in the midst of their reconversion campaigns, channeling the country back from the wartime pressures of personal sacrifice and domestic upheaval to a peacetime economy based on consumerism and family values. The advertisements suggested that television would serve as a catalyst for the return to a world of domestic love and affection—a world that must have been quite different from the actual experiences of returning GIs and their new families in the chaotic years of readjustment to civilian life.

The returning soldiers and their wives experienced an abrupt shift in social and cultural experiences. Horror stories of shell-shocked men circulated in psychiatric journals. In 1946, social workers at VA hospitals counseled some 144,000 men, half of whom were treated for neuro-psychiatric diseases.[12] Even for those lucky enough to escape the scars of battle, popular media such as film noir showed angst-ridden, sexually unstable men, scarred psychologically and unable to relate to the familial ideals and bureaucratic realities of postwar life (the tortured male hero in *Out of the Past* [1946] is a classic example). The more melodramatic social problem films such as *Come Back Little Sheba* (1952) and *A Hatful of Rain* (1957) were character studies of emotionally unstable, often drug-dependent, family men. Such images, moreover, were not confined to popular fiction. Sociological studies such as William H. Whyte's *The Organization Man* (1956) presented chilling visions of white-collar workers who were transformed into powerless conformists as the country was taken over by nameless, faceless corporations.[13] Even if his working life was filled with tension, the ideal man still had to be the breadwinner for a family. Moreover, should he fail to marry and procreate, his "manliness" would be called into question. According to Tyler May: "Many contemporaries feared that returning veterans would be unable to resume their positions as responsible family men. They worried that a crisis in masculinity could lead to crime, 'perversion' and homosexuality. Accordingly, the postwar years witnessed an increasing suspicion of single men as well as single women, as the authority of men at home and at work seemed to be threatened."[14] Although the image of the swinging bachelor also emerged in this period—particularly through the publication of *Playboy*—we might regard the "swinger" image as a kind of desperate, if confused, response to the enforcement of heterosexual family lifestyles. In other words, in a heterosexist world, the swinger

image might well have provided single men with a way to deflect popular suspicions about homosexuality directed at bachelors who avoided marriage.[15]

Meanwhile, women were given a highly constraining solution to the changing roles of gender and sexual identity. Although middle- and working-class women had been encouraged by popular media to enter traditionally male occupations during the war, they were now told to return to their homes where they could have babies and make color-coordinated meals.[16] Marynia Farnham and Ferdinand Lundberg's *The Modern Woman: The Lost Sex* (1947) gave professional, psychological status to this housewife image, claiming that the essential function of woman was that of caretaker, mother, and sexual partner. Those women who took paid employment in the outside world would defy the biological order of things and become neurotics.[17] One postwar marriage guidebook even included a "Test of Neurotic Tendencies" on which women lost points for choosing an answer that exhibited their desire for authority at work.[18] The domestic woman needed to save her energy for housekeeping, childrearing, and an active (monogamous) sex life with her husband.[19] The ways in which people interpreted and applied such messages to their own lives is difficult to discern, but their constant repetition in popular media did provide a context in which women could find ample justification for their early marriages, child-centeredness, reluctance to divorce, and tendency to use higher education only as a stepping stone for marriage.[20]

Even if people found the domestic ideal seductive, the housing shortage, coupled with the baby boom, made domestic bliss an expensive and often unattainable luxury. In part, for this reason, the glorification of middle-class family life seems to have had the unplanned, paradoxical effect of sending married women into the labor force in order to obtain the money necessary to live up to the ideal. Whereas before the war single women accounted for the majority of female workers, the number of married women workers skyrocketed during the 1950s.[21] Despite the fact that many women worked for extra spending money, surveys showed that some women found outside employment gave them a sense of personal accomplishment and also helped them enter into social networks outside family life.[22] At the same time, sociological studies such as Whyte's *The Organization Man* and David Reisman's *The Lonely Crowd* (1950) showed that housewives expressed doubts about their personal sacrifices, marital relationships, and everyday lives in alienating suburban neighborhoods. Although most postwar middle-class women were not ready to accept the full-blown attack on patriarchy launched in Simone de Beauvoir's *The Second Sex* (1949; English translation, 1952), they were not simply cultural dupes. Indeed, as the work of feminist historians such as Elaine Tyler May and Rochelle Gatlin suggests, postwar women both negotiated with and rationalized the oppressive aspects of the family ideal.

The transition from wartime to postwar life thus resulted in a set of ideological and social contradictions concerning the construction of gender and the family unit. The image of compassionate families that advertisers offered the public might well have been intended to serve the "therapeutic" function that both Roland Marchand and T. J. Jackson Lears have ascribed to advertising in general. The illustrations of domestic bliss and consumer prosperity presented a soothing alternative to the tensions of postwar life.[23] Government building policies and veteran mortgage loans sanctioned the materialization of these advertising images by giving middle-class families a chance to buy into the "good life" of ranch-style cottages and consumer durables. Even so, both the advertising images and the homes themselves were built on the shaky foundations of social upheavals and cultural conflicts that were never completely resolved. The family circle ads, like suburbia itself, were only a temporary consumer solution to a set of complicated political, economic, and social problems.

In the case of television, these kinds of advertisements almost always showed the product in the center of the family group. While soft-focus or dreamy mists were sometimes used, the manufacturers' claims for picture clarity and good reception seem to have necessitated the use of sharp focus and high contrast, which better connoted these product attributes. The product-as-center motif not only suggested the familial qualities of the set, but also implied a mode of use: the ads suggested television be watched by a family audience.

A 1951 advertisement for Crosley's "family theatre television" is a particularly striking example. As is typical in these kinds of ads, the copy details the technical qualities of the set, but the accompanying illustration gives familial meanings to the modern technology. The picture in this case is composed as a *mise-en-abyme:* in the center of the page a large drawing of the outer frame of a television screen contains a sharp focus photograph of a family watching television. Family members are dispersed on sofas on three sides of a room, while a little boy, with arms stretched out in the air, sits in the middle of the room. All eyes are glued to the television set, which appears in the center lower portion of the frame, in fact barely visible to the reader. According to the logic of this composition, the central fascination for the reader is not the actual product, which is pictured only in minuscule proportions on the lower margin of the page, but rather its ability to bring the family together around it. The ad's *mise-en-abyme* structure suggests that the Crosley console literally contains the domestic scene, thereby promising not just a television set but an ideal reflection of the family, joined together by the new commodity.[24]

Even families that were not welcomed into the middle-class melting pot of postwar suburbia were promised that the dream of domestic bliss would come true through the purchase of a television set. *Ebony* continually ran advertisements that displayed African-Americans in middle-class living rooms, enjoying an evening of television. Many of these ads were strikingly similar to those used in white consumer magazines—although often the advertisers portrayed black families watching programs that featured black actors.[25] Despite this iconographic substitution, the message was clearly one transmitted by a culture industry catering to the middle-class suburban ideal. Nuclear families living in single-family homes would engage in intensely private social relations through the luxury of television.

Such advertisements appeared in a general climate of postwar expectations about television's ability to draw families closer together. In *The Age of Television* (1956), Leo Bogart summarized a wide range of audience studies on the new medium that showed numerous Americans believed television would revive domestic life. Summarizing the findings, Bogart concluded that social scientific surveys "agree completely that television has had the effect of keeping the family at home more than formerly."[26] One respondent from a Southern California survey boasted that his "family now stays home all the time and watches the same programs. [We] turn it on at 3 P.M. and watch until 10 P.M. We never go anywhere."[27] Moreover, studies indicated that people believed television strengthened family ties. A 1949 survey of an eastern city found that long-term TV owners expressed "an awareness of an enhanced family solidarity."[28] In a 1951 study of Atlanta families, one respondent said, "It keeps us together more," and another commented, "It makes a closer family circle." Some women even saw television as a cure for marital problems. One housewife claimed, "My husband is very restless; now he relaxes at home." Another woman confided, "My husband and I get along a lot better. We don't argue so much. It's wonderful for couples who have been married ten years or more. . . . Before television, my husband would come in and go to bed. Now we spend some time together."[29] A study of mass-produced suburbs (including Levittown, Long Island, and Park Forest, Illinois) found similar patterns as women expressed their confidence that television was "bringing the romance back." One woman even reported, "Until we got that TV set, I thought my husband had forgotten how to neck."[30]

Typically also, television was considered a remedy for problem children. During the 1950s, juvenile delinquency emerged as a central topic of public debate. Women's magazines and child psychologists such as Dr. Benjamin Spock, whose *Baby and Childcare* had sold a million copies by 1951, gave an endless stream of advice to mothers on ways to prevent their children from becoming antisocial and emotionally impaired. Not only was childrearing literature big business, but the state had taken a special interest in the topic of disturbed youth, using agencies such as the Continuing Committee on the Prevention and Control of Delinquency and the Children's Bureau to monitor juvenile crimes.[31] Against this backdrop, audience research showed that parents believed television would keep their children off the streets. A mother from the Southern California survey claimed, "Our boy was always watching television, so we got him a set just to keep him home."[32] A mother from the Atlanta study stated, "We are closer together. We find our entertainment at home. Donna and her boyfriend sit here instead of going out now."[33] Such sentiments were popularized in a *Better Homes and Gardens* survey in which parents repeatedly mentioned television's ability to unify the family. One parent even suggested a new reason for keeping up with the Joneses. She said, "It [television] keeps the children home. Not that we have had that problem too much, but we could see it coming because nearly everyone had a set before we weakened."[34]

NOTES

1. *Better Homes and Gardens,* September 1949, p. 38.
2. In some cases, the television set was actually placed in the fireplace. Here, the objects were made to share the same system of meaning so that the familial values traditionally attributed to the fireplace were now also attributed to the television set. *See,* for example, *House Beautiful,* May 1954, p. 72. . . .
3. *House Beautiful,* September 1954, p. 153.

4. Television sets were often adorned with objects that connoted intellectual pursuits and high art, values traditionally associated with the piano. See, for example, *Ladies' Home Journal,* April 1951, p. 132. . . .

5. *Better Homes and Gardens,* March 1953, p. 72.

6. *House Beautiful,* January 1953, p. 76.

7. Kathi Norris, "How Now," *TV World,* August 1953, p. 54.

8. While the home magazines recommended substituting the television set for the piano, other evidence suggests that piano ownership might still have been significant for postwar families. Sales figures for the entire market show that the sale of pianos actually rose from 136,332 in 1940 to 172,531 in 1950, and by 1960 sales had increased to 198,200. Although these sales statistics alone cannot tell us how significant this rise was for the domestic market per se, they do caution us against assuming that the piano was actually phased out during the postwar years. See *Statistical Reference Index,* Music USA: 1982 Review of the Music Industry and Amateur Music Participation/American Music Conference, Report A22751 (Bethesda, MD: Congressional Information Service, 1983), p. 4. Also note that the National Piano Manufacturers Association saw radio as largely responsible for a 300 percent increase in sales during the late 1930s. The Association claimed, "Millions of listeners, who otherwise might never have attained an appreciation of music, are manifesting an interest in musical culture and endeavoring to become participants themselves." Cited in Davis, "Response to Innovation," p. 138.

9. George Nelson and Henry Wright, *Tomorrow's House: A Complete Guide for the Home-Builder* (New York: Simon and Schuster, 1946), p. 80.

10. *Better Homes and Gardens,* August 1950, p. 45.

11. Roland Marchand, *Advertising the American Dream* (Berkeley: University of California Press, 1985), pp. 248–54.

12. Elaine Tyler May, *Homeward Bound: American Families in the Cold War Era* (New York: Basic Books, 1988), p. 78.

13. William H. Whyte, Jr., *The Organization Man* (1956; Reprint, Garden City, NY: Doubleday, 1957).

14. Tyler May, *Homeward Bound,* p. 88.

15. See Barbara Ehrenreich, *The Hearts of Men: American Dreams and the Flight from Commitment* (Garden City, NY: Doubleday, 1983).

16. As Maureen Honey shows in her study of women's wartime magazine fiction, the Office of War Information gave suggestions to the magazine editors on ways in which to encourage married middle-class women to work. Honey, however, shows that magazines suggested wartime work for women was temporary, to be discarded when the GIs returned. Still, as Honey also shows, many women did not want to leave their jobs when men returned home. See *Creating Rosie the Riveter: Class, Gender and Propaganda During WWII* (Amherst: University of Massachusetts Press, 1984). . . .

17. Marynia Farnham and Ferdinand Lundberg, *The Modern Woman: The Lost Sex* (New York: Harper and Bros., 1947).

18. Jean and Eugene Benge, *Win Your Man and Keep Him* (New York: Windsor Press, 1948), p. 10. Cited in Tyler May, *Homeward Bound,* pp. 80–81.

19. Although feminine ideals and attitudes toward sexuality had changed considerably since the nineteenth century, the ideal woman of the 1950s shared a common problem with her Victorian ancestors—she was placed in the impossible position of taking on several incompatible roles at the same time. The efficient housewife was somehow supposed to transform herself into an erotic plaything for her husband at night. Even mothering was presented in terms of divided consciousness. . . .

20. In the early 1950s, the median marriage age ranged between twenty and twenty-one; the average family started having children in the beginning of the second year of marriage and had three to four children. For birthrates, see Rochelle Gatlin, *American Women Since 1945* (Jackson, MS: University Press of Mississippi, 1987), pp. 51, 55, 61. . . .

21. For labor force statistics, see Gatlin, *American Women Since 1945,* pp. 24–48. . . .

22. A 1955 survey showed that while most women worked for financial reasons, 21 percent worked to fulfill "a need for accomplishment" or to keep busy and meet people; even the women who worked for economic purposes cited the benefits of companionship and a sense of independence. A 1958 survey showed that almost two-thirds of married women cited their jobs as their chief source of feeling "important" or "useful," while only one-third mentioned housekeeping. See Gatlin, *American Women Since 1945,* p. 33. . . .

23. Marchand, *Advertising the American Dream,* pp. 335–59. . . .

24. *American Home,* October 1950, p. 25. For other examples of the product-as-center motif, see *House Beautiful,* November 1949, p. 1; *Ladies' Home Journal,* October 1948, p. 115; *House Beautiful,* February 1949, p. 1.

25. For examples, see *Ebony,* March 1950, p. 7; *Ebony,* August 1953, p. 3; *Ebony,* December 1955, p. 103. Advertisements in *Ebony* also showed white viewers and white actors on screen.

26. Bogart, *Age of Television,* p. 101. As a cautionary note, I would suggest that in his attempt to present a global, synthetic picture of the television audience, Bogart often smooths over the contradictions in the studies he presents. This attempt at global synthesis goes hand in hand with Bogart's view that the television audience is a homogeneous mass and that television programming further erases distinctions. He writes, "The levelling of social differences is part of the standardization of tastes and interests in which the mass media give expression, and to which they also contribute. The ubiquitous TV antenna is a symbol of people seeking—and getting—the identical message" (p. 5). Through this logic of mass mentalities, Bogart often comes to conclusions that oversimplify the heterogeneity of audience responses in the studies he presents.

27. Edward C. McDonagh, et al., "Television and the Family," *Sociology and Social Research* 40 (4) (March–April 1956), p. 117.

28. John W. Riley, et al., "Some Observations on the Social Effects of Television." *Public Opinion Quarterly* 13 (2) (Summer 1949), p. 232. This study was cosponsored by Rutgers University and CBS.

29. Raymond Stewart, cited in Bogart, *Age of Television,* p. 100.

30. Harry Henderson, "The Mass-Produced Suburbs: I. How People Live in America's Newest Towns," *Harper's,* November 1953, p. 28.

31. For more on this and other aspects of the public concern over juvenile delinquents, see James Gilbert, *A Cycle of Outrage: America's Reaction to the Juvenile Delinquent in the 1950s* (New York: Oxford University Press, 1986). . . .

32. McDonagh, et al., "Television and the Family," p. 116.

33. Stewart, cited in Bogart, *Age of Television,* p. 100.

34. *Better Homes and Gardens,* October 1955, p. 209.

CHAPTER **34**

Television Transforms the News

Mitchell Stephens

Mitchell Stephens is a professor of journalism and mass communication at New York University. He has written books and numerous articles that deal with the nature and social implications of news.

Radio gave newsmongers back their voices; television restored their faces. Indeed, the television newscast seems to resemble that most ancient of methods for communicating news: a person telling other people what has happened.

But this resemblance, as with much of what we see when we first examine this most powerful of news media, can be misleading.

A method for transforming moving pictures into and out of electronic signals, using a rotating disk with spiral perforations, had been devised as early as 1884 by Paul Nipkow of Germany. By the 1920s experimenters in Britain and the United States had succeeded in sending such signals through the air to receivers, and the rotating disk was soon replaced by an electronic scanning system. The technology of television was perfected by radio networks. And by 1941 CBS was broadcasting two fifteen-minute newscasts a day to a tiny audience on its New York television station.[1]

The problem faced by the producers of early television news broadcasts, most of whom were veterans of radio, was how to fill the screen. Those first newscasts on CBS were "chalk talks," with a newsman named Richard Hubbell standing, pointer in hand, in front of a map of Europe. Picture quality was so poor that it was difficult to make out Hubbell, let alone the map. When Pearl Harbor was attacked, CBS did not ignore its handful of television viewers, but for visuals they had to make do with a shot of an undulating American flag, blown by a fan in the studio.[2]

The development of television was placed on hold by the Second World War, but by 1949 Americans who lived within range of a couple of the approximately one hundred television stations that now dotted the country could *watch* the *Kraft Television Theater* or *Howdy Doody*, and choose between two fifteen-minute newscasts—*CBS TV News*, with Douglas Edwards, and NBC's *Camel News Caravan*, with John Cameron Swayze. The visuals on these newscasts consisted mostly of what would become known as "talking heads": shots of the somber Edwards or the boutonniered Swayze reading to the camera. (Don Hewitt, the director of the CBS newscast, was constantly searching for a way to increase the newscaster's eye contact with the camera, but Edwards drew the line at Hewitt's suggestion that he learn to read his script in Braille.)[3]

What film there was of news events was supplied by newsreel companies. (Television journalism was seen initially as an amalgam of radio news and movie newsreels.) Coverage of events was severely limited by the scarcity of film crews, by the bulkiness of their 16mm or 35mm cameras, by the time-consuming process of developing the film and transporting it to New York, and by the limitations of the genre—the newsreel emphasized on-scene photography, not on-scene reporting. Since filmed reports might not be aired for days after they were shot, film tended to be reserved for planned events and timeless features. Nonetheless, viewers were captivated simply by the opportunity to witness, from their living rooms, a ribbon cutting, a submarine christening, the dedication of a dam, a beauty contest or, on the first installment of Edward R. Murrow and Fred Friendly's hallowed *See It Now* in 1951, live shots of the Brooklyn Bridge and the Golden Gate Bridge side by side.[4]

Even with this primitive equipment, television journalism obviously possessed a power to re-create the sights and sounds of events that went well beyond anything even the most verbally skilled of their predecessors might have achieved, and it was not long before they were more fully exploiting that power. In 1949 a former radio journalist and former movie cameraman set out to cover a balloon race for France's first television news program. They were reporting on the race from the vantage point of their own balloon when storm winds swept it onto a high-tension wire. The two newsmen escaped with camera rolling, and film of their balloon exploding and burning provided the first great example of the potential of this new news medium in France. "*Le journal télévisé*" originally was broadcast three times a week; by the end of the year, it was aired twice a day.[5]

In the United States CBS and NBC began producing their own film reports in the 1950s. Camera crews were stationed in the largest cities; their film flown to New York by plane.[6] Correspondents in Washington and a few other cities might also appear live via a cable hookup. The quadrennial political conventions were covered; the earliest stirrings of the space program were covered, as were the initial struggles of the civil rights movement.[7] Occasionally, the "anchorman" (a term apparently first used to describe

Walter Cronkite's central role in CBS's convention coverage in 1952) himself ventured out of the studio on a story. In 1956 Hewitt's aggressiveness, Edwards's fame and some fortuitous timing secured a place for Edwards and a film crew in a Navy plane circling the Italian liner *Andrea Doria* as it sank off the coast of Nantucket. The film, combined with Edwards's eyewitness narration, led off CBS's newscast that evening, provided further evidence of the potential power of this medium.[8]

That power was realized in the 1960s. John Kennedy defeated Richard Nixon on television; Lee Harvey Oswald was shot on television; presidents dissembled, protesters protested, in front of the cameras, indeed with their eyes fixed upon the cameras. In August of 1965 a CBS reporter, Morley Safer, accompanied a group of United States Marines in Vietnam on a "search and destroy" mission to a complex of hamlets called Cam Ne. The Marines, who faced no resistance, held cigarette lighters to the thatched roofs and proceeded to "waste" Cam Ne. And this, too, appeared on television.[9]

Television news was no tool of radicals. Safer's report, the exception rather than the rule in television coverage of Vietnam, caused considerable consternation among the management at CBS; the network would make an effort in the following days to air more positive stories about the war.[10] Television journalists in the United States were subject not only to the moderating influence of their own allegiance to a working definition of the ethic of objectivity but to the moderating influence of their corporate owners, their government regulators (the Federal Communications Commission) and their corporate sponsors. (The film cameras that fed the *Camel News Caravan* had dared not happen upon any NO SMOKING signs.)[11]

In England, the nonprofit British Broadcasting Corporation—controlled by a board of governors appointed by the government and financed by an annual license fee on radio and television sets—maintained a similarly moderate tone. In France, where television has until recently been entirely under government control, television journalists placed a stricter interpretation upon their obligations to their superiors and became more open partisans of government policies. French President Charles De Gaulle once explained that "my enemies have the press, so I keep television."[12]

Nevertheless, television news, where it was free from direct censorship, was too sensitive an instrument to ignore the tremors radiating through the United States and Western Europe in the 1960s and early 1970s. And the workings of television news were not yet transparent enough to public relations experts employed by the established institutions that its reports might have been prevented from amplifying some of those tremors. Perhaps on television in these years the "human spirit," to use Harold Innis's terms, was breaking through before a new "monopoly of knowledge" had a chance to consolidate itself. Society, in the United States at least, has not since appeared on the television screen in such a state of disarray.

The morning after CBS aired Morley Safer's filmed report on Cam Ne, the network's president, Frank Stanton, was awakened by a telephone call. "Frank, are you trying to fuck me?" a voice said. "Frank, this is your president, and yesterday your boys shat on the American flag." This brief, unsolicited piece of journalism criticism, contributed by the president of the United States, Lyndon Johnson, is an indication of the political pressure under which television news operates. That Stanton, a good friend of the president, is reported to have "had it in for Safer" for a time after the call is an indication that journalistic principles may occasionally have sagged under the pressure.[13] Johnson's deep concern with one piece of news film on one network newscast also helps demonstrate another point: the extent to which television news had come to fascinate, if not obsess, the nation. President Johnson stationed three television sets in his office, so he could monitor coverage on all three networks. Many an evening, after Walter Cronkite would finish anchoring the *CBS Evening News,* Cronkite would find his secretary waiting to hand him the telephone: "White House on the line."[14]

And now, though it has been around for decades, television news continues to fascinate leaders and citizenry alike; it continues—like those French newsmen in a balloon—to make news as it covers news. Our interest in this "pretty toy" has, if anything, increased as it has brought us images of inner-city riots and of men hopping on the moon; images, in color and via increasingly portable videotape equipment, from the scene of famines and earthquakes, from John Dean's doorstep; images, via satellite, from Iran; images, live and then replayed endlessly on videotape, of a space shuttle disintegrating. We remain fascinated, too, by the irreverence with which television seems to treat the news—by its mix of bantering sportscasters, cavorting weathercasters, over-exposed celebrities, beatings, stabbings, crashes, and sobbing mothers invited to explain to a microphone how it feels to have lost all.

The perfect expression of this fascination may have been a scene during the intensely covered New Hampshire presidential primary in 1984 when television news cameras reported on the phenomenon of television news cameras reporting on the presence of so many television news cameras. And enthralled as we are with this seemingly omnipotent product of our seemingly omnipotent technology, we tend to overstate some of its accomplishments—pretty and ugly.

To begin with, despite the presence of satellites and twenty-four-hour cable news services, the television audience is hardly unique in its interest in news in general, or in events over the oceans in particular; nor is this audience, to recap another point, ... uniquely well informed about all aspects of the world. A television camera is trained on the president of the United States every moment that he spends in public, but in the larger television "markets," at least, such cameras are rarely in a position to supply news of neighborhood occurrences to the residents of what is left of such neighborhoods.

Some of the criticism television journalism inspires is equally short-sighted. Journalists did not become encumbered by celebrity for the first time when Barbara Walters was offered a million dollars to work for ABC television news; Horace Greeley was well enough known to obtain the Democratic nomination for president, and James Gordon Bennett, Henry Morton Stanley, Nellie Bly, Joseph Pulitzer and William Randolph Hearst are all examples of journalists who achieved considerable renown without appearing on television. Nor did news and entertainment meet and mate for the first time on often giggly, often frivolous, local television newscasts in the United States, their affair dates back at least as far as criers and minstrels. Television news, in other words, did not inject a foreign substance—playfulness—into the news; news has been enjoyed for as long as it has been exchanged.

Like the penny papers of the 1830s, the yellow journals of the 1880s and 1890s and the tabloids of the 1920s, television has succeeded in attracting a new audience to the news. Once television sets became affordable, news became available to audiences of many millions, including even those lacking the energy, skill or maturity to read a newspaper or concentrate on a radio narrative. (Television newscasts are, if anything, easier to watch than news events themselves, in the sense that it is easier to turn the set on than to walk outside and into the street.)

From this perspective, it is remarkable that television journalists have not adopted more sensationalistic techniques to cater to this largest of mass audiences. Local newscast producers in the United States have discovered the drawing power of murders, fires, gossip and fluff; but as a rule they include somewhat less blood, sex and depravity in their newscasts than can be found in some entertainment programs, and somewhat less than Joseph Pulitzer, for example, squeezed into his *New York World* in 1883.[15]

Crime is reported with great industriousness on television, but these stories of misbehavior tend to be told in the friendly but earnest equitone that has, give or take the occasional quip, become the voice of the medium worldwide; television journalists rarely resort to the overheated prose—teeming with adjectives, admonitions and sobriquets—of the tabloid journalist. And while celebrity scandals, quack diets and unidentified flying objects have occasionally found their way onto the television schedule, we have not yet seen the freaks and dismemberments that characterize some supermarket tabloids.

Perhaps *viewing,* rather than reading about, a freak or a real individual screaming for mercy would be too sensational even for a news audience; simply glimpsing a forlorn mother's sobs can be difficult enough to bear. Perhaps television cameras are not yet sufficiently swift and dexterous to capture life's rawest moments, moments newspaper reporters can recall with the still formidable magic of words. Perhaps that triumvirate of governors—corporate owners, corporate sponsors and government regulators—directs news producers away from the more extreme examples of the seamy and sordid. Or perhaps such techniques have simply never been needed in the comfortable environs of broadcast news: the *World* was losing about $40,000 a year when Pulitzer purchased it and began fighting for circulation; most commercial television stations in the United States turn a substantial profit (though networks have been hurt in recent years by competition from cable television and home videotapes). Television may be so simple and seductive a news medium that it attracts an economically viable audience without resort to the more exaggerated forms of sensationalism. Or perhaps such techniques are simply waiting to be discovered by some aggressive television journalists in some future ratings war. Whatever the explanation, as popular forms of journalism go, television newscasts have remained relatively tame.

The charge that these newscasts treat events with particular superficiality is more difficult to refute. Television newswriters have room for fewer words than their newspaper counterparts—their stones are measured in seconds, not column inches. Moving pictures (particularly the ever-more-popular moving graphics) certainly contribute information of their own, but to the extent that depth of coverage correlates with volume of words, television stories are undeniably shallower than most newspaper stories. And since their words are intended for a less acute, less painstaking sense—hearing—television newswriters must forswear the more complex formulations a newspaper reporter might hazard. But these are differences of degree.

Journalists, whatever their medium, tend to swim close to the surface—concerned with the splashes and waves more than the underlying currents. Whether communicating by print, newsletter or cry, journalists are not often endowed with the time or the endurance to delve deeper. More thorough discussions may accompany breaking news coverage—in extended newspaper series or columns, in television documentaries or interview programs, in magazine articles. But here too the hurry and fascination with the moment that permeates most newsrooms, and is indeed inherent in the journalistic enterprise, appears to discourage longer perspectives and more searching analyses.

Recently, a writer visiting an Eskimo village in Canada's Northwest Territories was asked by one of the residents how long he planned to stay. Before the writer could answer, the Eskimo suggested, in English: "One day—newspaper story. Two days—magazine story. Five days—book."[16] It is not clear whether that Eskimo was familiar yet with the three-hour, hit-and-run operations mounted by television news crews, with their complex equipment and harried schedules, but he hardly required acquaintance with a television reporter to grasp the journalist's tendency toward superficiality.

Television is also routinely accused of having debased contemporary politics. But newspapers had faced similar accusations before television cameras began to steal the attention and abuse. When reporters were first beginning to cover Parliament in England in the late eighteenth century, one of its members, William Windham, fumed that politicians were being treated like "actors." "What was to become of the dignity of the House," Windham demanded, "if the manners and gestures, and tone and action of each member were to be subject to the license, the abuse, the ribaldry of newspapers?"[17]

Television favors candidates who are attractive, skilled at producing a newsworthy fifteen-second statement and able to afford airtime for political commercials. Modern newspapers have favored candidates whose views are easily capsulized in headlines, and in the days before circulation measured in the hundreds of thousands, publishers demonstrated a less subtle bias—toward parties and candidates willing to help subsidize their operations.

Our impatience with television's view of politics represents, in part, a longing for an era when the news regularly achieved the depth, impartiality and seriousness of the civics lesson—an era that never was.[18] Journalists throughout history have been as prone to oversimplification as the politicians about whom they write. Certainly, there is substantial room for improvement in television's coverage of politics, but such efforts should not be based on a false nostalgia.

Of course, television has had some profound effects on journalism. Particularly noticeable are the changes it has imposed upon newspapers. With broadcast newscasts now routinely beating them to breaking news, newspapers increasingly are emphasizing news features and more analytical approaches to events. They are moving away from pure news reporting toward some hybrid of news, opinion, history and pop sociology. (Network television newscasts may now have to move in the same direction in the face of competition from lengthier, more frequent local and cable television newscasts.)[19] Television (along with radio) also deserves some credit for the modern American newspaper's return to less constricted writing styles—at the expense of the five Ws lead, the inverted pyramid and even the sobriquet. The anecdotes or turned phrases that now lead off so many front-page stories are there to compensate for the breaking news lost to broadcast journalists,

but they are also there in imitation of broadcast journalists, who have long recognized that their wordings, written to be read aloud, had to sound conversational.[20] Television's influence on newspapers is nowhere more apparent than in the national daily *USA Today*—a colorful confection of graphics and short, breezy stories.

But perhaps the most significant effect the television newscast has had on journalism has been the added distance it has placed between news purveyor and audience (in this it has continued the work of the newspaper). Television news is deceptive; it looks so friendly. The vast pool of live, videotaped and computer-generated images available to television newscasts have never succeeded in forcing the "talking head" of the newscaster from the screen. Audiences apparently prefer having their news delivered by a familiar, affable, *human* presence—these apparent throwbacks to criers or busybodies. Yet, the television screen is too flat and impenetrable for this to be much more than mimicry. No news medium offers less of the *actual* interaction and neighborly contact characteristic of spoken news than does television.

It is possible that the increasing number of channels made possible by cables and satellite dishes will drive television newscasts toward the smaller, demographically segmented audiences now sought by many radio stations. But for now, television speaks predominantly to the large communities of nation or metropolitan area. The chances of a member of those communities being heard—still a vague possibility for newspaper readers through a letter or a canceled subscription—have almost entirely disappeared with television. This is one-way news.

Television viewers live in a world of mediated reality. Increasingly they talk and think about people they have not met, places they have not been. Television has, in McLuhan's terminology, "extended" dramatically our access to news but, as cars weaken the legs they have "extended," reliance on television news may have weakened our ability to hear and tell our *own* news. We borrow facts, perceptions, even opinions from newscasters, and we borrow the newscasters themselves—with whom we fancy ourselves on a first-name basis—as surrogate busybodies, surrogate friends. It is important to remember, as we allow one of these well-known, well-dressed personalities to present our news, that the exchange of news has not always been a spectator sport, that the pursuit of news once encouraged even nonjournalists to move, observe, investigate, remember and talk, that for an individual to be fully informed, it was once necessary to leave the house.

One accomplishment of television seems impossible to overstate: it brings a wealth of news into our homes with astounding speed and immediacy. The development of television news has capped centuries of improvements in the means of news dissemination and news gathering, centuries in which the perennial shortage of reliable information about current events has been transformed into a surplus. We can learn more and see more of a President Reagan or Princess Diana than most of Thoreau's contemporaries could have dreamed of learning and seeing of President Pierce or Princess Adelaide. But we pay a price.

SELECTED BIBLIOGRAPHY

Barnouw, Erik. *A Tower in Babel, A History of Broadcasting in the United States.* I. New York: 1966.

———. *The Image Empire, A History of Broadcasting in the United States.* III. New York: 1970.

———. *Tube of Plenty: The Evolution of American Television.* New York: 1975.

Epstein, Edward Jay. *Between Fact and Fiction: The Problem of Journalism.* New York: 1975.

Gates, Gary Paul. *Air Time: The Inside Story of CBS News.* New York: 1979.

Halberstam, David. *The Powers That Be.* New York: 1979.

Lanson, Gerald, and Mitchell Stephens. " 'Trust Me' Journalism." *Washington Journalism Review,* November 1982, pp. 43–47.

———. "Jell-O Journalism: Reporters Are Going Soft in Their Leads." *Washington Journalism Review,* April 1982, pp. 21–23.

MacDonagh, Michael. *The Reporter's Gallery.* London: 1913.

Miguel, Pierre. *Histoire de la Radio et de la Télévision.* Paris: 1984.

Reasoner, Harry. *Before the Colors Fade.* New York: 1981.

NOTES

1. Barnouw, *Tube of Plenty,* 5, 48–49, 86; Gates, 55.
2. Gates, 55.
3. Barnouw, *Tube of Plenty,* 102, 112–113; Gates, 59–60, 66, 76.
4. Barnouw, *Tube of Plenty,* 102, 168–171; Gates, 59–60, 67–68.
5. Miguel, 193–194.
6. Barnouw, *The Image Empire,* 42.
7. For an account of some of these early efforts, see Reasoner.
8. Gates, 73–74, 79.
9. Halberstam, 448–490; Gates, 165–170.
10. Epstein, 213–214; Halberstam, 491.
11. Barnouw, *Tube of Plenty,* 170.
12. Cited, Paul Lewis, "French TV Battle Grows as Rightist Wins Contract," *New York Times,* February 25, 1987.
13. Halberstam, 490–491. This story is also told in Gates, 128, although Gates does not specifically connect Johnson's call to Safer's report on Cam Ne.
14. Barnouw, *Tube of Plenty,* 388.
15. Some examples of headlines from the first week after Pulitzer took control: Screaming for Mercy, Love and Cold Poison, While the Husbands Were Away; *New York World,* May 12, 16, 17, 1883.
16. Cited, Herbert Mitgang, "Barry Lopez, a Writer Steeped in Arctic Values," *New York Times,* March 29, 1986.
17. Cited, MacDonagh, 293–295.
18. In the first half of the eighteenth century, English periodicals featured the work of Addison, Steele, Swift, Defoe and Johnson. But it was during this apparent "golden age" that Defoe complained that his fellow journalists left readers "possessed with wrong notions of things, and wheedled to believe nonsense and contradictions," and that Dr. Johnson suggested that the press "affords ... too little" information "to enlarge the mind."
19. See Lanson, " 'Trust Me' Journalism."
20. For a critique of one aspect of this change in writing style—the use of "soft leads"—see Lanson, "Jell-O Journalism."

CHAPTER 35

Two Cultures—Television versus Print

Neil Postman and Camille Paglia

The late Neil Postman was chair of the Department of Communication Arts and Sciences at New York University. Of his many books, three relate directly to the history of communication: The Disappearance of Childhood, Amusing Ourselves to Death, *and* Technopoly. *Camille Paglia teaches at the University of the Arts in Philadelphia. Her books—notably* Sexual Personae, Sex, Art and American Culture, *and* Tamps and Vamps—*as well as numerous essays on media-related themes are not without controversy.*

W"hat I see as dangerous here," he said, "is the discontinuity of emotion that television promotes, its unnatural evocation, every five minutes, of different and incompatible emotions."

"You leave a restaurant," she said, "and get killed by a falling air conditioner. A tornado hits a picnic. There is no sense to reality. Television is actually closer to reality than anything in books. The madness of TV is the madness of human life."

So went the conversation between two cultural critics. Neil Postman and Camille Paglia, taking up an argument that has vexed nearly everyone in this century—the struggle for preeminence between words and pictures, today between books and television. This conflict is uniquely American—a debate so dense with prejudices that it has turned almost all of us into liars: "I don't watch TV" is now so common a dissembling among those who read that it has become a kind of mantra. And "I read that book" is a euphemism acceptable among recent generations to mean simply that one has heard of the title.

Neil Postman is one of the most original writers in defense of the book. A professor of communication arts at New York University and the author of *Amusing Ourselves to Death: Public Discourse in the Age of Show Business,* Postman is a scholar, raised in the pretelevision world, whose eloquence owes much to the classical declarative prose of Strunk and White. He argues that reading is an ordered process requiring us to sit at a table, consume ideas from left to right, and make judgments of truth and falsehood. By its nature, reading teaches us to reason. Television, with its random, unconnected images, works against this linear tradition and breaks the habits of logic and thinking. Postman has said that the two most dangerous words in this century are "Now . . . this"—that strange verbal doo-dad uttered by television anchors to ease the transition from a report on a natural disaster to a commercial about your need— desperate need, in fact—for an electric toothbrush.

Those who argue from the other side usually make a weak and unconvincing case. With the possible exception of Marshall McLuhan, anyone writing about television has done so with apologies. Recently, a new critic has emerged named Camille Paglia. She is a professor of humanities at the Philadelphia College of the Arts and is currently finishing a critical history of culture that ranges from the cave paintings of Altamira to the Rolling Stones concert at Altamont. Volume One, entitled *Sexual Personae: Art and Decadence from Nefertiti to Emily Dickinson,* was recently nominated for a National Book Critics Circle Award. Paglia was born after World War II, an accident to which she ascribes great significance. To hear her talk is to confirm her theory about the influence of the modern media: She speaks in a rush of images, juxtapositions, and verbal jump cuts. She argues that instead of criticizing television, most academics and other cultural critics simply turn up their noses dismissively at its enormous power—a kind of intellectual denial. Television, Paglia says, is the culture. And, she asks, by what and whose criteria is the latest Madonna any less meaningful an icon than the last? To those who argue that kids who watch television can't recall any of the facts mentioned on it, she wonders whether we have ever *watched* television. Perhaps we are doing something else when we stare at the screen. Perhaps the remembrance of facts has nothing to do with television's significance or effect.

Since no two thinkers have in recent time made such compelling cases, *Harper's Magazine* decided to introduce them. We sent each author a copy of the other's book and asked each to read it. One cold winter night in December, we asked them to dine in the private Tasting Room of New York City's Le Bernardin restaurant—a small, glass room located inside the kitchen of Chef Gilbert Le Coze. Throughout the conversation Bruno Jourdaine served a *menu dégustation* beginning with seviche of black bass and poured glasses of St. Veran Trenel (1988). We began the dinner with a blessing in the form of two readings from the Bible.

> *"Thou shalt not make unto thee any graven image."*
>
> —*Exodus 20:4*

> *"In the beginning was the Word, and the Word was with God, and the Word was God."*
>
> —*John 1:1*

Camille Paglia: But John got it all wrong. "In the beginning was nature." That's the first sentence of *my* book. Nature—violent, chaotic, unpredictable, uncontrollable—predates and stands in opposition to the ordered, structured world created by the word, by the law, by the book-centered culture of Judeo-Christianity. The image—which is pagan and expressive of nature's sex and violence—was outlawed by Moses in favor of the word. That's where our troubles began.

Remember that when the Ten Commandments were handed down on Mount Sinai, Moses had just led the Jews out of Egypt. They had followed Joseph down there several hundred years before and had become resident workers, then slaves. Over time, Judaism had gotten a little mixed up with the local Egyptian cults—a syncretism not unlike Santería in the Caribbean, with its blend of voodoo and Catholicism. When Moses tried to get his people to leave Egypt, there was resistance: "What are we *doing*? Moses, you're crazy. What homeland are you talking about?" The Ten Commandments were an attempt to clarify what is Hebrew, what is Jewish.

The Second Commandment implies that the Hebrew God has no shape, that He is pure spirit. Egyptian gods often appeared in animal form. The pagan cults of Egypt, Babylon, and Canaan worshiped such idols—for example, the Golden Calf. So Moses is saying, "We do not worship the gods of nature but a God who is above nature, a God who *created* nature. The ultimate God."

And the prohibition against graven images didn't forbid just pagan idols. It banned *all* visual imagery, of anything on earth or in the heavens. Moses knew that once a people begin to make images of any kind, they fall in love with them and worship them. Historically, the Second Commandment diverted Jewish creative energy away from the visual arts and into literature, philosophy, and law.

Neil Postman: It is curious that of the first three, so-called establishing commandments, two of them concern communications: the prohibitions against making graven images and taking the Lord's name in vain. Yet this makes sense if you think about the problems of constructing an ethical system 3,000 years ago. It was critical to tell the members of the tribe how to symbolize their experience. That is why Moses chose writing—using a phonetic alphabet, which the Jews no doubt borrowed from the Egyptians— to conceptualize this nonvisual, nonmaterial God. Writing is the perfect medium because, unlike pictures or an oral tradition, the written word is a symbol system *of* a symbol system, twice removed from reality and perfect for describing a God who is also far removed from reality: a nonphysical, abstracted divinity. Moses smartly chose the right communications strategy. With the Second Commandment, Moses was the first person who ever said, more or less, "Don't watch TV; go do your homework."

Most important, the written word allows for the development of a God who is, above all things, *mobile.* To invent a God who exists only in the word and through the word is to make a God that can be taken anyplace. Just as writing is portable speech, Moses' God is a portable God, which is fitting for a people setting forth on a long journey.

Paglia: That is why Jewish culture is one of the founts of Western tradition and why Western culture is so intellectually developed. Jewish thought is highly analytical, as is Greco-Roman philosophy. Both are very Apollonian. But the Greco-Roman tradition is also one of pagan idolatry. Early Christianity, which first proselytized among the poor, outcast, and unlearned, needed to use visual imagery, which became more and more pronounced in the Middle Ages and early Renaissance. Out of this came the renegade priest Martin Luther, who correctly diagnosed a lapse from authentic early Christianity in medieval Catholicism. Catholics are never told to read the Bible. Instead, they have to listen to the priest commenting on excerpts from the Bible, usually just the New Testament.

Postman: Luther called the invention of the printing press the "supremist act of grace by which the Gospel can be driven forward." And it was. As a result of Luther's Reformation, the intellectual geography of Europe flipped. Until then Venice, in the south of Europe, was the leading printing center and one of the world's intellectual capitals. Then the Catholic Church got nervous about it, because of the possibilities of further heresy, and began to restrict the printing press. And then, within a year of each other, Galileo died and Newton was born. The intellectual power of Europe moved from the south to the north. England, Scandinavia, Germany became the realm of the word, and the south returned to spectacle. Catholicism resorted increasingly to ornament and beautiful music and painting. To this day we think of Spain, Italy, and southern France as centers of great visual arts, from the Escorial to the Sistine Chapel. The north, home of the austere Protestant, concentrated on the word, until it found its greatest fulfillment here in the first political system built on the word alone: no divine right of kings, no mysticism, just a few pages of written text, the American Constitution.

Paglia: The polarity in Europe got more and more rigid. In the north, book, book, book; but in the Counter-Reformation of southern Europe, unbelievably lurid images—like Bernini's St. Teresa having a spiritual orgasm. My first childhood memories are of images, fantastic images, created by the Catholic Church. The statues are polychromatic, garish. In my church stood a statue of St. Sebastian, nude, arrows piercing his flesh, red blood dripping down. Who can wonder where *my* mind came from? Here were spectacular pagan images standing right next to the altar. In the beginning, you see, were sex and violence.

Early Christianity was very masculine. Just two male gods and a neuter—the Father, the Son, and the Holy Ghost. But the popular imagination couldn't tolerate that, so in the Middle Ages it added the Virgin Mary. Go reread the Bible and see how small a role Mary plays in the Gospels. Almost none. She is a survivor of the great goddess cults of antiquity. I interpret the most essential elements of Italian Catholicism as pagan. Martin Luther saw the latent paganism of the Catholic Church and rebelled against it. The latest atavistic discoverer of the pagan heart of Catholicism is

Madonna. This is what she's up to. She doesn't completely understand it herself. When she goes on *Nightline* and makes speeches about celebrating the body, as if she's some sort of Woodstock hippie, she's way off. She needs *me* to tell her. But this is what she's doing—revealing the eroticism and sadomasochism, the pagan ritualism and idolatry in Italian Catholicism.

Protestantism today continues to be based on the word and the book. That's why Protestant ministers in church or on television always stress the Bible. They shout, "*This* is all you need." And they wave it, they flap it, they even slam it around. The Protestant needs no priest, no hierarchy. There is nothing between you and God. Protestants want a close and chatty relationship with Jesus: "Have you accepted Christ as your *personal* Savior?" And they sing, "He walks with you and He talks with you." For Protestants, Jesus is a friend, the Good Shepherd.

The Italian Catholic Jesus can't speak. He's either preliterate—a baby in the arms of Mary—or comatose—a tortured man on a cross. The period when Christ is literate, when he can speak, is edited out of southern Catholicism.

. . . baked sea urchin . . .

Postman: It helps to understand your point if we remember what happens every time Moses leaves. He comes back and the whole tribe has lapsed into idol wsorship. He is always complaining to Aaron, "What the hell did you do while I was gone?" The image is so seductive. Catholics are known for keeping little images on the dashboard of their cars, and nowadays you find them among Jews as well. Many reform temples now have more and more interesting visual designs. The Second Commandment held for a long time. Jews weren't known for their achievements in the visual arts until this century.

This proves my point about the life of the word and the image: Humans are not biologically programd to be literate. In John Locke's essay on education, he insists that the body must become a slave to the mind. One of my students, upon hearing that quotation, said, "I know just what he means." And she told me

how she can only read lying on her side while holding the book against the wall and, as a result, only reads the right-hand page of any book. This is the challenge of literacy: to get children accustomed to sitting still, to abiding in a realm that is unnaturally *silent*. That is the world of the word. How can silence compete with television?

Paglia: But, Neil, people who are naturally disposed to reading may not be as physically active as others. There is an important difference here. I teach dancers. They are sometimes poor readers or even dyslexic. But they are brilliant at other, older forms of feeling and expression. Some people are inclined to the sedentary life that reading requires, others are not. That is why the entire discourse on sex and gender in academe and in the media is so off, because teachers and writers are not nearly as athletic or rambunctious as others.

Postman: The literate person does pay a price for literacy. It may be that readers become less physically active and not as sensitive to movement, to dance, and to other symbolic modes. That's probably true. It's a Faustian bargain. Literacy gives us an analytic, delayed response in perceiving the world, which is good for pursuits such as science or engineering. But we do lose some part of the cerebral development of the senses, the sensorium.

Paglia: And some people have more developed sensoriums than others. I've found that most people born before World War II are turned off by the modern media. They can't understand how we who were born after the war can read a book and watch TV at the same time. But we can. When I wrote my book, I had earphones on, blasting rock music or Puccini and Brahms. The soap operas—with the sound turned down—flickered on my TV. I'd be talking on the phone at the same time. Baby boomers have a multilayered, multitrack ability to deal with the world. I often use the metaphor of a large restaurant stove to describe the way the mind works. There are many burners, and only one of them is the logical, analytical burner. And, Neil, I think we agree that our contemporary education system neglects it.

One reason American academic feminism is so mediocre is that these women can't think their way out of a wet paper bag. They have absolutely no training in logic, philosophy, or intellectual history, so they're reduced to arguing that we should throw out Plato and Aristotle because they're dead white males, or some such nonsense. That's so dopey and ignorant. People born before World War II can't understand those of us raised in the fragmented, imagistic world of TV. We can shut off one part of the brain and activate another. Scientists, psychologists, and IQ testers haven't caught up with these new ways of perception.

Postman: Camille, I think we actually agree on the evidence. Only you think it is all just fine and will be a liberating development. Television and the other visual media will enlarge the sensorium and give people a fuller repertoire of means of expression. Marshall McLuhan used to refer to people like me and others as POBs: Print-Oriented Bastards—literates who had their right hemispheres amputated or atrophied. You should adopt the term, Camille; your analysis is absolutely correct. Only I tend to see this development as ominous.

Bertrand Russell used to utter a lovely phrase. He said that the purpose of education was to teach each of us to defend ourselves against the "seductions of eloquence." In the realm of the word, we learn the specific techniques used to resist these seductions: logic, rhetoric, and literary criticism. What worries me is that we have not yet figured out how to build defenses against the seductions of imagery. The Nazi regime was only the most recent example of seducing, through words and images, one of the most *literate* populations on earth. I remember Hitler's rantings. Now, I won't ask you how old you are.

Paglia: I'm forty-three. I was born in 1947. And you graduated from college in 1953. I checked! I wanted to know, because I think this information is absolutely critical to how one views the mass media. I graduated from college in 1968. There are only fifteen years between us, but it's a critical fifteen years, an unbridgeable chasm in American culture.

            . . . shrimp and basil beignets . . .

Postman: Well, I remember the imagery of the 1940s, when an entire political machine was pressed into the service of imagistic propaganda. In America it is somewhat different. There is a machine producing such images, but it is capitalism, and the output is the commercial. The process is the same. Have you seen the commercial for Hebrew National frankfurters? It shows Uncle Sam while a narrator declares how good and healthy frankfurters are because Uncle Sam maintains such high standards. Then Uncle Sam looks up as the narrator adds that Hebrew Nationals are even better than other frankfurters because they must answer to a higher authority.

Paglia: I love that ad! It's wonderful. Hilarious.

Postman: Here is what bothers me. Symbols *are* infinitely repeatable, but they are not inexhaustible. If you use God to sell frankfurters, or if you use the face of George Washington to sell discount car tires, you drain the symbol of the very meanings, Camille, that you so astutely discover and explicate in your book. You look at a painting and analyze its levels of meaning, its ambiguities, its richness. But what happens if people see the same image a thousand times, and always to sell tight jeans?

Paglia: I would argue exactly the opposite. In the Hebrew National ads the invocation of Uncle Sam and God reinforces their symbolic meaning and helps young people have a historical perspective on their own culture.

Ads shaped the imagination of my generation. The Hebrew National image of Jehovah—that he's invisible, a voice inspiring his children to high standards—is faithful to tradition. It's a fabulous ad. And, by the way, it's true—kosher franks *are* better! I believed this ad and bought the franks! I love ads as an art form. To me, there is no degradation in this particular ad at all.

Postman: Perhaps you're not taking it seriously enough, Camille. By age twenty, the average American has seen 800,000 television advertisements, about 800 a week. I am not talking about radio, print, or any other kind of advertisement. I am referring only to television advertisements. Television commercials are now the most powerful source of socialization, and the schools ought to take them seriously.

Some advertisements are good, of course. I don't think Madonna would serve too well. But I think of Jimmy Stewart selling soup. In that advertisement, the producers used his voice only because that voice is sufficient to symbolize what he stands for—the embodiment of the thoroughly decent American. So the use of that imagery is fine. But in the Hebrew National advertisement, a sense of the sacred is being eliminated, or exploited by redirecting it to the profane world.

Paglia: If Jehovah had never expressed Himself about table manners, I would support you. But the Bible shows that Jehovah instructed the Jews at great length about what foods to eat and how to prepare and serve them.

Postman: And, of course, Jehovah also forbade shellfish—everything we're eating tonight!

Paglia: This is the point. Kosher ritual preparation is dictated by the Bible. Nothing in the Hebrew National ad distorts or lies about Jewish tradition.

Postman: Suppose you saw a commercial that showed Jesus looking at a bottle of Gallo wine and saying, "When I turned the water into wine in Cana, it wasn't nearly as good as this Gallo Pinot Noir." What does that do to the meaning of Jesus Christ for Christians? You seem very enthusiastic about the use of these images, but I think the *secularization* of these symbols and religious icons is dangerous.

Paglia: To you, coming from the Judeo-Christian tradition, this looks secular. If you look at it from my perspective, popular culture is an eruption of paganism—which is also a sacred style. In your book, you skip from 1920 to television. I think you leap over a critical period—the great studio era of Hollywood movies in the 1930s and 1940s. Cinema then was a pagan cult full of gods and goddesses, glamour and charisma. It was a style devoted to the sacred and the numinous. So it's not that the sacred has been lost or is being trivialized. We are steeped in idolatry. The sacred is everywhere. I don't see any secularism. We've returned to the age of polytheism. It's a rebirth of the pagan gods.

What I argue in my book is that Judeo-Christianity never defeated paganism but rather drove it underground, from which it constantly erupts in all kinds of ways. Ancient Greco-Roman culture harnessed the dynamic duality of the Apollonian and the Dionysian principles. We've inherited the Apollonian element of the Greco-Roman tradition. The history of Western civilization has been a constant struggle between these two impulses, an unending tennis match between cold Apollonian categorization and Dionysian lust and chaos.

That's why you can always tell whether a critic was born before or after World War II by the way he or she speaks of the twentieth century. To you who grew up knowing life as narrative exposition and who saw the end of an era with Fitzgerald and Hemingway—and you're right, there was a great shift, and the novel is now dead as a doornail—it's the Age of Anxiety. But the death of the novel was also the beginning of movies. I date the modern age from the first sound pictures in 1928. I call the twentieth century the Age of Hollywood.

There's a huge generational difference here. For those of us born after the war, our minds were formed by TV. Take Susan Sontag, born in 1933. There are fourteen years between her and me. It doesn't seem like much, but it's like an abyss between us. In the 1960s she was writing briefly about popular culture, but then she backed off and has spent the rest of her life saying, "I'm serious, I'm serious. Gotta find that ultimate Eastern European writer!" A few years ago, she boasted in *Time* that she had no TV and had to rent one when a guest came to visit. My TV is constantly fluttering. It's a hearth fire in the modern home. TV is not something you *watch*; it is simply on, all the time.

. . . seared scallops in truffle
vinaigrette . . .

Postman: If you keep this up, Camille, I'm going to need either more wine or a cigarette. Do you mind if I smoke?

Paglia: Not at all. Neil, in your book you mentioned tests in which people didn't remember any facts from a news program they had watched thirty minutes earlier on TV. But they weren't testing the right part of the brain. Watching TV has nothing to do with thought or analysis. It's a passive but highly efficient process of storing information to be used later. The proper analogy is to interstate driving or football. You know, baseball was *the* sport of the pre–World War II era. Academics love it. It's the ultimate academic sport—linear, logical, slow. Football, especially as *remade* for TV with slow motion and replays, is the sport of my generation. There's a lot of writing about baseball but hardly any good stuff about football. When a quarterback pulls back from the line and quickly checks out the field, he's not thinking, he's *scanning,* the very thing we do when we watch TV. It's like the airline pilot sweeping his eyes across his bank of instruments or the driver cruising down the interstate at high speed, always scanning the field, looking; for the drunk, the hot rod, the police, or the slow old lady in the Cadillac—watch out for *her.* None of these people—the quarterback, the pilot, the driver—is *thinking.* They're only reading the field and working by instinct, deciding in an instant where to throw the ball or steer the jet or car. The decision is made by intuition, not by ratiocination.

Postman: It's called pattern recognition.

Paglia: Oh, really? Perfect! And that's why you can't picture Susan Sontag driving a car. You know what I mean? Can you imagine Susan Sontag behind the wheel? Forget it. It's like a *New Yorker* cartoon: *Susan Sontag buys her first car!*

Postman: Of course, I agree: Reading a book and "reading" television are two completely different cerebral activities. I can remember hearing print-oriented people complain that the problem with a show like *Charlie's Angels* is that it didn't honor the Aristotelian unities of time, place, and action. Or that it didn't have any *true* character development.

Paglia: You liked *Charlie's Angels?*

Postman: As a matter of fact, I did, but I am bringing it up as an example of how people misread television. Print-oriented people can't

understand such a show because they try to judge it by the measures of literature. I came to understand *Charlie's Angels* when I realized that the entire show was about *hair.*

Do you remember that at the end of the show there was a two-minute segment in which the disembodied voice of Charlie explained to the angels *what the entire show had been about.* I imagine that the show was written by a bunch of former English majors. And I see them confounded by the fact that they have just written a show that is basically about hair and doesn't fit any of the categories that they have been taught count. So at the end, they shoehorn in a vestigial narrative. Once I saw an episode in which, in order to explain everything, the voice at the end had to mention characters and action that hadn't even been *in* the program: "She killed him because years ago he had stolen money and given it to a third person . . ." Those sixty seconds before the credits—when the show was actually already over—were meant to give a show about hair a sense of logic or coherence.

Paglia: *TV Guide* once said about the actresses on *Knots Landing*—my favorite prime-time show—that "they act with their hair." I love it! Soap operas also are mainly about hair, you know. Very pagan—the worship of beauty. And do you realize that the Farrah Fawcett hairdo of *Charlie's Angels* can still be seen today in every shopping mall in America? Though that show has been off the air for ten years, it has this incredible ongoing influence. Farrah herself has moved on to battered-wife roles, but her old Seventies hairstyle is still the dominant look for boy-crazy girls in American high schools. Awesome, really.

Postman: We agree on the influence of popular culture as expressed through visual images. Everyone has a right to defend his or her own culture, and I feel sure there will be a cost to the kind of culture I value. It may be that your sensorium has been enlivened while mine has atrophied. But let's look at my tradition and see what it has accomplished. Consider that in 1776 Thomas Paine sold, by the most conservative estimates, 300,000 copies of *Common Sense.* That is the equivalent of selling 30,000,000 copies—a feat attainable only today by Danielle Steel or Tom Wolfe. Camille, do you think we will pay a price for this more fully developed sensorium?

Paglia: In your book you say that there was a high literacy rate during the American Revolution. But does that mean people actually *read* books? Political and literary books? Or was it that they could just sign their names? Your portrait of the highly literate nineteenth century also sort of ignores the trashy sentimental novels, ladies' fashion magazines, and the dime western. I agree with you that our country was founded as an Enlightenment experiment. The framers of the American Constitution were true intellectuals. But I think your book puts undue stress on that period, which was, as I see it, a kind of privileged moment. Comparing our period with that one—when there was a high degree of cultural awareness and political activity—makes us think we're slipping into a decline. But maybe we're just returning to the norm. I think the world as it is now is the way it always was.
 . . . black bass in coriander nage . . .

Postman: I'm not certain it was only a privileged moment, although you are right in suggesting that a high literacy rate creates a somewhat abstracted view of the world. Our culture paid a price for literacy, and it will pay a price for its transformation into a visual culture. We are, for example, rapidly losing any sense of sacrality. The reason the Ayatollah Khomeini struck most Americans as either a complete riddle or a lunatic is that he was actually a *truly religious* person. And we can no longer understand what such a person is like.

Paglia: Exactly. Whenever Qaddafi would spend days in his tent, the Western media would sneer and ridicule him. I couldn't believe it. Does no one understand the ethical meaning of the desert in Bedouin culture? It's like our Walden Pond. Hasn't the media ever seen *Lawrence of Arabia?* There are two lessons in the Salman Rushdie case. First, artistic freedom is a value only in the democratic Western tradition. Second, to millions of people in the world, religion is a matter of life and death.

Postman: Camille, I think these observations support my argument that what I call the secularization of imagery depletes religious symbolism: not only the frequency of the image but also the ignominious tie between the image and commercialization. That is why we in the West can't understand why someone would risk his life in an attempt to kill Salman Rushdie. To us, it's crazy. To the martyr, it is the path to heaven.

Paglia: Rather than your total secularization, I see the repaganization of Western culture. In the realm of politics, I think pop culture—the vehicle of the pagan eruption—plays a crucial role. Popular culture has the function of purging politics of many of its potential demagogues. Elvis Presley, an enormously charismatic figure, was able to build his empire in the politically neutral realm of pop culture.

Postman: Are you saying that Hitler might have been a Hollywood star in America?

Paglia: Today, you have other ways for extraordinarily charismatic people to create their worlds. There are other ways to rule the universe. Before popular culture, the only realm that allowed that kind of power of personality was politics.

Postman: I see the confluence between television and politics a little differently. The first television president was, obviously, John Kennedy. But the first *image* president was Ronald Reagan. They were very different figures. Kennedy, Jimmy Carter, even Mario Cuomo are very much identified with regions of the country. They were and are developed personalities that play well on television. But Reagan and even Bush are different. Remember how no one knows what state Bush is from and how Reagan's being from California seemed irrelevant. These are personalities onto whom a full spectrum of voters are able to project their personal image of a president. Whatever a president is supposed to be, then that is what Reagan or Bush is.

Paglia: As a television persona, Reagan was avuncular and nostalgic—a return to the happy, innocent, pre–World War II era of base-ball, before the chaos and disasters of the Six-ties. He was simple, kindly, even-tempered, sometimes goofy. He got into his pajamas right after dinner. He ate jelly beans. He called his wife "Mommy." He never aged. His hair never got gray. To liberal writers and academics, these things seemed stupid and ludicrous. They were off reading his policy papers, missing the whole point of his popularity. Our president is both the political and the symbolic head of our government, serving in jobs that in England, for example, are separately represented by the prime minister and the queen. The president symbolizes the nation in psychodramatic form.

Postman: A nation as heterogeneous as ours gropes to find comprehensive symbols and icons to pull us together. Ronald Reagan was such an image. Every Christmas you hear people say, "Happy Holidays." We try to be so polite and inclusive. We are a fragile polity desperate for unifying images. But, paradoxically, we can destroy ourselves by exhausting the available icons.

Paglia: Another such image is the national weather map, which is shown, naturally, on TV. Here's this patchwork country of Chinese and Chicanos and African-Americans and Jews and Italians, and then there's this map with beauti-fully sweeping curved lines of air pressure stretching from sea to shining sea, pulling us together. The weatherman and the president are our two titular heads.

These images and their meaning become obvi-ous once you know how to read TV. One more example. Remember, during the 1988 election, how everyone was calling George Bush a wimp? And he was a wimp, constantly trotting after Reagan and in his shadow. What a ninny, I would think; he'll never win the election. Then came the day when Ronald Reagan made his last visit to the Republican convention, and Bush named Dan Quayle as his running part-ner for vice president. It was the most stunning moment of TV transformation I've ever seen, but no one in the media picked it up. After Reagan left, remember the outdoor scene when Bush named Quayle? The press hysterically rushed off to report the story of how silly,

stupid, and rich Quayle was. But the story was not that George had picked a jerk. The story was that George Bush, emerging as a new man, had picked a *son*. Bush had made a complete *rite de passage* on television and for television. Remember how Quayle was jumping around, acting like a puppy—even grabbing Bush by the shoulder? Later that day at the indoor press conference, Bush was amazingly stern and con-fident. He cut reporters off, he was completely in charge. He was this totally new person, a man no one had seen before. It was then I knew he was going to be president. I called people up and told them, but no one believed me. If you didn't know how to read TV or weren't watch-ing, you missed it completely.

Postman: And my point, Camille, which you are overlooking, is that Roger Ailes engineered that entire effect. We were all manipulated into having just that very perception.

Paglia: What I am talking about is nothing that Roger Ailes could have created. It was a side of Bush that predated Roger Ailes. We all have many personas, and we can pick and choose which to make public. But we cannot create them. Roger Ailes could not have saved Michael Dukakis.

    . . . roast monkfish on savoy cabbage . . .

Postman: Granted. If you read Bush's résumé, it is one of the most macho documents of recent times—first baseman at Yale, youngest Navy pilot, shot down in combat, head of the CIA. But when Ailes saw him acting like a ninny on television—and television does have a way of showing the authentic soul—I agree, he went to work on the indecisive wimp and promoted the image of the macho guy so that you and others would pick it up. And then that image was repeated and repeated, washing away any memory of a past impression.

Paglia: In your book you speak of television as being a medium of flashing images with only an eternal present and no past. I disagree. It's just the opposite. TV is a genre of reruns, a for-mulaic return to what we already know. Every-thing is familiar. Ads and old programs are constantly recycled. It's like mythology, like the Homeric epics, the oral tradition, in which the listener hears passages, formulae, and epithets repeated over and over again. There is a joy in repetition, as children know when they say, "Mommy, tell me that story again." TV is a medium that makes us feel "at home."

If you go back to the Fifties, when movies lost their cultural centrality to TV, you'll see that the great sacred images—the huge, cold images of cinema—were being miniaturized, familiarized, and domesticated by the television screen. The box became part of the family, and the shows reflected it: *Father Knows Best* and *Leave It to Beaver*. Ads are the same way. I put one of my favorite ads in my book—Luciana Avedon crooning, "Camay has coconut-enriched lather." I adored that ad! Of course, ads you hate are like torture. You want to die. So TV is about repetition and compulsion. It's like prayer, like the Catholic Rosary, repeated over and over again. That's what ads are: soothing litanies that make us feel safe and familiar and at home in the strange modern world.

Postman: So idolatry has triumphed. I think Luther would join Moses in saying that the cult of the word is defenseless in the face of the image.

Paglia: Moses got his people out of Egypt, out of the land of the pagan image. That was the only way. Judaism could not have flourished in Egypt. Today, either you live in a cabin in northern Canada or you try to control TV. And I believe we *should* try to control it, by the way. Liberals are wrong when they say, "Parents should just turn off the TV set." You can't. TV is everywhere. It's bigger than politics. It's bigger than the Church.

Postman: This is where education comes in, Camille. I believe that educational theory should be what I call "ecological"; that is, education should supply what the rest of the culture is not supplying. In this case, I think the only defense against the seductions of imagery is a literate education. If children are educated in the traditions of the word, then perhaps they will be able to make discriminating choices in the chaotic realm of the image.

Paglia: To me the ideal education should be rigorous and word-based—logocentric. The student must learn the logical, hierarchical system. Then TV culture allows the other part of the mind to move freely around the outside of that system. This is like the talent you need for internal medicine. An internist has to be intuitive. He knows there are about a half dozen different systems in the body, all interrelated. His mind has to weave in and out and around them and more or less guess what's wrong. This is the mental flexibility that a word-based education and a TV-based culture can develop. All parents should read to their children, from infancy on. Education is, by definition, repressive. So if you're going to repress, then repress like hell. I don't believe in the Dewey or Montessori methods—"We want to make this pleasant." There is nothing pleasant about learning to read or to think. The teachers used to shake me and yell at me to stay in line or sit still in my seat. I didn't like it, but I recommend it.

Postman: In *Aspects of the Novel,* E. M. Forster wrote that if you say the king died and the queen died, you don't have a story. But if you say that the king died *because* the queen died, you have a story. I find that television undermines these simple word-based connections. The whole idea of language is to provide a world of intellectual and emotional continuity and predictability. But many of my students no longer understand, for example, the principle of contradiction. I was talking to one student the other day about a paper in which he asserted one thing to be true in the first paragraph and the exact opposite to be true three paragraphs later. He said, "What's the problem?"

This habit derives from television, which tells you that there was a rape in New York and then it tells you there was an earthquake in Chile and then it tells you that the Mets beat the Cardinals.

Paglia: Well, Neil, that's life.

Postman: That's insanity.

Paglia: Not to me. In your book you say TV is Dadaist in its random, nihilistic compilation of unrelated events. I say it's surrealist—because *life* is surreal! You leave a restaurant and get killed by a falling air conditioner. A tornado hits a picnic. There's no sense to reality. It simply happens. Television is actually closer to reality than anything in books. The madness of TV is the madness of human life.

Postman: Here is what I would like: When our young student is watching Dan Rather say that 5,000 people died in an earthquake in Chile and then Dan says, "We'll be right back after this word from United Airlines," I would like our student to say, "Hey, wait a second, how could he ask me to make such an emotional switch?"

Paglia: My answer is this: Buddha smiles. He sees the wheel of reincarnation and accepts the disasters of the universe. That's the way it should be. There's no way we can possibly extend our compassion to 5,000 dead people. By juxtaposing such jarring images, TV is creating a picture of the world that is simply true to life. We are forced to contemplate death the way farmers do—as just another banal occurrence, no big deal. Nature can crack the earth open and swallow thousands, and then the sun shines and the birds sing. It's like going from an airplane crash to a hemorrhoids ad. In TV, as in nature, all have equal weight.
      . . . carousel of caramel desserts

Postman: What I am focusing on is our emotional response to those things. We all know that nurses who work in hospitals make jokes. They see the absurdity of death routinely. But they don't see anywhere near the number of deaths the television viewer sees. What I see as dangerous here is a discontinuity of emotion that television promotes, its unnatural evocation, every five minutes, of different and incompatible emotions.

Paglia: By moving from disaster to commercial, TV creates the effect of Greek tragedy: emotion, then detachment; contemplation of loss, then philosophical perspective. At the end of *Hamlet,* there are four corpses strewn all over the stage.

Postman: But no one is laughing—although I will admit that in the graveyard scene, when

Hamlet makes the "Alas, poor Yorick" speech, he *is* laughing. But my point is, just after Horatio's final soliloquy, at least on television, we would then see the Hebrew National spot or perhaps a commercial for Danish pastry.

Paglia: To make that radical switch from disaster to detachment is, I think, a maturing process. If you fully responded emotionally to every disaster you saw, you'd be a mess. In fact, you'd be a perpetual child, a psychological cripple. Wisdom by definition is philosophical detachment from life's disasters.

Postman: Injecting humor into otherwise insane catastrophes is comic relief. It is what we must do unless we want to go mad. But the effect I am talking about on the television news is different.

Paglia: I know that you see "amusement" as a bad thing wherever it shows up. You said in your book that teaching has finally been reduced to a branch of popular entertainment and that students won't sit still for anything that's not as funny as Big Bird on *Sesame Street.* And you cite Plato, Cicero, and Locke as educational philosophers who would insist on seriousness. I respectfully disagree. Plato's dialogues, which follow the Socratic method, a conversational give-and-take such as we're having here, are in fact very entertaining. There's a lot of comedy in Plato. Socrates is always pretending to be the most ignorant person there, and so on.

I think Jesus was a brilliant Jewish stand-up comedian, a phenomenal improvisor. His parables are great one-liners. When an enemy, trying to trap him, asks him about paying taxes, Jesus says, "Show me the coin of the tribute. Whose image is on it?" "Caesar's," the guy replies. "Then render unto Caesar the things that are Caesar's and unto God the things that are God's." I think that line got applause and laughs.

Postman: You studied with Harold Bloom too long.

Paglia: Bloom used to say, "Teaching's a branch of show biz!" One last point—there are the koans, the teachings of the great Buddhist masters. They often took the form of slapstick. The novice comes in and says, "Tell me about life, master," and the elder whacks him on the head. Or says something surreal, like "Beanstalk!" So we do have many examples of teaching by great sages using humor or stand-up improv—Plato, Jesus, Buddha.

Postman: No one is saying not to use humor in the classroom. I guess we are talking about magnitude. It is one thing to use humor to reveal an idea you are developing. But now it is used simply to win the student's attention. Consequently, drawing an audience—rather than teaching—becomes the focus of education, and that is what television does. School is the one institution in the culture that should present a different worldview: a different way of knowing, of evaluating, of assessing. What worries me is that if school becomes so overwhelmed by entertainment's metaphors and metaphysics, then it becomes not content-centered but attention-centered, like television, chasing "ratings" or class attendance. If school becomes that

way, then the game may be lost, because school is using the same approach, epistemologically, as television. Instead of being something different from television, it is reduced to being just another *kind* of television.

Paglia: Our dialogue has reached one major point of agreement. I want schools to stress the highest intellectual values and ideals of the Greco-Roman and Judeo-Christian traditions. Nowadays, "logocentric" is a dirty word. It comes from France, where deconstruction is necessary to break the stranglehold of centuries of Descartes and Pascal. The French have something to deconstruct. But to apply Lacan, Derrida, and Foucault to American culture is absolutely idiotic. We are born into an imagistic and pagan culture ruled by TV. We don't need any more French crap from ditsy Parisian intellectuals and their American sycophants. Neil, we agree on this: We need to reinforce the logocentric and Apollonian side of our culture in the schools. It is time for enlightened repression of the children.

CHAPTER **36**

TV in the Net-age

Henry Jenkins

"Henry Jenkins is Director of the Comparative Media Studies Program at MIT and the Peter de Florez Professor of Humanities. His most recent books include Convergence Culture: Where Old and New Media Collide *and* Fans, Bloggers and Gamers: Exploring Participatory Culture.*"*

ZAPPERS, CASUALS, AND LOYALS

Industry insiders often deploy the distinction among zappers, casuals, and loyals: this distinction manages to blur together how, why, and what consumers watch. Zappers are people who constantly flit across the dial—watching snippets of shows rather than sitting down for a prolonged engagement. Loyals actually watch fewer hours of television each week than the general population:

they cherry pick those shows that best satisfy their interests; they give themselves over fully to them; they tape them and may watch them more than one time; they spend more of their social time talking about them; and they are more likely to pursue content across media channels. Loyals watch series; zappers watch television. Loyals form long-term commitments; zappers are like the folks at cocktail parties who are always looking over their shoulders to see if someone more interesting has just entered the room. Casuals fall somewhere in between; they watch a particular series when they think of it or have nothing better to do. They generally watch it from start to finish but are more apt to wander away if it starts to bore them. They may be more likely to conduct conversations or do other household activities over the show rather than give it their full attention.

No given viewer is exclusively a loyal, a casual, or a zapper; most watch television in different ways on different occasions. The most discriminating viewer will zap around the dial in a hotel room or at the end of a hard day. And sometimes zappers get hooked into a series and watch it every week. Nobody knows for sure yet whether the new media environment has produced more zappers, casuals, or loyals. For one thing, A. C. Nielsen's continued focus on entire program blocks rather than more microscopic units of time means that they have no real way of measuring zapping or, indeed, the fluctuating loyalties of more casual viewers.

Throughout much of the 1990s, industry analysts overstressed the significance of the zappers. For example, Phillip Swann asserts in his book, *TV.Com: How Television Is Shaping Our Future:* "Few viewers today can sit through an entire program without picking up the remote and checking out another channel. . . . Today's viewer needs constant gratification: if she's not entertained or intrigued for any stretch of time, she will flip the dial."[1] Swann thinks interactive television should and will be designed for zappers. In Swann's future, variety and magazine shows will almost entirely displace dramas, and

the few remaining series will be shrunk to thirty minutes or less. According to Swann, "[There will be] fewer occasions where people sit down and watch a show from beginning to end without interruptions. People will start watching TV shows the way they read books: a little at a time. . . . The concept of 'appointment television'—arranging to be home at a precise time to watch a particular program—will soon be a thing of the past."[2] Refusing to bow out just yet, the networks want to hold on to appointment viewing by constructing new forms of programming that demand and reward immediate attention, and they want to build up viewer loyalty by intensifying the affective appeal of their programs.

Industry research now suggests that loyals are much more valuable than zappers. According to a study done by Initiative Media, the average network program was identified as a "favorite series" by only 6 percent of its viewers. But, in some cases, as many as 50 or 60 percent of viewers may rank a program as their favorites. Early evidence suggests that these loyals have a higher rate of brand recall (a key concern of advertisers) and are much less likely to be lured away from the networks toward competing cable content (a key concern of programmers). Loyals are twice as likely to pay attention to advertisements and two to three times more likely to remember product categories than more casual viewers. And they are between 5 to 20 percent more likely to recall specific sponsors—not huge numbers, perhaps, but big enough that they can give a competitive edge to advertisers who consistently target shows with a high degree of viewer loyalty. Historically, networks ignored those fan bases in making decisions about renewing series, seeing fans as unrepresentative of the general public; but advertisers are increasingly realizing that they may be better advised investing their dollars behind shows that have a high favorability than shows that have high ratings. As this research impacts programming decisions, the media industry is trying to generate content that will attract loyals, slow down zappers, and turn casuals into fans.

At first glance, *American Idol* looks like it was designed for zappers. Each episode breaks down into bite-size units of only a few minutes' duration as each of the competing performers sings and is judged. To some degree, reality series are built up of "attractions," short, highly emotionally charged units that can be watched in or out of sequence. But the series is designed to support and sustain multiple levels of engagement.

· *American Idol* is designed to pull in every possible viewer and to give each a reason not to change the channel. Many elements loyals find repetitive ensure the program's continued accessibility to casuals—things like the recaps of the previous episodes, the recurring profiles of the contestants, the rereading of key quotes from the judge's assessments. Each of these segments reorient casuals to the contest's basic mechanics or provide the background that's needed to appreciate the dramatic conflicts in that night's episode. As they move into their final weeks and more casuals are drawn into the snowballing phenomenon, *American Idol* and many other reality shows may devote an entire episode to the season's highlights, designed to provide an easy entry point. Beyond this, each episode is constructed to allow a satisfactory entertainment experience. In *American Idol,* each Tuesday night episode includes performances by all of those contestants still in the competition. Each episode also includes a cliffhanger, so *American Idol* viewers are encouraged to tune in the following night to see how the voting went. These unresolved elements are intended to pull casuals toward a more committed relationship.

As for loyals, perhaps the single most important factor separating reality from other kinds of nonfiction programming is serialization. Talent contests are a well-established genre in American broadcasting, going back at least as far as *Major Bowies' Original Amateur Hour* on radio in the 1930s. What *American Idol* added to the mix, however, was the unfolding of the competition across a season, rather than in the course of a single broadcast. Or to be more accurate, serialized

talent competitions had already sprung up on cable networks, such as MTV and VH1, but FOX brought them over to the major networks and made them prime-time entertainment. In serializing the talent competition, *American Idol* is simply following a trend that runs across all contemporary television—a movement away from the self-contained episodes that dominated broadcasting for its first several decades in favor of longer and more complicated program arcs and more elaborate appeals to series history. Serialization rewards the competency and mastery of loyals. The reason loyals watch every episode isn't simply that they enjoy them; they need to have seen every episode to make sense of long-term developments.

Every reality series starts out with a cast larger than most audience members can grasp and most of those characters will receive relatively limited airtime. As the winnowing process occurs, however, certain characters will emerge as audience favorites, and a good producer anticipates those interests and rewards them by providing those characters with more airtime. Viewers move from thinking of the characters as generic types toward thinking of the characters as particular individuals. Viewers get to know the contestants, learn their personality, their motives for competing, their backgrounds, and, in some cases, other members of their families. In *American Idol,* viewers watch them improve or crash and burn. This may be why *American Idol* has become such a powerful marketing tool for launching the careers of young performers compared to earlier televised talent competition.

TALK AMONG YOURSELVES!

There has historically been a tendency within industry discourse to focus either on mass, undifferentiated audiences (of the kinds that get measured by the ratings system) or individual consumers. Marketing researchers now speak about "brand communities," trying to better understand why some groups of consumers form intense bonds with the product and, through the product, with fellow consumers. In one study that helped to define the concept of "brand community," marketing professors Albert M. Muniz Jr. and Thomas C. O'Guinn concluded: "Brand communities carry out important functions on behalf of the brand, such as sharing information, perpetuating the history and culture of the brand, and providing assistance [to other users.] They provide social structure to the relationship between marketers and consumer. Communities exert pressure on members to remain loyal to the collective and to the brand."[3] These brand ethnographers research specific groups of highly committed consumers (such as Harley-Davidson riders, Apple Computer users, or Saturn drivers) or what they call "brandfests," social events (either commercially sponsored or grassroots) that pull together large numbers of consumers.

As these brand communities move online, they are able to sustain these social connections over long periods and thus to intensify the role the community plays in their purchasing decisions; they expand the number of potential consumers who interact with the community and help to move casual consumers into a more intense engagement with the product. Marketing professor Robert Kozinets sees these online consumption communities, whether focused on a single product or a cluster of related products (coffee, wine, cigars), as places "where groups of consumers with similar interests actively seek and exchange information about prices, quality, manufacturers, retailers, company ethics, company history, product history, and other consumption-related characteristics."[4] In short, they are something like Pierre Lévy's knowledge communities applied to consumer decision making. Participation within such communities does not simply reaffirm their brand affiliation but also empowers these groups to assert their own demands on the company. As Kozinets explains, "Loyal consumers are creating their tastes together as a community. This is a revolutionary change. Online, consumers evaluate quality together. They negotiate consumption standards. Moderating product meanings, they brand and rebrand together. Individuals place great weight on the judgment of their fellow community of consumption members. . . . Collective responses temper individual reception of marketing communications. . . . Organizations of consumers can make successful demands on marketers that individual consumers can not."[5]

Just as the social dynamic of these online communities reaffirm and/or redefine their individual members' brand loyalties, a similar social dynamic shapes the ways people consume media and products within their families or with friends. A team of researchers from MIT's Comparative Media Studies Program and Initiative Media joined forces to document audience response to the second season of *American Idol*.[6] The MIT team sent researchers into homes and dorm rooms to observe people watching television; we did one-on-one interviews with a range of different consumers; we did surveys through the official *American Idol* Web sites; and we monitored discussions within the fan community. The Initiative team ran large-scale surveys and focus groups and collected aggregate data from the official *Idol*-on-FOX home page. We wanted to better understand how people integrated the experience of watching *American Idol* into the rest of their social interactions.

The Initiative Media/MIT research team found that in almost every social space where *American Idol* was watched, viewers of different degrees of commitment were present.

In one family setting, for example, the two youngest children (girl, 9; boy, 7) were among the first into the family room for the start of *American Idol;* they generally watched the last few minutes of *Lizzie McGuire* (Disney, 2001) before turning the channel to FOX, As the program started, both routinely raised their voices to announce to those throughout the house that "it's starting!" As the opening segments began, they recalled last week's performances and made comments about what the judges are wearing or how their hair looks. By the end of the first segment, the mother had usually arrived and stood at the door. Typically, she would come and go for the first thirty minutes of the program, working in the kitchen or running up and down the stairs. Such distracted viewing is fairly common for women; even those fairly committed to the program must respond to competing demands on their attention in the early evening hours.[7] The father would typically enter the broadcast in progress and the older daughter would only occasionally view the program, allowing other family members to bring her up to speed as needed. The son's attention would wander during the commercial break and he would begin to zap around the dial and they might miss the start of the next program segment unless the mother and daughter called him back to FOX on time. Finally, as the entire family was sitting in front of the television during *American Idol's* recap in the last five minutes of the program, they would debate the contestant before the mother would call in the vote. The conversation never ended in disagreement, although in later weeks the young girl became more vocal about whom she expected to win, waffling between Ruben and Clay. The father took it all in and endorsed the family's choice based on the snippets of performance he saw in the recap.

Through family conversation, the loyals pulled the casuals into the fold and held on to the attention of the would-be zapper; they announced when the program was on and updated those who have missed segments. In the absence of such reinforcement, some of the family members probably would not return each week, yet even the most casual participants see watching the series as a family ritual. One of the effects of expanding audience participation is to give such families more different ways to engage with the content; discussing who to vote for becomes part of the viewing experience and provides an incentive for everyone to watch the recap if not the individual performances. Researchers have found that such shared rituals or mutual evaluations are central to the sense of affiliation members feel to the group, and it makes sense that similar rituals would be played out in individual households.[8] *American Idol* can become family entertainment because it lies at the intersection between youth and adult tastes, allowing everyone to show some expertise. Most of the contestants are in their teens or twenties. To broaden its focus, the show brings in aging pop stars as guest judges and coaches: Burt Bacharach, Billy Joel, and Olivia Newton-John appeal not to the kids who compete but to their parents'—or even their grandparents'—generation.

The researchers who observed college students watching *American Idol* in a dorm common area found similar patterns: different students had different investments in the various contestants and carried on debates from week to week about their relative merits. Catch phrases might be dropped ironically into the conversation. People who had missed some episodes could reenter the series with the help of their friends because they knew the rules of the competition and had some passing familiarity with the contestants. Some people wandered into the commons area with no prior plans of watching the series and got sucked in. The number of committed viewers grew week by week as the competition mounted and as watching the series became more central to the social life of the dorm community. Interestingly, the final episodes conflicted with final exams, so the group taped them, made a pact not to look at the results, and scheduled time to watch them together.

Across a range of studies, Initiative Media has found that different genres of entertainment provoke different degrees or kinds of social interactions. Drama viewers are the most likely to view alone, comedy to view with family members, and reality viewers to view with friends. Demographically, 18–34-year-old viewers have the most varied habits, depending on program genre. Adults over 50 either view alone or with family, but rarely with friends, while 35–49-year-olds are most consistent, viewing all genres primarily with family members. People watching in groups pay more attention to the program content, are less likely to shift channels mid-broadcast, and are more likely to access program-related Web sites. Of course, as those viewers move onto the Web, some are choosing to discuss their interpretations and assessments of the programs via online fan communities. Social viewing, then, would appear to be an important driver behind brand and content extension.

A survey of 13,280 *American Idol* viewers, conducted through the official FOX Web site, found that the majority of fans discovered the series on the basis of word-of-mouth and watched it regularly because other people they knew were also watching it. (On the zapper side of the equation, the same study found that significantly more viewers stumbled onto the series while channel-surfing than tuned in consciously on the basis of prior awareness.) While historically men make the viewing decisions during the primetime hours, only slightly more women (32 percent) than men (31 percent) said they started watching the show because other family members were watching it. Altogether, 78 percent of *American Idol* viewers surveyed said that they watched the show with family or friends, and 74 percent reported that they talked about the show with friends during the week between episodes.

Such conversations extended beyond the initial viewing group to friends, workmates, or more distanced relatives. As one respondent told us, "My mother lives in Africa, my aunt lives in Russia, but they are able to watch the show on the Armed Forces Network over the weekend. My other aunts, scattered about the country, will create tests and drop stupid hints that all come clear when they finally get to watch the show. It's a family viewing occurrence, which I don't usually have the opportunity to do." Even if they missed individual episodes, study participants made a conscious effort to keep up with developments to participate in casual conversations with peers and coworkers. Consequently, many more people know about *American Idol,* follow its development, and even get exposed to its marketing message than actually sit down and watch.

Phone companies, across the board, observed a marked increase in traffic on Tuesday nights following the broadcasts. In the third season's final week, Verizon reported an increase of 116 million calls, a 7 percent increase over a typical Tuesday, and SBC saw 100 million more calls, an 80 percent increase over a normal weeknight.[9] In all likelihood, this increase was not simply stimulated by the large number of people who were voting, but also indicates the number of people chatting about the program content.

HOW GOSSIP FUELS CONVERGENCE

One of the survey respondents captures the spirit of these conversations: "[Watching *American Idol*] helps me to relax because it gives me something to talk about with friends that doesn't effect our lives in any big way; therefore, it is an easy thing to discuss." Historically, gossip has been dismissed as "worthless and idle chatter," but over the past several decades, feminist scholars have begun to reappraise the place of gossip in women's community, and subsequent writers have extended it to talk about interactions within a much broader range of communities. Writing in 1980, Deborah Jones described gossip as "a way of talking between women in their roles as women, intimate in style, personal and domestic in topic and setting."[10] Gossip, she argued, allowed women to talk about their common experiences, share expertise, and reinforce social norms. While the fluidity of gossip makes it difficult to study or document, Jones suggests that gossip is an important resource that women historically have used to connect their personal experiences within a larger sphere beyond their immediate domestic environment. The specific content of gossip is often less important than the social ties created through the exchange of secrets between participants—and for that reason, the social functions of gossip hold when dealing with television content. It isn't who you are talking *about* but who you are talking *with* that matters.

Gossip builds common ground between participants, as those who exchange information assure one another of what they share. Gossip is finally a way of talking about yourself through critiquing the actions and values of others.

As cyberspace broadens the sphere of our social interactions, it becomes even more important to be able to talk about people we share in common via the media than people from our local community who will not be known by all of the participants in an online conversation. Into that space step the complex, often contradictory figures who appear on reality television. Reality television provides consumers with a steady stream of ethical dramas, as contestants are forced to make choices about whom to trust and what limits to set on their own behavior. Viewers can argue about whether Joe Millionaire picked the right woman or The Donald fired the right apprentice, whether it's OK to lie your way to success on *Survivor,* and whether Clay, Ruben, or Kimberley sang best on *American Idol.* In a focus group study of reality television viewers conducted by Initiative Media, 60.9 percent of the respondents said that the ethical conduct of the contestants was a central topic of their discussions around such series. By way of contrast, 67 percent discussed the outcomes, 35 percent discussed strategies, and 64 percent discussed personalities. Rather than being morally debasing, ethically dubious on-air conduct frequently encourages a public discussion of ethics and morality that reaffirms much more conservative values and assumptions. In a multicultural society, talking through differences in values becomes a mechanism by which different social groups can learn more about how they each see the world, so there is a real value in gossip that extends into virtual rather than face-to-face communities. The reality contestants put themselves forward to be judged by their audience; and through their judgments, the audience reaffirms their own shared values by expressing outrage over their social transgressions, and they learn about their differences by sharing notes about how they respond to shared ethical dramas.

American Idol viewers debate whether the contest should be decided on the basis of "pure talent," or whether it is legitimate to draw on other factors, such as personality or appearance, which are often key to defining commercial success. Consider, for example, the self-righteous indignation expressed by one *American Idol* viewer who wrote to the CMS/Initiative Media research team convinced that we had a direct pipeline back to the producers. This message followed an episode where fan favorite and ultimate winner Ruben Studdard unexpectedly ranked near the bottom:

> Do you really think the American public believes for one second that Ruben could possibly be voted into the bottom? Ruben has never had one negative comment said about him nor has he ever not been excellent. He has never missed a tune. . . . It is very cruel to mislead these young people into trusting you are going to be honest and fair. This is a talent show, isn't it? Hence the word TALENT SHOW. . . . So do the right thing and seriously look at who is counting those votes and maybe check to see if they actually know how to count. If you are rigging the show you will probably burn in hell for being so stupid. (A true and honest American).

What was striking to us about this comment, apart from its cynicism about the voting process, was its moral intensity; its firm belief that the outcome of a talent competition should be read in terms of questions or justice, honesty, and equity. Another respondent referenced her "responsibility" to monitor the results to see "whether America has chosen and voted fairly . . . whether or not America really votes based on real talents or just tits and asses."

Assessment is a two-part process: first, discussions about the performances, and then discussions about the outcomes. Among the most committed and socially linked members of a consumption community, these evaluative standards are arrived at collectively, just as the members of the family we described pooled their individual tastes to make a collective decision about who should win. Such a process tends to pull toward a consensus over time, and then, over a longer time, the consensus no longer seems to be something that was disputed or haggled over; it is the commonsense outcome. We can see this as part of the process through which collective intelligence generates shared knowledge. Some critics, such as Cass Sunstein, argue that this process of consensus formation tends to decrease the diversity of perspectives that any community member encounters; people tend to flock toward groups that share their existing biases, and over time they hear less and less disagreement about those core assumptions.[11] At the same time, this consensus-forming process increases the likelihood that these brand and fan communities will speak up when corporate interests cross the group's consensus. In the course of a season of *American Idol,* total consensus may not have been achieved, but most members of the online community saw season 2 as a contest between Clay and Ruben, making the buildup toward the season finale that much more powerful. The community expressed outrage, however, when voting went against the perceived consensus, as occurred one week when Ruben was almost bumped (the incident provoking the above response) or as occurred frequently throughout the third season.

Because the characters are real people whose lives continue beyond the series borders, viewers are left feeling like there is more and more they might know about them, which provides an incentive to track down additional information through multiple media channels. This search for the hidden "truth" of reality television is what motivated the spoiling described in chapter 2. The Initiative Media survey found that 45 percent of *American Idol's* loyals went onto the Web in search of more information about the program, and it is generally agreed that reality television is one of the primary drivers of traffic to network Web sites.

These networks build upon synergies within the entertainment corporations to ensure that talk about their hit reality series continues throughout the week. The contestants are featured prominently on morning and late-night talk shows and on network affiliated chatrooms. The results of at least the top rated reality series are seen as news events that will be covered even by rival networks. In the case of *American Idol,* for example, *USA Today, Entertainment Weekly,* and AOL each conducted its own independent audience surveys designed to second-guess the likely results before they are aired in the network. Online gossip magazines, such as *The Smoking Gun,* have sought to tap public interest of the series, digging out old criminal records or divorce proceedings involving contestants. In some cases, reality series market access to exclusive content which further expands the viewing experience. Given the pervasiveness and diversity of such publicity, any given fan is apt to know something his friends do not, thus creating an incentive to share knowledge.

This publicity also has the effect of making some viewers more apt to want to watch the episodes as they are aired so they can avoid finding out the outcomes in a less dramatically compelling fashion. For other consumers, such coverage keeps their interest alive even if they are unable to watch some installments and makes it more likely they will tune in for the final episodes of a particular run.

CONTESTING THE VOTE

So far, we have focused our discussion on those factors that ensure viewer loyalty to *American Idol,* but as Heyer's speech suggests, sponsors are seeking to transfer viewer loyalty from entertainment properties onto their brands. The majority of the people our research team interviewed were acutely aware that *American Idol* was serving as a testing ground for branding strategies and were eager to offer their opinions about the experiments as they unfolded. Product placements and program-themed commercials became an acknowledged part of the *American Idol* phenomenon, something people, in some cases, tuned in to see—much as the Super Bowl has become as much a showcase for advertising as a sporting event. Coca-Cola spoofed the uncompromising honesty of judge Simon Cowell, depicting him as forced by a mobster to read an endorsement for Vanilla Coke; Ford created new musical segments each week featuring the program contestants; AT&T created a campaign that mimicked *Legally Blonde* (2001) and showed an air-headed teenager going around the country encouraging people to participate in the call-in voting process. Sponsors are not simply seeking the chance to advertise their products; they are seeking to brand the content so that the red of the *American Idol* set becomes inseparable from Coca-Cola's sponsorship of the series, so that the Ford spots featuring the contestants becomes part of the evidence fans mobilize in support of their favorite performers, and so that AT&T's text-messaging system becomes the preferred vehicle for voting.

NOTES

1. Phillip Swann, *TV.Com: How Television Is Shaping Our Future* (New York: TV Books, 2000), pp. 9–10.
2. Ibid., p. 31.
3. Albert M. Muniz Jr. and Thomas C. O'Guinn, "Brand Community," *Journal of Consumer Research*, March 2001, p. 427.
4. Kozinets, "E-Tribalized Marketing?" p. 10.
5. Ibid., p. 12.
6. Preliminary findings were reported in David Ernst, Stacey Lynn Koerner, Henry Jenkins, Sangita Shresthova, Brian Thiesen, and Alex Chisholm, "Walking the Path: Exploring the Drivers of Expression," presented at the Advertising Research Foundation/ESOMAR Conference, June 2003.
7. David Morley, *Family Television: Cultural Power and Domestic Leisure* (London: Routledge, 1996).
8. James H. McAlexander, John W. Schouten, and Harold F. Koenig, "Building Brand Community," *Journal of Marketing*, January 2002, pp. 38–54.
9. Deborah Starr Seibel, "*American Idol* Outrage: Your Vote Doesn't Count," *Broadcasting & Cable*, May 17, 2004, p. 1.
10. Deborah Jones, "Gossip: Note on Women's Oral Culture," *Women's Studies International Quarterly* 3 (1980): 194–195.
11. Cass Sunstein, *Republic.Com* (Princeton, N.J.: Princeton University Press, 2002).

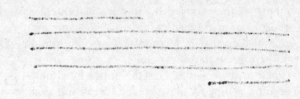

PART EIGHT

New Media and Old in the Information Age

The ENIAC, an early analog computer. *"Collections of The University of Pennsylvania Archives."*

Our final section deals with the computer, now in its seventh decade of development, and the internet. Hazarding judgment on the consequences of this medium for our own time and for an immediate future most of us will live to see is no easy task. The electronic computer marks the development of a technology which, like moveable type printing, has influenced and in turn been influenced by other technologies—hence the title of this section. Computers got their start in large organizations, aiding administration, scientific research, and the military. Following the development of microchip technology in the seventies, computer circuitry permeated industry and commerce and became a mainstay of household appliances, from stoves to television sets and games. With the emergence of the personal computer, an individual working at home now has access to information-processing capacities that previously had been the sole preserve of large institutions. Today we are witnessing the rapid proliferation of networks—best typified by the global internet, corporate intranets, and the World Wide Web—permitting an expanding range of administrative uses, research, education, public expression, art, social activity and commerce.

In order to understand the implications of all of this we can draw upon insights from past media revolutions. We know, for instance, that new media frequently bypass difficulties, bottlenecks or barriers encountered in older media. In the later Middle Ages, for instance, print helped democratize the reading public. It lessened the control over literacy exercised by scribes and religious orders. The resulting changes profoundly reorganized the ways in which knowledge circulated in society. Likewise, in the promotion of electronic communications in the twentieth century, such as broadcasting has led researchers to see an equivalent bypassing of the institution of the book and the newspaper in providing access to information. Perhaps one of the most controversial areas of the bypass effect with computers was the use of hand-held calculators in the classroom to circumvent traditional memory-based mathematical operations. As Walter Ong has pointed out, there are intriguing parallels here with Plato's critique of writing as an "artificial" aid, one which Plato argued could lead to the erosion of mental capacities, specifically memory.

Despite the dramatic implications of the computer today, we must not forget that aspects of it have been formed from traditional ways of structuring information found in previous media. The computer program is a case in point. Morse code was also a program, one that standardized the transmission of telegraphic messages. Likewise, vernacular grammars and Arabic numbers were programs that facilitated the use and accelerated the influence of the printing press. The index in printed books is yet another example. The index gave rise to the text as a work of reference. The resulting dictionaries, encyclopedias, and manuals of grammar helped promote the use of standardized classification systems for knowledge. These reference works can be compared to contemporary electronic databases, such as google, for the storage and retrieval of a wide range of knowledge and information.

In terms not just of the storage and retrieval, but the movement of military, industrial, and commercial information, the computer can be compared to the telegraph's creation of a "wired world". The computer based linking of stock markets and currency exchanges on a global basis recalls the telegraph's role in transforming the commodity price and marketing system of a century ago. And just as the earlier systems of railway traffic regulation and forward ordering depended on telegraphy, so tightly linked systems such as air traffic and inventory controls are increasingly dependent on the coordinating capabilities of the computer.

In our first selection, "The Control Revolution," the communications historian James Beniger proposes that the computer's greatest impact has been on other media. He argues that the capacity of the computer to digitize the output of all other communication and information media will make it into a new "generalized medium" in the twenty-first century. This is because computers can treat previously discrete forms of communication as technically the same. Thus, numbers, words, pictures, and sounds can be coded digitally by the computer, stored, or transmitted, then reproduced on demand in a virtual facsimile of the original. This convergence of our previously discrete representational systems of textual and audio-visual materials signals major changes in how such materials will be categorized, catalogued, and stored in the future.

Monopolies are a recurring theme in media developments, and monopolies of communication and information—whether technological or organization based—seldom enjoy unfettered power. Rather they are constantly threatened by change and competition, chaotic developments, and the rise of alternative resources. We might point to the role of cable television and satellites as decentralizing forces in disrupting the television monopoly that had been established in the United States by the 1960s—and of course in many other parts of the world. We could point to audio and video cassettes during the seventies in much the same spirit, as overcoming the fixed time regimes of listening and viewing and providing an alternative as well to the previous impermanency of broadcast products. Closer to the present, new portable media players and wireless telephony raise yet other examples. We should also keep in mind the role that amateurs have played in providing crucial support for electronic communications and computing, which resonates with what others in this text have said of earlier media development. As an example, we could point to the Homebrew Computer Club, from which the world of personal computing directly emerges in the 1980s.

Lev Manovich extends Beniger's thesis of a new generalized media, suggesting that new media are now emerging from the capabilities of the computer to transform both the presentation and distribution of media. For him, web sites, virtual worlds, virtual reality, multimedia, computer games, and computer animation all qualify as forms of new media; and together will eventually reshape the visual language used by contemporary culture. Manovich also stresses the historical continuities between old and new media. In his excerpt, "How Media Became New," he suggests some historical continuities between the computer and photography, noting for instance that one of the earliest models for the computer, the nineteenth century Jacquard loom, which used punch cards to control the pattern of the weave and could in fact weave images, can be seen as an early image synthesizer, one that seems to prefigure the visual preoccupations of twentieth century media.

We could also point to some provocative links between computers and print. As many of our excerpts have shown, the conventions that surround the prevailing media at any time are in part the result of limitations in what that media can do. Thus the computer seems destined to have major consequences for the printed word, perhaps most directly in reshaping the ways in which we access information, dramatically improving capabilities for retrieving information. We may still depend upon intermediaries to find what we want, but the written goods are no longer tied primarily to the physical form of the book, the newspaper, or the journal. Even the library as the ultimate warehousing system for words of all kinds may itself take on an altered if still critical role in orientating us to these new informational spaces and as a source for guidance and investigative resources.

Our next selection focuses upon the most obvious example of a new media space or environment, the internet itself. The history of the internet is only now getting the attention it deserves. Janet Abbate's work stresses that the internet is the product of many players and is a tale of collaborations and conflicts worthy of a Shakespearean drama. Her excerpt, "The Popularizing of the Internet," carefully places the development of the internet and its supporting technologies in an international context, showing how the internet grew from powerful synergies that transcended borders, boundaries, and barriers placed in the way of its development. The World Wide Web, she argues, continues that trend, and she points out some similarities with the internet's earlier history.

In our next essay, Jay David Bolter and Richard Grusin offer a perspective on perhaps the most successful internet format, that of the World Wide Web. Bolter and Grusin echo Marshall McLuhan's provocative aphorism that old media tend to become the content of new media. However, they deepen the logic considerably by inviting us to consider the interconnectedness of media old and new. Their idea of "remediation" is intended to alert us to the ways in which media continually borrow from and refashion the representations of older media: but also the countervailing tendency, in which older media in turn can borrow from and refashion emerging media. We can see, for example, in the development of electronic versions of print publications—as well as in blogging, podcasts, twitter and the use of portable handheld devices—some of the ways newspapers and television continue to adopt and adapt to the audio-visual attributes of the Web. The popular appeal of the World Wide Web, Bolter and Grusin argue, arises from the way in which it plays with the interconnection of text and image. In their treatment of older media there is also an appreciation for the emergent possibilities within those older forms. They see, for instance, in the illuminated manuscripts of the Middle Ages and early twentieth century photomontages a prototype for the hypermedia windowing environment of the Web.

Bolter and Grusin's essay stands as a useful caution for us today when so many aspect of new media are presented as revolutionary breaks with the past. Although the computer and the internet have combined in the last decade to produce a powerful and provocative form of electronic communication, this new media does not yet have a settled shape.

As Manuel Castells and his co-authors show in our final entry the term mobile communications is somewhat of a misnomer. The important feature of new wireless technologies is not, as in the wireless of old, that they move with us through time and space, but in their connectivity. Their dominant feature is the links they provide to the various elective networks with which we surround ourselves. The authors note that these devices blur rather than transcend space and time while being used for everything from dating to rallying movements for political dissent. Of particular note is how the authors assess some of the differences between the adoption of these technologies in the United States and the rest of the world. What wireless devices do you employ and how do you see that usage in light of the analysis provided in this chapter?

The internet, like the other communications media we have explored in the previous sections, both enables new forms of human action and expression at the same time it disables others. This has been a recurring theme in many of the contributions. The conclusion Harold Innis drew from his analysis of the role of writing in the early civilizations of the

Middle East seems applicable to the contemporary convergence of computers with electronically enhanced expression and experience. Media, Innis proposed, can never be truly neutral within the human environment. By their very application media refashion the choices, the preoccupations, and the interaction of individuals, groups, nations and societies; and media give shape to the form that information and knowledge take in society and to the ways in which they circulate. In turn, of course, every society can shape and give direction, within limits, to the media that develop. This perspective is a fitting final formulation for students of media, a reminder that our exploration of media change must always be joined to an appreciation of their ongoing social consequences.

CHAPTER 37

The Control Revolution

James Beniger

James Beniger is professor of communications at the University of Southern California. His book The Control Revolution *is widely regarded as an important theoretical and historical investigation of technology's role in the management of industrial society.*

Few turn-of-the-century observers understood even isolated aspects of the societal transformation—what I shall call the "Control Revolution"—then gathering momentum in the United States, England, France, and Germany. Notable among those who did was Max Weber (1864–1920), the German sociologist and political economist who directed social analysis to the most important control technology of his age: bureaucracy. Although bureaucracy had developed several times independently in ancient civilizations, Weber was the first to see it as the critical new machinery—new, at least, in its generality and pervasiveness—for control of the societal forces unleashed by the Industrial Revolution.

For a half-century after Weber's initial analysis bureaucracy continued to reign as the single most important technology of the Control Revolution. After World War II, however, generalized control began to shift slowly to computer technology. If social change has seemed to accelerate in recent years (as argued, for example, by Toffler 1971), that has been due in large part to a spate of new information-processing, communication, and control technologies like the computer, most notably the microprocessors that have proliferated since the early 1970s. Such technologies are more properly seen, however, not as causes but as consequences of societal change, as natural extensions of the Control Revolution already in progress for more than a century.

Revolution, a term borrowed from astronomy, first appeared in political discourse in seventeenth-century England, where it described the restoration of a previous form of government. Not until the French Revolution did the word acquire its currently popular and opposite meaning, that of abrupt and often violent change. As used here in Control Revolution, the term is intended to have both of these opposite connotations.

Beginning most noticeably in the United States in the late nineteenth century, the Control Revolution was certainly a dramatic if not abrupt discontinuity in technological advance. Indeed, even the word *revolution* seems barely adequately to describe the development, within the span of a single lifetime, of virtually all of the basic communication technologies still in use a century later: photography and telegraphy (1830s), rotary power printing (1840s), the typewriter (1860s), transatlantic cable (1866), telephone (1876), motion pictures (1894), wireless telegraphy (1895), magnetic tape recording (1899), radio (1906), and television (1923).

Along with these rapid changes in mass media and telecommunications technologies, the Control Revolution also represented the beginning of a restoration—although with increasing centralization—of the economic and political control that was lost at more local levels of society during the Industrial Revolution. Before this time, control of government and markets had depended on personal relationships and face-to-face interactions; now control came to be reestablished by means of bureaucratic organization, the new infrastructures of transportation and telecommunications, and system-wide communication via the new mass media. By both of the opposite definitions of *revolution,* therefore, the new societal transformations— rapid innovation in information and control technology, to regain control of functions once contained at much lower and more diffuse levels of society—constituted a true revolution in societal control.

Here the word *control* represents its most general definition, purposive influence toward a predetermined goal. Most dictionary definitions imply these same two essential elements: *influence* of one agent over another, meaning that the former causes changes in the behavior of the latter; and *purpose,* in the sense that influence is directed toward some prior goal of the controlling agent. If the definition used here differs at all from colloquial ones, it is only because many people reserve the word *control* for its more determinate manifestations, what I shall call "strong control." Dictionaries, for example, often include in their definitions of control concepts like direction, guidance, regulation, command, and domination, approximate synonyms of *influence* that vary mainly in increasing determination. As a more general concept, however, *control* encompasses the entire range from absolute control to the weakest and most probabilistic form, that is, any purposive influence on behavior, *however slight.* Economists say that television advertising serves to control specific demand, for example, and political scientists say that direct mail campaigns can help to control issue-voting, even though only a small fraction of the intended audience may be influenced in either case.

Inseparable from the concept of control are the twin activities of information processing and reciprocal communication, complementary factors in any form of control. Information processing is essential to all purposive activity, which is by definition goal directed and must therefore involve the continual comparison of current states to future goals, a basic problem of information processing. So integral to control is this comparison of inputs to stored programs that the word *control* itself derives from the medieval Latin verb *contrarotulare,* to compare something "against the rolls," the cylinders of paper that served as official records in ancient times.

Simultaneously with the comparison of inputs to goals, two-way interaction between controller and controlled must also occur, not only to communicate influence from the former to the latter, but also to communicate back the results of this action (hence the term *feedback* for this reciprocal flow of information back to a controller). So central is communication to the process of control that the two have become the joint subject of the modern science of cybernetics, defined by one of its founders as "the entire field of control and communication theory, whether in the machine or in the animal" (Wiener 1948, p. 11). Similarly, the pioneers of mathematical communication theory have defined the object of their study as purposive control in the broadest sense: communication, according to Shannon and Weaver (1949, pp. 3–5), includes "all of the procedures by which one mind may affect another"; they note that "communication either affects conduct or is without any discernible and probable effect at all."

Because both the activities of information processing and communication are inseparable components of the control function, a society's ability to maintain control—at all levels from interpersonal to international relations—will be directly proportional to the development of its information technologies. Here the term *technology* is intended not in the narrow sense of practical or applied science but in the more general sense of any intentional extension of a natural process, that is, of the processing of matter, energy, and information that characterizes all living systems. Respiration is a wholly natural life function, for example, and is therefore not a technology; the human ability to breathe under water, by contrast, implies some technological extension. Similarly, voting is one general technology for achieving collective decisions in the control of social aggregates; the Australian ballot is a particular innovation in this technology.

Technology may therefore be considered as roughly equivalent to that which can be done, excluding only those capabilities that occur naturally in living systems. This distinction is usually although not always clear. One ambiguous case is language, which may have developed at least in part through purposive innovation but which now appears to be a mostly innate capability of the human brain. The brain itself represents another ambiguous case: it probably developed in interaction with purposive tool use and may therefore be included among human technologies.

Because technology defines the limits on what a society *can* do, technological innovation might be expected to be a major impetus to social change in the Control Revolution no less than in the earlier societal transformations accorded the status of revolutions. The Neolithic Revolution, for example, which brought the first permanent settlements, owed its origin to the refinement of stone tools and the domestication of plants and animals. The Commercial Revolution, following exploration of Africa, Asia, and the New World, resulted directly from technical improvements in seafaring and navigational equipment. The Industrial Revolution, which eventually brought the nineteenth-century crisis of control, began a century earlier with greatly increased use of coal and steam power and a spate of new machinery for the manufacture of cotton textiles. Like these earlier revolutions in matter and energy processing, the Control Revolution resulted from innovation at a most fundamental level of technology—that of information processing.

Information processing may be more difficult to appreciate than matter or energy processing because information is epiphenomenal: it derives from the *organization* of the material world on which it is wholly dependent for its existence. Despite being in this way higher order or derivative of matter and energy, information is no less critical to society. All living systems must process matter and energy to maintain themselves

counter to entropy, the universal tendency of organization toward breakdown and randomization. Because control is necessary for such processing, and information, as we have seen, is essential to control, both information processing and communication, insofar as they distinguish living systems from the inorganic universe, might be said to define life itself—except for a few recent artifacts of our own species.

Each new technological innovation extends the processes that sustain life, thereby increasing the need for control and hence for improved control technology. This explains why technology appears autonomously to beget technology in general (Winner 1977), and why, as argued here, innovations in matter and energy processing create the need for further innovation in information-processing and communication technologies. Because technological innovation is increasingly a collective, cumulative effort, one whose results must be taught and diffused, it also generates an increased need for technologies of information storage and retrieval—as well as for their elaboration in systems of technical education and communication—quite independently of the particular need for control.

As in the earlier revolutions in matter and energy technologies, the nineteenth-century revolution in information technology was predicated on, if not directly caused by, social changes associated with earlier innovations. Just as the Commercial Revolution depended on capital and labor freed by advanced agriculture, for example, and the Industrial Revolution presupposed a commercial system for capital allocations and the distribution of goods, the most recent technological revolution developed in response to problems arising out of advanced industrialization—an ever-mounting crisis of control.

NEW CONTROL TECHNOLOGY

The rapid development of rationalization and bureaucracy in the middle and late nineteenth century led to a succession of dramatic new information-processing and communication technologies. These innovations served to contain the control crisis of industrial society in what can be treated as three distinct areas of economic activity: production, distribution, and consumption of goods and services.

Control of production was facilitated by the continuing organization and preprocessing of industrial operations. Machinery itself came increasingly to be controlled by two new information-processing technologies: closed-loop feedback devices like James Watt's steam governor (1788) and preprogrammed open-loop controllers like those of the Jacquard loom (1801). By 1890 Herman Hollerith had extended Jacquard's punch cards to tabulation of U.S. census data. This information-processing technology survives to this day—if just barely—owing largely to the corporation to which Hollerith's innovation gave life, International Business Machines (IBM). Further rationalization and control of production advanced through an accumulation of other industrial innovations: interchangeable parts (after 1800), integration of production within factories (1820s and 1830s), the development of modern accounting techniques (1850s and 1860s), professional managers (1860s and 1870s), continuous-process production (late 1870s and early 1880s), the "scientific management" of Frederick Winslow Taylor (1911), Henry Ford's modern assembly line (after 1913), and statistical quality control (1920s), among many others.

The resulting flood of mass-produced goods demanded comparable innovation in control of a second area of the economy: distribution. Growing infrastructures of transportation, including rail networks, steamship lines, and urban traction systems, depended for control on a corresponding infrastructure of information processing and telecommunications. Within fifteen years after the opening of the pioneering Baltimore and Ohio Railroad in 1830, for example, Samuel F. B. Morse—with a congressional appropriation of $30,000—had linked Baltimore to Washington, D.C., by means of a telegraph. Eight years later, in

1852, thirteen thousand miles of railroad and twenty-three thousand miles of telegraph line were in operation (Thompson 1947; U.S. Bureau of the Census 1975, p. 731), and the two infrastructures continued to coevolve in a web of distribution and control that progressively bound the entire continent. In the words of business historian Alfred Chandler, "The railroad permitted a rapid increase in the speed and decrease in the cost of long-distance, written communication, while the invention of the telegraph created an even greater transformation by making possible almost instantaneous communication at great distances. The railroad and the telegraph marched across the continent in unison . . . The telegraph companies used the railroad for their rights-of-way, and the railroad used the services of the telegraph to coordinate the flow of trains and traffic" (1977, p. 195).

This coevolution of the railroad and telegraph systems fostered the development of another communication infrastructure for control of mass distribution and consumption: the postal system. Aided by the introduction in 1847 of the first federal postage stamp, itself an important innovation in control of the national system of distribution, the total distance mail moved more than doubled in the dozen years between Morse's first telegraph and 1857, when it reached 75 million miles—almost a third covered by rail (Chandler 1977, p. 195). Commercialization of the telephone in the 1880s, and especially the development of long-distance lines in the 1890s, added a third component to the national infrastructure of telecommunications.

Controlled by means of this infrastructure, an organizational system rapidly emerged for the distribution of mass production to national and world markets. Important innovations in the rationalization and control of this system included the commodity dealer and standardized grading of commodities (1850s), the department store, chain store, and wholesale jobber (1860s), monitoring of movements of inventory or "stock turn" (by 1870), the mail-order house (1870s), machine packaging (1890s), franchising (by 1911 the standard means of distributing automobiles), and the supermarket and mail-order chain (1920s). After World War I the instability in national and world markets that Durkheim had noted a quarter-century earlier came to be gradually controlled, largely because of the new telecommunications infrastructure and the reorganization of distribution on a societal scale.

Mass production and distribution cannot be completely controlled, however, without control of a third area of the economy: demand and consumption. Such control requires a means to communicate information about goods and services to national audiences in order to stimulate or reinforce demand for these products; at the same time, it requires a means to gather information on the preferences and behavior of this audience—reciprocal feedback to the controller from the controlled (although the consumer might justifiably see these relationships as reversed).

The mechanism for communicating information to a national audience of consumers developed with the first truly mass medium: power-driven, multiple-rotary printing and mass mailing by rail. At the outset of the Industrial Revolution, most printing was still done on wooden handpresses—using flat plates tightened by means of screws—that differed little from the one Gutenberg had used three centuries earlier. Steam power was first successfully applied to printing in Germany in 1810; by 1827 it was possible to print up to 2,500 pages in an hour. In 1893 the New York *World* printed 96,000 eight-page copies every hour—a 300-fold increase in speed in just seventy years.

The postal system, in addition to effecting and controlling distribution, also served, through bulk mailings of mass-produced publications, as a new medium of mass communication. By 1887 Montgomery Ward mailed throughout the continent a 540-page catalog listing more than 24,000 items. Circulation of the Sears and Roebuck catalog increased from 318,000 in 1897 (the first year for which figures are available) to more than 1 million

in 1904, 2 million in 1905, 3 million in 1907, and 7 million by the late 1920s. In 1927 alone, Sears mailed 10 million circular letters, 15 million general catalogs (spring and fall editions), 23 million sales catalogs, plus other special catalogs—a total mailing of 75 million (Boorstin 1973, p. 128) or approximately one piece for every adult in the United States.

Throughout the late nineteenth and early twentieth centuries uncounted entrepreneurs and inventors struggled to extend the technologies of communication to mass audiences. Alexander Graham Bell, who patented the telephone in 1876, originally thought that his invention might be used as a broadcast medium to pipe public speeches, music, and news into private homes. Such systems were indeed begun in several countries—the one in Budapest had six thousand subscribers by the turn of the century and continued to operate through World War I (Briggs 1977). More extensive application of telephony to mass communication was undoubtedly stifled by the rapid development of broadcast media beginning with Guglielmo Marconi's demonstration of long-wave telegraphy in 1895. Transatlantic wireless communication followed in 1901, public radio broadcasting in 1906, and commercial radio by 1920; even television broadcasting, a medium not popular until after World War II, had begun by 1923.

Many other communication technologies that we do not today associate with advertising were tried out early in the Control Revolution as means to influence the consumption of mass audiences. Popular books like the novels of Charles Dickens contained special advertising sections. Mass telephone systems in Britain and Hungary carried advertisements interspersed among music and news. The phonograph, patented by Thomas Edison in 1877 and greatly improved by the 1890s in Hans Berliner's "gramophone," became another means by which a sponsor's message could be distributed to households: "Nobody would refuse," the United States Gramophone Company claimed, "to listen to a fine song or concert piece or an oration—even if it is interrupted by a modest remark, 'Tartar's Baking Powder is Best' " (Abott and Rider 1957, p. 387). With the development by Edison of the "motion picture" after 1891, advertising had a new medium, first in the kinetoscope (1893) and cinematograph (1895), which sponsors located in busy public places, and then in the 1900s in films projected in "movie houses." Although advertisers were initially wary of broadcasting because audiences could not be easily identified, by 1930 sponsors were spending $60 million annually on radio in the United States alone (Boorstin 1973, p. 392).

The mass media were not sufficient to effect true control, however, without a means of feedback from potential consumers to advertisers, thereby restoring to the emerging national and world markets what Durkheim had seen as an essential relationship of the earlier segmental markets: communication from consumer to producer to assure that the latter "can easily reckon the extent of the needs to be satisfied" (1893, p. 369). Simultaneously with the development of mass communication by the turn of the century came what might be called *mass feedback* technologies: market research (the idea first appeared as "commercial research" in 1911), including questionnaire surveys of magazine readership, the Audit Bureau of Circulation (1914), house-to-house interviewing (1916), attitudinal and opinion surveys (a U.S. bibliography lists nearly three thousand by 1928), a Census of Distribution (1929), large-scale statistical sampling theory (1930), indices of retail sales (1933), A. C. Nielsen's audiometer monitoring of broadcast audiences (1935), and statistical-sample surveys like the Gallup Poll (1936), to mention just a few of the many new technologies for monitoring consumer behavior.

Although most of the new information technologies originated in the private sector, where they were used to control production, distribution, and consumption of goods and services, their potential for controlling systems at the national and world level was not overlooked by government. Since at least the Roman Empire, where an extensive road system proved equally suited for moving either commerce or troops, communications infrastructures have served to control both economy and polity. As corporate bureaucracy came to control increasingly wider markets by the turn of this century, its power was increasingly checked by a parallel growth in state bureaucracy. Both bureaucracies found useful what Bell has called "intellectual technology":

> The major intellectual and sociological problems of the post-industrial society are . . . those of "organized complexity"—the management of large-scale systems, with large numbers of interacting variables, which have to be coordinated to achieve specific goals . . . An *intellectual technology* is the substitution of algorithms (problem-solving rules) for intuitive judgments. These algorithms may be embodied in an automatic machine or a computer program or a set of instructions based on some statistical or mathematical formula; the statistical and logical techniques that are used in dealing with "organized complexity" are efforts to formalize a set of decision rules. (1973, pp. 29–30)

Seen in this way, intellectual technology is another manifestation of bureaucratic rationality, an extension of what Saint-Simon described as a shift from the government of men to the administration of things, that is, a further move to administration based not on intuitive judgments but on logical and statistical rules and algorithms. Although Bell sees intellectual technology as arising after 1940, state bureaucracies had begun earlier in this century to appropriate many key elements: central economic planning (Soviet Union after 1920), the state fiscal policies of Lord Keynes (late 1920), national income accounting (after 1933), econometrics (mid-1930s), input-output analysis (after 1936), linear programming and statistical decision theory (late 1930s), and operations research and systems analysis (early in World War II).

In the modern state the latest technologies of mass communication, persuasion, and market research are also used to stimulate and control demand for governmental services. The U.S. government, for example, currently spends about $150 million a year on advertising, which places it among the top thirty advertisers in the country; were the approximately 70 percent of its ads that are presented free as a public service also included, it would rank second—just behind Procter and Gamble (Porat 1977, p. 137). Increasing business and governmental use of control technologies and their recent proliferation in forms like data services and home computers for use by consumers have become dominant features of the Control Revolution.

THE INFORMATION SOCIETY

One major result of the Control Revolution had been the emergence of the so-called Information Society. The concept dates from the late 1950s and the pioneering work of an economist, Fritz Machlup, who first measured that sector of the U.S. economy associated with what he called "the production and distribution of knowledge" (Machlup 1962). Under this classification Machlup grouped thirty industries into five major categories: education, research and development, communications media, information machines (like computers), and information services (finance, insurance, real estate). He then estimated from national accounts data for 1958 (the most recent year available) that the information sector accounted for 29 percent of gross national product (GNP) and 31 percent of the labor force. He also estimated that between 1947 and 1958 the information sector had expanded at a compound growth rate double that of GNP. In sum, it appeared that the United States was rapidly becoming an Information Society.

Over the intervening twenty years several other analyses have substantiated and updated the original estimates of Machlup (1980, pp. xxvi–xxviii); Burck (1964) calculated that the information sector

had reached 33 percent of GNP by 1963; Marschak (1968) predicted that the sector would approach 40 percent of GNP in the 1970s. By far the most ambitious effort to date has been the innovative work of Marc Uri Porat for the Office of Telecommunications in the U.S. Department of Commerce (1977). In 1967, according to Porat, information activities (defined differently from those of Machlup) accounted for 46.2 percent of GNP— 25.1 percent in a "primary information" sector (which produces information goods and services as final output) and 21.1 percent in a "secondary information" sector (the bureaucracies of noninformation enterprises).

The impact of the information society is perhaps best captured by trends in labor force composition. As can be seen in Figure 1 and the corresponding data in Table 1, at the end of the eighteenth century the U.S. labor force was concentrated overwhelmingly in agriculture, the location of nearly 90 percent of its workers. The majority of U.S. labor continued to work in this sector until about 1850, and agriculture remained the largest single sector until the first decade of the twentieth century. Rapidly emerging, meanwhile, was a new industrial sector, one that continuously employed at least a quarter of U.S. workers between the 1840s and 1970s, reaching a peak of about 40 percent during World War II. Today, just forty years later, the industrial sector is close to half that percentage and declining steadily; it might well fall below 15 percent in the next decade. Meanwhile, the information sector, by 1960 already larger (at more than 40 percent) than industry had ever been, today approaches half of the U.S. labor force.

At least in the timing of this new sector's rise and development, the data in Figure 1 and Table 1 are compatible with the hypothesis that the Information Society emerged in response to the nineteenth-century crisis of control. When the first railroads were built in the early 1830s, the information sector employed considerably less than 1 percent of the U.S. labor force; by the end of the decade it employed more than 4 percent. Not

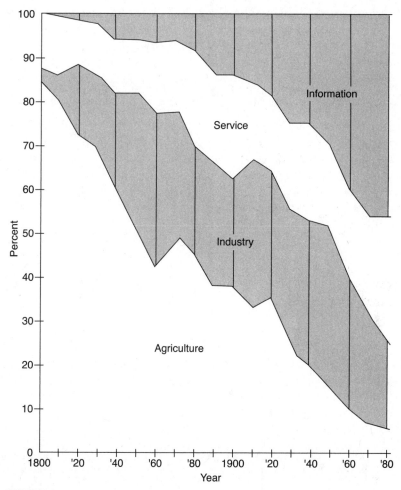

FIGURE 1   U.S. civilian labor force chart. *Reprinted by permission of Harvard University Press.*

until the rapid bureaucratization of the 1870s and 1880s, the period that . . . marked the consolidation of control, did the percentage employed in the information sector more than double to about one-eighth of the civilian work force. With the exception of these two great discontinuties, one occurring with the advent of railroads and the crisis of control in the 1830s, the other accompanying the consolidation of control in the 1870s and especially in the 1880s, the information sector has grown steadily but only modestly over the past two centuries.

Temporal correlation alone, of course, does not prove causation. With the exception of the two discontinuities, however, growth in the information sector has tended to be most rapid in periods of economic upturn, most notably in the postwar booms of the 1920s and 1950s, as can be seen in Table 1. Significantly, the two periods of discontinuity were punctuated by economic depressions, the first by the Panic of 1837, the second by financial crisis in Europe and the Panic of 1873. In other words, the technological origins of both the control crisis and the consolidation of

Table 1   U.S. Experienced Civilian Labor Force by Four Sectors, 1800–1980

	Sector's Percent of Total				
Year	Agricultural	Industrial	Service	Information	Total Labor Force (in millions)
1800	87.2	1.4	11.3	0.2	1.5
1810	81.0	6.5	12.2	0.3	2.2
1820	73.0	16.0	10.7	0.4	3.0
1830	69.7	17.6	12.2	0.4	3.7
1840	58.8	24.4	12.7	4.1	5.2
1850	49.5	33.8	12.5	4.2	7.4
1860	40.6	37.0	16.6	5.8	8.3
1870	47.0	32.0	16.2	4.8	12.5
1880	43.7	25.2	24.6	6.5	17.4
1890	37.2	28.1	22.3	12.4	22.8
1900	35.3	26.8	25.1	12.8	29.2
1910	31.1	36.3	17.7	14.9	39.8
1920	32.5	32.0	17.8	17.7	45.3
1930	20.4	35.3	19.8	24.5	51.1
1940	15.4	37.2	22.5	24.9	53.6
1950	11.9	38.3	19.0	30.8	57.8
1960	6.0	34.8	17.2	42.0	67.8
1970	3.1	28.6	21.9	46.4	80.1
1980	2.1	22.5	28.8	46.6	95.8

Sources: Data for 1800–1830 are estimated from Lebergott (1964) with missing data interpolated from Fabricant (1949); data for 1860–1870 are taken directly from Porat (1977); data for 1980 are based on U.S. Bureau of Labor Statistics projections (Bell 1979, p. 185).

control occurred in periods when the information sector would not have been expected on other economic grounds to have expanded rapidly if at all. There is therefore no reason to reject the hypothesis that the Information Society developed as a result of the crisis of control created by railroads and other steam-powered transportation in the 1840s.

A wholly new stage in the development of the Information Society has arisen, since the early 1970s, from the continuing proliferation of microprocessing technology. Most important in social implications has been the progressive convergence of all information technologies—mass media, telecommunications, and computing—in a single infrastructure of control at the most macro level. A 1978 report commissioned by the President of France—an instant best-seller in that country and abroad—likened the growing interconnection of information-processing, communication, and control technologies throughout the world to an alteration in "the entire nervous system of social organization" (Nora and Minc 1978, p. 3). The same report introduced the neologism *telematics* for this most recent stage of the Information Society, although similar words had been suggested earlier—for example, *compunications* (for "computing + communications") by Anthony Oettinger and his colleagues at Harvard's Program on Information Resources Policy (Oettinger 1971; Berman and Oettinger 1975; Oettinger, Berman, and Read 1977).

Crucial to telematics, compunications, or whatever word comes to be used for this convergence of information-processing and communications technologies is increasing digitalization: coding into discontinuous values—usually two-valued or binary—of what even a few years ago would have been an analog signal varying continuously in time, whether a telephone conversation, a radio broadcast, or a television picture. Because most modern computers process digital information, the progressive digitalization of mass media and telecommunications content begins to blur earlier distinctions between the communication of information and its processing (as implied by the term *compunications*), as well as between people and machines. Digitalization makes communication from persons to machines, between machines, and even from machines to persons as easy as it is between persons. Also blurred are the distinctions among information types: numbers, words, pictures, and sounds, and eventually tastes, odors, and possibly even sensations, all might one day be stored, processed, and communicated in the same digital form.

In this way digitalization promises to transform currently diverse forms of information into a generalized medium for processing and exchange by the social system, much as, centuries ago, the institution of common currencies and exchanges rates began to transform local markets into a single world economy. We might therefore expect the implications of digitalization to be as profound for macrosociology as the institution of money was for macroeconomics. Indeed, digitalized electronic systems have already begun to replace money itself in many informational functions, only the most recent stage in a growing systemness of world society dating back at least to the Commercial Revolution of the fifteenth century.

SELECTED REFERENCES

For works of primarily historical interest, generally those published before 1960, citation is to the year of *first* publication except for ancient texts. When the text used was not this edition, page numbers and other references are to the edition (including year of publication) listed after the publisher. In the citation "Kant 1788," for example, the year refers to the first German publication; references are to the English-language edition published by Bobbs-Merrill in 1956. Citations to works in languages other than English are to translations whenever available.

Abbott, Waldo, and Richard L. Rider. 1957. *Handbook of Broadcasting: The Fundamentals of Radio and Television,* 4th ed. New York: McGraw-Hill.

Bell, Daniel. 1973. *The Coming of Post-Industrial Society: A Venture in Social Forecasting,* New York: Basic Books.

———. 1979. "The Social Framework of the Information Society." Pp. 163–211 in *The Computer Age: A Twenty-Year View,* ed. Michael L. Dertouzos and Joel Moses. Cambridge, Mass.: MIT Press.

Berman, Paul J., and Anthony G. Oettinger. 1975. *The Medium and the Telephone: The Politics of Information Resources.* Working Paper 75–8 (December 15). Cambridge, Mass.: Harvard University Program on Information Technologies and Public Policy.

Boorstin, Daniel J. 1973. *The Americans: The Democratic Experience.* New York: Random House, Vintage.

Briggs, Asa. 1977. "The Pleasure Telephone: A Chapter in the Prehistory of the Media." Pp. 40–65 in *The Social Impact of the Telephone,* ed. Ithiel de Sola Pool. Cambridge, Mass.: MIT Press.

Burck, Gilbert. 1964. "Knowledge: The Biggest Growth Industry of Them All." *Fortune* (November): 128–131ff.

Chandler, Alfred D., Jr. 1977. *The Visible Hand: The Managerial Revolution in American Business.* Cambridge, Mass.: Belknap Press of Harvard University Press.

Durkheim, Emile. 1893. *The Division of Labor in Society,* trans. George Simpson. New York: Free Press, 1933.

Fabricant, Solomon. 1949. "The Changing Industrial Distribution of Gainful Workers: Some Comments on the American Decennial Statistics for 1820–1940." *Studies in Income and Wealth,* vol. 11. New York: National Bureau of Economic Research.

Lebergott, Stanley. 1964. *Manpower in Economic Growth: The American Record since 1800.* New York: McGraw-Hill.

Machlup, Fritz. 1962. *The Production and Distribution of Knowledge in the United States.* Princeton, N.J.: Princeton University Press.

———. 1980. *Knowledge: Its Creation, Distribution, and Economic Significance,* vol. 1. Princeton, N.J.: Princeton University Press.

Marschak, Jacob. 1968. "Economics of Inquiring, Communicating, and Deciding." *American Economic Review* 58(2): 1–8.

Nora, Simon, and Alain Minc. 1978. *The Computerization of Society: A Report to the President of France.* Cambridge, Mass.: MIT Press, 1980.

Oettinger, Anthony G. 1971. "Compunications in the National Decision-Making Process." Pp. 73–114 in *Computers, Communications, and the Public Interest,* ed. Martin Greenberger. Baltimore: Johns Hopkins University Press.

Oettinger, Anthony G., Paul J. Berman, and William H. Read. 1977. *High and Low Politics: Information Resources for the 80's.* Cambridge, Mass.: Ballinger.

Porat, Marc Uri. 1977. *The Information Economy Definition and Measurement.* Washington: Office of Telecommunications, U.S. Department of Commerce.

Shannon, Claude E., and Warren Weaver. 1949. *The Mathematical Theory of Communication.* Urbana: University of Illinois Press.

Thompson, Robert Luther. 1947. *Wiring a Continent: The History of the Telegraph Industry in the United States, 1832–1866.* Princeton, N.J.: Princeton University Press.

Toffler, Alvin. 1971. *Future Shock.* New York: Bantam Books.

U.S. Bureau of the Census. 1975. *Historical Statistics of the United States, Colonial Times to 1920.* 2 vols. Washington: U.S. Government Printing Office.

Wiener, Norbert. 1948. *Cybernetics: or Control and Communication in the Animal and the Machine.* Cambridge, Mass.: MIT Press, 2nd ed., 1961.

Winner, Langdon. 1977. *Autonomous Technology: Technics-out-of-Control as a Theme in Political Thought.* Cambridge, Mass.: MIT Press.

CHAPTER **38**

How Media Became New

Lev Manovich

Lev Manovich is associate professor in the Visual Arts Department at the University of California, San Diego.

On August 19, 1839, the Palace of the Institute in Paris was filled with curious Parisians who had come to hear the formal description of the new reproduction process invented by Louis Daguerre. Daguerre, already well known for his Diorama, called the new process *daguerreotype.* According to a contemporary, "a few days later, opticians' shops were crowded with amateurs panting for daguerreotype apparatus, and everywhere cameras were trained on buildings. Everyone wanted to record the view from his window, and he was lucky who at first trial got a silhouette of roof tops against the sky."[1] The media frenzy had begun. Within five months more than thirty different descriptions of the technique had been published around the world—Barcelona, Edinburgh, Naples, Philadelphia, St. Petersburg, Stockholm. At first, daguerreotypes of architecture and landscapes dominated the public's imagination; two years later, after various technical improvements to the process had been made, portrait galleries had opened everywhere—and everyone rushed to have her picture taken by the new media machine.[2]

In 1833 Charles Babbage began designing a device he called "the Analytical Engine." The Engine contained most of the key features of the modern digital computer. Punch cards were used to enter both data and instructions. This information was stored in the Engine's memory. A processing unit, which Babbage referred to as a "mill," performed operations on the data and wrote the results to memory; final results were to be printed out on a printer. The Engine was designed to be capable of doing any mathematical operation; not only would it follow the program fed into it by cards, but it would also decide which instructions to execute next, based on intermediate results. However, in contrast to the daguerreotype, not a single copy of the Engine was completed. While the invention of the daguerreotype, a modern media tool for the reproduction of reality, impacted society immediately, the impact of the computer was yet to be seen.

Interestingly, Babbage borrowed the idea of using punch cards to store information from an earlier programmed machine. Around 1800, J. M. Jacquard invented a loom that was automatically controlled by punched paper cards. The loom was used to weave intricate figurative images, including Jacquard's portrait. This specialized graphics computer, so to speak, inspired Babbage in his work on the Analytical Engine, a general computer for numerical calculations. As Ada Augusta, Babbage's supporter and the first computer programmer, put it, "The Analytical Engine weaves algebraical patterns just as the Jacquard loom weaves flowers and leaves."[3] Thus a

programmed machine was already synthesizing images even before it was put to processing numbers. The connection between the Jacquard loom and the Analytical Engine is not something historians of computers make much of, since for them computer image synthesis represents just one application of the modern digital computer among thousands of others, but for a historian of new media, it is full of significance.

We should not be surprised that both trajectories—the development of modern media and the development of computers—begin around the same time. Both media machines and computing machines were absolutely necessary for the functioning of modern mass societies. The ability to disseminate the same texts, images, and sounds to millions of citizens—thus assuring the same ideological beliefs—was as essential as the ability to keep track of their birth records, employment records, medical records, and police records. Photography, film, the offset printing press, radio, and television made the former possible while computers made possible the latter. Mass media and data processing are complementary technologies; they appear together and develop side by side, making modern mass society possible.

For a long time the two trajectories ran in parallel without ever crossing paths. Throughout the nineteenth and the early twentieth centuries, numerous mechanical and electrical tabulators and calculators were developed; they gradually became faster and their use more widespread. In a parallel movement, we witness the rise of modern media that allow the storage of images, image sequences, sounds, and texts in different material forms—photographic plates, film stock, gramophone records, etc.

Let us continue tracing this joint history. In the 1890s modern media took another step forward as still photographs were put in motion. In January 1893, the first movie studio—Edison's "Black Maria"—started producing twenty-second shorts that were shown in special Kinetoscope parlors. Two years later the Lumière brothers showed their new Cinématographie camera/projection hybrid, first to a scientific audience and later, in December 1895, to the paying public. Within a year, audiences in Johannesburg, Bombay, Rio de Janeiro, Melbourne, Mexico City, and Osaka were subjected to the new media machine, and they found it irresistible.[4] Gradually scenes grew longer, the staging of reality before the camera and the subsequent editing of samples became more intricate, and copies multiplied. In Chicago and Calcutta, London and St. Petersburg, Tokyo and Berlin, and thousands of smaller places, film images would soothe movie audiences, who were facing an increasingly dense information environment outside the theater, an environment that no longer could be adequately handled by their own sampling and data processing systems (i.e., their brains). Periodic trips into the dark relaxation chambers of movie theaters became a routine survival technique for the subjects of modern society.

The 1890s was the crucial decade not only for the development of media, but also for computing. If individual brains were overwhelmed by the amount of information they had to process, the same was true of corporations and of governments. In 1887, the U.S. Census Bureau was still interpreting figures from the 1880 census. For the 1890 census, the Census Bureau adopted electric tabulating machines designed by Herman Hollerith. The data collected on every person was punched into cards; 46,804 enumerators completed forms for a total population of 62,979,766. The Hollerith tabulator opened the door for the adoption of calculating machines by business; during the next decade electric tabulators became standard equipment in insurance companies, public utility companies, railroad offices, and accounting departments. In 1911, Hollerith's Tabulating Machine Company was merged with three other companies to form the Computing-Tabulating-Recording Company; in

1914, Thomas J. Watson was chosen as its head. Ten years later its business tripled, and Watson renamed the company the "International Business Machines Corporation," or IBM.[5]

Moving into the twentieth century, the key year for the history of media and computing is 1936. British mathematician Alan Turing wrote a seminal paper entitled "On Computable Numbers." In it he provided a theoretical description of a general-purpose computer later named after its inventor: "the Universal Turing Machine." Even though it was capable of only four operations, the machine could perform any calculation that could be done by a human and could also imitate any other computing machine. The machine operated by reading and writing numbers on an endless tape. At every step the tape would be advanced to retrieve the next command, read the data, or write the result. Its diagram looks suspiciously like a film projector. Is this a coincidence?

If we believe the word *cinematograph,* which means "writing movement," the essence of cinema is recording and storing visible data in a material form. A film camera records data on film; a film projector reads it off. This cinematic apparatus is similar to a computer in one key respect: A computer's program and data also have to be stored in some medium. This is why the Universal Turing Machine looks like a film projector. It is a kind of film camera and film projector at once, reading instructions and data stored on endless tape and writing them in other locations on this tape. In fact, the development of a suitable storage medium and a method for coding data represent important parts of the prehistory of both cinema and the computer. As we know, the inventors of cinema eventually settled on using discrete images recorded on a strip of celluloid; the inventors of the computer—which needed much greater speed of access as well as the ability to quickly read and write data—eventually decided to store it electronically in a binary code.

The histories of media and computing became further entwined when German engineer Konrad Zuse began building a computer in the living room of his parents' apartment in Berlin—the same year that Turing wrote his seminal paper. Zuse's computer was the first working digital computer. One of his innovations was using punched tape to control computer programs. The tape Zuse used was actually discarded 35mm movie film.[6]

One of the surviving pieces of this film shows binary code punched over the original frames of an interior shot. A typical movie scene—two people in a room involved in some action—becomes a support for a set of computer commands. Whatever meaning and emotion was contained in this movie scene has been wiped out by its new function as data carrier. The pretense of modern media to create simulations of sensible reality is similarly canceled; media are reduced to their original condition as information carrier, nothing less, nothing more. In a technological remake of the Oedipal complex, a son murders his father. The iconic code of cinema is discarded in favor of the more efficient binary one. Cinema becomes a slave to the computer.

But this is not yet the end of the story. Our story has a new twist—a happy one. Zuse's film, with its strange superimposition of binary over iconic code, anticipates the convergence that will follow half a century later. The two separate historical trajectories finally meet. Media and computer—Daguerre's daguerreotype and Babbage's Analytical Engine, the Lumière Cinématographie and Hollerith's tabulator—merge into one. All existing media are translated into numerical data accessible for the computer. The result: graphics, moving images, sounds, shapes, spaces, and texts become computable, that is, simply sets of computer data. In short, media become new media.

This meeting changes the identity of both media and the computer itself. No longer just a calculator, control mechanism, or communication device, the computer becomes a media processor. Before, the computer could read a row of numbers, outputting a statistical result or a gun trajectory. Now it can read pixel values, blurring the image, adjusting its contrast, or checking whether it contains an outline of an object. Building on these lower-level operations, it can also perform more ambitious ones— searching image data-bases for images similar in composition or content to an input image, detecting shot changes in a movie, or synthesizing the movie shot itself, complete with setting and actors. In a historical loop, the computer has returned to its origins. No longer just an Analytical Engine, suitable only for crunching numbers, it has become Jacquard's loom—a media synthesizer and manipulator.

NOTES

1. Quoted in Beaumont Newhall, *The History of Photography from 1839 to the Present Day,* 4th ed. (New York: Museum of Modern Art, 1964), 18.
2. Newhall, *The History of Photography,* 17–22.
3. Charles Eames, *A Computer Perspective: Background to the Computer Age* (Cambridge, Mass.: Harvard University Press, 1990), 18.
4. David Bordwell and Kristin Thompson, *Film Art: An Introduction,* 5th ed. (New York: McGraw-Hill), 15.
5. Eames, *A Computer Perspective,* 22–27, 46–51, 90–91.
6. Ibid., 120.

CHAPTER 39

Popularizing the Internet

Janet Abbate

Janet Abbate teaches in the Science and Technology in Society program at Virginia Tech.

THE GLOBAL PICTURE

Today, few if any countries are without at least one connection to the Internet. How did this worldwide expansion occur? Though the Internet originated in the United States, it did not simply spread from the United States to the rest of the world. Rather, its global reach resulted from the convergence of many streams of network development. Starting in the 1970s, many other nations built large data networks, which were shaped by their local cultures and which often served as agents and symbols of economic development and national sovereignty. The question was not whether these countries would adopt an "American" technology; it was whether and how they would connect their existing national or private networks to the Internet.

Since the early 1970s the ARPANET and the Internet had included sites outside the United States; University College London had an ARPANET connection for research purposes, and ARPA's Satellite Network linked the United States with a seismic monitoring center in Norway. The defense portion of the Internet also connected many overseas military bases. But the Internet's ownership by the U.S. government was an obstacle to connecting it with civilian networks in other nations. ARPA and NSF managers feared that such connections would be perceived by the American public as giving away a taxpayer-subsidized resource to foreigners, and citizens of other countries might regard the encroachment of U.S.

networks as a form of imperialism. Overseas, grassroots user-supported networks with lower political profiles, such as BITNET and UUCP, spread faster than the Internet.

Before privatization, therefore, it was difficult to expand the Internet abroad by adding host sites to the U.S.-run networks; connecting the Internet to networks in other countries was much more promising. By the mid 1970s, state-run networks were being built in a number of countries, including Canada, Germany, Norway, Sweden, Australia, New Zealand, and Japan (Carpenter et al. 1987). In addition to these national networks, there were several efforts to build multinational networks across Europe in support of the creation of a European Union. These included the European Informatics Network (established in 1971) and its successor, Euronet. Some of the networks were, like the ARPANET, designed for research and education; others provided commercial network services.

France Telecom, with its Minitel system (introduced in 1982), was the first phone company to offer a network service that provided content as well as communications. Since few people in France owned or had access to computers at that time, the phone company encouraged widespread use of Minitel by giving its customers inexpensive special-purpose terminals they could use to access the system. Minitel allowed millions of ordinary people to access online telephone directories and other commercial and recreational services (including online pornography, a popular attraction that received much public comment and that the U.S.-government-run Internet could not have openly supported).

One of the world's leading sites for computer networking was CERN, the European laboratory for particle physics. Owing to the peculiar needs of its users, CERN had a long history of networking (Carpenter et al. 1987). Experimentalists in high-energy physics must travel to accelerator sites such as CERN. While there, they generate huge amounts of data. In the early 1980s, to make it easier to transfer such data around its laboratory in Geneva, CERN installed local-area networks. Physicists also need to communicate with and transfer data to their home institutions. To accommodate this need, CERN joined various wide-area networks, including EARN (the European branch of BITNET), the Swiss public data network, and HEPNET (a U.S.-based network for high-energy physics).

Networks outside the United States had few links to the Internet while it was under military control. But when the National Science Foundation set up its civilian NSFNET, foreign networks were able to establish connections to it, and thus to gain access to the rest of the Internet. Canada and France had connected their networks to the NSFNET by mid 1988. They were followed by Denmark, Finland, Iceland, Norway, and Sweden later in 1988; by Australia, Germany, Israel, Italy, Japan, Mexico, the Netherlands, New Zealand, Puerto Rico, and the United Kingdom in 1989; and by Argentina, Austria, Belgium, Brazil, Chile, Greece, India, Ireland, South Korea, Spain, and Switzerland in 1990 (MERIT 1995). By January of 1990 there were 250 non-U.S. networks attached to the NSFNET, more than 20 percent of the total number of networks. By April of 1995, when the NSF ceased operating it, the Internet included 22,000 foreign networks—more than 40 percent of the total number (ibid., file history.netcount). The system had truly become international in scope, though its membership remained highly biased toward wealthy developed countries.

The other industrialized nations approached networking rather differently than the United States. In the United States, the federal government operated military and research networks, but public network services were provided on a commercial basis. In other countries, the public networks were government-run monopolies, so network decisions involved overtly political maneuvers as well as business considerations. In many countries, people viewed the expansion of U.S. networks such as the Internet with alarm, seeing it as further evidence of U.S. economic dominance in the computing industry. Thus, while many people inside and outside the United States favored expanding the Internet around the world, politically charged differences between network systems presented a number of barriers.

One technical obstacle was incompatibilities among network systems. Initially, many networks outside the United States had used proprietary network systems or protocols designed by their creators. Most state-run networks eventually adopted the official CCITT or ISO protocols, which they regarded as the only legitimate standards; few if any used TCP/IP.

In the mid 1980s, however, many private network builders outside the United States began adopting TCP/IP, perhaps because they had become impatient with the slow introduction of ISO standards. In November of 1989, a group of TCP/IP network operators in Europe formed RIPE (Réseaux IP Européens, meaning European IP Networks). Similar in concept to the CIX (and perhaps providing a model for that system), RIPE connected its member networks to form a pan-European Internet, each network agreeing to accept traffic from the other members without charge. RIPE also provided a forum for members to meet, discuss common issues, and work on technical improvements. By 1996, RIPE had as members more than 400 organizations, serving an estimated 4 million host computers (RIPE 1997).

While the Internet protocols were gaining popularity outside the United States, many network operators wanted to reduce the United States' dominance over the Internet. One contentious issue was the structure of the Domain

Name System. Since the ultimate authority to assign host names rests with the administrators of the top-level domains, other countries wanted to have their own top-level domains. Responding to these concerns, ISO promoted a domain name system in which each country would have its own top-level domain, indicated by a two-letter code such as "fr" for France or "us" for the United States.[1] Within these top-level domains, national governments could assign lower-level domains as they saw fit. The new system provided autonomy and symbolic equality to all nations. However, the old Internet domain names based on type of organization (educational, military, etc.) were not abolished. In the United States, most organizations continued to use them, rather than adopting the new "us" domain (Krol 1992, p. 28).

Since the Internet originated in the United States, its "native language" is English—a fact that has caused some resentment among other linguistic groups. The dominance of English on the Internet has led to political disputes over what is often seen as American cultural or linguistic imperialism. In the mid 1990s, for example, the French government, which had put in place a number of measures to maintain French-language content in the media, required every Web site based in France to provide a French version of its text. Internet users whose native languages do not use the Roman alphabet have struggled to get support for extended character sets (Shapard 1995).

Finally, the expansion of the Internet has been limited by global disparities in the telecommunications infrastructure that underlies network access. In 1991, for instance, the number of telephone lines per 100 inhabitants in industrialized nations ranged from 20 (in Portugal) to 67 (in Sweden); in much of South America, Africa, and the Middle East, there were fewer than 10 lines per 100 inhabitants, and China, Pakistan, India, Indonesia, and Tanzania—countries with a huge percentage of the world's population—had fewer than one line per 100 people (Kellerman 1993, p. 132). Clearly, the unequal distribution of wealth among nations will continue to shape the

Internet's worldwide role. The Internet, as a medium of instantaneous communication, might overcome geographic distance, but it cannot simply erase political or social differences.

THE WORLD WIDE WEB

In the 1980s the Internet's infrastructure grew impressively, but network applications lagged behind: email and file transfer were still the most common activities, and there were few user-friendly applications to attract novices. One factor that discouraged wider use of the Internet was its drab text-only interface, which contrasted sharply with the attractive graphical interfaces found on many personal computers. CompuServe, America Online, and Prodigy took advantage of the personal computer's graphic capabilities to provide attractive, user-friendly interfaces, thus setting a precedent for providing online information that incorporated images. Some software developers were also trying to create more graphics-oriented interfaces for Unix workstations (notably the X Windows system, developed at MIT in the mid 1980s), but many users of time sharing machines were still confined to text-based network interfaces.

Another drawback to using the Internet was the difficulty of locating and retrieving online information. File-transfer programs were available, but the user had to know the names of the desired file and its host computer, and there was no automated way to get this information. In former times it had been the ARPANET Network Information Center's role to provide information on network resources, and even then the information it had provided had often been inadequate. The privatized Internet had no central authority to create a directory of resources, and in any case the size of the Internet would have made the task of maintaining such a directory impossible.

In the early 1990s, new services made it easier to locate documents on the Internet. One such service was the gopher system, developed at the University of Minnesota. The gopher software allowed information providers to organize their information in a hierarchy of related topics; users of the system could select topics from menus, rather than having to know and type in the names of computers and files. Another widely used system was the Wide-Area Information Server, developed by the Thinking Machines Corporation. Instead of using a menu system, WAIS allowed users to search for documents whose text contained specified words; the titles of the documents would be displayed, and the user could retrieve the documents (Schatz and Hardin 1994, pp. 895–896). Services such as gopher and WAIS took a step in the direction of organizing information by content rather than location. There were still many obstacles to finding information on the Internet, however. There was no way to link information found in different documents, and the various protocols that had evolved for exchanging information were not compatible; no one program could handle formats as diverse as ftp, mail, gopher, and WAIS.

All these issues were addressed by a new Internet application that became known as the World Wide Web. The Web would fundamentally change the Internet, not by expanding its infrastructure or underlying protocols, but by providing an application that would lure millions of new users. The Web also changed people's perception of the Internet: Instead of being seen as a research tool or even a conduit for messages between people, the network took on new roles as an entertainment medium, a shop window, and a vehicle for presenting one's persona to the world.

BUILDING THE WEB

The Web did not spring from the ARPA research community; it was the work of a new set of actors, including computer scientists at CERN, the staff of an NSF supercomputer center, and a new branch of the software industry that would devote itself to providing Web servers, browsers, and content.

The first incarnation of the Web was created in 1990 by Tim Berners-Lee, Robert Cailliau, and others at CERN. Berners-Lee appreciated the value of networking; however, he saw a severe limitation in the fact that, though personal computers were becoming increasingly image oriented, most uses of the Internet were still limited to text. He envisioned a system that would help scientists collaborate by making it easy to create and share multimedia data (Berners-Lee et al. 1994, p. 82; Comerford 1995, p. 71). CERN had adopted TCP/IP in the early 1980s in order to provide a common protocol for its various systems, so Berners-Lee designed the new service to run over the Internet protocols.

The computing tradition on which Berners-Lee drew was far removed from the military roots of the ARPANET and the Internet: the hacker counterculture of the 1960s and the 1970s. In 1974, Ted Nelson, a vocal champion of this counterculture, had written a manifesto, *Computer Lib*, in which he had urged ordinary people to learn to use computers rather than leaving them in the hands of the "computer priesthood." More to the point, Nelson had proposed a system of organizing information that he called "hypertext." Hypertext would make it possible to link pieces of information, rather than having to present the information in a linear way.

Berners-Lee planned to create a hypertext system that would link files located on computers around the world, forming a "world wide web" of information. To the idea of hypertext he added the use of multimedia: his system included not only text-based information but also images, and later versions would add audio and video. (See Hayes 1994, p. 416; Schatz and Hardin 1994.) The Web's use of hypertext and multimedia drastically changed the look and feel of using the Internet.

In Berners-Lee's vision, the Web would create "a pool of human knowledge" that would be easy to access (Berners-Lee et al. 1994, p. 76). Before achieving this goal, however, Berners-Lee and his collaborators had to address a number of technical challenges. First, they had to create a shared format for hypertext documents, which they called hypertext markup language (HTML).[2] To allow the Web to handle different data formats, the designers of HTML specified a process of "format negotiation" between computers to ensure that the machines agreed on which formats to use when exchanging information. "Our experience," Berners-Lee (1993a) observed, "is that any attempt to enforce a particular representation . . . leads to immediate war. . . . Format negotiation allows the web to distance itself from the technical and political battles of the data formats." Like the ARPANET's designers before them, the Web team chose to create a system that could accommodate diverse computer technologies.

The layered structure of the Internet meant that Berners-Lee could build his new application on top of the communications services provided by TCP/IP. His group designed the hypertext transfer protocol (HTTP) to guide the exchange of information between Web browsers and Web servers. To enable browsers and servers to locate information on the Web, there also had to be some uniform way to identify the information a user wanted to access. To address this need, they created the uniform resource locator (URL)—a standard address format that specifies both the type of application protocol being used and the address of the computer that has the desired data. An important feature of the URL was that it could refer to a variety of protocols, not just HTTP. This would make it possible to use the Web to access older Internet services, such as FTP, gopher, WAIS, and Usenet news. The accommodation of all Internet services—present and future—within a single interface would be an important factor in making the Web system versatile and user friendly (Berners-Lee et al. 1994, p. 76; Berners-Lee 1993b; Schatz and Hardin 1994, pp. 896–897).

In December of 1990 the first version of the Web software began operating within CERN. Berners-Lee's system was an instant hit with CERN users. It took more than an inspired invention, however, to create an application that would bring the Internet mass popularity. It also required the right environment: widespread access to the Internet (made possible by privatization) and the technical means for users to run the Web software (provided by the personal computer).

Personal computers had brought computing to masses of ordinary Americans in the 1980s, and a decade later they laid the foundation for the popular embrace of the Web. The popularization of the Internet could have occurred without the personal computer. France's widely used Minitel system, for instance, relied on inexpensive home terminals for its user interface. But Minitel did not allow users to create their own content—a distinctive feature of the World Wide Web. The Web depended on significant computer power at the user's end of the connection. In addition, the time and energy that individuals had invested in learning to use their personal computers would make it easier for them to acquire the skills needed to access the Web. Thanks to the spread of graphical user interfaces via the Macintosh and Windows operating systems, instructions such as "point and click" seemed obvious rather than perplexing to novice Web users. For non-expert users in particular, the Internet-based Web represented the convergence of personal computing and networking.

NOTES

1. According to Barry Leiner (email to author, 29 June 1998), the country-code system had actually been envisioned by the original designers of DNS, but the impetus to adopt it as the standard way of designating domains seems to have come from outside the United States.
2. HTML was based on an existing ISO standard called the Standard Generalized Markup Language. SGML is specified in ISO Standard 8879 (1986); HTML is specified in RFC 1866 (1995).

REFERENCES

Berners-Lee, Tim. "W3 Concepts." Web page http://www.3.org/pub/WWW/Talks/General/Concepts.html, 1993a.

Berners-Lee, Tim. "W3 Protocols." Web page http://www.3.org/pub/WWW/Talks/General/Protocols.html, 1993b.

Berners-Lee, Tim, et al. "The World-Wide Web." *Communications of the ACM* 37(8): 76–82, 1994.

Comerford, Richard. "The Web: A Two-Minute Tutorial." *IEEE Spectrum* 32: 71, 1995.

Carpenter, B. E., et al. "Two Years of Real Progress in European HEP Networking: A CERN Perspective." *Computer Physics Communications* 45: 83–92, 1987.

Hayes, Brian. "The World Wide Web." *American Scientist* 82: 416–420, 1994.

Kellerman, Aharon. *Telecommunications and Geography.* New York: John Wiley, 1993.

Krol, Ed. *The Whole Internet User's Guide & Catalogue.* San Francisco: O'Reilly & Associates, 1992.

MERIT. "Merit Retires NSFNET Backbone Service." Web page http://nic.merit.edu/nsfnet/news.releases/nsfnet.retired, 1995.

RIPE. "About RIPE." Web page http://www.ripe.net/info/ripe/ripe.html, 1997.

Schatz, Bruce R., and Joseph B. Hardin. "NCSA Mosaic and the World Wide Web: Global Hypermedia Protocols for the Internet." *Science* 265: 895–901, 1994.

Shapard, Jeffrey. "Islands in the (Data)Stream: Language, Character Codes, and Electronic Isolation in Japan." In *Global Networks,* ed. L. Harasim. Thousand Oaks, CA: Sage, 1995.

CHAPTER **40**

The World Wide Web

Jay David Bolter and Richard Grusin

Jay David Bolter is professor of language, communications, and culture at the Georgia Institute of Technology. Richard Grusin is professor and chair of the Department of English at Wayne State University.

The World Wide Web has already passed through several stages, each of which refashions some earlier media. The Web today is eclectic and inclusive and continues to borrow from and remediate almost any visual and verbal medium we can name. What is constantly changing is the ratio among the media that the Web favors for its remediations; what remains the same is the promise of immediacy through the flexibility and liveness of the Web's networked communication. The liveness of the Web is a refashioned version of the liveness of broadcast television.

TEXT AND GRAPHIC DESIGN

The Internet itself, as a communications system and as a cultural symbol, remediates the telegraph. We still picture the Internet as a reticule of electric lines covering the industrialized world, as the telegraph first did in the nineteenth century, even though the Internet today consists of a variety of data links, including lines above ground, buried cables, and microwave and satellite links. Prior to the World Wide Web, the services of the Internet (such as email and simple file transfer)

Editors' Note: URLs in this essay may be out of date. The stability and the persistence of URLs and the content they point to has become a significant controversy and issue of concern for users of the World Wide Web.

refashioned principally alphabetic media (the book, the letter, the technical report). Although it was possible to transmit digital graphics, most users were limited to ASCII text. And because the Internet could not pretend to offer the range of materials available in print, it had to rely on speed of communication as the only advantage in its remediation. This speed was most telling in electronic mail, by far the most popular use of the Internet even into the early 1990s.

In its obscure first years, the Web too remediated only textual communication. A CERN physicist, Tim Berners-Lee, proposed the World Wide Web hypertext service so that scientists could more readily share their papers and numerical data. The earliest browsers, such as Lynx, presented only text on web pages. . . . However, in 1993, Marc Andreessen and colleagues at the University of Illinois created the first graphical browser, the forerunner of Netscape, which permitted static images to appear along with text on the page. . . . This apparently minor addition had two momentous consequences. First, the Web began to engage a much larger audience of users, including most academics and researchers, who were already using email, and soon a large fraction of technically literate people throughout the industrialized world. Without graphics on the World Wide Web, there would not now be tens of millions of Internet users, nor would there be much interest from the business community. The second consequence, related to the first, was that the World Wide Web could now refashion a larger class of earlier media. In addition to the letter and the scientific report, it could now remediate the magazine, the newspaper, and graphic advertising. Internet magazines and news services became popular and important genres. The tradition to which web designers now looked for inspiration was graphic design for print, and the principles of web page design became similar to those for laying out magazine articles, advertisements, and title pages. . . . Even the differences, such as the smaller space and poorer resolution of the computer screen, were analyzed in a vocabulary provided by graphic design.

Graphic designers brought to the Web their obsession with visual perfection, which expressed itself in this new medium as a need to control the placement and color of every pixel on the users screen. (This obsession was not shared by the computer programmers who built the first generation of web sites and browsers. They placed a higher value on user control and customization.) As always, these remediations combined respect and rivalry. While it was clear that the computer screen could not compete with the printed page in precision, the Web did have in its favor speed of delivery and point-and-click interactivity. At the same time, as the numbers of both servers (information sources) and clients (the audience) continued to grow, the Web became an increasingly important remediator of all sorts of printed information. It began to resemble a conventional public library in the scope of its materials, while public libraries themselves were expanding their definition of appropriate materials and even including Internet terminals in reading rooms.

Traditional graphic design could not account for moving images, so the Internet and World Wide Web necessarily passed into a new phase when they began to deliver animation, fuller interactivity, and digital video and audio. The old remediations were not abandoned. The Web still refashions the personal letter, the book, and the magazine, but now it also refashions and reforms CD-ROM or DVD multimedia, radio, film, and television. It rivals all these forms by promising greater immediacy and by recontextualizing them in the encompassing electronic environment of cyberspace.

THE VARIETY OF REMEDIATIONS ON THE WORLD WIDE WEB

There are a number of possible strategies for remediation, from respectful to radical, and designers for the World Wide Web have adopted each of these strategies at various times. There have been and remain many web sites that highlight other media without any apparent critique. This respectful attitude is most common in remediations of more venerable media: the printed book, static graphics, paintings, and photographs. The purpose of Project Gutenberg is to collect pure verbal versions of "classic" texts; the site adds little in the way of graphic ornamentation, so as not to distract from the alphabetic texts themselves. . . . Its editor, Michael Hart, has called the computer a "Replicator Technology," because it can reproduce texts infinitely and without adding errors (http://www.promo.net/pg/history.html January 13, 1998). Hart's replication is nothing other than respectful remediation. CETH—the Center for Electronic Texts in the Humanities—is another example of respectful remediation (http://www.ceth.rutgers.edu/ January 13, 1998). Such textual databases in fact preceded the introduction of the Web and at first relied on earlier services of the Internet or even digital tape to achieve their respectful remediations of the book. We can also point to the web site for the American Memory Project of the Library of Congress (http://lcweb2.loc.gov/amhome.html January 13, 1998), which preserves documents, prints, and early photographs, as well as some early films and sound recordings. . . . And there are many virtual museums and art galleries that offer a sampling of digitized images, often laid out in some arrangement that reflects the physical space of the building itself.

Perhaps developers of these web sites and our popular culture at large are inclined to be respectful precisely because these media are regarded as played out and therefore not likely to threaten the new digital media. In reproducing classic texts made for print or oil paintings hanging on a museum wall, the Web can fulfill an archival function without giving up its own claim to being revolutionary. Web designers feel less need to compete with "classic" authors or photographers

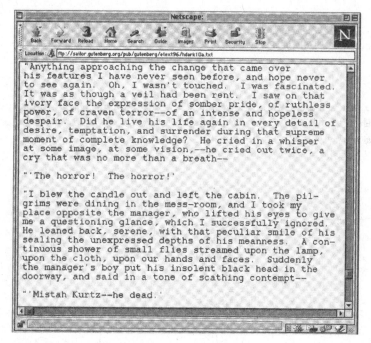

Heart of Darkness from Project Gutenberg. http://www.promo.net/pg/
Project Gutenberg is a registered trademark of Michael S. Hart. Reprinted by permission.

A Civil War photograph: *Atlanta, Ga. Trout House, Masonic Hall, and Federal encampment on Decatur Street.* © *Courtesy of the Library of Congress, Prints & Photographs Division. American Memory. http://lcweb2.loc.gov/ammen/.*

because these modes of representation already seem complete. There are also film archives, as in the American Memory Project, although the Web's relationship to film is more complicated and contentious.

The remediation of print is by no means sacrosanct in this new medium. Web newspapers, magazines, and encyclopedias, for example, do seek to improve on the printed versions. Thus, the encyclopedia in CD-ROM, DVD, or Web form makes predictable claims to both transparency and hypermediacy. All electronic encyclopedias are hypermediated and can claim to move the reader to desired information more efficiently by means of string searches or by hyperlinks. This hypermediacy is the main improvement offered by most web encyclopedias—for example, by the

Britannica Online, which, although it contains some video, is primarily a collection of textual articles with static graphics. . . . The CD-ROM or DVD encyclopedias, however, promise a new transparency through the animation, video, and audio that cannot appear in a printed version. The user can hear Martin Luther King's voice or the cry of a particular exotic bird; she can see digitized video of a volcanic eruption or the first landing on the moon. The claim here is that the electronic encyclopedia can bring her closer to the event by offering such transparent media instead of mere prose. Such multimedia encyclopedias are also beginning to appear on the Web.

Web and Internet applications refashion the newer perceptual media of radio, television, and telephone more aggressively than they refashion print. With radio and television, the claim is not that the Internet provides a new transparency, although the quality of the audio (if not video) is already approaching the level that broadcasting or cable can provide. However, on the Internet, the listener has greater control over her listening or viewing experience of radio. It is an immediacy that she achieves through the hypermediacy of the windowed interface. She now listens to Internet radio with a mouse in one hand while she looks at a web

Wikipedia screenshot © 2000, 2001, 2002 Free Software Foundation, Inc.

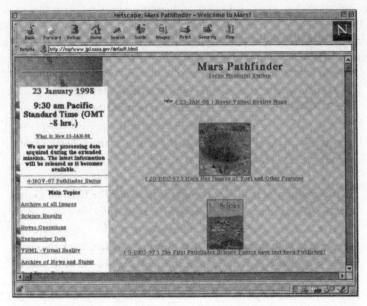

The Mars Pathfinder web site. *http://mpfwww.jpl.nasa.gov. © 1998, Courtesy of NASA/JPL/Caltech.*

page; she reads rubrics as she listens and may change the order of the materials by clicking on the links provided. Similar interfaces for Internet television already exist and will no doubt flourish as soon as the bandwidth to the home can handle full-screen, full-motion images. With the Internet phone services, more senses come into play, as the user makes, retrieves, and modifies calls through a graphical user interface. The main claim of improvement, however, is economic: the Internet phone is cheaper to use for long-distance calls.

WEB CAMERAS

Like other digital media, the Web may radically remediate its predecessors while failing to acknowledge them at all. The so-called web cameras only occasionally acknowledge their cultural role as "television only better." Apparently frivolous, web cameras are in fact deeply revealing of the nature of the Web as a remediator. Trained on some corner of the world—a hamster in a cage, a coffee machine,

or the traffic on an expressway—web cameras take up the monitoring function of television and video. Broadcast television and closed-circuit video still perform this cultural task both publicly and privately. Security cameras guard the interior and exterior of buildings and private homes, while we have come to expect that news networks such as CNN will provide us with a constant video stream for any important natural or human disaster. Television monitors the commonplace as well as the disastrous; it both transforms the commonplace into an event (the Weather Channel) and makes the disastrous commonplace (with its endless coverage of developing tropical storms or forest fires).

Now the Web and related services on the Internet have begun to supplement and rival broadcast television in this role. Because streaming video on the Web is relatively cheap, we can now afford to monitor quotidian events more closely than ever. And, as always, the Internet can offer its user an interactivity that is not available with conventional broadcast television. At some sites the visitor can even adjust the camera's view herself.

In comparison with the viewing of film, the monitoring function of television is relatively private, since we watch television in our living room rather than in a public place. An indication of this difference is the way in which the VCR turns film into television. Watching a film amid the distractions and conversations of the living room often becomes an experience of casual monitoring rather than intense viewing. Yet the World Wide Web offers an even more private experience than television, because the individual browser is often alone with her machine, and in any case only one person can conduct the interaction. Web cameras are in some ways better monitors than television, and indeed there are even web sites that allow the viewer to monitor television shows as they progress. Web cameras are now often in stop motion, but full-motion video eventually will put the Web in direct competition with broadcast and cable television. . . .

Web cameras would seem to operate under the logic of transparency, as each provides an unedited stream of images that makes some part of the physical world transparent to the Internet. Many cameras are pointed at nature sites such as mountains and beaches, despite the fact that, except for the daily changes in lighting and seasonal changes in the weather, there are few changes to monitor. The function of these nature cameras is to put the viewer in touch with the exotic or the remote, a service performed by photography and film in the last hundred years. Thus, a series of "robot cameras" on Maui track the conditions in paradise at sixty-minute intervals . . . , while another camera takes the viewer to the perpetually frozen Mawson Station in Antarctica. . . . In 1997, when the Mars Pathfinder became the first spacecraft to land on another planet after the widespread deployment of the Web, the site operated by the Jet Propulsion Laboratory became the world's most distant and exotic web camera. . . . The site received millions of "hits" in the first days after the landing, even though there was nothing to see but a rocky desert and an undifferentiated sky. The only movement was made by the spacecraft's own automated rover, as it raced across the surface of the planet at speeds of less than two feet per minute taking pictures and measurements of the rocks and soil. For most of the public, who have no knowledge of geology, the fascination could only have been with the reality of media—the fact that scientists had succeeded in putting several cameras on Mars. What the scientists then asked us to watch—and we responded enthusiastically—were these media in operation.

Web cameras reveal again our fascination with media. What other motive can there be for transmitting around the world an endless stream of images of one's goldfish? Such a site serves no imaginable practical or aesthetic purpose; the designer can only be demonstrating to herself and to us the monitoring function of the Internet. Once again, transparent immediacy passes into hypermediacy, for if these web cameras make part of the physical world available, they also mediate that corner of the physical world by bringing it into cyberspace. They make Maui, Antarctica, and Mars nodes on the Internet. Many of these sites explore the aesthetic of hypermediacy by multiplying the camera images on one page. They may present several images by the same camera taken over time; they may build a panorama from the images of several closely aligned cameras . . . or they may simply present unrelated images. One site lets the browser make her own web jukebox by placing any three cameras side by side. . . . These techniques make us conscious of each web camera as a mediating technology. The "Guinea Pig Television" site goes further in playfully acknowledging the Web's remediation of television, because the designer has put the animals on view inside the graphic frame of a television set. . . .

The cultural expectation that the Web remediate all earlier media means that the web interface can never be completely transparent. The strategy that dominates on the Web is hypermediacy, attaining the real by filling each window with widgets and filling the screen with windows. Hypermediacy is also the predominant strategy of broadcast television. Insofar as the Web is like television, it is committed to monitoring the real and the quotidian. Indeed, while television may still (barely) distinguish between the physical reality and its mediated presentation, the Web is even more aggressive in breaking down that barrier and insisting on the reality of mediation itself. Everything, from the snow fields of Antarctica to the deserts of Mars, finds its way on to the Web.

A Mobile Network Society

—Manuel Castells et al.

Manuel Castells is professor of Communication and the Wallis Annenberg Chair in Communication Technology and Society at the Annenberg School for Communication, University of Southern California and Professor Emeritus of Sociology and Planning at the University of California, Berkeley.

RELENTLESS CONNECTIVITY

The key feature in the practice of mobile communication is connectivity rather than mobility. This is because, increasingly, mobile communication takes place from stable locations, such as the home, work, or school. But it is also used from everywhere else, and accessibility operates at any time. So, while in the early stages of wireless communication it was a substitute for the fixed-line phone when people were on the move, mobile communication now represents the individualized, distributed capacity to access the local/global communication network from any place at any time. This is how it is perceived by users, and this is how it is used. With the diffusion of wireless access to the Internet, and to computer networks and information systems everywhere, mobile communication is better defined by its capacity for ubiquitous and permanent connectivity rather than by its potential mobility.

NETWORKS OF CHOICE

Mobile communication has considerably improved the chances, opportunities, and reach of interpersonal sociability and shared practices. People—particularly, but not only, young people—build their own networks of relationships, usually on the basis of their face-to-face experiences, interests, and projects, and then keep them constantly open by using wireless communication, more often than the fixed-line Internet. Thus, peer groups become reinforced in this hybrid space of interaction of physical, online, and wireless communication.

But the technology also allows for a rapidly changing network, adding individuals to or deleting individuals from the network, according to the evolving projects and moods of each individual in the network. So that networks expand, overlap, and are modified following a decentralized multiple entry/exit structure of communication. An extremely malleable pattern of communication follows, highly sensitive to the evolution of orientations among the participants in the communication process. Thus, at the same time, we observe stepped-up communication, the increased rootedness of electronic communication in face-to-face experience, and the complete dependency of the composition of the communication networks on the desires of the communicating subjects. Social choice, including communication choice, continues to be framed by institutions and social structure. But within these obvious limits, wireless communication considerably enhances the choice of interlocutors, and the intensity and density of interaction.

INSTANT COMMUNITIES OF PRACTICE

One of the most important communicative practices we have observed is the emergence of unplanned, largely spontaneous communities of practice in instant time, by transforming an initiative to do something together into a message that is responded to from multiple sources by convergent wills in order to share the practice. This is, of course, most evident in flash political mobilizations, some of which we have analyzed in this book. But it is not limited to sociopolitical uses. It is manifested as well in professional projects, in cultural experiences, in countercultural expressions, in party going, in family reunions, in the celebrations of sports fans, in religious gatherings, and so on. In other words, the general trend observed in our societies for ad hoc groupings to take precedence over formal structures of interaction and participation, be it family traditions, civic associations, or political parties, finds its technological platform in this capacity to call for action or for meeting or for sharing—in instant time.

It is important to emphasize that these communities can only be formed if the message aimed at constituting them resonates in a network of affinity. In other words, communities of practice, in the mobile society as elsewhere, express the latent existence of common interests and/or values. But on the basis of this latent structure, communities of

practice can be formed instantly by a message that strikes a chord along a network of receptive subjects. We currently lack the evidence to evaluate the resilience of these instantly formed communities over time. However, it is an important question, particularly for the understanding of new forms of social mobilization, which should be taken up by researchers.

THE BLURRING OF THE SOCIAL CONTEXT OF INDIVIDUAL PRACTICE

Wireless communication does not transcend space and time, as is often stated in terms of an apparently commonsense observation. It blurs, rather than transcends, spatial contexts and time frames. And it induces a different kind of space—the space of flows—made of the networked places where the communication happens, and a new kind of time—timeless time—formed from the compression of time and the desequencing of practices through multitasking. This is what emerges from a number of studies on the social dimensions of wireless communication. These studies show that there is a new spatial context and a new time dimension in which the communication takes place. It is the space and time of the communicating individuals, which is a material form, as material as any other space and time, but it is chosen by the communicating subjects.

Furthermore, since communication is at least bilateral and potentially multiple (networks of wireless communication), the time/spatial context is formed by the frame chosen by the initiator of the communication, the frame of the solicited communicator, and the set of relationships objectively existing between the two or more time/spatial contexts. Besides, not only are time and space blurred (not eliminated, but blurred) but organizational contexts and social practices are often mixed. This is the case with communication that takes place in airports or stations with the family, office, and friends. Or the multiple use of mobile devices from the car, from trains, or from waiting rooms. Or dating on the move. Or the multimedia use of the mobile device (image taking and sending, audio retrieving and playing, data transmission, Interpersonal communication) mixed in chosen time/space contexts.

So the system of mobile communication enables the blurring, mixing, and recomposing of a variety of social practices in a variety of time/space contexts. But the blurring process is not undetermined. It is centered on the communicating individual. So it is an individually centered production of the material and social process of communication. In so doing, networks of individual interaction tend to free themselves from organizations, institutions, norms, and material constraints, on the basis of personal convenience and suitability to individual projects. As a result, there is an extraordinary strengthening of the culture of individualism (meaning the primacy of individual projects and interests over the norms of society or reference groups) in material terms. Therefore, individualism rather than mobility is the defining social trend of the mobile society because it not only allows users to communicate on the move, but also to communicate from immobility, as is shown in a number of important studies on the benefits of mobile communication in enhancing the communicative capacity of disabled persons.

One consequence of this development is that traditional norms of courtesy have to be redefined in the new context. Since people build their own private space by simply ignoring others around them, a new m-etiquette (and its implicit norms of cultural domination) is struggling to be adopted, specifying when it is proper to isolate oneself from the social environment and when it is not, when it is acceptable to expose one's personal life in the middle of an audience of strangers and when it is not, or when pupils can talk to or e-mail their buddies in the classroom and when they cannot.

In sum, the blurring of time, space, and activities into a new frame of chosen time, space, and

multipurpose communication dematerializes social structure and reconstructs it around individually centered networks of interaction. This is not the fading away of time, but the emergence of chosen time, and of compressed time, to fit the multitasking of communication. This is not the end of distance, but the definition of interaction in a space of communication flows structured around spatial nodes of opportunity. And this is not the confusion of all social practices, but the constitution of a set of practices around the interests, values, and priorities of each individual. It is the blurring of the preexisting social structure of communication, but it is also the relentless definition of new channels and forms of communication. More important than communication on the move is the rise of moving communication patterns.

Blackberry curve ricardo/zone41.net

ACCESS TO THE WIRELESS NETWORK AS A SOURCE OF PERSONAL VALUE AND AS A SOCIAL RIGHT

We know that the value of a network increases exponentially with its size and the intensity of interaction between its nodes. From the observation of social behavior in wireless communication networks, we also verify this general rule of network logic. Users become dependent on mobile communication very quickly. They tend to be always on, and find ways to reduce the cost of communication. When government regulations, technological standards, and business pricing systems favor the diffusion of wireless communication, it becomes explosive. People in general, but particularly young people, find a major source of personal value in wireless communication. And they go to extraordinary lengths to make an effort to access the network. Thus, prepaid cards and call-time rentals have led the diffusion of use in developing countries and among low-income segments of the population in advanced countries. In China, the Little Smart phone systems have made major inroads among working people, far from the trendy professionals of Shanghai, as our fieldwork among migrant workers in the Pearl River Delta shows. In Japan, i-mode became a major success by tailoring not only habits and needs, but pricing systems to its young user population. And in Europe, the relative affordability and flexibility of mobile-phone payment systems explain to a large extent the fast diffusion of wireless communication. In contrast, the U.S. example of misguided competitive strategies, lack of communicating standards, and misunderstanding of the pricing needs of young users and the poorer segments of the population have hampered the diffusion of the technology, with potential serious consequences down the line, in terms of the learning curve and service availability, for both companies and users in general.

In sum, wireless communication technology seems to be the most rapidly adopted technology, and the one that most users have quickly found indispensable to their lives, particularly among young people. As soon as regulatory, technological, and affordability obstacles are overcome, there is an explosion in usage. This places a serious burden on regulators because, in the absence of an affirmative policy favoring diffusion, those countries, areas, and people left behind will clearly suffer from lack of connection to a fundamental network. It is also clear that when wireless communication and the Internet come together, as in the experience of i-mode in Japan, and in new developments in Korea, the effect of increasing communication is amplified. We can even say that the blockage in Internet diffusion that Japan and other Asian countries were experiencing is being solved through wireless Internet connections. However, given the technical and business difficulties experienced by WAP and mobile Internet access in Europe and the United States, it becomes increasingly clear, by looking at patterns of social use, that the true convergence of wireless communication and the Internet will be the critical question in the next phase of the Information Age.

Suggested Readings

PART I

Chiera, Edward. *They Wrote on Clay.* Chicago: University of Chicago Press, 1975.

Childe, Gordon. *Man Makes Himself.* New York: Mentor, 1951.

Giedion, Siegfried. *Space, Time and Architecture.* Cambridge, MA: Harvard University Press, 1967.

Kramer, Samuel Noah. *History Begins at Sumer.* New York: Doubleday, 1959.

Landmark Media. *Signs of the Times.* Video. Nd.

Marshack, Alexander. *The Roots of Civilization.* New York: McGraw-Hill, 1982.

Rudgley, Richard. *The Lost Civilization of the Stone Age.* New York: Simon & Schuster, 1999.

Schmandt-Besserat, Denise. *Before Writing.* Houston, TX: University of Texas Press, 1992.

Schramm, Wilbur. *The Story of Communication.* New York: Harper and Row, 1988.

Ucko, Peter, and Andree Rosenfeld. *Paleolithic Cave Art.* New York: McGraw-Hill, 1967.

PART II

Clanchy, Michael. *From Memory to Written Record: England 1066–1307.* Cambridge, MA: Harvard University Press, 1979.

Davis, Natalie Zemon. *The Return of Martin Guerre.* Cambridge, MA: Harvard University Press, 1983.

Drucker, Johanna. *The Alphabetic Labyrinth.* London: Thames and Hudson, 1995.

Eco, Umberto. *The Name of the Rose.* New York: Warner Books, 1983.

Films for the Humanities and Sciences. *A World Inscribed: The Illuminated Manuscript.* Films Media Group. Nd.

Goody, Jack. *The Logic of Writing and the Organization of Society.* New York: Cambridge University Press, 1988.

Havelock, Eric. *The Literate Revolution in Greece and Its Cultural Consequences.* Princeton, NJ: Princeton University Press, 1987.

Logan, Robert. *The Sixth Language.* Toronto: Stoddart, 2000.

Robinson, Andrew. *The Story of Writing.* London: Thames and Hudson, 1995.

Sampson, Geoffrey. *Schools of Linguistics.* Stanford, CA: Stanford University Press, 1980.

PART III

Arnaud, Jean-Jacques. *Name of the Rose.* Cristalda Films. 1986.

Darnton, Robert. *The Great Cat Massacre and Other Episodes in French Cultural History.* New York: Basic Books, 1984.

Darnton, Robert. *Revolution in Print—The Press in France, 1775–1800.* Berkeley: University of California Press and the New York Public Library, 1989.

Eisenstein, Elizabeth. *The Printing Revolution in Early Modern Europe.* New York: Cambridge University Press, 1983.

Febvre, Lucien, and Henri-Jean Martin. *The Coming of the Book: The Impact of Printing, 1450–1800.* London: New York Books, 1979.

Films for the Humanities and Sciences. *Print History.* Films Media Group. Nd.

Ivins, William. *Prints and Visual Communication.* London: Routledge & Kegan Paul, 1953.

Joyce, William, et al., eds. *Printing and Society in Early America.* Worcester, MA: American Antiquarian Society, 1983.

McLuhan, Marshall. *The Gutenberg Galaxy.* New York: Signet, 1969.

McMurtrie, Douglas. *The Book.* London: Oxford University Press, 1967.

Mumford, Lewis. *Art and Technics.* New York: Columbia University Press, 1952.

Wood, Amanda. *Knowledge before Printing and after: The Indian Tradition in Changing Kerala.* Oxford: Oxford University Press, 1985.

Part IV

Altick, Richard Daniel. *The English Common Reader: A Social History of the Mass Reading Public, 1800–1900*. Chicago: University of Chicago Press, 1957.

Carey, James. *Communication as Culture*. Boston: Unwin Hyman, 1989.

Grosvenor, Edwin S., and Morgan Wesson. *Alexander Graham Bell*. New York: Abrams, 1997.

Knightley, Phillip. *The First Casualty*. New York: Harcourt Brace Jovanovich, 1975.

PBS Home Video. *The Great Transatlantic Cable*. PBS Educational Video. 2005.

Pool, Ithiel de Sola. *The Social Impact of the Telephone*. Cambridge, MA: MIT Press, 1977.

Schivelbusch, Wolfgang. *Disenchanted Night*. Los Angeles: University of California Press, 1988.

Schudson, Michael. *Discovering the News: A Social History of American Newspapers*. New York: Basic Books, 1978.

Standage, Tom. *The Victorian Internet*. New York: Walker and Co., 1998.

Stephens, Mitchell. *A History of News: From the Drum to the Satellite*. New York: Viking, 1988.

Thompson, Robert L. *Wiring a Continent: The History of the Telegraphic Industry in the United States*. Princeton, NJ: Princeton University Press, 1947.

Williams, Raymond. *The Long Revolution*. New York: Columbia University Press, 1961.

Part V

Boorstin, Daniel. *The Image*. New York: Atheneum, 1978.

Chandler, Alfred A. *The Visible Hand*. Cambridge, MA: Harvard University Press, 1977.

Cohen, Paula Marantz. *Silent Film and the Triumph of the American Myth*. New York: Oxford University Press.

Fowles, Jib. *Starstruck: Celebrity Performers and the American Public*. Washington, D.C.: The Smithsonian Institution, 1992.

Goldberg, Vicki. *The Power of Photography*. New York: Abbeville, 1991.

History Channel. *The Edison Effect*. A&E Entertainment. 1994.

Kern, Stephen. *The Culture of Time and Space: 1880–1918*. Cambridge, MA: Harvard University Press, 1983.

Marchand, Roland. *Advertising the American Dream—Making Way for Modernity, 1920–1940*. Berkeley: University of California Press, 1985.

Peterson, Theodore. *Magazines in the Twentieth Century*. Urbana: University of Illinois Press, 1964.

Schudson, Michael. *Advertising: The Uneasy Persuasion*. Los Angeles: University of California Press, 1984.

Sklar, Robert. *Movie-Made America: A Cultural History of American Movies*. New York: Vintage Books, 1994.

Williams, Rosalynd. *Dream Worlds*. Berkeley: University of California Press, 1982.

Part VI

Allen, Woody. *Radio Days*. Orion Pictures. 1987.

Barnouw, Eric. *A History of Broadcasting in the United States*. New York: Oxford University Press, 3 vols., 1966–1970.

Briggs, Asa. *The History of Broadcasting in the United Kingdom*. London: Oxford University Press, 1966.

Covert, Catherine, and John Stephens, eds. *Mass Media between the Wars*. Syracuse: Syracuse University Press, 1984.

Crisell, Andrew. *Understanding Radio*. New York: Methuen, 1986.

Culbert, David. *News for Everyman*. Westport, CT: Greenwood Press, 1976.

Douglas, Susan. *Listening In: Radio and the American Imagination*. New York: Random House, 1999.

Hilmes, Michele. *Radio Voices: American Broadcasting, 1922–1952*. Minneapolis: University of Minnesota Press, 1997.

Hilmes, Michele, and Jason Loviglio, eds. *The Radio Reader: Essays in the Cultural History of Radio*. New York: Routledge, 2002.

Lewis, Tom. *Empire of the Air—The Men Who Made Radio*. New York: HarperCollins, 1991.

Nachman, Gerald. *Raised on Radio*. Berkeley: University of California Press, 2000.

Sterling, Christopher, and John M. Kittross, *Stay Tuned: A Concise History of American Broadcasting*. 3rd ed. Mahwah, NJ: LEA, 2001.

Stone, Oliver. *Talk Radio*. Universal Pictures. 1988.

PART VII

Barnouw, Erik. *Tube of Plenty: The Evolution of American Television*. New York: Oxford University Press, 1990 (1970).

Boddy, William. *Fifties Television*. Urbana: University of Illinois Press, 1990.

Bodroghkozy, Aniko. *Groove Tube*. Durham, NC: Duke University Press, 2001.

Briggs, Asa. *The History of Broadcasting in the United Kingdom*. London: Oxford University Press, 1966.

Clooney, George. *Good Night, and Good Luck*. Warner Independent Pictures. 2005.

Fiske, John. *Television Culture*. London: Methuen, 1987.

Lumet, Sydney. *Network*. Warner. 2006.

McLuhan, Marshall. *Understanding Media*. Cambridge, MA: MIT Press, 1994 (1963).

Newcombe, Horace, ed. *Television: The Critical View*. New York: Oxford University Press, 2006.

Postman, Neil. *Amusing Ourselves to Death*. New York: Dell, 1986.

Redford, Robert. *Quiz Show*. Baltimore Pictures. 1994.

Rutherford, Paul. *When Television Was Young: Primetime Canada, 1952–67*. Toronto: University of Toronto Press, 1990.

Smith, Anthony. *Television: An International History*. New York: Oxford University Press, 1998.

Tichi, Cecelia. *Electronic Hearth: Creating an American Television Culture*. New York: Oxford University Press, 1992.

Williams, Raymond. *Television and Society*. London: Fontana, 1979.

PART VIII

Beniger, James. *The Control Revolution*. Cambridge, MA: Harvard University Press, 1986.

Bolter, Jay David, and Richard Grusin. *Remediation*. Cambridge, MA: MIT Press, 1999.

Hollins, Timothy. *Beyond Broadcasting: Into the Cable Age*. London: BFI, 1984.

Mitchell, William. *City of Bits*. Cambridge, MA: MIT Press, 1996.

O'Donnell, James J. *Avatars of the Word*. Cambridge, MA: Harvard University Press, 1998.

Poole, Ithiel de Sola. *Technologies of Freedom*. Cambridge, MA: Harvard University Press, 1983.

Poster, Mark. *The Second Media Age*. Cambridge: Polity Press, 1995.

Postman, Neil. *Technopoly: The Surrender of Culture to Technology*. New York: Vintage, 1993.

Weizenbaum, Joseph. *Computer Power and Human Reason*. New York: W. H. Freeman, 1976.

Zuboff, Shoshana. *In the Age of the Smart Machine*. New York: Basic Books, 1988.

Credits

1999 by MIT Press. Reprinted by permission of MIT Press.

40. "The World Wide Web" by Jay David Bolter and Richard Grusin is from *Remediation: Understanding New Media* by Jay David Bolter and Richard Grusin. Copyright © 1999 by MIT Press. Reprinted by permission of MIT Press.

41. "A Mobile Network Society" is from *Mobile Communication and Society* by Manuel Castells, Mireia Fernandez-Ardevol, Jack Linchuan Qiu, and Araba Sey, Copyright 2006 by the MIT Press. Reprinted with permission.

Index

315